THE UNIVERSAL ENEMY

Stanford Studies *in* Middle Eastern
and Islamic Societies *and* Cultures

THE UNIVERSAL ENEMY

Jihad, Empire, and the Challenge of Solidarity

Darryl Li

STANFORD UNIVERSITY PRESS
Stanford, California

STANFORD UNIVERSITY PRESS
Stanford, California

Printed in the United States of America on acid-free, archival-quality paper

Library of Congress Cataloging-in-Publication Data

Names: Li, Darryl, author.
Title: The universal enemy : jihad, empire, and the challenge of solidarity / Darryl Li.
Other titles: Stanford studies in Middle Eastern and Islamic societies and cultures.
Description: Stanford, California : Stanford University Press, 2019. | Series: Stanford studies in Middle Eastern and Islamic societies and cultures | Includes bibliographical references and index.
Identifiers: LCCN 2019012268 | ISBN 9780804792370 (cloth ; alk. paper) | ISBN 9781503610873 (pbk. ; alk. paper) | ISBN 9781503610880 (epub)
Subjects: LCSH: Jihad—Political aspects—Bosnia and Herzegovina. | Panislamism. | Solidarity—Religious aspects—Islam. | Muslim soldiers—Bosnia and Herzegovina. | Yugoslav War, 1991–1995—Participation, Muslim. | Yugoslav War, 1991–1995—Participation, Foreign. | Yugoslav War, 1991–1995—Bosnia and Herzegovina.
Classification: LCC BP65.B54 L5 2019 | DDC 320.55/7—dc23
LC record available at https://lccn.loc.gov/2019012268

Cover design: Kevin Barrett Kane

Cover art: Omar Khouri

Typeset by Kevin Barrett Kane in 10.5/14.4 Brill

Contents

Terms of Engagement

All translations from Arabic, Bosnian/Croatian/Serbian, French, Italian, and Urdu/Hindi are my own unless otherwise specified.

Arabic or Urdu names are transliterated according to a modified version of the system used by the Library of Congress, unless the individual has settled on a spelling of their own. Diacritics are generally limited to quotations, translation glosses, bibliographic references, and the list of terms below. Pluralization of such words will usually follow English conventions rather than those of the original languages unless otherwise specified (for example, "mujahids" rather than "mujahidun/mujahidin").

I have done my best to use non-English language terms only to the extent necessary. When such words appear for the first time, they are italicized to draw the reader's attention. All such italicized terms are also listed below for reference.

Arabic	*Bosnian*	*Meaning*
Akhlāq	Ahlak	Virtues
Amīr	Emir	Commander; leader
Anṣār	Ensar	The Partisans, or Helpers: the people of Medina who sheltered Muhammad, the prophet of Islam, and his followers and then joined the Muslims; in this book, often used to refer to foreign Muslims fighting in the Bosnian jihad

Arabic	*Bosnian*	*Meaning*
Daʿwa	Dawa	Propagation of the Islamic faith
Farḍ	Farz	Religious duty
Fatwā	Fetva	Islamic legal opinion
Fiqh	Fikh	Islamic jurisprudence
Ḥadīth	Hadis	Reported statement by the Prophet Muhammad or one of his companions; such statements are, along with the text of the Quran, an important source of authority
Karāma	Karama	Miraculous occurrence bestowed by God upon His friends
Katība	Odred	Battalion, detachment
Kunyā	—	Kinship name used in Arabic, starting with either "Abū" (father of) or "Umm" (mother of)
Madhhab	Mezheb	School of fiqh
Muhājir	Muhadžir	Emigrant: One of Muhammad's followers who fled with him from Mecca. In contemporary Arabic, this term is used for migrants in general. In Bosnian, it denotes people escaping persecution
Mujāhid	Mudžahid	One who engages in jihad
—	Nišan	Grave marker, usually upright and made of stone with name and dates of birth and death written on it
Sīra	Sira	Genre of biographies of the Prophet Muhammad
Sunna	Sunnet	The way of the prophet and his companions, as documented in the Quran and hadith
Umma	Ummet	Community of Muslims; in modern usages, this has a global connotation

Following is a list of organizations and other entities referred to in this book. Quite a few of them have names and acronyms in multiple languages or scripts. Here, they are alphabetized according to the names under which they will appear in the body of the book; those names are written in boldface. For languages written in Latin script, acronyms are given in the original language. In Arabic, acronyms are used less frequently, hence acronyms given are for the name translated into English.

Ahl-i Ḥadīth: South Asian Islamic revivalist movement that rejects deference to established schools of Islamic jurisprudence (madhhabs); strong doctrinal overlaps with Salafis in the Arab world and often conflated with them.

Revival of Islamic **Heritage Society** (Arabic: Jamʿiyyat Iḥyāʾ al-Turāth al-Islāmī, Bosnian: Organizacija preporoda Islamske tradicije): Kuwaiti Salafi political and charitable organization.

HVO (Hrvatsko vijeće obrane): Croat Defense Council; most powerful militia of Bosnian Croat nationalist forces.

Islamic Group (al-Jamāʿa al-Islāmiyya): Social movement and armed opposition group that sought to establish an Islamic state in Egypt.

IZ (Islamska zajednica): Islamic Community; official body overseeing Islamic religious institutions in Bosnia.

The **Katiba** (Arabic: Katībat al-Mujāhidīn, Bosnian: Odred Elmudžahedin): Mujahids' battalion in the Bosnian army.

Muslim Forces (Muslimanske snage): Militias in the early stages of the Bosnian war that stressed proper observance of Islamic ritual and piety requirements, later folded into the **7th Muslim Brigade** of the Bosnian army; not to be confused with the Bosnian army itself, whose ranks were predominantly composed of individuals identifying with the Muslim or Bosniak nationality but without necessarily committing to any particular practice orientation.

SDA (Stranka demokratske akcije): Largest Bosniak nationalist political party.

SHC (Arabic: al-Hay'a al-ʿuliyā li-jamʿ al-tabarruʿāt lil-Būsna wal-Harsak, Bosnian: Visoki Saudijski komitet za pomoć Bosni i Hercegovini): Saudi High Committee for Bosnia, the largest foreign Islamic NGO to operate in Bosnia in the aftermath of the war.

TO (Teritorijalna odbrana): Territorial Defense militias in socialist Yugoslavia, some of which later formed part of the basis for the Bosnian army.

Dramatis Personae

Following is a list of people who appear in multiple chapters of this book. Some are public figures, but most are individuals I interviewed. Of the latter, some prefer to be named because they feel that publication of their narratives in this book serves their interests. But others cannot be identified here due to fear of arrest, deportation, or worse. In cases of doubt I have chosen to maintain anonymity. For the sake of clarity, the names that will be used most consistently in the book are in bold and the list is alphabetized accordingly. Pseudonyms assigned in this book for the purposes of disguising identities are in *italics*. Several people here, including public figures, are identified by their *kunyas*, which are widely used in jihad activism.

Mahmud Bahadhiq (**Abu ʿAbd al-ʿAziz**): Leader of one of the earliest groups of Arabs to fight in Bosnia.

Abu ʿAli al-Maghribi: Moroccan mujahid disabled during a 1993 battle.

Imad al-Husin (**Abu Hamza** al-Suri): Syrian who studied in Yugoslavia prior to the war; worked as interpreter in the Katiba.

Abu al-Harith al-Libi: Libyan physician who came to the war from Vienna; first amir of the Katiba.

Abu al-Maʿali al-Jazaʾiri: Algerian who came to the war from France; succeeded Abu al-Harith as amir of the Katiba.

Abu al-Zubayr al-Ha'ili: Saudi, led a smaller group of mujahids independent of the Katiba.

Ayman Awad: Syrian, emigrated to Yugoslavia for study in early 1980s; joined the Katiba as an interpreter.

'Abd Allah **'Azzam** (1941–1989): Palestinian jurist and activist; most prominent Arab supporter of the Afghan jihad; founded and ran the Services Office to coordinate Arab and other foreign Muslim volunteers in the Afghan jihad.

Fadhil al-Hamdani: Iraqi, studied in Yugoslavia from 1979 onward; joined the Katiba as an interpreter.

Imad el-Misri: Proselytizer and mujahid, head for some time of the Katiba's school, and author of the pamphlet *Notions That Must Be Corrected.*

Alija **Izetbegović** (1925–2003): Bosnian Muslim nationalist leader; founder and president of the Party of Democratic Action (SDA), president of Bosnia-Herzegovina (1992–1996), Bosniak member of the presidency of Bosnia-Herzegovina (1996–2000).

Jusuf: Bosnian who ran away from home as a teenager to join the Katiba.

Mehmud: Bosnian factory worker and soldier who transferred from the 7th Muslim Brigade to join the Katiba.

Nezim Halilović (**"Muderis"**): Preacher, Islamic school teacher, al-Azhar graduate, and founder of a militia in Konjic later called the 4th Muslim Light Brigade.

Muhsin: One of the senior Bosnians in the Katiba.

Anwar **Sha'ban** (1956–1995): Egyptian, arguably the most influential person in the Katiba, preacher and director of the Islamic Cultural Institute in Milan.

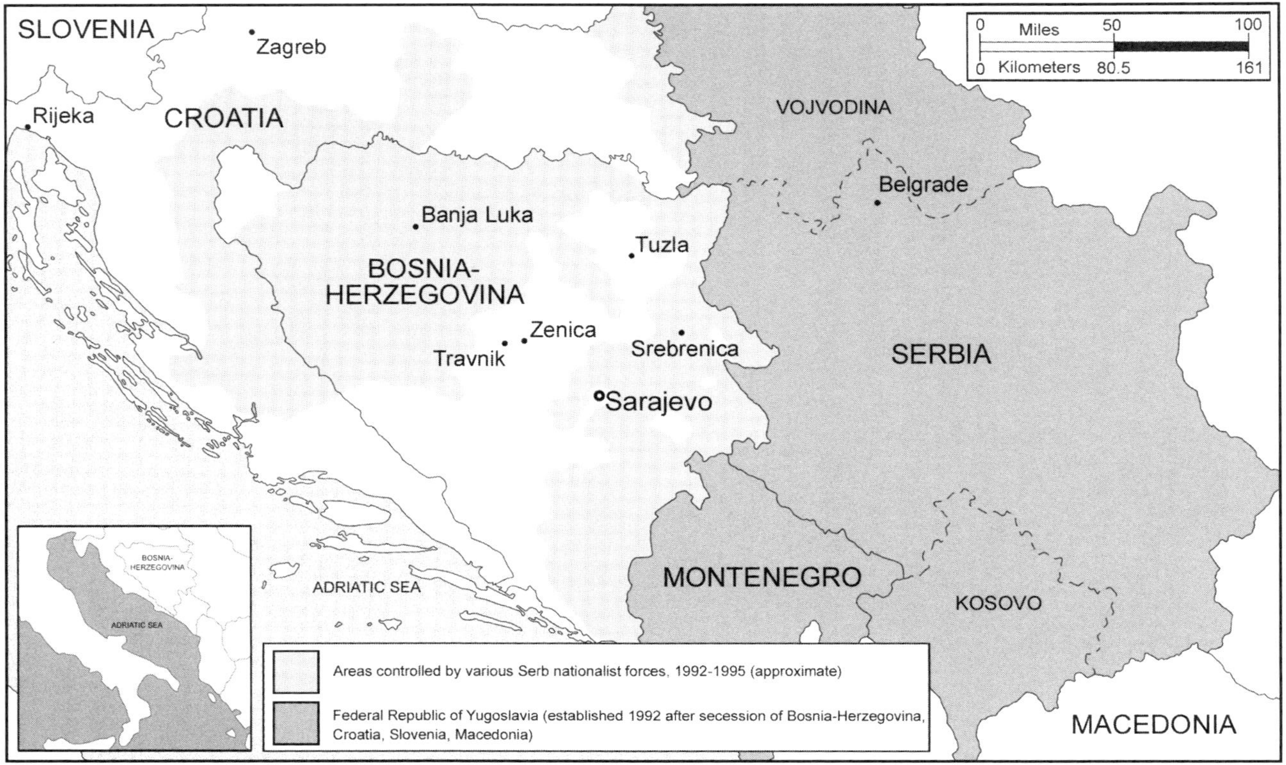

FIGURE 1. The end of Yugoslavia (1991–2009). Map by Dale Mertes.

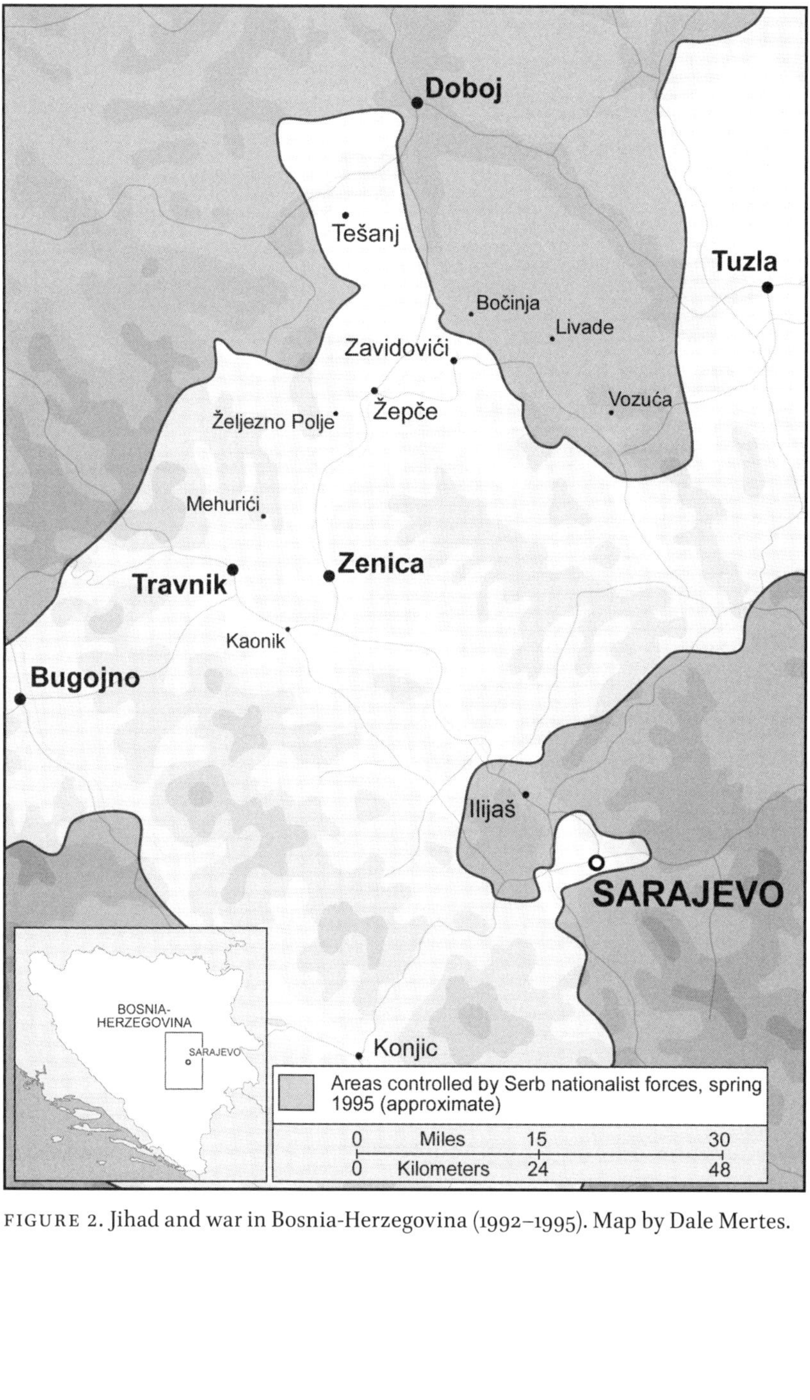

FIGURE 2. Jihad and war in Bosnia-Herzegovina (1992–1995). Map by Dale Mertes.

THE UNIVERSAL ENEMY

INTRODUCTION

THE NOONTIME AIR WAS SWELTERING, THE OUTDOOR MARKET packed, and Fadhil was not in the best of moods. It was a summer day in Zenica, an industrial city in central Bosnia-Herzegovina, in 2007. Fadhil wore a t-shirt and jeans and had short hair and stubble on his face. He told me his story over a cup of Bosnian coffee in a cramped kiosk near the stall where he worked as a peddler. Fadhil was raised in Baghdad and came to the country then known as Yugoslavia in 1979, eventually enrolling in Zenica University's prestigious metallurgy department. In those days, Yugoslavia was a leading state in the Non-Aligned Movement, seeking a path separate from the two blocs that divided the world in the Cold War. Industrial knowledge from Yugoslavia's mines, refineries, and factories was in high demand among many recently decolonized countries. Flush with oil revenue, the Iraqi state subsidized travel for students like Fadhil to Yugoslavia, which in turn welcomed Arabs and others from what today is called the Global South. At some point in the 1980s, Fadhil slowed the pace of his studies: he had to work part-time as a vendor to support himself, was getting married to a Muslim woman from Zenica, and didn't want to go home, where he would almost certainly have been drafted to fight in the war against Iran.

Fadhil's attempt to avoid one war, however, put him in the midst of another, this time much closer to his front door. His adopted country began to split apart through the emergence of nationalist political forces; his friends and neighbors now considered themselves Muslims, Croats, and Serbs first rather than Yugoslavs.[1] In January 1993, he volunteered for the newly formed Bosnian army "to defend myself and my children" even though as a foreigner he was exempt from conscription. And because Fadhil prayed regularly and did not drink—unlike many of the Bosnians he knew who identified as Muslim—he preferred to join a unit with other pious fighters, most of whom had recently arrived from abroad. Fadhil's patterns of observance also changed: he grew a longer beard and quit smoking.

Fadhil was one of several thousand foreign Muslims who fought in Bosnia in the name of jihad. Most of them ended up in a special detachment, called in Bosnian "Odred Elmudžahedin" but more commonly known even among the locals who joined as the *Katiba*, the Arabic word for battalion. The men hailed from dozens of countries, easily as many as those that sent peacekeepers to Bosnia for the United Nations (UN) or took part in the coalition that would invade Fadhil's homeland a decade later. Most were Arabs, either coming directly from the Gulf states or migrant workers from north Africa living in Italy. A smaller number were raised in Europe or the United States of Arab, Turkish, or South Asian backgrounds, as well as some converts. Their motivations, orientations toward Islamic piety, and class backgrounds varied widely and confound any straightforward attempt at correlating individuals to social variables or nationalities. At its maximum strength in the final months of the war, the Katiba officially comprised around one thousand men—approximately half foreign, half Bosnian. It chose its own leaders, raised its own funds from abroad, and had its own religious education program, which adhered largely to the Salafi orientation to Islam.[2] At the same time, the unit served under the flag of the avowedly multi-ethnic nation-state of Bosnia-Herzegovina.

Fadhil acquired Bosnian citizenship on the basis of his army service; in the fifteen years since arriving in Zenica he had earned a degree, started a family, and fought for his adopted country, so it made sense to him at the time. "I didn't have plans to go anywhere else, so why not?" After the war ended in late 1995, Fadhil earned his diploma but had to take more exams to get the professional qualifications he was seeking, so he kept working as a vendor to pay the bills. Fadhil's many legal troubles began after the September 2001 attacks in New York and Washington, when local authorities commenced a long-running campaign to expel Arabs who had fought in the war. By the time we first met, Fadhil was appealing the revocation of his citizenship while also waiting on his application for a foreigner's residency permit—after having lived in the country for more than half of his life. Despite his lack of any criminal record and his having been featured in human rights reports and Western newspapers, he saw little hope for the future. And he has never worked in metallurgy.

I asked Fadhil if he felt Bosnian. "When you know you're wanted, it's different," he answered, staring out the window and stubbornly wiping sweat from his brow every few seconds. Now, after the years of harassment, he was fed up and irritable and even contemplated returning to Iraq despite the bloodletting going on there. But his Arabic was peppered with Bosnian words, a trace of having spent so much of his life in the country. "I still have dignity [Ar: karāma]. If I stay, who knows what will happen? In a few more years, there may be another citizenship review [B: revizija]. I'm tired of *ghurba*." This last word connotes foreignness in Arabic but also strangeness, or better yet estrangement.

Feelings of strangeness and estrangement have long suffused conversations about Muslims who in recent decades have traveled great distances to fight under the banner of jihad: most notably in Afghanistan since 1979, but even more after the 1991 end of the Cold War in places such as Kashmir, Iraq, the Philippines, Chechnya, Somalia, and Syria. The roving participants in transnational jihads are often cast as the enemy of mankind—the latest in the ignoble lineage of the *hostis humani generis* stretching back to pirates and other figures of outlawry who have been subjected to radical forms of exclusion and demonization. They allegedly stand opposed not just to "the West" but to multiculturalism, to tolerance, to the very idea of common humanity itself. The jihad fighter—especially the one who travels across national boundaries—is a *universal* enemy. This is not due to an implacable hostility to humanity on his part, but because he has been declared as such by those whose right to speak in the name of the universal is often taken for granted. This book argues that such jihads are more usefully thought of as universalist projects in their own right; as we will see, to do so is neither to pay them a compliment nor to put them in the dock. Rather, this approach requires asking what it means to claim the mantle of the universal and dealing with the violence that making such claims often entails. Exploring such issues allows us to rethink and connect conversations about Islam, international law, empire, race, and war in unexpected ways. *The Universal Enemy* is therefore an anthropology of universalism: it attempts to understand how universalist claims are made and enacted, especially by people who are not ordinarily associated with ideas of the universal. Unlike most of what has been written on this topic, this book brackets questions of explaining and solving the "problem" of jihad and instead asks how these jihads can help us see the broader world differently than we may have otherwise.

JIHAD AND WORLD ORDER

This book explores the lives and times of men who came to Bosnia for jihad, those described as "transnational volunteers," "foreign fighters," and, of course, "terrorists." I will refer to them generally as *mujahids*, the Arabic-origin term for those who participate in jihad that can be translated, if not very elegantly, as "struggler" or "one who exerts effort."[3] Not every mujahid crosses borders—indeed, most people claiming this label do not—but those who do are of special interest. Participating in armed forms of solidarity without the permission of any nation-state—fighting in "other people's wars"—is treated as suspect in a world order that favors the model of the citizen-soldier as the paradigm for legitimate violence.[4] Yet this is the concrete issue raised by the mujahids under discussion here, one that has often been overlooked by conversations about establishing an Islamic state or implementing divine law, or *shariʿa*. In some senses, Fadhil's story, which will be explored further in this study, is unusual, since he lived in Bosnia before the war and stayed when it ended. But it is precisely this anomaly—that he did not come for jihad, but rather one could say that jihad came to him in a way—that is helpful in unsettling many prevalent assumptions about this phenomenon.

Following the arc of Fadhil's life reveals some of the larger issues at stake. His participation in jihad was important and not something he has ever regretted, but it was embedded in other activities: study, work, marriage, prayer, lots and lots of waiting, and imprisonment, both figurative and literal. Fadhil's trajectory has been marked by the Non-Aligned Movement, by attempts to incarnate some notion of a global Islamic community (*umma*), and by the myriad interventions of the US-led "International Community." Fadhil's experiences underscore that the story of the jihad in Bosnia is simultaneously one of settling in a particular place and getting to know its people, in encounters shaped and reshaped by much larger forces. *The Universal Enemy* is an account of world politics whose protagonists move beneath and between governments.[5] It tells the story of this jihad by tracing a series of peregrinations between the Balkans, the Middle East, and elsewhere as they intersect with and shed light on a shifting world order.

That world order is the era of what can be loosely understood as American empire. The United States is a settler polity that has also long engaged in alien rule over foreign territories while also cultivating various forms of influence over weaker countries. After the 1991 demise of the Soviet Union, its global role transformed into one of unipolar dominance. Washington's favored style of hegemony, originally developed in the western hemisphere, was now extended to much of the wider world: informal dependency and vassalage through a series of power relations mediated by debt, military assistance, and development aid, provided either directly or through multilateral institutions. While this influence varied enormously in degree from place to place, it operated through the juridical form of putatively independent, equal, and freely consenting sovereign nation-states. In the Arab world in particular, Washington was free to pursue military intervention without significant contestation from other global powers for nearly a quarter-century, from the 1991 war on Iraq until 2015, when Russian forces openly joined the fighting in Syria.

In this world order, there have been two primary ways of characterizing armed conflicts: localized ethnic wars and a globally threatening militant Islam.[6] The former, marked by the "post–Cold War," is presented as peripheral, regionally confined, and destabilizing in only a distant sense, producing hordes of hapless victims in need of mercy and management. While the West may decide to intervene on one side or another, formally it projects an image of neutrality as a referee or policeman committed only to lofty values such as humanitarianism. The latter, framed as "post-9/11," produces the figure of the terrorist as the one the world must band together to defeat. Here, self-defense for the United States or the West is conveniently elided into a defense of all humanity. Together, these two framings represent conjoined and mutually justifying aspects of the world order.[7] The management of ethnic conflict impels action in the register of compassion, but with pragmatic benefits such as preserving regional stability or preventing refugee flows. The Global War on Terror (GWOT) mobilizes the language of self-protection, but happens to be for the good of all, given the centrality of the United States to world order. Two kinds of war—humanitarian intervention and war on terror—are proffered by the left and right hands of empire, respectively.

There is perhaps no place that better exemplifies the relationship between these two intertwined understandings of war in a US-dominated world than Bosnia-Herzegovina. The armed conflicts accompanying the dissolution of the Socialist Federal Republic of Yugoslavia (1991–2001) and especially in Bosnia (1992–1995) as one of its six constituent parts captivated the attention of the West.[8] A cascading logic of nationalism and partition led to widespread atrocities in the service of creating new demographically pure territories—the events that introduced the term *ethnic cleansing* into global media discourse.[9] The protracted nature of the fighting, especially the nearly four-year siege of the capital city of Sarajevo by Serb nationalists seeking to secede from Bosnia, was perhaps the most vivid symbol of dashed hopes for a harmonious post–Cold War dispensation. Media images of a European city under assault and emaciated men—emaciated *white* men, to be precise—behind barbed wire converged with the half-century commemorative recasting of World War II as a crusade against evil as embodied by the mass atrocity of the Holocaust. The failures of the UN peacekeeping operation, the most ambitious and expensive ever at the time, severely strained the organization's credibility as well as that of the Atlantic Alliance. The Bosnian war ended on terms unsatisfying for most concerned: with the country quasi-partitioned under a protectorate run by the United States and the European Union in a constitutional system structured in a way so as to virtually guarantee paralysis along nationalist lines. Mass atrocities would be punished through international tribunals targeting individuals, but the territorial projects made possible by those atrocities were institutionalized. More broadly, the wars of Yugoslav succession were a vital part of the remaking of the European project: they formed a backdrop of "Balkan" chaos that provided a contrast with and justification for the newly emergent and prosperous European Union. As a spectacle of white-on-white violence on the world stage, the wars presented what could be safely treated as a crisis internal to the West over its ability to maintain order and face down the specter of absolute evil.

There are many works seeking to explain the breakup of Yugoslavia and the rise of nationalism or its diminutive form, ethnicity. This book is not one of them. Instead, it seeks a broader horizon that takes into account global hierarchies of race: like the dominant literature, it analyzes the Balkans' marginal position at the edges of Europe but it goes further by highlighting the region's links to the darker-skinned peoples to the south and east. The generation of scholarship that emerged from the ashes of Yugoslavia has been largely dedicated to challenging narratives about nationalism, even to the extent of neglecting the ravages of neoliberal capital in the region.[10] This literature laments how southeast Europe has been harmfully depicted as exotic, backward, and violent, like Asia and Africa.[11] However cogent the critique, whenever ex-Yugoslavs actually encounter nonwhite peoples from those other regions—either as migrants or while traveling themselves—they can suddenly become quite European enough. The scholarship's *comparison* of the Balkans to the nonwhite parts of the world has left few tools for probing the region's actual *connections* to them. The result has been a history ultimately by, for, and about white people, however incomplete or precarious that whiteness may be.

This inattention to race bears directly on understanding one of the major geopolitical issues of the day.[12] For Bosnia was not merely the paradigmatic site of post–Cold War ethnic conflict and humanitarian intervention. It was also an early battleground for GWOT, and one that brought to light the expansive scope and seemingly unbounded reach of that campaign. Among the first captives to arrive in the infamous prison at the Guantánamo Bay naval base in Cuba in January 2002 were six Algerians living in Bosnia, seized far from the zone of active warfare in Afghanistan. They had been arrested in the weeks after 9/11 by local authorities acting at the behest of the United States, which accused them of belonging to a global Islamic conspiracy led by al-Qaʿida. When a Sarajevo court ordered the men released three months later due to lack of evidence, they were instead handed over to the United States. Unlike previous cases of covert abductions overseas by Washington, this instance of capture was openly justified in domestic US courts under an expansive legal theory of war, the same one used for detentions on the battlefields of Afghanistan. The landmark 2008 US Supreme Court decision establishing habeas corpus rights for detainees in Guantánamo,

Boumediene v. Bush, bears one of these men's names.[13] The litigation that led to *Boumediene* fueled a morality tale throughout the first decade of this century about the history of habeas corpus and an American struggle to balance security and freedom. It was a saga whose heroes and heroines were mostly white American judges and lawyers, and it was one that faded with a whimper after the Supreme Court ruling, even as the Guantánamo prison looks set to remain open for the indefinite future.

Returning to the original facts of the *Boumediene* case, the scene of the crime as it were, these mysterious Arabs in Bosnia seemed bizarre and racially out of place. For proponents of GWOT, they embodied the omnipresence of the new enemy; for critics, their abduction was a sign that Washington was willing to stop nowhere and at nothing in its pursuit of chimerical threats. But both lacked a context in which to make sense of the presence of these men. This book is, among other things, a history of the circulations and encounters across region, race, and culture that made *Boumediene* possible. The six Algerians served as a reminder that even within the US-dominated world order, other forms of transnational solidarity were at work, syncopated to the historical rhythms described above. These included echoes of diverse pan-Islamic mobilizations—from the late-nineteenth-century through the 1979–1989 Soviet war in Afghanistan—in shifting relations of competition, collaboration, and confrontation with various imperial projects.[14] The most familiar stories about Bosnia have presented squabbling local nationalist factions, with the Western powers standing above them, whether hailed as saviors or decried as meddlers. Missing from this story of natives and colonizers has been a view from another boat, a perspective that responds to empire through diasporic rather than strictly parochial terms.[15]

The Bosnia crisis also riveted the attention of Muslims worldwide, especially those living within the West. For these audiences, the resonant historical parallels were not so much with the Holocaust but with the colonization of Palestine or even the fifteenth-century Spanish conquest of Andalusia.[16] As a European country where Muslims were a plurality, Bosnia was (over)loaded with symbolic significance from both ends. The fact that so many Bosnians are Muslim was a sign of the West's universality, while their whiteness was a sign of Islam's universality. This makes Bosnia a helpful site for thinking about how the racialization *of* Muslims in the Global War on

Terror resonates with processes of racialization *between* Muslims as well.[17] Both promises of universality were, of course, conditional and limited; Bosnians, as Europeans, received more concern than Rwandans being slaughtered wholesale on a continent to the south, but this provided little consolation as they starved under siege, dodged snipers, and watched the town of Srebrenica overrun and its Muslim male population massacred with the rest scattered into exile, all under the watchful eye of the International Community.

And solidarity from Muslims worldwide brought its own dilemmas. Its most visible form arrived in the mujahids who fought as part of or alongside the Bosnian army.[18] In addition, there were many aid organizations and proselytizers; some of them also participated in combat, while others kept their distance. The mujahids committed various atrocities during the war, including executing enemy prisoners. And both fighters and aid workers have been accused of attempting to impose forms of religious practice labeled as "Wahhabi" and described as backward and illiberal. At the war's end, the vast majority of the foreign Muslim volunteers left: some to new war zones, others to seek asylum in Europe, yet others to return home. A few stayed in Bosnia as civilians, married, and started families. Nevertheless, their presence continued to stir controversy, serving as fodder in debates between partisans of Croat, Serb, and Bosniak nationalisms. For Bosnia's Muslims, opinion has been divided between those who stress the Arabs' alleged contributions and those who see them as troublemakers validating the very caricatures and stereotypes that all Muslims must face.[19]

This book argues that the most useful way of understanding the contentious phenomenon of the jihad in Bosnia is through the lens of universalism. Thinking more clearly about questions of universalism will help to make the jihad legible in political terms rather than in pathologizing or moralistic ones.[20] To tell this story, I have resorted to a kind of ethnographic history from below—one that unfolds across different regions and seeks grounding in local contexts without being limited by them. Such an approach also sheds light on other universalist projects, especially more powerful ones organized along nation-state lines. It traces the Non-Aligned Movement, United Nations peacekeeping, and the Global War on Terror in ways rarely apprehended before and provides a set of terms for comparing them.

To speak of jihad as universalism is not a form of praise: universalisms—as many have noted and this study further confirms—invariably entail violent hierarchies and erasures, even if they hold out exhilarating possibilities. To take only the most obvious of exclusions, the universalism discussed here is also a deeply masculinized one that relies on the peregrinations of men while presuming women to be stationary. My concern here is to highlight the structural dilemmas that universalisms share.[21] Perhaps the starkest way to bring this out is to juxtapose mujahids and peacekeepers. Both seek to incarnate particular ways of imagining the human community, bringing together diverse constituencies, especially in facing locals who may be reluctant, hostile, or opportunistic. Both tend to stumble through the local language and oscillate between marveling at the hospitality they have seen and the duplicity that sometimes follows. Both exercise power across boundaries—juridical, racial, and so on—raising serious questions of responsibility and difference. Both offer favored locals resources and the opportunity to become one of them through travel. Both are accused by critics of unrealistic devotion to ideals as well as base motivations that cheapen those ideals. Both are admired for assuming risks despite the apparent lack of an "organic" link to these sites of conflict and face suspicion over their motives for the same reason. Both are engaged in bringing projects of social transformation with questionable local legitimacy, and struggle over how aggressively to pursue those programs and how much to interfere in local dynamics. But in most conversations in the West, it is the mujahids who are described as "foreign fighters" irreconcilable to local context, while other people with guns who are no less foreign are seen to incarnate an International Community that necessarily includes the local but exceeds it at the same time. This book seeks to understand and unsettle the conditions that make this contrast seem intuitively obvious to so many. Doing so requires developing a clearer sense of how to usefully think about universalism.

THE PRACTICE OF UNIVERSALISM

"Hey," one of Mahdi's companions on the front line perked up one evening, sniffing the air. "What's that? Do you smell that?" They were two Black Britons of Jamaican origin fighting alongside the Taliban in Afghanistan; Mahdi was also a veteran of the Bosnian jihad, which he joined shortly after embracing Islam in the early 1990s. While others tried to pick up the scent themselves, Mahdi's friend continued to marvel: "Is that . . . [sniff, sniff] is that . . . [sniff, sniff]" and then the punchline: " . . . *fish 'n chips?!*" It had been months since either fish or chips, both very much beloved, had been anywhere near Mahdi's mind, and the joke reached out to mercilessly tickle him as if from another world years later as we discussed his past in a south London coffee shop. "It was just so wonderful," Mahdi said wistfully after being spent with laughter. "It was a reminder that we had a past. That we had a life, before everything in this jihad. And it made us all the more happy that we had become Muslims."

Mahdi's madeleine moment calls to mind how media coverage of foreign fighters often revels in discovering attachments to tokens of Western consumerism, as if playing video games or enjoying fast food is a scandalous betrayal of their values. After all, jihadists are held to be committed to re-creating a mythical vision of life in seventh-century Arabia. More generally, pan-Islamic visions have often been condemned to failure because actual Muslims have conflicting interests; because Islam has nothing to offer nonbelievers; because a religion that started with some Arabs in the desert centuries ago is limited by definition. These critiques are echoes of an old argument that universalism—at least those forms marked as undesirable—flattens human differences regardless of context or nuance in the service of dehumanizing, coercive political projects. In a parallel context, human rights has long been faulted for failing to capture the diverse ways in which societies conceive of justice; underwriting the exclusion of certain critics as enemies of humanity; and perpetuating a fraud since it is based on treaties written by dead white men anyway. The burdens of this critique do not fall upon all with equal force: human rights ideology remains resilient in the face of all manner of refutation, while the dismissal of jihad produces a peculiar kind of oblivion—the kind that makes possible puzzlement or surprise at the idea that a jihadist can also like fish and chips.

The impulse to refute universalism will always remain valuable as a tool of critique, especially when such claims are deployed in the service of power. But the object of critique is often universal*ity*, the notion that a particular normative claim, empirical assertion, or explanatory theory is applicable or valid in all cases. This approach tends to overlook and misapprehend the effects of universal*ism* as a structure of aspirations.[22] And it is far less useful in accounting for invocations of the universal whose provenance is not necessarily Western, whose idiom is not necessarily liberal. Here, the analytical challenge lies not only in unmasking the problems of universalist claims but also in making sense of their precarious emergence and unlikely purchase.[23] Thinking of universalism as practice—and not simply as ideology—reminds us that the categories of universal and particular in any given situation relate in complex and shifting ways. For Mahdi, conversion to Islam and participation in violence in its name did not require him to erase or forsake Britishness; indeed, awareness of the gap between his background and his commitment to Islam could even be a source of joy. Universalism does not and cannot demand total homogeneity; rather, it is a claim to transcend difference, which therefore requires means to regulate and redefine it.

One useful way to understand the practice of universalism is to start with the suffix, *ism*. Ultimately derived from ancient Greek, *ism* is a marker of nominalization, often giving rise to a concept or a category. This might lead us to developing an ideology, a genealogy, a theory. It would lead us to ask whether something is universal or is not. Instead, we will venture from the reminder that *ism* is also the Arabic word for "name." We can ask in a given situation who is speaking in the name of the universal and what makes it possible for them to do so in a way that seems authoritative or even self-evident. Doing so directs attention toward the practical challenges and dilemmas that ensue, especially from the constant redefinition of the universal and the particular and the line that both divides and conjoins them.[24]

Let us take another example. Ismail Royer, a white middle-class Christian from St. Louis, Missouri, converted to Islam and traveled to Bosnia for jihad during his first year of college. Two decades later at an office in downtown Washington, D.C., he recounted a day during the war when he and some other mujahids sat down for lunch. They were underneath a tent, divided into small groups, each clustered around a shared plate of meat and rice. Suddenly, Ismail heard a voice from behind him call out in Arabic, "Hey! You an American?!" The object of address was unmistakable: Ismail was the only American in a group of mostly Gulf Arabs. Equally unmistakable was the contempt in the question, casually tossed into the air between bites of food by someone who didn't even bother to turn around and speak to him directly. As a white convert, Ismail was accustomed to being accepted and indeed celebrated by Middle Eastern Muslims, but here the subtext was clear: he was being singled out as different, his dedication to Islam and the jihad questioned. Moreover, the lack of any justification or explanation accompanying the question signaled that it came from someone assuming the right to speak—or in this case to interrogate and accuse—in the name of an unmarked universal whose terms are safely presumed among this group to be Muslim. Aware that he was being tested, Ismail grunted, with matching nonchalance, "Yeah. You Saudi?" Ismail explained to me the logic of his riposte: nationality was generally a neutral category in the jihad. Mujahids were often identified by their citizenship, and Ismail had no problem being known as "Ismail the American." This was only a problem for those coming from Saudi Arabia; since their country is named after a dynastic ruling family, calling them "Saudi" implied an uncomfortable degree of personal fealty or subservience unbecoming those with a strong tribal identity. They instead preferred monikers denoting their region, such as the Hijaz or Najd. Ismail's reply poked at this sore spot without overreacting in a way that would betray any insecurity over his own Muslimness. The impudent bully was momentarily startled and all the mujahids guffawed in appreciation. Ismail successfully challenged the Saudi's assumption of the right to speak in the name of the universal: if the man had sought to put Ismail in his (national) place, Ismail returned the favor while gently reminding him that neither of them identified too strongly with their citizenships. The two would go on to become good friends.

Universalisms entail several things, which tend to come together under jumbled, shifting, and unlikely historical circumstances. They involve loose sets of ideals directed at all of humanity, which can be drawn from any number of places, such as a religious tradition or a set of theoretical texts; let us call this an *idiom*. Too often the discussion of universalism begins and ends at the level of idiom, as when "Islam," "liberalism," and "Marxism" are glossed as comparable universalisms, each following easily from an underlying written code. Universalism is something that should be approached as specific and concrete; there is no single "Islamic universalism" or "Western universalism" as such, but rather multiple universalist projects whose primary idioms may describe themselves as broadly Islamic or Western and which strive for the ability to invoke such categories with a force that is convincing. Instead of employing universalism as shorthand for civilization or other discredited monolithic categories, this book tries to build its analysis up from smaller scales, following how the players in this story cobble together ideas, institutional forms, and practices that they deem Islamic.

As discussed above, thinking anthropologically about universalism also requires identifying a *horizon of belonging*, a category that includes some people and treats all others as theoretically capable of incorporation. Even this inclusion, of course, is inevitably striated with all sorts of hierarchies and exclusions: most notably, the Bosnian jihad called for help from Muslims around the world yet always found ways to discourage women from coming to fight. While writing this book, the most common note of skepticism I encountered from colleagues was the question of how something could be both Islamic and *truly* universal. But universalism in this book is a question of aspiration, not a claim of empirical reality, normative validity, or explanatory power. The idea of a universalism that speaks to all of humanity with little assurance or even concern that anyone is actually listening should be familiar. International human rights lawyers promulgate new rules as universal in full awareness that most of the world's population may be unaware of or even oppose them. Diplomats frequently chide, implore, and demand on behalf of the "International Community" regardless of how many people identify with that community. For those who traveled to fight in Bosnia, Islam also carried a message for all of mankind. In this view, the umma is both the subset of humanity that has accepted Islam as well as humanity's ultimate horizon through the possibility—however remote or hypothetical—of conversion.[25] And indeed, as the examples of Mahdi and Ismail remind us, at least a handful of those who fought had only just become Muslim.

Universalisms' promise to transcend differences between people does not necessarily propose to erase those differences or to preserve them, but it must have mechanisms to *process* them. Social cleavages and antagonisms around gender, nationality, race, and class were not ignored by the jihad, but rather repolarized and managed in a variety of ways. This book examines some of the concrete practices and institutions that enabled a group of Muslims in Bosnia to debate, stand together, and fall out with each other, thus creating new social formations and reshaping old ones. This puts difference at the center of the story about universalism instead of casting it as contingent practice subservient to textualized religious truths, norms, or ideals. Universalisms also require some *theory of authority* that can regulate the use of violence and adjudicate which differences are contingent and which mark an absolute limit.

Speaking in the name of the universal is also far more likely to be effective if attached to an *institutional formation* of some kind. For the jihad in Bosnia, the Katiba was such a formation, although not all foreign mujahids joined it (Ismail was a reject, perhaps arousing too much suspicion of being a spy). In general, of course, the most common institutional form for making universalist claims that actually stick is the nation-state. The nation-state, even in its most xenophobic manifestations, always makes universalist claims: the nation is a concrete embodiment of a universal notion of freedom or human belonging or something else and presupposes the existence of other nations as well. Indeed, nation-states often can participate in different universalist projects at once: in the case of wartime Bosnia-Herzegovina, appeals to the liberal international legal order and to the umma were both common. And, as we shall see, Islamic solidarity was itself a broad category taking many different and even conflicting forms.

The outsized weight of the nation-state as a political formation in the contemporary era means that the best-known universalisms tend to be state-based: let us call these *internationalisms*, universalist projects that are explicitly organized on an inter-state basis. If the first half of the book follows the practice of universalism to make the jihad in Bosnia legible in terms beyond pathos and morality, the second half juxtaposes the jihad to three internationalisms in particular: socialism in the states of the Non-Aligned Movement (NAM), United Nations peacekeeping, and the US-led Global War on Terror. In each of these cases, the lens of a transregional ethnographic history from below reveals new dimensions: this book will follow the NAM through the eyes of Arab students in Yugoslavia rather than the typical pageants of postcolonial summitry; it will regard UN peacekeepers not as totems of independent states but as heirs to histories of colonial soldiering; and it will trace the paths of GWOT captives through and against a global network of prisons rather than as mere victims of human rights abuses.

On several occasions so far, I have resorted to examples from international law in order to illustrate ideas about universalism. This is hardly a coincidence: international law provides idioms for many of the best-known examples of universalism today. International law, of course, has also been widely criticized as an instrument of imperialism, as the premier example of false or harmful universalism.[26] Worth mentioning here are two major challenges to the nineteenth-century notion of an international legal order in which full formal participation was limited to Western states. C. H. Alexandrowicz, a Polish citizen of the Austro-Hungarian Empire who spent a significant part of his career in newly independent India, undermined this order's pretensions to universality. He adduced evidence of non-European participation as sovereign equals in the international legal order of the early modern period. Alexandrowicz showed how even many acts of colonial conquest were based on treaties concluded with local potentates—thereby confirming that no matter how craven, European powers nevertheless at some point conferred legal recognition upon native authorities.[27] The German Nazi jurist Carl Schmitt, on the other hand, warned that invocations of universal categories would provide new and even more compelling justifications for violence against the excluded. Such a move threatened to transform the enmity between any two states into a war of all against one in the name of humanity. He also averred that expanding the European order through decolonization would only result in an abstract universalism not grounded in concrete political orders.[28] The thrust of Alexandrowicz's work was to seek a more complete and just universality, while Schmitt seemed to question the desirability of universality altogether. Both of these critiques have shaped this book. Schmitt called attention to the work performed by invocations of the universal in justifying and enacting violence, while Alexandrowicz's attentiveness to the participation of "peripheral" actors in the legal order remains an exemplar of how empirical research can push against Eurocentric narratives. Nevertheless, attempts to theorize universalism within international law scholarship remained hampered by the field's more general focus on norms, texts, or the lives of elite jurists and have rarely been placed into a thick social or historical context.[29]

Drawing on ethnography and history, *The Universal Enemy* presents a counterpoint for consideration: a universalism that at first glance appears radically different from those typically studied in international law.[30] In doing so, it hopes to develop a sharper and more theoretically robust account of universalism in practice.[31] For international law is here more than a model for thinking about jihad. It has also informed my own professional and intellectual formation in ways that made this book possible. Further explanation is in order.

ETHNOGRAPHIC LAWYERING IN THE GLOBAL WAR ON TERROR

During my first research trip to Bosnia, in December 2006, I met Abu Hamza, a Syrian who was the public face of the Arab ex-mujahids in the country. Bosnia was at that time one of the few countries in which veterans of transnational jihad movements maintained a regular public presence and could meet with journalists and researchers in relative openness. Abu Hamza was, of course, suspicious at first—the only people who are interested in such topics, he told me, are spies. His caution was hardly misplaced: our meeting came only a few months after revelations in mainstream media of a network of secret CIA prisons in Thailand, Romania, Poland, and elsewhere used to torture alleged al-Qaʿida members. Arabs in Bosnia had been arrested, questioned, and in some cases deported; those who left the country also found themselves hunted down. A journalist who interviewed the wife of one of the six Algerians sent to Guantánamo turned out to be an undercover German intelligence officer. Abu Hamza recognized that the type of research I was attempting was not like an ordinary media interview, but was more akin to joining a family, marrying a daughter. And for that, he said, he would need a "token of friendship" [ʿarabūn al-ṣadāqa]. What did that mean? He smiled and said it was up to me to figure out what form that would take.

Since that first conversation with Abu Hamza in 2006, I have spent a total of one year in Bosnia, mostly in trips averaging one month in duration between 2009 and 2012 with visits until 2018. Roughly half of my time was in the capital, Sarajevo, where I lived in various neighborhoods, from the relatively affluent city center and Koševo Hill to the more working-class outlying area of Alipašino Polje. During the rest of my research, I was based in downtown Zenica, located about an hour's drive northwest of Sarajevo. Zenica was a major center for foreign Islamic solidarity efforts during the war, as it was the largest city under undisputed government control and better-connected to the outside world than besieged Sarajevo. The core research of this book is based on a biographical database consisting of over two hundred non-Bosnians who fought in the jihad, drawing from archival documents, primary source publications, and a network of interlocutors that included twenty-eight self-described mujahids—seventeen foreign, eleven Bosnian. Most of these were people with whom I had repeated, extended, and open-ended conversations over the course of multiple years, in Arabic or English. In addition, there were Arab aid workers and other migrants, Bosnian clerics, war veterans, journalists, and intellectuals. Nearly all of these were men; I was able to interview a few Bosnian women married to Arab mujahids and migrants as well and several children of such couples. Interviews were held in coffee shops, private homes, or the immigration detention center at Lukavica, which will be discussed in Chapter 7. Outside Bosnia, this research took me to Egypt, France, Italy, Kuwait, Malaysia, Pakistan, Saudi Arabia, the United Kingdom, the United States, and Yemen. Interviews were supplemented by archival research, mostly with Bosnian army documents collected by the UN war crimes tribunal for ex-Yugoslavia. Unlike most other transnational jihads, the one in Bosnia was affiliated with a nation-state and a regular army, leaving behind a considerable and uniquely detailed paper trail. And because the events of the war and the time of my fieldwork were separated by less than a generation, I could incorporate archival documents directly into some interviews—including with individuals who were mentioned in them.

As with many ethnographies, the bulk of the research for this book was conducted while I was a doctoral student in anthropology. But I was also undergoing a concurrent course of training and professionalization as an attorney, after having worked for several human rights organizations prior to graduate school. During that first meeting with Abu Hamza, I had intended to keep these two aspects of my background separate and approach potential interlocutors purely as an academic researcher. As time passed, it became clear that the work of anthropology and lawyering could not remain separate, and indeed that for me they could *only* proceed together in lockstep. This is because the Global War on Terror has been configured as an intensively litigious space—contrary to accusations of "lawlessness," it has been a campaign marked by an anxiousness to frame actions in legal terms, even if done so in ways that may seem to clash with liberal norms and commitments to the rule of law. As a non-Muslim citizen of the United States, I was not surprised to face suspicion; while a few people I contacted by phone angrily berated me as a spy before hanging up, most others politely stopped replying to messages after an initial meeting or conversation, leaving me to stew in uncertainty and self-doubt. Meanwhile, from many Bosnians, I experienced considerable racial curiosity and at times hostility as a person of East Asian origin, especially in smaller cities and towns, at a time when Chinese merchants were becoming an increasingly prevalent and resented sight.[32] But once I spoke English with a certain kind of accent and identified myself with well-known American universities, I was quickly shown the deference customarily accorded to "Internationals." Mention of my research topic would then shift conversations back to the register of suspicion that I was looking to besmirch Bosnia's international reputation by tying it to concerns about terrorism. Given all of this, the role of human rights lawyer seemed the most legible and least threatening identity to embrace in approaching potential interlocutors.

Accordingly, this book may be read as an anthropology of law, but it is also a product of ethnographic lawyering, drawing on the broad repertoire of technical skills, ways of reasoning, discourses of authority, even habits of bodily comportment that mark the legal profession. Most ethnographic encounters involve at least the pretense of some reciprocity between researchers and interlocutors: in this case, acting as a lawyer was the only thing I could offer that seemed useful. But inhabiting such a professional role entails entering into specific relationships of responsibility with clients that bring their own dilemmas. Academic research about one's own clients poses obvious methodological challenges, given the tension between representing a client and developing the critical distance from them upon which research depends. And it raises concerns about unethical exploitation of the attorney-client relationship as well. Navigating the demands of these different roles was a constant struggle. Thinking ethnographically with formal legal categories—generating theoretical insights from their use in everyday life—requires disentangling the most important types of lawyering that inflected this research.

The first form of lawyering was as *party counsel*, or representing clients in adversarial situations, such as litigation in the US federal courts. While in law school—and after my first research trip to Bosnia—I had the opportunity to join a legal clinic specializing in cases arising from the Global War on Terror.[33] In 2008, I found myself assigned to a team representing Ahmad Zuhair, a national of Saudi Arabia abducted in Lahore, Pakistan, and held without charge as an "unlawful enemy combatant" at Guantánamo. By an incredible coincidence, he had also spent time in the Balkans during the 1990s and was accused, among many other things, of having fought in the jihad—an allegation that he steadfastly denied, along with all the others leveled by the US government.[34] Mr. Zuhair and another captive maintained what was at the time the longest hunger strike ever at Guantánamo, leading the government to subject him to a regime of forced feeding that was in many respects another form of torture. Several times a day for four years, Mr. Zuhair was painfully strapped into a restraint chair, and a cold, unlubricated plastic tube was rammed up his nose in order to pump nutrients into his stomach. We filed emergency motions seeking relief for Mr. Zuhair and were fortunate enough to persuade a federal judge in Washington to order an independent medical expert to conduct a physical examination—the first time this was ever done at the prison.[35] In the meantime, we prepared to challenge the case against Mr. Zuhair, which required investigating the government's allegations, including those concerning his time in Bosnia. This entailed building on my own previous research to interview potential witnesses and locate relevant documents, as well as reaching out to Mr. Zuhair's family and acquaintances in other countries and discussing his case with him directly at the prison. I participated in one such visit in February 2009. Later that spring, just weeks before the scheduled court hearing that would determine the legality of Mr. Zuhair's detention, the US government unilaterally decided to transfer him to Saudi Arabia. He was held in a "rehabilitation center" in Riyadh—essentially another form of nonjudicial detention, albeit far less draconian than Guantánamo and, crucially, allowing family visits—before finally being released without charge several years later.

My experience working on Mr. Zuhair's legal team is an important part of the backdrop of this book. But you will not read any more about it here. Writing an ethnography of this experience that would successfully balance both the critical imperatives and ethical sensibilities that I seek to uphold would likely have been impossible. But there is no way to know for sure, because of a more immediate reason: most of the evidence used in Guantánamo detention cases is classified by the US government.[36] Then, like all other lawyers and paralegals defending Guantánamo captives, I had to travel to a "secure facility" near the Pentagon to see the evidence. We were not permitted to remove the files from the building; any written notes, including from meetings with clients at the base, were presumptively classified and could only be removed with government consent.[37] Any court filings referencing classified information had to be composed on government computers at the secure facility, which were not connected to the Internet. Accordingly, Mr. Zuhair's case only registers as an absence in the pages that follow.[38] While it is important to stress that none of the information in this book comes from these experiences, working on this case shaped the many questions and lines of inquiry that the project would take.

The second form of lawyering that inflects this study was my work as counsel for *amicus curiae*, Latin for "friend of the court." A long-standing institution of common law that has found its way into various international courts, the amicus is a third party who intervenes in a case with a court's permission, often in explicit support of one side.[39] In theory, however, their primary obligation is to the court itself, in order to help judges arrive at sound conclusions. I mobilized such interventions in two cases filed by Abu Hamza that were essentially test cases for the other Arabs in Bosnia. In the first case, the amicus was the Helsinki Committee for Human Rights in Bosnia-Herzegovina, a local NGO. I prepared a brief that the Helsinki Committee submitted to the Constitutional Court of Bosnia-Herzegovina describing the relevant international standards governing the revocation of citizenship.[40] In the second case, the amicus was the US-based organization Human Rights Watch, which submitted an intervention to the European Court of Human Rights analyzing the legal framework for immigration detention under European human rights law.[41] In both cases, Abu Hamza won partial victories, although not on the issues that amici addressed.[42]

Amicus curiae interventions provided a space of interaction with the law in which to balance concerns over method and ethics. Amicus briefs did not seek to argue the merits or facts of Abu Hamza's case, that obviously being the role of his own counsel. Instead, they deployed the prestige of these NGOs to bolster arguments to the courts about what the applicable legal standards should be. This afforded the possibility of maintaining certain broad normative stances—such as an opposition to torture or to arbitrary deprivation of citizenship—without committing myself to any specific opinion or perspective on what Abu Hamza or other mujahids had done. Lawyering for the amicus was hardly a neutral act, but it also allowed me to preserve some degree of critical distance from the parties themselves. In this way, I sought to place myself in the gap between supporting a "friend" of the court and providing the "token of friendship" [ʿarabūn al-ṣadāqa] requested by Abu Hamza.

Finally, there was the more general role of *human rights advocate*. While in Bosnia, I developed an informal (and unpaid) relationship with the local human rights NGO mentioned above, the Helsinki Committee. Over the course of my research, Abu Hamza and several other of my interlocutors found themselves placed in a newly built immigration detention center in Sarajevo. I was able to continue seeing them there, but only in my capacity as a consultant for the Helsinki Committee. While this work did not require being a licensed attorney, it nevertheless entailed inhabiting a certain NGO worker role that depends on a fluency in English and in the specific manner of speaking that invokes and repurposes international and European human rights law and its related forms of regulatory and technocratic implementation. During my visits, I was careful to delineate my two professional identities of researcher and advocate when speaking to detainees, and accordingly prioritized the human rights aspect of discussing their cases and conditions. Several were uninterested in taking conversations beyond that. Others were eager to speak about everything, reasoning that participating in my anthropological research would also be helpful to them in the long term through the altering of public perceptions and understandings.

While lawyering shaped this ethnography in many ways, the converse was true only to a lesser extent. The most logical space to bring my ethnography to bear in litigation has been in the familiar but somewhat limited role of the expert witness, and I have accordingly done so in court cases touching on the Bosnian jihad in the United States and the United Kingdom.[43] Educating judges about the social context out of which GWOT captives emerged has its uses, encouraging them to resist reflexively criminalizing everyday forms of wandering across the Global South in search of adventure, jobs, religious learning, or mere safety. Too often, however, ethnography helped me see what the law *cannot* do, at least not without massive and sustained political pressure. Notwithstanding the enormous attention paid to courts as guardians of rights, my anthropological sensibilities led me to appreciate how much of the dirty work of GWOT takes place in transnational spaces *between* governments that produced jails and killing fields designed to evade judicial scrutiny. Litigating against GWOT is a frustrating form of shadow-boxing, and that is something anthropology could do little to change from within the courtroom. Outside, one can only hope that the insights of this study may contribute to wider shifts in thinking and debate.

Chapter 1

MIGRATIONS

IN THE AUTUMN OF 1992, AS THE WORLD'S ATTENTION INCREASINGLY turned toward the war in newly independent Bosnia-Herzegovina, something piqued the curiosity of journalists passing through the center of the country. Word had spread that a small group of Arab "holy warriors," veterans of the recent jihad in Afghanistan, were fighting alongside Bosnian Muslims and had set up camp in the village of Mehurići. The foreigners stood out with their darker skin tones, manner of speech and dress, and outward markers of Islamic piety, such as long beards, abstention from alcohol, and rigorous adherence to the five daily prayers. A stream of reporters from London, New York, Kuwait, and Zagreb flocked to them. Some published photographs of their leader, known as Abu ʿAbd al-ʿAziz: a middle-aged, dark-skinned man wearing camouflage and a camping vest, his hair and beard dyed dark orange with henna (Figure 3). In some pictures, he is sitting placidly in a wooded field, in others he poses in a spotless white robe with smiling blond children. To many, Abu ʿAbd al-ʿAziz may have seemed to be the jihad's universalism made flesh, thanks to rumors of his having also fought in the Philippines, Kashmir, and "Africa." When asked about his nationality, he consistently answered only: "Islam."[1] And the passport that he did carry came from the state that strives to project an image of worldwide stewardship of the faith: Saudi Arabia.

At the same time, Abu ʿAbd al-ʿAziz maintained that his only mission was to defend his Muslim brethren, and he disclaimed one of the goals most commonly ascribed to foreign jihadists: establishing an Islamic state by force of arms. Lest one think this message was designed only to reassure non-Muslims, it was mainly directed at those arguing that Bosnian Muslims were insufficiently pious to merit armed solidarity. As Abu ʿAbd al-ʿAziz retorted in one of the Muslim Brotherhood's leading magazines, "Will we leave girls to be raped, children to be taken away by Crusaders, and youths to be killed and slaughtered while standing by and simply invoking [the excuse of] 'secularism'? Personally, I believe that a secular Muslim state is much better than a Crusader one."[2] Nor was Abu ʿAbd al-ʿAziz a fellow traveler of the group that would later be known as al-Qaʿida, and he was even careful never to openly criticize the House of Saud.[3] In short, Abu ʿAbd al-ʿAziz confounded typical narratives portraying "global jihad" or "Salafi jihadism" as forms of violence that, through an alchemy of piety and mobility, somehow defy any political logic or limitation.[4]

As Abu ʿAbd al-ʿAziz is perhaps the best-known foreign mujahid to fight in Bosnia—although, as we shall see, his notoriety greatly surpassed his role on

FIGURE 3. Abu ʿAbd al-ʿAziz in *Newsweek* magazine. Pascal Le Segretain/Sygma via Getty Images.

the ground—his story is a useful place to start in writing a history of this jihad, through folios of narrative stitched across languages and regions, rumors and fictions. The journalists who interviewed Abu ʿAbd al-ʿAziz started so often by asking *where* he was from; this chapter will instead focus on *how* he and others like him got there, in the broad sense of the historically inflected circuits of mobility that shaped their lives. This shift in perspective is necessary to understand the history of this universalist project, which also requires thinking beyond the category of the "foreign fighter." Posing the foreign fighter as a problem—or setting up a puzzle as asking why individuals fight in "other people's wars"—reinforces the nation as the default category for legitimate violence.[5] This is an old and prevalent way of thinking. Carl Schmitt once contrasted the true partisan, the nonstate rebel whose legitimacy stems from limiting his fight to his own home territory, with what he called the "motorized partisan": an irregular fighter who instead of defending home and hearth is set loose upon the world without geographical or legal constraint.[6] For Schmitt, the very possibility of humane warfare requires legal regimes with a clear spatial grounding—a founding act of appropriating and partitioning land in which the nation roots itself.[7] The genealogy of the term *foreign fighter* echoes this distinction: its use exploded into global media coverage during the occupation of Iraq, when the US military sought to divide its armed opposition between persuadable locals and fanatical outsiders.[8]

The methodological nationalism embedded in the foreign fighter category has left us with a literature that focuses on states either as origins or as destinations. In the former, alienated Muslim youth set off for distant lands of jihad only to boomerang back, better-trained and readier to wreak havoc than ever before.[9] In the latter, foreign fighters appear in conflicts between local factions as a sort of interruption, inscrutable and perhaps even monstrous.[10] Taken together, these two approaches rely on geographies of blame in which a process called "radicalization" always seems to happen off-stage: viewed from sites of departure, radicalization occurs while fighting abroad. Viewed from their destinations, fighters arrive being radicalized already.

This chapter, in contrast, presents a history of a universalism without reverting to the nation-state as its constituent unit. While nationality was certainly relevant among the mujahids, *foreign* and *local* were not the primary categories used in the jihad. Instead, the most common way of distinguishing someone like Abu ʿAbd al-ʿAziz from the Bosnian Muslims he fought alongside was to call him one of the *ansar*. This term, a collective noun, resonates with early histories of Islam: when Muhammad the prophet of Islam and his followers emigrated from Mecca, the people of Medina sheltered them, joined their ranks, and then set out with them to spread the faith. The emigrants from Mecca were called *muhajirs*; the helpers from Medina were the ansar, a term often rendered in English as "partisans."[11] Emigrant and partisan—muhajir and ansar, respectively—are both tropes of mobility and together disrupt Schmitt's easy distinction between the tentatively legitimate local fighter and the always-suspect foreigner.[12] In the pages that follow, we will see how ansar could be mobile without being rootless, how their movements were conditioned and shaped by overlapping historical patterns and thick webs of transregional social relations.

The category of ansar is just one example of the diverse, deeply rooted, and widely shared repertoire of tropes and institutional structures broadly deemed "Islamic" that were readily drawn upon to ground, legitimize, and organize the work of the jihad.[13] But writing a useful history here requires going beyond such idioms a universalist project may employ. No less necessary is attending to the patterns of historical movement that bring people together such that categories like ansar could emerge as something they all regarded in common as compelling.[14] Before properly regarding the tapestry of the jihad, we must examine some of the many threads out of which it was woven, threads that traversed and bound disparate geographies. The use of similar idioms across various jihads—notions like ansar or other sundry Arabic-language terms whose diligent cataloging and explication too often stand in for thinking about jihad—can project a false sense of "Islamic" continuity across cases. Yet mujahids did not move from Afghanistan to Bosnia as a single horde; indeed, it is highly likely that most of those who fought in Bosnia had never been to Afghanistan at all. Instead, mobilities need to be discerned in relation to their specific locations and histories. This chapter will highlight two of the major circuits that fed into the Bosnian jihad: one that coalesced around the western Indian Ocean and another that emerged across the Mediterranean Sea.[15] It will do so through following the life histories of two mujahids: its most infamous character, Abu ʿAbd al-ʿAziz, as well as an ordinary fighter from Morocco. Following the stories of these two men can broaden our conceptual horizons beyond the framing of the nation-state, but at the cost of adopting a more narrowly gendered perspective: while the diasporic and other forms of circulation discussed here set both men and women into motion, the jihad in Bosnia mobilized only men as ansar. In these accounts, it is men who cross geographical and moral thresholds while women are often the mothers, wives, and sisters who are left behind, returned to, or brought along.

Before proceeding with this historical reconstruction, however, we need to take one more step through the fog that has enveloped the subject of jihad and Abu ʿAbd al-ʿAziz in particular. The first challenge of this research has not been tracking down elusive or violent men, but rather making them legible as historical subjects, which requires sifting through the accumulated layers of discourse dumped on them in the Global War on Terror. If there is in these pages any journey into the heart of darkness, it is the darkness of the national security state. In other words, there is no talking about "terrorists" without first talking about terrorism expertise.

THE LEGENDS OF ABU ʿABD AL-ʿAZIZ

Across continents, languages, and media forms, Abu ʿAbd al-ʿAziz achieved considerable notoriety and became the stuff of legends. After spending a few months in Bosnia, he departed in late 1992 and traveled the world to give speeches, meet with journalists, and raise funds for the jihad from the Gulf states, Pakistan, and the United States. He even obtained an audience with Muhammad Nasir al-Din al-Albani, one of the most prominent Salafi scholars of the twentieth century.[16] The further away from Bosnia, the more his stature seemed to grow, far out of proportion to his actual influence on the ground. The Pakistani armed group Lashkar-e-Tayyiba called Abu ʿAbd al-ʿAziz "supreme commander" of the jihad in Bosnia as well as around the world, primary instigator of a mass armed Islamic revival that would "send a tide of concern [tashwīsh kī lahar] washing over the rulers of Europe."[17] In 2008, the United States Treasury labeled him a "Specially Designated Global Terrorist" on account of his financial support for Lashkar; the United Nations Security Council followed suit later that year by adding him to a sanctions list that requires member states worldwide to impose an arms embargo, travel ban, and asset freeze.[18] Before tracing Abu ʿAbd al-ʿAziz's journeys in the hopes of illuminating the outlines of the jihad, we must attend to these legends and their genesis, including through the production of terrorism expertise.

Abu ʿAbd al-ʿAziz's emergence in the English-speaking world as a globe-trotting arch-terrorist and the exploration of this legend marked the beginning of my own journey to write a history of this jihad. His introduction to these audiences came in a curious book, *Al-Qaida's Jihad in Europe: The Afghan-Bosnian Network*, that appeared in 2004. Its author, Evan Kohlmann, apprenticed under one of the earliest self-styled "terrorism experts," Steven Emerson, before striking out on his own.[19] Kohlmann's book is based almost entirely on English-language press clippings interwoven with court pleadings, along with a dash of plagiarism.[20] The book nevertheless helped Kohlmann launch a successful business as a terrorism consultant, trawling the internet (or rather, paying people who know Arabic and other relevant languages to do so) and developing a theory of online "radicalization." He became a sought-after expert witness in criminal prosecutions resulting in the imprisonment of multiple American Muslims, as well as a regular commentator for the MSNBC television network.

Like the book you are currently reading, *Al-Qaida's Jihad in Europe* devotes much of its first chapter to Abu ʿAbd al-ʿAziz. It gives his real name as Abdel Rahman al-Dosari and describes him not simply as leader of the Arab mujahids in Bosnia but also as an agent of al-Qaʿida responsible for turning the country into a staging ground for attacks on the West.[21] Some cursory internet searches, however, revealed that Kohlmann's sources would mention either al-Dosari or Abu ʿAbd al-ʿAziz, but none linked the two names as one person, nor could I find any other source that did so—other than those relying on Kohlmann's work, of course. But they were clearly different men: Abdel Rahman al-Dosari was a Salafi scholar and prominent critic of the House of Saud; Abu ʿAbd al-ʿAziz, on the other hand, was neither a religious scholar nor a public critic of the Saudi regime. There is another thing worth mentioning: al-Dosari died in 1979, over a decade before his alleged alter ego set off for jihad in Bosnia.[22] Yet without identifying Abu ʿAbd al-ʿAziz as al-Dosari, Kohlmann's thesis that Arab ansar in Bosnia were an extension of al-Qaʿida largely falls apart.

The legend of Abu ʿAbd al-ʿAziz as rendered by Evan Kohlmann was not simply an instance of incompetence or hackery: it also points to the symbiotic but fraught relationship between the national security state and outside experts. When Kohlmann began his work in the early years of the Global War on Terror, whatever knowledge the US government had about jihad-themed websites was likely very limited and tightly restricted. What prosecutors could not easily pry out of the intelligence agencies they could get from freelancers like Kohlmann instead, who as a private citizen was not governed by the secrecy rules of the bureaucracy. Further, investigative journalists have suggested that Kohlmann instigated the very prosecutions that would then retain him as a handsomely compensated expert witness.[23] These cases in turn generated opportunities to launder his "research"—by providing tips to the government that it would then repackage in its own public court filings. Even if later withdrawn or otherwise discredited, such allegations nevertheless had the imprimatur of being included in "government documents" and could find citational afterlives in the footnotes of more works of terrorism expertise.[24] Meanwhile, Kohlmann's erroneous conflation of al-Dosari and Abu ʿAbd al-ʿAziz was further recycled and propagated as authoritative by more respectable researchers based in universities and state-aligned defense research institutes.[25] Among the manifold ironies of this echo chamber of follies is that even when experts serve state imperatives they also act autonomously, indeed recklessly: Kohlmann's mistake seems to have been his alone and does not appear on US government terrorism lists. Terrorism experts are less faithful scribes of empire than they are enterprising vendors eagerly hawking new wares in the hopes of catching the eye of a fickle and easily distracted patron.

The legends of Abu ʿAbd al-ʿAziz as sketched above are constituted in very different ways: one largely through word of mouth, through faded newspaper clippings, audio recordings, and interviews that furtively resurface on the internet. The other, drawing partly from the subset of the first that exists in English, circulated in court testimony, prosecutors' pleadings, bureaucratic proscriptions, and works of terrorism expertise that move through the state. Both legends elevated Abu ʿAbd al-ʿAziz from a man who commanded at most a few dozen men in Bosnia for several months to an immensely powerful fighter of global reach. And both present him as an incarnation of a dangerous form of universalism: a one-man vector connecting Islam's Arab center to its Balkan periphery in a quest to found a global Islamic state, sailing on a current of petrodollars and piety. But there is another way to understand this history, one that is obscured in glossing Abu ʿAbd al-ʿAziz as "Saudi," or even as "Arab." For Abu ʿAbd al-ʿAziz was actually born Mahmud Bahadhiq in Hyderabad, in the Indian subcontinent, to parents from the Hadramawt region of southern Yemen.[26] The family was part of the larger Hadrami diaspora that has extended across the Indian Ocean and elsewhere for centuries, whose best-known son was Osama bin Laden.[27] This detail can help us overturn these legends and see Abu ʿAbd al-ʿAziz's story not in national terms but in transregional ones, and to sketch a different approach to placing universalisms in history.

PORTRAIT OF THE MUJAHID AS AN OLD MAN

After a decade of piecing together his story from newspaper clippings, excavated online postings, archival documents, and the narratives of others, I sat down with Abu ʿAbd al-ʿAziz, then in his early seventies. We had a pleasant chat in a more or less public place in Jeddah in the winter of 2014 while I was on a brief visit to Saudi Arabia. We were joined by his brother Khalid, a prominent physician whom I had interviewed by Skype several years earlier while Abu ʿAbd al-ʿAziz was still in prison. Abu ʿAbd al-ʿAziz had spent the better part of the previous decade incarcerated, but the buoyant sense of humor evident from his 1990s interviews remained: "I like to be happy and to tell people that there is also fun in jihad." Thanks to his being on US and UN terrorism lists, his bank accounts were frozen and he could not leave the country. Two decades had passed since the only photographs of him that I had seen were taken: now he wore spectacles and the almost pinkish dye in his hair was much more vivid than the orange henna of the early 1990s (Figure 4). Finding Abu ʿAbd al-ʿAziz was not particularly difficult, requiring little more than knowledge of Arabic, the ability to use an internet search engine, and some deductive reasoning. It was certainly more straightforward—and, for me, less ethnographically noteworthy—than untangling the footnotes and citations of the texts about him circulating through and around the US security state.

More than other fieldwork encounters—including those that took place in contexts of incarceration—this one was overdetermined by the law in one specific sense: through the foreclosure of the very possibility of reciprocity. This is because in 2010, the United States Supreme Court sanctioned an extraordinarily broad interpretation of the crime of material support for terrorism that would include even speech acts ordinarily protected by the First Amendment to the US Constitution if undertaken "in coordination with . . . a foreign terrorist organization."[28] In the context of my meeting with Abu ʿAbd al-ʿAziz this meant adopting a maximally cautious approach of avoiding any behavior that could be mischaracterized as "coordination," even small gestures such as coffee-buying, driving, and draft-sharing that anthropologists use to convince themselves that they can mitigate the disturbingly one-sided power relationships that often structure the act of "fieldwork." Under US law, the safest course of action was to conjure a relationship of pure parasitism: the collection of data in exchange for nothing.[29] Yet logics of exchange were not far from Abu ʿAbd al-ʿAziz's mind: after I showed him the quick photograph of him I had snapped on my phone, he chuckled and remarked dryly, "You can sell it."

Abu ʿAbd al-ʿAziz's enforced immobility follows several generations of transregional migration around the Indian Ocean. In the pages that follow, I hope to give some sense of this movement—not only its geographical range,

FIGURE 4. Abu ʿAbd al-ʿAziz in Jeddah, 2014. Photo by author.

but also how it could be seen as not so extraordinary for such a person. Abu ʿAbd al-ʿAziz's paternal grandfather, Ahmad Bahadhiq, left his home in the Wadi al-Aysar area of Hadramawt in the early twentieth century, crossed the Arabian sea, and found his way to the city-state of Hyderabad in southern India.[30] Abu ʿAbd al-ʿAziz and his brother did not know exactly why their grandfather left, but written histories allow some educated guesses. Wadi al-Aysar was conquered with great difficulty in 1898 by forces allied with the Quʿayti sultanate. The new rulers imposed heavy exactions on their vanquished foes, forcing many to sell their lands or go into exile.[31] One may be tempted to think of Ahmad Bahadhiq's move as one between nations—Yemen to India—or between regions—from the Middle East to South Asia. But it was also a journey through territory familiar to Hadramis, akin to "two rooms in the same house."[32] After all, Hyderabad had been a major destination for Hadramis since at least the late eighteenth century, where despite their limited numbers they became especially prominent in this large multi-ethnic city as soldiers, police officers, and private guards—a migrant military labor force that the British were anxious to surveil.[33] Tens of thousands of Hadramis and their descendants made the city their home. This migration had significant political ramifications as well: the Quʿaytis who conquered the Bahadhiqs' lands had themselves amassed their fortunes in Hyderabad. And like Hyderabad, the Quʿayti sultanate was a nominally independent kingdom under indirect British rule, albeit a much smaller one on the overseas fringe of the Indian empire.[34] Many of the Quʿaytis were absentee aristocrats, more accustomed to living in Hyderabad than in their ancestral homeland.

Nearly a half-century after Ahmad Bahadhiq crossed the sea to Hyderabad, the family moved again. On his deathbed, he told his son Muhammad—Abu ʿAbd al-ʿAziz's father—to go to the Hijaz, site of Islam's two holiest cities and under the rule of the House of Saud. Muhammad had grown up in Hyderabad, graduated from a government high school, and found a job as a clerk in the government. He married another Hadrami from the Baghazal clan; the family was part of Hyderabad's cosmopolitan Muslim middle class, and their children grew up speaking Arabic, Urdu, and English. Even decades later, Abu ʿAbd al-ʿAziz's accent in English retained distinctively Urdu characteristics, such as the semivowel medial "v" in words like "government."[35] The family's Indian Arab social world was violently rearranged with the end of British rule in South

Asia: decolonization did not just birth the two newly independent states of India and Pakistan, it also led to the absorption of hundreds of princely states, of which Hyderabad was the largest. In September 1948, the Indian army marched into the city, suppressed several competing insurgencies, and accepted the surrender of its Hadrami-led army. The Hadramis' place in the new order was unclear: some left for Pakistan, while early attempts by India to repatriate those born in Yemen also ran aground.[36] Those who stayed became a marginalized community in the city, later associated with organized crime and professional sports, especially wrestling. With their status and prospects diminished, the Bahadhiqs came to see their future elsewhere. But instead of crossing the newly forged border between the nation-states of India and Pakistan, Muhammad took to the ocean, finding it to be a more suitably traversable threshold. He journeyed to the gulf coast of Saudi Arabia by ship and made his way by land to Jeddah, as thoroughly cosmopolitan a city as Hyderabad was. A few years later, he sent for his wife and for some of his children—the oldest son stayed behind in India with a prosperous maternal uncle to complete his studies.

Mahmud Bahadhiq, who would later be known to the world as Abu ʿAbd al-ʿAziz, was around ten years old when he arrived in Jeddah. The family may not have felt especially out of place, as the cosmopolitan port city boasted large and long-standing Hadrami and Indian populations and trade ties with the subcontinent, including Hyderabad.[37] Within a few years of settling in the Hijaz, the Bahadhiqs received Saudi citizenship, something that became far more difficult to obtain in subsequent decades. The early years weren't easy; the boys worked as street vendors, hawking cigarettes and watermelon seeds in coffee shops or at football matches. With his language skills and work experience, the father readily found work at the US Embassy, which around that time moved to a new compound on the northern outskirts of the city. He died of tuberculosis in 1962, and his widow continued to work from home, stuffing and addressing envelopes containing copies of the embassy's Arabic newsletter. In the meantime, the boys managed to visit India a few times, except now they flew, arriving via Bombay in 1965 to see their uncle. For Mahmud, it was the start of decades of travel: after completing high school in Syria in 1967, he applied to be a pilot for Saudia Airlines, which was training its first generation of pilots to replace the Americans provided by the ARAMCO oil company. He remembered being impressed with the smart uniforms he saw on pilots in Syria, with their neckties and stripes. Colorblindness disqualified him from the job, but he was instead hired as a secretary and eventually worked his way up to middle management—a job that would take him all over the world. Several years later, Mahmud visited Egypt for the first time, and while calling on the family of a colleague in Mansura met the woman who would become his first wife, ʿAzza—"you can write it," he pointed at my notebook as he mentioned her name. They wed in 1973.

For Abu ʿAbd al-ʿAziz, the shift to jihad came with middle age. By the mid-1980s, Abu ʿAbd al-ʿAziz was nearing early retirement from Saudia Airlines, which gifted him with a Rado wristwatch that an envious fellow mujahid in Bosnia would "borrow" years later.[38] He and ʿAzza, already active in charitable causes, were at the time caught up in the general mood of solidarity with the Afghan jihad prevalent in Jeddah. Abu ʿAbd al-ʿAziz decided to check things out for himself: he traveled to Pakistan on holiday and spent a few weeks in a training camp financed by bin Laden. The decision to travel and fight may seem either pathological or heroic when left in the margins of grand geopolitical narratives of "global jihad." Those accounts have focused on the billions of dollars spent by the United States and Saudi Arabia in the 1980s to drive the war in Afghanistan but have had much less to say about the parallel networks of activism built on a confluence of migratory ties shaped and driven by oil, capital, and piety across the Indian Ocean and the Arab world. The Hijaz region became an important site for these mobilizations through the multiple opportunities for networking afforded by the Hajj pilgrimage, Saudi-sponsored pan-Islamic organizations, and Jeddah's cosmopolitan communities and its massive new airport, opened in 1981. When understood against this backdrop, Abu ʿAbd al-ʿAziz emerges clearly not simply as a Saudi national radicalized into joining other people's wars, but as a third-generation migrant with a genealogy extending from Hadramawt to Hyderabad to the Hijaz, command of multiple languages, and a career in civil aviation that allowed him to travel widely.

Abu ʿAbd al-ʿAziz told me that in Afghanistan he only spent one night at the front in 1988, where he could hear sounds of gunfire in the distance. Instead it was Pakistan that ended up drawing his interest, in contrast to most other Arab mujahids who treated it as a way station or rear base for the Afghan jihad. While traveling through Pakistan and practicing the half-forgotten Urdu of his childhood, he linked up with activists from the Ahl-i Hadith, a reformist school of Islamic thought originating in South Asia.[39] Abu ʿAbd al-ʿAziz had attended lectures by one of their leading preachers, Ehsan Elahi Zaheer, in Saudi Arabia. The Ahl-i Hadith, however, had at best a tepid attitude toward the Afghan jihad. So in Abu ʿAbd al-ʿAziz's telling, it was he who convinced some Ahl-i Hadith activists to participate in jihad and establish an organization for this purpose, whose most notorious instantiation would be known as Lashkar-e-Tayyiba.[40] Lashkar's commitment to taking up arms rendered it an outlier in the broader Ahl-i Hadith scene, itself one of the smaller streams of Islamic reformism in the country: its scholastic nature and lack of a broad social base facilitated its co-optation by the Pakistani military as a proxy militia for the war in Kashmir.[41] Abu ʿAbd al-ʿAziz's financial contributions to Lashkar, which he estimated as at most amounting to a few tens of thousand dollars per year during the 1990s, likely paled in comparison to the subventions from Pakistan's military. But what he could distinctively offer in contrast to a national army was a sense of being part of a global struggle, through his Arabness and a record of fighting in other regions—the further away from Afghanistan and Kashmir, the better.

In March 1992, Bosnia-Herzegovina declared independence from Yugoslavia, and the next month, the Marxist government in Kabul fell to the Afghan mujahidin. Just as one struggle seemed to come to an end, another presented new opportunities to burnish one's credentials in jihad. That summer, Abu ʿAbd al-ʿAziz set out alongside four friends from Jeddah with experience in Afghanistan to explore prospects. They traveled to Croatia via Germany and Austria and spent about a month in Zagreb surveying the situation before meeting people who agreed to take them into Bosnia to meet a new militia calling itself the Muslim Forces, whose story will be explored in the next chapter. Abu ʿAbd al-ʿAziz returned to Jeddah to raise more funds while his comrades entered Bosnia and linked up with the Muslim Forces near Travnik.[42] Abu ʿAbd al-ʿAziz rushed to join them, spending the summer and autumn in Bosnia fighting and proselytizing. The journalists and aid workers soon followed, many of them sponsored by the organizations, capital, and knowledge that congealed in the Hijaz for the Afghan jihad.

When Abu ʿAbd al-ʿAziz departed Bosnia in December 1992, he parlayed his experiences into a speaking and fundraising tour throughout the Arab world as well as the United States and the United Kingdom. As is often the case in solidarity movements, Abu ʿAbd al-ʿAziz's entrepreneurial spirit enabled him to make a name for himself as a spokesman for the Bosnian cause, especially to more distant and less-informed publics. Pakistan would provide his most important audience: in January 1993, he attended a special meeting in which Lashkar's parent organization appointed him as the head of its department for "global jihad," although he seems not to have had much else to show for it.[43] He continued regular visits to Pakistan until the early 2000s, eventually purchased a house in Muridke, near Lashkar's headquarters, and even sent some of his children to university in Pakistan.

Abu ʿAbd al-ʿAziz's grandstanding stirred its own resentments and suspicions, which he gently avoided addressing in our meeting. More than two years after his departure from Bosnia, Abu ʿAbd al-ʿAziz allegedly continued to describe himself to journalists as the leader of the jihad there, prompting the Katiba to correct the record in a letter to as important a donor as Qatar's Minister of Religious Endowments: "We understood from Abu ʿAbd al-ʿAziz's comments that he wants to be seen as the commander of the mujahids throughout the whole world; we can comment on what concerns us and he is not the commander of the mujahids in Bosnia." [44] Whether he was intentionally exaggerating his importance or not, Abu ʿAbd al-ʿAziz did not seem to mind the publicity so much.

By the early 2000s—when the Saudi state had become far more suspicious of traveling jihad activists—he turned to the then-emergent medium of the internet, fielding questions in online forum discussions about sundry matters of jihad. Is parental permission required to join the fight? Is jihad a hindrance or an opportunity for marriage? He shared anecdotes about his meeting with Bosnian president Alija Izetbegović and a letter from his wife to their son providing encouragement and support as he embarked on his own first jihad. He penned a humorous essay playing on the stereotypes about different nationalities he encountered—wisecracking Egyptians with their funny accents, authoritarian Libyans who took after their leader Qaddafi, Britons obsessed with order and punctuality.[45]

If we follow Abu ʿAbd al-ʿAziz's genealogical chain of peregrinations—from Hadramawt to Hyderabad to the Hijaz to Afghanistan and Pakistan and then to Bosnia—a distinctive kind of diasporic sensibility emerges. In recounting his family story, Abu ʿAbd al-ʿAziz described India as a "golden bird," a land promising riches not only for the British empire but for Hadramis as well. Hadramis, in his telling, are itinerant merchants in search of "halal income" who are wary of entanglements in local politics. "The Hadramis never like to stay in one country. If there is any problem, they travel. They leave. They don't like to interfere, just business." As questionable and self-serving as this statement may be, it also resonates with his stance that the jihad must support Bosnian Muslim goals, regardless of whether they wanted an Islamic state. In both cases, mobility has a specific and morally inflected purpose (defending Muslims, generating "halal" income) and one should avoid the risks of becoming too embroiled in local situations. At the same time, his use of transactional language—Hyderabad as a place to make money, telling me that I could sell his photograph—and almost crass sense of humor evince a particular register of the Hadrami diaspora. While the best-known itinerant Hadramis historically have been scholars and *sayyids*—those claiming descent from the Prophet Muhammad—Abu ʿAbd al-ʿAziz identifies as a modest tribesman. He described sayyids as people for whom you had to stand whenever they enter a room, for no good reason.[46] Similarly, Abu ʿAbd al-ʿAziz's attitude toward being Hadrami was rather matter-of-fact: while it was relevant to his narration of his genealogy, he would never suggest that it gave him some kind of inherent inclination or talent for jihad. The relationship between his diasporic existence and the universalism he embraced was an important but ultimately contingent one.[47]

As important, mobility informed Abu ʿAbd al-ʿAziz's public persona, from acolytes and detractors alike. His Pakistani beneficiaries invoked the stereotype of Gulf Arabs as profligate and licentious in praising Abu ʿAbd al-ʿAziz for instead being "rapturously intoxicated with jihad [jihād ke nashe meñ mast]." [48] For audiences already exposed directly or through family and friends to conspicuous consumption in Gulf societies, the reference would have been especially pertinent. From the other side, one pseudonymous online detractor ridiculed Abu ʿAbd al-ʿAziz as "one of the shaykhs of the purse" looking to buy his way to glory. This author compared him to other Saudis who "send out labor contractors to bring them Indians, Filipinos, and Egyptian rubes," and claimed he rented mujahids from the motley hordes squatting on the outskirts of Mecca's great mosque.[49] In this argument, the cosmopolitan populations of the Hijaz become evidence not of Islam's universality but of a lack of roots and principles. Carl Schmitt would have understood this critique all too well. Yet the thick web of connections and currents that shaped both Abu ʿAbd al-ʿAziz's life and the possibilities of his engagement with jihad belie Schmitt's conception of the "motorized partisan" as mere weaponized anomie. Even when I met him, with his passport seized and bank accounts frozen, Abu ʿAbd al-ʿAziz nevertheless continued to reach out across boundaries in his own ways, using his Urdu to proselytize to South Asian workers in Jeddah. It was these lifetimes of migration, these attempts to ride and stay afloat on the shifting and at times violent currents of history, that made Abu ʿAbd al-ʿAziz an unsurprising figure to emerge as an early—but not uncontested—representative of the jihad in Bosnia.

MUJAHID WITH A WALKMAN

One day in September 1992, Abu ʿAbd al-ʿAziz was at the mujahids' camp in the village of Mehurići. He greeted a Moroccan newcomer who had just arrived by bus from Italy and wanted to join the jihad. Abu ʿAbd al-ʿAziz asked a few simple questions about where he came from, if anyone sent him, if he had any military experience, if he had chosen a *kunya* for himself.[50] The newcomer decided to be called Abu ʿAli al-Maghribi—ʿAli after his father since he had no children himself and al-Maghribi (the Moroccan) to distinguish himself from any other Abu ʿAli. Never having handled a weapon, Abu ʿAli had to wait until there were enough recruits to put together a training course. He spent the next week or so in the village, praying and studying the Quran. When the number of arrivals reached twenty or so, they started two weeks of training with basic infantry weapons such as Kalashnikovs and rocket-propelled grenades. Before heading to the front, each man had to hand over his passport and money for safe-keeping and to draw up a will.[51] While sitting with me in a Zenica restaurant fifteen years later, Abu ʿAli couldn't recall much about his will except that the first person it addressed was his mother. "I started with my mother because she's more emotional, if you die she'll start crying straight away. So I wrote, telling her not to cry, if I'm martyred you should cheer, not weep.'"[52] Soon enough Abu ʿAbd al-ʿAziz was gone, off raising funds and promoting the jihad, and Abu ʿAli and the remaining few dozen mujahids braced themselves for winter.

If Abu ʿAbd al-ʿAziz was swept along to Bosnia by currents of history that swirled around the Indian Ocean, Abu ʿAli came from an equally significant itinerary for the jihad, across the Mediterranean Sea. A large segment of the Arabs who participated in the Bosnian jihad like Abu ʿAli did not arrive from the Middle East but were already living in western Europe: France, the United Kingdom, Germany, Austria, and most important, Italy. By following the experiences of migratory routes such as those traced by Abu ʿAli, we can see how the jihad in Bosnia was in many key ways a European phenomenon. Moreover, the northward migrations to which Abu ʿAli belonged were intensifying at a time when the idea of Europe was being reconfigured from the divided confrontation space of the Cold War to a zone of capitalist cosmopolitanism and prosperity contrasted with its clannish, impoverished Balkan periphery. At the same time, the European project was increasingly questioned from within by politically self-aware and assertive Muslim communities. For many Muslims in Europe, the Bosnian war presented not only a cause with which they could identify and show solidarity, but a test of Europe's own stated commitment to tolerance, secularism, and multiculturalism. This was the case especially for those who grew up exposed to—or bombarded by—these values. A jihad veteran from suburban London with Pakistani immigrant parents once told me about first seeing news footage from the Omarska concentration camp while in high school. "I thought to myself, hang on: this reminds me of the Holocaust. I studied it in school, I read Anne Frank. I used to think that these things only happened many years ago, but what would I do if this happened again in my time?" He only learned later that Muslims were involved in the war.

Abu ʿAli was born in a small city in central Morocco and had pursued Islamic studies for two years in university before dropping out and working in a customs office in Casablanca. He decided to seek work abroad in 1992 and went to France on a tourist visa—he also had siblings in Canada and elsewhere in Europe so the decision to migrate was hardly an unusual one. After a few weeks visiting relatives in France, Abu ʿAli slipped into Italy and worked as a street vendor in the southern city of Potenza. Italy was a seam joining two different maritime zones: one across the Mediterranean linking it to north Africa, the other across the Adriatic to the Balkans.[53]

The number of Moroccans in Italy jumped from sixteen thousand to nearly seventy-eight thousand between 1987 and 1990.[54] Tunisians also came in significant numbers after Italy helped Zine El Abidine Ben Ali come to power in 1987. Ben Ali presided over massive privatization of state companies and a steep devaluation of the Tunisian currency, dramatically increasing migration from the southern shore. Egyptians, too, came in large numbers from Iraq after the 1991 war and UN sanctions regime caused employment opportunities there to dry up. Much of the migration, unlike in earlier periods, went north to Milan and Turin, where Arabs found jobs in manufacturing, construction, agriculture, street peddling, and food service industries.[55]

These passages over land and sea were experienced by some as journeys along a path of moral enlightenment as well. In Abu ʿAli's recounting, the Moroccans he found in Potenza did not keep to a proper lifestyle as ordained by the faith, so he moved on to Turin, in the north. There, he met an imam he knew from university back home, who showed him videos of atrocities against Muslims in Bosnia. Abu ʿAli then decided to join the fight. He sent all his money back to his family, keeping only 2,000 Deutschmarks for himself, and bought a bus ticket. On the bus to Slovenia, Abu ʿAli was not worried about being arrested. Moroccans didn't need visas to enter ex-Yugoslavia at that time and after all, he reasoned, what would the Italian authorities do if he was trying to exit their country? The border guards looked at him askance for wanting to leave the safety of western Europe for a Balkan war zone: "Don't you know there's a war going on over there?" "That's where I want to go!" he told them.

In some important ways, however, Abu ʿAli was not leaving Europe behind, but was carrying it with him into the war. For veterans of Afghanistan coming from the Gulf, Bosnia was a markedly "European" jihad. Because so many of the fighters were migrants who had been living in Europe, all the classic stereotypes followed. They were seen as morally loose and tied to the comforts of consumerism—a type that came to be known derisively as "a mujahid with a Walkman," a reference to the Japanese-made portable audio cassette players that were popular in the late twentieth century. Europe was glossed as the cause of any undisciplined or embarrassing behavior—acts that other observers often attribute to Islamic zealotry instead. Perhaps the most notorious of the mujahids, Kamal Karay from Tunisia, was widely reputed to have been involved in criminal activity while in Italy. In Bosnia, he was kicked out of the Katiba for reasons that were never clear: accusations that came up in people's stories and in archival documents included disobeying orders, coercing Bosnian Muslims to practice Islam "properly," and mistreatment of Croat civilians.[56] After the war, he stayed and continued to get in trouble with the law, including reports of domestic violence and a murder conviction for killing an Egyptian in Zenica. He was a colorful figure in the regional media, implicated in a plot to assassinate the Pope (likely on the basis of mistaken identity) and temporarily absconding while on furlough from prison.[57]

From the other end, some mujahids decried what they called a "Peshawar" mind-set, after the frontier city in Pakistan that was the main base for the Afghan jihad. Peshawar attitudes and ways of thinking were those associated with factionalism and fanaticism. Efforts to support the Bosnian jihad throughout the Muslim world encountered increasing skepticism resulting from the growing infighting between the mujahidin groups in Afghanistan. Arab volunteers were criticized for succumbing to the same centrifugal forces: Peshawar in the 1990s was home to perhaps dozens of competing groups of Islamist exiles from various countries, and some sought to use the opportunities posed by chaos in Afghanistan to pursue their own agendas.[58] The mujahids in Bosnia from Abu ʿAbd al-ʿAziz onward presented their efforts as comparatively more organized, disciplined, and in sync with a credible local authority. There were obvious structural reasons for these differences, of course. In Afghanistan, the jihad was a guerrilla struggle aimed at denying a regime's control over the populace, using mainly hit-and-run attacks on conventional forces from a safe haven in a neighboring country. Things quickly degenerated in the attempted shift to regular warfare and conquest of urban centers. In contrast, the war in Bosnia was one of nationalist consolidation and ethnic cleansing: the enemy didn't seek to rule Muslims but to expel or eliminate them. Relative to Afghanistan, there were more or less clearly demarcated lines of confrontation, and warfare was more hierarchically organized, albeit often in separate besieged enclaves that left local commanders with considerable autonomy from central authorities.

The "Europeanization" of the jihad was well under way before the end of its first year with efforts to consolidate and institutionalize the presence of ansar. Around this time, those who emerged as the Katiba's political leaders were educated professionals living in Europe, none of whom had fought in Afghanistan. The first *amir* of the Katiba, Abu al-Harith, was a Libyan physician residing in Austria who arrived in Bosnia sometime in 1992. His deputy and successor, Abu al-Maʿali, was an Algerian who finished university studies in economics and was working in Italy before joining the jihad. They will feature prominently in the following chapters, but the question of Europe—both the way that this concept shaped the jihad and how the jihad prompts a rethinking of its racial and geographic dimensions—perhaps loomed largest in the itinerary and entailments of the man who was arguably the most respected Arab mujahid in Bosnia. Anwar Shaʿban, head of Milan's Islamic Cultural Institute (ICI—Istituto Culturale Islamico), worked to support both relief efforts and the jihad in Bosnia while preaching to his largely working-class congregation of Arab migrants. Like many Egyptian Islamist activists of his generation, Shaʿban was educated as an engineer: he completed a degree in marine engineering from Alexandria University and was largely self-taught in Islamic subjects. Shaʿban arrived in Milan in 1989 after spending several years teaching in Kuwait. He took up the job of building up ICI, whose founders had split off from the older and more Muslim Brotherhood–oriented Islamic Center (Centro Islamico). ICI acted as a communications node for the Katiba, relaying its faxed newsletters to the outside world and guiding volunteers on how to enter Bosnia. When supporters outside the region could not reach the Katiba by phone, they would sometimes call Milan instead. Shaʿban visited Bosnia in 1992, and the Katiba continued to seek his advice; upon relocating to Zenica in 1995—and, unusually, bringing his family along—he quickly became the unit's leading authority on Islamic matters.[59] In the meantime, ICI developed a reputation as a stronghold for exiled members of Egypt's Islamic Group and drew intense police scrutiny, including the extensive wiretaps that have made some of the research for this book possible.[60] Police raided the mosque in June 1995, shortly after Shaʿban's departure for Bosnia. For years thereafter, ICI remained one of the most prominent targets of the Italian state's efforts against "radical Islam." One of Shaʿban's successors as head of ICI, al-Husayni Hilmi ʿArman (Abu ʿImad), was arrested on multiple occasions before finally being deported in 2013. ʿArman's deputy, Hassan Mustafa Nasr (Abu Omar), was kidnapped by the CIA in 2003 and rendered to Egypt, causing an international scandal.[61]

In parallel with the intrigues of exile groups and the secret police services that chased them, some laborers, students, and other migrants found in the jihad a path to spiritual self-improvement. A common theme in the narrative style of mujahid biographies emphasizes past sins to underscore redemption through jihad. Famous among the mujahids was the bulky Egyptian head cook, who had honed his skills working in a restaurant in Italy. Bosnian mujahids remembered him shouting, "Yalla, manjeria!" [It: *mangiare*] whenever meals were ready. It was also in Italy where he did drugs and ran with women before finding the straight path. But perhaps the most vivid example of the archetype of a man who traded passages over the sea for journeys of the soul would be Tabarnak, a well-traveled Algerian ship captain living in Italy who was wealthy, successful, and married to a Christian woman. One story in Arabic holds that a chance encounter with a "righteous man" [rajul min ahl al-khayr] who suggested he seek jihad in Bosnia changed the course of his life. That same day, Tabarnak gave his wife an ultimatum to convert to Islam and join him or divorce; she chose the latter and he abandoned his wealth and nice houses for jihad in Bosnia. Eventually he would fall in battle in Tutnjevac in the northeast of the country; locals reportedly renamed the hill where he died in his honor.[62] Tabarnak's story seems typical of the so-called "born again" who come to affirm their faith with renewed vigor, as seen in his choice of jihad over his wife in the Arabic hagiography summarized above. But such stories need not be seen as a refusal of all things European in favor of an inflexible, ethereal Islam. In one Bosnian narration, Tabarnak is remembered for his ability to connect with locals. "Tabarnak was special. Knowledgeable, capable, and versatile, he grasped our customs in a 'snapshot' ['snimao' je naše običaje] and loved talking to the youth and giving them guidance and advice for life."[63]

Similarly, Abu ʿAli's narration of his journey from Morocco through France, Italy, Slovenia, Croatia, and Bosnia was not just a passage through space, but also a story of his own development as a man, a Muslim, and a human being. Having stopped his studies of Islam while back in Morocco, he took up jihad as a substitute—"jihad is when one's faith is at its greatest and is most tested"—while in Europe, on a path that would take him through further tribulations. As the months passed, conditions became more difficult. By early 1993, the border with Croatia was mostly closed as Bosnian Muslim and Croat forces increasingly turned on each other, transforming their joint fight against Serb nationalists into a three-way conflict instead. After months of guard and patrol duty, the mujahids started going on the offensive and Abu ʿAli participated in several skirmishes. One day in June 1993, some men from a Bosnian militia calling itself the Green Berets (Zelene beretke) brought Abu ʿAli and some other Arabs along for an assault on a Croat position. "They liked to have Arabs with them on the line, it scared the enemy," he recalled. Abu ʿAli was on the left flank as they crept through the woods at dawn toward their objective when the enemy opened fire with machine guns from only a few meters away. Abu ʿAli was hit by a bullet in the arm and a rocket-propelled grenade seared the side of his head as it flew past him. The others told him that when they saw his body thrown into the air by the resulting explosion they reckoned him dead. Abu ʿAli's injuries left him badly maimed, and he spent weeks in a hospital unconscious or unable to recognize people. He rejoined the jihad after a year in rehabilitation, but only in an administrative capacity; his combat days were forever behind him.

When I met him in Zenica fourteen years after his injury, Abu ʿAli continued to walk with a limp, was deaf in one ear, and had only limited use of his left arm. On damp and rainy days, his arm would hurt even more. Abu ʿAli had no regrets about the war and repeatedly stressed to me the power of his faith, insisting one never knows when death will come and that therefore one must live life as properly as possible every day. He showed me videos expounding on this theme, with Islamic anthems in English with Bosnian subtitles playing over footage of jets colliding at an air show and race cars spinning out of control and knocking over spectators, all culminating in a computer-generated animation of a tsunami-like wave crashing down upon a city. Another tape came from Saudi Arabia, with images of men whose corpses had rotted within hours of death as a sign of their lack of piety during life.

In the weeks that we regularly saw each other, the life he recounted was one indelibly marked by migration, piety, and injury all together. When the war ended, he did not know what to do with himself. Most of the Arab mujahids were leaving, but some Bosnians counseled him to stay so he could collect disability benefits from the army. A Bosnian friend took him to a displaced persons camp in Bistričak to find a wife. He married a woman from Banja Luka's ethnically cleansed Muslim community. They had their respective criteria: he wanted someone who prayed, wore hijab, and had never married. She wanted someone who was educated and had declined a wealthy Saudi suitor on those grounds. Migrant and refugee, these two strangers to Zenica wed and set about finding a place to live while waiting for Abu ʿAli's disability payments to come through. For several years, they squatted in a flat whose previous occupants were Croats—whether they fled or were expelled was murky, as is often the case. They had no furniture, ate aid rations out of cans, and had to borrow utensils from neighbors. "That's how I started: from scratch [min ṣifr]," he recalled with a smile. For Abu ʿAli, starting the jihad was marked by bidding farewell to his mother and ending it coincided with finding a spouse; the shift in emphasis from being a son to being a husband was accomplished through the geographical and moral distances covered through his journey.

Abu ʿAli continued his struggles to root himself in Bosnia. Obtaining citizenship and disability benefits required many fruitless visits to bureaucrats, generals, and politicians, not too subtly reminding them of a debt owed to him by the state, whose note of credit was the scars on his body. Even after the benefits came through, housing was a problem. The Croat owner of his flat returned in 1999, so Abu ʿAli and his family took up in another place around the corner, from which they were also evicted a few years later. Abu ʿAli decided that he had to build his own home, and for that he needed land. The relevant ministries denied his requests for a property assignment, so for five consecutive weeks, Abu ʿAli traveled to Sarajevo to try to catch President Alija Izetbegović during Friday prayers, only to be turned back each time. Visits to Jordanians in the NATO peacekeeping force also went nowhere. Finally, Abu ʿAli found an American woman working with an international organization who told him that her portfolio was women's issues but that she was willing to help him. The two went back to the very same municipal office that had rejected his request earlier, except this time with an American in his corner he was assigned a plot of land straightaway. Meanwhile, a Bosnian ex-army officer whom Abu ʿAli knew from the war loaned him cash to buy building materials. Abu ʿAli went to a mosque—the one across the street from where he told me this story—and asked if anyone could help him build his house. A few men volunteered, one of whom brought friends and relatives from a nearby village. One weekend, Abu ʿAli brought the building materials and some food and together with the villagers they put up the basic structure of the house over the course of a few days. According to Abu ʿAli, this help was an explicit act of reciprocity. They told him, "You helped us during the war, so we'll help you." For Abu 'Ali, these fortuitous interventions—the American woman who helped him, the villagers who put up his house—were not coincidences, but divinely ordained.[64]

In the meantime, however, the Europe that Abu 'Ali left behind caught up to him in Bosnia. When he first crossed from Italy to ex-Yugoslavia across the erstwhile Iron Curtain in 1992, the European Community had not yet transformed into the European Union. Twelve years later, an EU peacekeeping force was in Bosnia, and it sent a squad of Italian Carabinieri to Abu 'Ali's house to search for weapons. When we first met, Abu 'Ali delighted in mockingly reenacting their fruitless search of each place in and around the house: the kitchen, the firewood pile, a plastic bag of old clothes, under the hood of his car, each time ending with the refrain, "Where are the weapons? There aren't any weapons!" Despite the lack of any criminal charges, the escalating state harassment brought on by the Global War on Terror continued to erode the precarious life he had built for himself in Bosnia. The Bosnian government revoked Abu 'Ali's citizenship in 2007. A year later and fearing deportation to Morocco, Abu 'Ali fled, making his way westward somehow to France, his initial point of entry into Europe, where he would eventually obtain asylum. I do not know if his wife and children were able to join him. During a visit to Paris several years later, I reached out through a mutual friend to see if we could meet, but he demurred, explaining that he was having leg pains and was very tired. I could only begin to imagine.

Chapter 2

LOCATIONS

IN THE FALL OF 1993, A CURIOUS BOOKLET APPEARED IN CENTRAL Bosnia under the title *Notions That Must Be Corrected*. It was around this time that unfamiliar forms of Islamic piety—often labeled as "Wahhabi"—began to stand out in the area: long beards, face veils and headscarves, new styles of prayer. The men in particular acquired a reputation for harassing Muslims they deemed insufficiently observant. These developments were widely attributed to the influence of Arab "guests," specifically those bringing funds from the Gulf. *Notions That Must Be Corrected*, for example, bore the logo of Kuwait's leading Salafi organization, the Revival of Islamic Heritage Society.[1] It was printed in the local language, but the author, Imad el-Misri, was an Egyptian who had recently arrived in the country for jihad and for *daʿwa*. "I came to Bosnia," the pamphlet begins, "and found strange notions of Islam, things that the Muslims [here] think are part of the faith, but they surely are not." El-Misri ticked off a long list of errors, such as visiting shrines in search of saintly intercession with God; socializing between members of the opposite sex outside the bonds of family; the shaving or trimming of beards; smoking; and listening to music. He faulted some local Islamic scholars for failing to set this right.[2]

Predictably, the text provoked heated responses from Muslim political and religious elites, who saw this foreigner not as a scholar, but as an upstart. Writing in *Preporod*, the official magazine of the Islamic Community

(Islamska zajednica, or IZ), a Bosnian imam blasted el-Misri as a "self-declared mujtahid" [samozvani mudžtehid] and was astounded at the focus on criticizing people's manner of prayer in a country where most Muslims did not even practice.[3] Meanwhile, the prominent Muslim nationalist Džemaludin Latić, writing in the magazine of the ruling SDA political party, accused el-Misri of harming Muslims by fomenting strife [fitna] and encouraging a form of Islam that would serve the purposes of those seeking to portray them as backwards fanatics.[4] Perhaps the harshest response to *Notions That Must Be Corrected* came all the way from Munich, where an imam in the Bosnian diaspora wrote a book hammering el-Misri for his lack of specific citations and imploring the Arabs to go back to their own countries, lest they cause the "Afghanistanization" of Bosnia.[5]

The debate over *Notions That Must Be Corrected* is but one example of the recurring trope pitting Arabian Salafi Islam against traditional Bosnian Islam. The former has often been denigrated as emerging from the desert, rigid, rootless, literalistic, barbaric, the latter celebrated as a creature of mountains and forests, tolerant, autochthonous, flexible, and European. In the logic of liberalism and its weaponized variant in the Global War on Terror, the opposition here is between an Islam that is frightening and one that is potentially redeemable. From the converse perspective of someone like el-Misri, Salafi Islam is more authentic and pure, while Bosnian Islam is compromised and adulterated. The terms here resonate with debates in various contexts around the world that are often structured through an opposition of religion versus nation, cosmopolitan versus parochial, center versus periphery, global versus local, and, ultimately, the universal versus the particular. Yet in the controversy described above, both sides were keen to define the universal on their own terms. Imad el-Misri's exposition of the basic tenets of Islam emphasized that worship of a single god is part of human nature and that whereas "earlier prophets were sent to their tribe, city, or people, Muhammad was sent for all of humanity."[6] Bosnian critics did not take issue with this sentiment, but they were also doing more than merely defending their right to be different from Arabs. Latić wrote that el-Misri and others like him "may be Arabian a hundred times over, but they are still far from the rule [hukm] of Islam. They could come to Bosnia for us to teach them, not for them to teach us!"[7] Bosnians could claim that their practices embodied the true universality of Islam while characterizing their opponents as merely particular, or ethnically Arab.

The universal and the particular are often posited as distinct categories, with the local as the place where these two are somehow reconciled. Yet this book is not straightforwardly about Bosnia, nor can it afford to merely treat Bosnia as an inert backdrop for some global phenomenon, readily interchangeable with Afghanistan, Chechnya, or other lands reduced to neatly comparable "case studies." Instead, in this chapter Bosnia is a locus where multiple universalist projects quite literally take place—take *a* place *in* a specific place—and in doing so are part of a process of remaking that place as they are remade in turn. This chapter will approach location as a question of locus, as an active site in flux that is redefined in its relationships to the universal rather than as a fully formed given that confronts it. It will show how "foreign" texts like *Notions That Must Be Corrected* were also constituted through local processes, and how local [domaći] fighters were not simply parochial. Doing so will require confronting questions of nationalism and secularism, and the shifting names—here, most notably Bosnia, Bosnia*n*, Bosnia*k*—that they appropriate.

The clerics and commentators who challenged Imad el-Misri were far from the only Bosnians staking a claim to defining the universal terms of Islam. The early 1990s witnessed the emergence of a significant revivalist movement among younger Muslims, one that enjoyed an ambiguous relationship with the resurgent nationalisms in the region. Its adherents participated in the war in a way that sought to publicly inscribe their actions within terms of Islamic piety. For them, to use the term *jihad* (or *džihad*) was not merely to signify that the war was Islamically justified, but to seek a distinct way of waging war grounded in some notion of Islamic belief and practice. Otherwise, Muslim nationalism—by reducing Islam to a mere identity—carried with it the danger of moral and spiritual decay. Some of the Muslims involved in this movement joined the ansar and eventually constituted a majority of the Katiba's rank and file. These Bosnian Muslims have been rendered invisible in debates like the one described above that set Arab extremists against Bosnian moderates; or, if they are acknowledged, it is as the mere dupes and appendages of the foreign interlopers.

For example, one mujahid, Jusuf, spent his time during the war as a child soldier—perhaps the ultimate category of a person said to be incapable of acting on their own volition.[8] Jusuf was born in Bugojno, a town in central Bosnia of a little more than twenty thousand before the war. His father worked in the local bank and his mother in a factory; they came from nearby villages during what he called the town's "golden age" in the 1970s, when it was rapidly industrializing and prosperous (Josip Broz Tito, Yugoslavia's longtime ruler, had his private hunting grounds nearby).[9] When the war broke out, Jusuf began taking a greater interest in prayer, but his family was not particularly religious; his grandmother on one side was devout and known for the beauty of her Quranic recitation, while his grandfather on the other side made and sold plum brandy. In November 1993, after having lost two uncles to the war, Jusuf decided to join the fight, going against his family's wishes. As he was only sixteen years of age, the army wouldn't accept him—but the Katiba would. Jusuf resolved to take things into his own hands: along with two friends, he walked to Travnik, trudging in the snow for eleven hours. They arrived and spent the night in the local high school, which was crowded with refugees from Prijedor. "It was not a pretty sight," he told me seventeen years later at a cafe in Sarajevo's old city. "There were women and children crying, wearing dirty clothes, crammed into narrow spaces, maybe twenty men to a single room." Exhausted, Jusuf and his buddies collapsed into sleep. The next morning, they had breakfast. "We had eggs," he recalled, breaking out into a broad smile. "That, I remember." They walked another three hours to Mehurići and linked up with the ansar. There, he took Islam classes with none other than Imad el-Misri.

For Bosnians like Jusuf, joining the jihad was a way to fight for a nation that defined itself as both Bosnian and Muslim, and in a manner compatible with their faith, without ceding their ability to be critical of the dominant spokesmen for either cause. It also marked a willful transition to manhood, one that defied paternal authority in the service of cultivating new masculinized pieties. All too often, debates take the universal and the particular as categories with fixed referents in the world and merely argue over which side should be given more or less weight. Lost is any examination of what is entailed by the very act of drawing a line dividing the universal from the particular, especially the contests over how that line is drawn and redrawn. The previous chapter dealt with Muslims traveling to Bosnia for jihad, striving to apprehend their mobility without casting them as rootless. Now we will turn to the Bosnian side of the equation, to understand the local without reducing it to an inert object simply acted upon by others.

NAMES AND NATIONS

Universalism and nationalism have always had an ambivalent relationship. Nationalism is often cast as the worst kind of particularism, as narrow and chauvinistic. Yet insofar as universalism recognizes and operates through certain kinds of difference, nationalism also serves as one of the main ways for organizing this difference. To take the example at hand, the phenomenon of Bosnians turning to Muslim nationalism is a sign that they will reject liberal universalism; but at the same time, the cultivation of a specifically Bosnian form of Islam is also presented as an antidote to unmoored forms of extremism. Those arriving in Bosnia to help in the name of a global umma experienced this dilemma on inverted terms. For them, nationalism was often something counterposed against Islamism and against transnational Muslim solidarity. And yet nationalism was also the primary formation by which the Muslims they wanted to help were expressing their identity *as Muslims*.

For Salafis in particular, this anxiety over the vicissitudes of universalism was mostly expressed through the idiom of piety. Many Salafis might have winced at the tone of Imad el-Misri's polemic, but they shared the belief that Bosnian Muslims needed their spiritual guidance. In the Salafi debates that informed the jihad as well as aid and daʿwa efforts, any such deviance was often explained by centuries of misrule, from the impure Hanafi Islam of the Ottomans through the outright atheism of socialist Yugoslavia.[10] This alleged backwardness was posited as a reason to help: guiding wayward Bosnian Muslims to the correct path was not only important in itself, but would provide them with the spiritual strength necessary to defend themselves against mass atrocities and emerge victorious. For Imad el-Misri, Abu ʿAbd al-ʿAziz, and other mujahids who are the subject of this book, religious reform and participation in combat were equally necessary and indeed mutually reinforcing. But for many Salafis, the local Muslims' alleged lack of proper Islamic education could also be a reason for skepticism about the jihad as such. Muhammad Nasir al-Din al-Albani, one of the most prominent Salafi scholars of the twentieth century, rebuffed an entreaty from Abu ʿAbd al-ʿAziz to endorse the jihad, stressing that Bosnian Muslims needed daʿwa first and foremost. "You cannot conduct jihad with those who do not share your creed [ʿaqīda]. You may be fighting [tuqātil] but you are not engaging in jihad." What were the results, al-Albani asked rhetorically, after ten years of so-called jihad in Afghanistan? Fragmentation and infighting. "So we are not interested in armed jihad in Bosnia," al-Albani said, instead counseling his visitor "to stay on the path of daʿwa through the good word." Proselytizers could carry arms for self-defense but not participate in any attacks.[11]

In Yugoslavia, being Muslim was marked by logics of both nationalism and secularism.[12] On the eve of the war, 16 percent of Yugoslavia's population was classified as "muslimani," a confessional category used for people of Muslim backgrounds, scattered across the country's six constituent republics—Slovenia, Croatia, Bosnia-Herzegovina, Serbia, Macedonia, Montenegro—and speaking a variety of languages. About half of these were also considered "Muslimani"—the capitalized "M" meant to designate a national group consisting of people of Muslim background living mostly in Bosnia and whose mother tongue was the language then called Serbo-Croatian. Other muslimani included non-Slav minority groups, especially Albanians, who had even fewer constitutional rights. Both of these "Muslim" categories were tenuous: many muslimani were not practicing or considered themselves atheists and many potential Muslimani instead opted to identify as Yugoslavs. And substantial numbers of people had parents from different nationalities or confessional backgrounds.

The Muslim nationality was officially recognized by the regime starting in the 1960s, and it was the culmination of a long-running debate over how to classify Bosnia's Muslim Slavs, who since the nineteenth century had been regarded as backward in developing national consciousness compared to Serbs and Croats.[13] Yet unlike Yugoslavia's other constituent nations—Serbs, Croats, Montenegrins, Slovenes, Macedonians—these Muslims did not have a territorial space in which they enjoyed legally recognized primacy or a demographic majority. So while Croatia, for example, was designated as the state of the Croat people only, Bosnia was constitutionally defined as the state of Muslims, Serbs, and Croats alike. Hence the term *Bosniak* came to be preferred over *Muslim* during the war, as it implies a more explicit territorial rootedness in and claim to a specific place.

Yugoslavia was built not only on nationalism, but also on secularism, a logic of governance that continuously attempts to reconstitute and manage the boundary between categories of the religious and nonreligious.[14] The IZ has been a key instrument of secularism in Bosnia: it is the central body governing the administration of Islamic affairs, managing mosques, Islamic schools, and other functions.[15] Under socialism, the IZ was caught between serving all Yugoslav Muslims as a confessional category—nearly half of whom were Albanians or

Macedonians—and the increasingly strident nationalist demands from Bosnian Muslims.[16] Historically, nationalism among Bosnian Muslims was led by professional classes with only limited support from Islamic scholars. This was hardly surprising, as the IZ traces its origin to late nineteenth-century efforts by Austro-Hungarian colonial administrators to centralize management of Muslim religious affairs in a state whose dominant public values were no longer defined with reference to Islam.[17] After Bosnia was absorbed into the Kingdom of Yugoslavia in 1918, the IZ's authority was extended throughout the rest of the country. The IZ was in some ways a microcosm of Yugoslavia itself by virtue of its considerable linguistic and national diversity—unlike the Serbian Orthodox Church and the Catholic Church in Croatia, both of which were more closely tied to their respective national projects. The IZ struggled to maintain its autonomy from the state, especially after the socialist regime expropriated most of its endowed properties (waqf), closed down most Islamic schools, and abolished shariʿa courts. Despite these various forms of state surveillance, pressure, and co-optation, the IZ became more active from the 1970s onward, through campaigns of building or renovating mosques, the gradual opening of new educational institutions such as the Faculty of Islamic Studies in Sarajevo, the legalization of Sufi orders, and greater freedom to publish religious texts.[18]

The logic of universalism always plays out in lived situations striated by unequal relations of power. This engenders a tension between universalism acting as a means for the powerful to justify their agendas versus it providing a framework for the less powerful to participate and wield influence: universalism as cover for power, universalism as constraint on power. Recall the endless and mind-numbing debates among the American foreign policy elite over unilateralism versus multilateralism. This logic also inflected Yugoslavia: it was a federation of co-equal nations, but with the Serbs as the single most powerful national group in a multicentric order. Whether Yugoslavia was a vehicle for Serb domination or a way to fetter Serb power was always a recurring question and cause for existential concern. For Muslims within Yugoslavia, the IZ mirrored this dynamic, except with the Bosnian Muslims in the dominant position vis-à-vis other Muslims who identified with the Albanian, Macedonian, or other nations. This was especially the case in the province of Kosovo, where in terms of institutionalized Islam, it was Bosnian clerics who were the primary face of Serb-led Slav chauvinism.[19]

For both Yugoslavia and the IZ, this tension ended in an implosion of the universal, whereby dominant groups sought to act openly in their own interests without giving up their hold on central institutions. Serb nationalists seized control of the army and used it to support Serb secessionists in Croatia and Bosnia, while at times claiming to fight in the name of preserving Yugoslavia. The IZ underwent a parallel process of fragmentation from the center after the mass ethnic cleansing of Muslim communities by Serb forces in eastern Bosnia and the siege of Sarajevo pushed Bosnian Muslim clerics to close ranks against the leadership, which was aligned with the collapsing socialist regime.[20] In April 1993, thirteen months after Bosnia declared independence from Yugoslavia, a separate autonomous IZ for Bosnia was established. This new-old body inherited the existing Sarajevo-based facilities as well as most of the resources and personnel of the all-Yugoslavia IZ. It also retained authority over the administration of Islamic affairs in Croatia, Slovenia, and the Sandžak region of Serbia.[21] The move was part secession and part coup, founding a new institution while also claiming to restore the Bosnia-only IZ that had existed before Yugoslavia.

This reconfigured, more nationalist-oriented Bosnian IZ sought to contribute to the war effort in several ways: by boosting spiritual morale in the army, engaging in aid and relief efforts, rallying the Bosnian Muslim diaspora overseas, and participating in diplomatic outreach to Muslim communities and governments worldwide. But first it had to consolidate its authority over the organization of Islamic affairs, including against foreign influences. In December 1993, Mustafa Cerić, then still only the acting head of the IZ, issued his second *fatwa* in office, reaffirming the community's adherence to the Hanafi *madhhab* (school of Islamic jurisprudence). The fatwa's preamble noted the "frequent occurrence of deviations from the Hanafi madhhab in certain religious practices, especially recently, upon coming into contact with Muslims from other madhhabs, whether in the country or abroad in exile [muhadžerluk]."[22] For supporters of the (quite literally) besieged Bosniak national project in the early 1990s, even piety-based criticisms from fellow Muslims could be threatening. In an early response to *Notions That Must Be Corrected*, Islamic scholar Enes Karić explicitly compared Salafi proselytizing to hostile nationalist projects that sought to erase Bosniak identity: "[N]ot only do Serbs and Croats see us as just an empty space, but so do our Islamic brothers." Referring to newly arrived Islamic proselytizing literature, Karić complained,

"[Y]ou don't see a single word about Bosnia or about one of the main duties [farz] of our Bosniaks: preserving Bosnia as a state!"[23]

The dilemma facing Bosnian Muslims can be thought of as one of crosscutting universalisms. From some universalist projects they faced suspicions of being *too* nationalist in their narrow particularity, either not truly secular and tolerant enough for liberals, or insufficiently pious and devout for Salafis. And in the view of many Serb and Croat nationalists they lacked any authentic national identity at all, which meant their lands could be legitimately taken.[24] The vicissitudes of Bosniak nationalism are thus a reminder that nationalism's relationship with universalist projects is always necessarily ambivalent. Although often cast as perhaps the most virulent form of narrow particularism, nationalisms always presuppose and indeed demand some kind of universalist vision.[25] They make claims to embody ideals such as freedom and self-determination that belong to humanity; they simply wish to incarnate those ideals in particular places and with reference to particular people through the vehicle of the sovereign state. And if nationalism can realize the universal in any number of ways, it can also connect the particular to different kinds of universalism. In the case of Muslims in Bosnia, all of the things that made them deficient in terms of national categories—the overlap of apparently incongruous identities such as Muslimness and Europeanness—also multiplied potential points of connection with the outside world. They could speak in multiple universalist idioms: not simply Western versus Islamic, but within and across those categories as well. Bosnia, with the messiness of its categories and names, should be understood as an exemplar, and not an exception, of the ambiguities of nationalism and universalism.

Beyond their many attempts to find allies and supporters in the West, leading Bosnian Muslim politicians and clerics were actively engaged in cultivating relations with Muslims worldwide. The pages of Bosnian periodicals from the war were filled with reports of solidarity delegations and interviews with luminaries from throughout the Muslim world of various doctrinal and political orientations. In the broad set of ties, Salafis were only one strand among many, and the issue of ansar coming to fight was marginal at best. The bulk of this pan-Islamic activism took place within the framework of nation-states: it was either explicitly directed by governments or, even when led by popular forces, organized along national lines.

These included diplomatic efforts, contributions to peacekeeping forces, aid donations, and attempts to mobilize through the Organization of the Islamic Conference. Saudi Arabia in particular operated at the bilateral level with large-scale financial contributions as well as through its sponsorship of and influence over pan-Islamic NGOs such as the Muslim World League.[26] Iran was also a major contributor of aid and sent arms, in defiance of the UN embargo—but with tacit US assent.[27] Beyond governments, Islamist political parties and movements were also vocal in calling for stronger action from their governments and from the international community, as well as in raising funds and sending aid. Hizballah lost several fighters in Bosnia who were working with the government—a fact it repeatedly brought up decades later during the war in Syria to rebut allegations of sectarian motivation.[28] Ahmad al-Malt, a physician and one-time deputy head of the Egyptian Muslim Brothers, was active in solidarity efforts and visited Bosnia in 1994.[29] Necmettin Erbakan, who would later serve briefly as Turkey's first Islamist prime minister before being deposed in a military coup, urged his country to bomb Belgrade.[30] That Islamist opposition movements often framed their solidarity with Bosnia as demands for state action—often calculated to embarrass ruling regimes—only underscores how prevalent is the tendency to turn to states as the primary agents of universalism. Pan-Islam and nationalism were mutually reinforcing, and pan-Islamic projects were as diverse as nationalisms.

CLAIMING THE NAME

Imad el-Misri may have found things in Bosnia not to his liking, but it was a place where things were anything but settled. Categories of nation and religion were still very much in flux and under contestation. Arriving in a war zone where governmental and spiritual authority were highly fragmented, the ansar found their readiest interlocutors and allies in a set of militias led by young Muslim preachers and clerics emerging in central Bosnia's small cities and medium-sized towns. These fighting units stood out in their self-denomination as "Muslim" not merely in the national sense, but in a commitment to Islamic piety as well, by banning alcohol and fornication and encouraging regular prayer. They made common cause with Arab Salafis but would also part ways, leaving neither side unchanged.

Perhaps best-known in this regard was the Muslim Forces [Muslimanske snage], a militia that first emerged early in the war in the Travnik area. Travnik is a town in the Lašva valley, and its municipal area had about seventy thousand inhabitants before the war, predominantly Muslims and Croats. As the capital of the Ottoman province [eyalet] of Bosnia for much of the eighteenth and nineteenth centuries, Travnik had a strong tradition of Islamic education, but its three-hundred-year-old *medresa* was closed during the socialist era.[31] The medresa is housed in a nineteenth-century structure built in the Austro-Hungarian Moorish style after the original site was demolished to make way for a railroad. It was put to a variety of uses during the school's closure; in the 1980s it housed a furniture store for the Šipad company.[32] The medresa was only reopened during the war; its restoration, like the establishment of the Muslim Forces, was part of a broader effort to reclaim certain public spaces as "Islamic." I was sitting in the teachers' conference room at the medresa one day in 2007 when Ahmed Adilović, a teacher there and an imam at Travnik's Many-Colored Mosque [Šarena džamija], recounted to me the founding of the Muslim Forces:

> When the war started, I wasn't obliged to join the army because I was an imam. Nevertheless, one can't witness those kinds of massacres and atrocities and just do nothing. So in May 1992 some friends and I, a small group of about twenty, decided that we should defend Bosnia and the people with respect for the rights of Muslims. By this I mean that we had behind us fifty years of communist government, which resulted in the expulsion of religion from our lives [ṭard al-dīn min al-ḥayāt].
>
> We confronted these problems of the war and said we would join the army, but our unit had rules against drinking, fornication, all that is forbidden in Islam. This was a purely voluntary group, we didn't compel or conscript anyone. Other units had problems like this, not just lack of arms but mockery [sukhriyya] of religion, drinking, and so on. Half a year later, there were two hundred of us. We were called the Muslim Forces, though we were very small.

Adilović smiled wryly as he made this last observation: "We were called the Muslim Forces, though we were very small." It encapsulated their marginal position, as well as their aspiration to speak in the name of the universal, to lay a claim to defining "Muslim" in terms distinct from those of the nationalist project. Although the Bosnian army embraced Muslim nationalism, it still often enough spoke in terms of a civic Bosnian identity and included considerable numbers of non-Muslims. But more important, even the most ardent Muslim nationalists were not necessarily practicing, and some openly indulged in ritually proscribed activities such as consuming alcohol. As Mahmut Karalić, one commander in the Muslim Forces, explained in an interview, "The Muslims in the army of Bosnia are Muslims in name [only] and few of them are believers. Most keep away from Islam, and so we wished to keep separate our forces so that our foundation [aṣl] would be sound."[33] These militias denominated themselves as "Muslim" to claim the name as one attached to pious practices as much as to a national identity. The Muslim Forces in Travnik worked quickly to build up support from outside. They hosted Abu ʿAbd al-ʿAziz and his small band of ansar when they arrived in the summer of 1992, gave interviews to visiting Arab journalists, and raised funds from the Bosnian diaspora in Austria.[34]

The other major locus for the Muslim Forces was Zenica, the largest city under the uncontested control of the Bosnian government. Unlike Travnik, Zenica was very much a new city: it grew exponentially during the socialist era thanks to its steelworks facility, the third-largest in Europe. The eclecticism of Zenica's rapidly growing population was also reflected in the composition of its Islamic community, including the young preachers, scholars, and mystics who would join the war effort in creating a Muslim Forces militia. These included Karalić, a graduate of *hadith* studies from the Islamic University in Medina and a mystic and healer;[35] Halil Mehtić, the city's mufti and head of Ilmijje, the official union of imams; and Halil Brzina, a former steelworks employee who was also a shaykh in the Naqshbandi Sufi order. In early 1993, while the all-Yugoslav IZ was still paralyzed by the war, Mehtić teamed up with Hasan Makić—a graduate of Muhammad ibn Saud Islamic University in Riyadh who had recently been released from Serb concentration camps—to co-author a pamphlet that sought to lay out proper Islamic morals for combatants and commanders. *Instructions to the Muslim Fighter* was described in an IZ newsletter as a "manual of Islamic ethics and Bosnian patriotism."[36] It exhorted Bosnian Muslims to fight for both homeland and faith at once, and stressed the importance of piety [pobožnosti] in warfare as necessary for national resilience and martial efficacy. The book bragged that pious fighters don't need alcohol, for "drinking only lets people get a false courage that allows them to conceal their cowardice or satisfy their passions, giving Satan cause to seduce them and turn them away from what is dear to God."[37]

Elsewhere, in the Herzegovinian town of Konjic, an imam and recently returned graduate of al-Azhar University in Cairo, Nezim Halilović (also known as Muderis), founded a similar unit of his own that later became the 4th Muslim Light Brigade.[38] Muderis was probably the most politically successful of this generation of militant clerics, continuing to position himself as an internal critic of the IZ who urged the leadership to open up to younger generations while still ascending the ranks. Muderis later served as head administrator of religious endowments (waqf), ran the office for coordinating the hajj, and retained a perch leading the Friday prayers at the Saudi-built King Fahd mosque in Sarajevo.

These piety-oriented militias were the outgrowth of an Islamic revival movement that predated the war and found itself critically engaged with both mainline Bosnian Muslim nationalism and the IZ. Described by the British anthropologist Cornelia Sorabji during her fieldwork in Bosnia in the mid-1980s as "new mystics," the movement was diffuse but characterized by a focus on individual practice and personal behavior over political change; an embrace of scripturalism coupled with a tolerance of Sufi mysticism; and a strong sense of identification with the global umma, especially as represented by imaginations of the Arab world and Turkey. This tendency stressed the divide between Muslims who are conscious believers and Muslims by nationality as much as the distinction between the Muslim, Serb, and Croat nations. Women in the movement were often marked by dress practices such as covering their hair or, more rarely, their faces.[39] At the same time, the new piety movements were doctrinally inchoate: some participants were Sufis, but many did not adhere strictly to anything more specific than Sunni Islam. Under these circumstances, they shared an elective affinity with Salafi ansar who arrived during the war not on the basis of common doctrinal approaches but simply because they both engaged in a public practice of religion that was otherwise rare in the country. And as the war continued, the presumed commonalities became strained as both sides learned more about each other, as we shall soon see.

These units attracted men who found the army to be lacking in Islamic morals and the IZ to be lacking in nationalism. When Bosnia-Herzegovina declared independence in March 1992, it gained rapid recognition as a sovereign state from the international community. But on the ground, authority was highly fragmented and localized, and constantly shifting. Key institutions struggled to develop under conditions of war, siege, and ethnic cleansing. Perhaps most important was the army, or rather the lack of one. Instead, much of the early fighting in the name of the Bosnian republic was done by socialist-era local Territorial Defense militias (Teritorijalna odbrana, TO), the Patriotic Leagues that grew out of the SDA's own security apparatus, and criminal gangs.[40] In addition, there were Bosnian Croat militias—some of whom included considerable numbers of Muslims—that fought in a tense alliance with forces loyal to Sarajevo, until the two sides turned on each other for much of 1993.[41] Meanwhile, Islamic institutions—especially before the 1993 split resulting in an independent Bosnian IZ—were criticized for being compromised by the socialist regime and, like the regime, serving more as a bureaucratic apparatus than as a source of spiritual leadership.[42] The exemption of imams from compulsory army service was also a sore point for much of the population.

The first waves of Bosnians who joined the ansar often passed through these pious militias. One of these young men was Muhsin, who moved from unit to unit during the war as part of a search for spiritual and martial camaraderie. Before the war, he was like many young people who did not fit into neat categories of practicing and nonpracticing. "I used to think it was funny that I would drink beer and then go to the mosque later," he recalled. But it also meant, he stressed, that he knew Islam in his own way before ever meeting any Arabs. When the war broke out, Muhsin left his university studies in Sarajevo and quickly returned to his hometown. He joined a local defense militia that included both TO and HVO units, a ragtag affair in which there were not enough guns to go around. As with other Bosnians I met who joined the ansar after serving elsewhere in the army, the experience left him underwhelmed: eager to join the fight, he found other units to be too timid to take the offensive. He recalled vividly one time when there was a call for ten volunteers to launch a diversionary attack on the Serb forces, and only two or three soldiers stepped forward.

After a few months, Muhsin drifted to one of the Muslim Forces militias, which he described as still mostly informal and based on the practical needs of pious soldiers. "Let us say you are on the [front] line at night and you want to pray, and the person on guard next to you is drinking, and swearing," he explained. "It was very normal that people who don't drink alcohol and who want to pray, that they want to be with similar people. Especially in the most dangerous job possible, you want to be free of such uncomfortable situations." Muhsin's unit was deployed to a tiny village surrounded on three sides by Serb forces. It was during this difficult time that he first encountered the ansar, a small band of seven or eight men that included Imad. They had been looking for a place where they could fight but also have their religious practices accommodated. Muhsin was fascinated by the foreigners, with whom he communicated mostly in English. Some, such as a Saudi who worked at the Jeddah airport, he came to admire; others, such as Imad and another Saudi who later showed up in a video beheading prisoners, less so. He also saw Abu ʿAbd al-ʿAziz give a lecture in the main mosque of the town of Bugojno. "He said a lot but kept it simple. Most people either say very little or they say a lot but it's not simple." The ansar collectively made an impression on Muhsin as individuals knowingly risking their lives to help Bosnia while some Bosnians were unwilling to defend their own homes.

By early 1993, the various Muslim Forces militias were merged into a new unit, the 7th Muslim Brigade, and professional military officers took control while retaining clerics for the purposes of providing inspiration and raising morale.[43] The unit was headquartered in Zenica but its first battalion was located in Travnik, where Muhsin joined up. His experience there was very different: the unit was keen to fight and "even smoking was frowned upon. Even to be lazy was not okay. It was Spartan from a military point of view, and Sufi from a spiritual point of view." Muhsin recalled an arduous march from Travnik to Bijelo Bučje in which so many soldiers had volunteered to carry equipment and supplies that there was nothing left for him to pick up. He thought to himself that he would be happy to die amongst such people. There were no ansar in the unit, but Muhsin believed that they had been influenced by the example that the ansar had set in terms of dedication to piety and military discipline. And he continued to encounter those Arabs who tended to be clustered around the Muslim Forces even after it became the 7th Muslim Brigade. Several months later, Muhsin joined a mixed unit of ansar and Bosnians that would later become the nucleus of the Katiba. For Muhsin, the appeal of joining the ansar had little to do with embracing Salafi doctrine in any specificity and more about how they shared his general orientation toward finding a way to participate in a nationalist war on pious terms.

Muhsin was proud of how the Katiba was able to reconcile different approaches, in the best tradition of what Islam stood for. In one of our first conversations, in 2012, he noted that people were complaining about Chinese immigrants in Bosnia taking away jobs from locals—a growth in hostility over the years that I personally experienced while walking down the street—and dismissed this as backwardness. "All rich countries have welcomed immigrants to help build those societies; we should be doing the same. Like Darwin said, even though I don't completely agree with him, new bacteria new forms of life take things from outside in order to develop and to become stronger." Muhsin continued,

> Islam developed like that. It spread universal ideas, not a culture. It spread an intention for justice, social order, appreciation of life. It went all the way to the far east, to Indonesia. Islam came but the domestic cultures stayed. The Persians stayed in their culture. The Turks stayed in their culture. The Bosnians too. We just took what is universal, what is from God.
>
> One problem in Islam is knowing when something is universal and not just embedded in ideology and culture. I'm not against culture. But you cannot spread culture. When Turks or Arabs spread culture, they were spreading their national identity in the name of Islam.
>
> The Katiba was an interesting story in this regard. No one can understand the challenges of the Katiba and its main achievements. From one group of people who come from different countries, their own movements, their own džemats [communities]. They came to Bosnia and even I am still surprised at how it was established and functioned, despite the discussions, quarrels, some conflicts.

Muhsin's trajectory was not that of a mere "local" element that suddenly experienced the universal descending from above. His journey through different military units and the development of his relationship with Islam proceeded in the same contingent, experimental, serendipitous arc as that of the Bosnian

Muslim piety militias and the ansar who encountered them. What was important was finding a way through the war that did not force him to choose between being a Bosnian patriot and a good Muslim and to instead develop a mechanism for making decisions between the universal and the particular. For him and several hundred other Bosnians, the Katiba would become that mechanism.

HOW TO READ A JIHAD

To see how universal and particular were co-constituted through encounters in the jihad, let us turn to the example of texts. Jihad is a phenomenon that has been largely commented on through readings of texts, often with little attention to how those texts are actually produced and used in the world. The underlying assumption of such approaches is that texts themselves are a kind of vector for ideology, delivered like missile payloads from centers of Islamic scholarship in the Arab world to the non-Arab periphery. In Bosnia, however, it is noteworthy that the most popular texts produced by the mujahids have very little to say about jihad at all. Instead of reading them as ideological blueprints, one must examine their utility to their readers, who valued them as technologies of piety that could facilitate a new and more up-to-date approach to practicing their faith—in this sense, they could appeal to those who were engaged in the fight as well as to those who were not. And, more important, such texts did not simply arrive as wholly formed imports; rather, they were endeavors of translation, annotation, copying, and editing produced collaboratively by ansar mujahids and their Bosnian interlocutors.

Let us return to the pamphlet that opened this chapter, *Notions That Must Be Corrected*. The book that has more than any other text stood for an alien Arabian form of Islam imported into Bosnia is as useful a place as any to rethink ideas of circulation. Imad el-Misri published it without the permission of the Katiba's leadership and perhaps even in an attempt to embarrass it.[44] The booklet appeared several months after Mehtić and Makić's *Instructions to the Muslim Fighter* and can rightly be read as an implicit rebuke to it as well as to the Muslim Forces, in light of tensions that will be discussed further in the next chapter. And although Imad's introduction was provocative, the bulk of the pamphlet has for the most part escaped discussion. The second half consists of a number of verbal formulae in Arabic to be used as supplications or invocations [duʿā, adhkār] in everyday acts: what to say and do when waking up from a dream, before sleep or performing ablutions, before and after meals, during illness, in rain, at sunset, and so on. Each invocation is written in transliterated Arabic—no Arabic script appears in the book—accompanied by Bosnian translation, all justified by reference either to a passage from the Quran or a hadith, each footnoted (though the latter in only general terms, by referring to the collection in which it is to be found, without a page or volume number).[45] There is little additional commentary or analysis, for the text presents itself as a pure distillation of the *sunna* without any unwarranted innovation from others.

The Bosnians I spoke to who appreciated *Notions That Must Be Corrected* emphasized the text's portability, organization, and brevity rather than el-Misri's incendiary commentary. For some mujahids, the simplified and referenced excerpts in manuals such as *Notions That Must Be Corrected* were far more sensible than those promulgated by the IZ, and more open to textual verification. An example is Mehmud, who was from a village outside Bugojno, where he worked in a factory for a few years before the outbreak of the war. He was quiet and practical-minded, with a strong autodidactic streak, his shelves lined with action novels by Robert Ludlum and Dean Koontz, through which he had learned much of his English. During the war, Mehmud enthusiastically accepted some religious teachings of Salafi ansar and one day brought in his son to show me differences in styles of prayer. At the same time, Mehmud hardly adopted Salafi norms wholesale: he kept a closely trimmed beard, his wife did not cover her face, and he mocked the famous fatwa by Saudi scholar bin Baz rejecting heliocentric views of the solar system. One day, Mehmud pulled *Ilmihal*—a catechism distributed by the IZ—off his shelves and showed me a section detailing multiple, needlessly complicated steps that he claimed were ordained for the process of ablutions before prayer. More important, Mehmud insisted, there were no citations to the sunna.

The invocations that constitute the second half of *Notions That Must Be Corrected* are adapted and translated from *The Fortress of the Muslim*, a popular Salafi pamphlet by a Saudi scholar, Sa'id bin 'Ali bin Wahf al-Qahtani, first published in the late 1980s and since translated into over forty languages.[46] *Notions That Must Be Corrected* appears to have introduced al-Qahtani's text to Bosnia.[47] *The Fortress of the Muslim* was itself extracted from a longer work by the same author whose purpose is somewhat incantatory, to provide prayers "that the Muslim may need in his life; in his days and his nights, from the time he wakes up in the early morning until he goes to sleep the next night." For al-Qahtani, the condensed version in *The Fortress of the Muslim* is only meant to provide minimal references, and anyone wishing to know more must return to the original texts herself. Al-Qahtani credited his analysis of hadith to three scholars: Nasir al-Din al-Albani, ʿAbd al-Qadir al-Arnaʾut, and Shuʿayb al-Arnaʾut.[48] All of them were part of the wave of Albanian migration to Syria between 1910 and 1930 around the collapse of the Ottoman Empire.[49] Thus the booklet's portability was hardly incidental; *Notions That Must Be Corrected* was a useful technology of piety for a universalist project. It was mobile, as conceived by al-Qahtani; accretive, through el-Misri's adaptations and additions; accessible and promising verifiability, as experienced by Mehmud; transgressive, through its provocations of the Bosnian Islamic authorities; and made of components that were themselves not pure essences, but extracts fashioned through human effort and selection, with their own genealogies. Moreover, the book that has come to represent the arrival of an alien, "Arab" Islam in the Balkans is itself built on work by scholars from that same region.[50]

Other texts that emerged in the jihad were similarly valued for their utility and were also collaboratively produced. The Katiba's first published book was *The Sealed Nectar*, a biography of the Prophet Muhammad, a genre called *sira*. This text was a product of pan-Islamic networks described in the previous chapter that pulled together and acted on diverse linguistic and doctrinal contexts as it crossed borders and seas. Like *Notions That Must Be Corrected*, it relies on modern hadith-oriented scholarship, but from South Asia instead of the Balkans. Its author, Safi al-Rahman Mubarakpuri, was an Indian scholar from the Ahl-i Hadith movement who taught at the Salafi University in Varanasi and the Islamic University in Medina before returning home to serve as president of India's national Ahl-i Hadith organization.[51] He came from a context of intense doctrinal disputation between Ahl-i Hadith and other Muslim reformist orientations.[52] Yet notwithstanding this sectarian background, *The Sealed Nectar*, Mubarakpuri's first book in Arabic, was aimed at a far broader audience: it won first prize in a 1979 sira contest organized by the Muslim World League and is heavily used in Saudi-sponsored proselytizing efforts around the world. It has been translated into English, French, Romanian, Russian, Sindhi, Spanish, Turkish, Urdu, and other languages.

The Katiba published a local edition of *The Sealed Nectar* in late 1994.[53] There was greater coordination with local Islamic authorities than with *Notions That Must Be Corrected.* The mufti of Travnik and a teacher at the University of Zenica's Islamic pedagogy faculty, who had both studied in Saudi Arabia, were listed as consulting editors. A medresa teacher in Visoko translated the text: Subhija Hadžimejlić-Skenderović was the first European woman to graduate from Cairo's Dar al-ʿUlum, where she learned Arabic in the 1960s. Her father had been chief judge of Visoko's shariʿa court before World War II and was also a Naqshbandi Sufi.[54] It is not clear if Hadžimejlić-Skenderović thought she was translating the book for the Katiba, a charity such as the Heritage Society, or some other purpose, but the case underscores the point that individual decisions to translate texts cannot be presumed to straightforwardly reflect ideological or doctrinal positions. This was especially true during the war, which ushered in an efflorescence of translations of religious texts from abroad. Mehmud the factory worker, for example, translated several books on Islamic topics from English to Bosnian, which he stumbled upon through friends. For him, translation was an excuse to read the books in the first place. In one case, the authorization was undertaken without even obtaining the author's permission, so when published he made sure to list a fake name for the translator.[55]

As for *The Sealed Nectar,* the Katiba serialized and broadcast readings from the book over Radio Hayat in Sarajevo and advertised its availability in the Bosnian army's official magazine.[56] Like the prayers in *The Fortress of the Muslim, The Sealed Nectar* appeals to readers as an up-to-date version of traditions of Islamic learning. Accessibility and simplicity were key features emphasized by many to whom I spoke. Unlike classic siras dotted with long fragments of archaic poetry, *The Sealed Nectar* starts with several chapters of historical and sociological context about tribes, rulership, religion, and culture of the Arabs. Mubarakpuri extracted neat bullet-pointed lists of historical stages, variables that explained events, and groups of actors—more like a modern school textbook. For Jusuf, who ran away as a teenager to join the Katiba and studied in Jordan after the war, the book stood out in his memory as substantively superior in terms of the research behind it:

> The thing with the earlier sira writers is that they were more limited in what they knew and what kinds of information they had access to. For example, let us say maybe that Ibn Ishaq did not know about what Bukhari knew, or Tirmidhi.

> He only knew about what he had access to in his own time. Also, these siras were based on proper isnad [chains of transmission between trusted narrators]. They would say: "So-and-so said, quoting so-and-so, quoting so-and-so . . . " and so on. Which means that sometimes they left in information that was weak. This author [Mubarakpuri] canvassed all the available siras, and took only what was best, most reliable. His method was more modern [aḥdath].

Although the book is unquestionably associated with the Saudis and Salafism and its narrative can be contested on many different grounds by various Muslim believers, it also appears to have been received in Bosnia without much controversy. This is somewhat striking in light of Mubarakpuri's history of polemical disputation with Hanafis back in India, which the Hanafi Bosnian scholars I met seemed to know nothing about. One day in 2010, I sat with Halil Mehtić, the Zenica mufti who had helped found the Muslim Forces. He criticized Salafis for trying to change Bosnian Muslim religious practices and stressed that Bosnia was a European country and could not emulate Arab ones. Yet when I asked Mehtić for his opinion on *The Sealed Nectar*, he replied, "It is a good book, and it is in agreement with what has been written in this field," drawing a sharp contrast with *Notions That Must Be Corrected*.[57]

The Sealed Nectar's accessibility and ubiquity gave it a life in Bosnia far beyond the Katiba, thanks to the Saudi High Committee (SHC) to Aid Bosnia-Herzegovina, the largest foreign Islamic charity operating in the country. The SHC republished the translation in its own name with a new cover, replacing the Katiba's introduction with one of its own.[58] Many Bosnian Muslims I met who knew the book encountered it through the SHC edition and had not heard of the role the mujahids played in bringing it to the country. *Preporod*, the IZ magazine which had denounced *Notions That Must Be Corrected*, ran a two-page spread on the translator of *The Sealed Nectar*, prominently featuring her work on that book—without any mention of the mujahids.[59] Thus was one of the many ironies of the experience of the Katiba: the book that achieved the greatest notoriety in shaping its public reputation was unauthorized, while the best-received book it actually published is rarely attributed to them.

Examining a third key text of the Bosnian jihad yields yet more incongruities. As mentioned earlier, books published in the jihad rarely dealt with military topics. The only one that did so at length was *The Factors for Victory and Defeat Throughout Our Islamic History*, a 1979 text by Shawqi Abu Khalil, a Palestinian who grew up in Syria.[60] The book was printed as a simple paperback with the Katiba's seal on the cover and was mentioned in several of its bulletins to the outside world. Like *The Sealed Nectar*, it was translated by Hadžimejlić-Skenderović and printed under the supervision of the Zenica mufti's office, most likely in the spring of 1995.[61] At first, Abu Khalil may seem a sharp contrast to Mubarakpuri: he was not a religious scholar, but a historian trained in Soviet Azerbaijan. Although not part of the interpretive communities of religious scholars and jurists whose writings were used by the Katiba, Abu Khalil was nevertheless engaged in a similar project of using modern scholarly methods to provide "updated" and portable texts that furthered a sense of Islamic identity. *The Factors for Victory and Defeat* methodically combs through the early centuries of Islam to extract a systematized list of variables explaining the outcomes of battles. But it was not focused on ritual or spiritual matters, so few of the mujahids I knew had any recollection of reading the book, and it seems not to have caught on in terms of reprints or wider distribution. It was not useful as an instrument of piety, and to the extent it had any traction, it was as part of outreach to troops in the regular Bosnian army. The most "militant" book published by the ansar, it turns out, was the one least remembered, and it was authored not by a Salafi nor even a religious scholar, but by a historian educated in a communist state. Like the other texts produced by ansar discussed here, *The Factors for Victory and Defeat* did not simply circulate fully formed like a coin, but was collaboratively reconstituted in a specific location.

ONCE AND FUTURE YUGOSLAVS

During my fieldwork in Bosnia, nationalist divisions had both hardened and deadened, weighing down the air like smog. As a political force, nationalism's avatars were largely discredited along with the rest of the political class, but it still retained a hold on everyday life. It was a category ridiculed and even despised by many, but was no more dispensable because of this.[62] The spaces where I spent most of my time, such as Sarajevo and Zenica, had recently been transformed from "mixed" cities into predominantly Muslim spaces, reflecting broader dynamics of partition and ethnic cleansing since the early 1990s. Bosnians who fought in the jihad were like secular Bosniaks I knew in the sense that they experienced a range of reactions and viewpoints on issues of nationalism and on non-Muslims, especially as the war receded further into memory. They embraced a pious orientation toward Islam incorporating an immanent moral critique of nationalism that could emerge in unexpected ways. This was a trace of their commitment to a universalism that, like liberalism, could accommodate Bosniak nationalism but also could tug it in a slightly different direction.

Many of these issues came up through my conversations with Mehmud. Mehmud grew up with little concern over national identity and once took me to his family burial plot to tell me the stories of how relatives managed to maintain good ties with both Serbs and Croats even during the darkest days of World War II. His uncle, with whom he was still close, was one of Tito's partisans and was a committed communist. As a child, Mehmud did not regularly pray or even believe in God. But he would ponder the nature of the universe while looking up at the stars at night and found himself contemplating bigger spiritual questions as he grew older, especially after his father's sudden death from cancer in 1992. When the war broke out, Mehmud joined the local TO and then a regular army unit. He was surrounded by soldiers who often drank and never prayed. It was toward the end of that year, 1992, when he caught his first glimpse of mujahids, in this case Bosniaks passing through from Travnik, and they made a strong impression: "They attracted me, their behavior, their justness." Later in 1993, after his unit prevailed in difficult fighting against the HVO, Mehmud decided to leave and seek out a more pious environment, joining the 7th Muslim Brigade and eventually the Katiba. The main impetus was him witnessing his comrades looting the homes of Croats who had fled the Bugojno area. "That wasn't right," Mehmud recalled. "In that period, I believed strongly in God. I was looking for people like me, people who were believers." At the same time, Mehmud supported the idea of expelling Croats from the area during the war, arguing that it was necessary to prevent the other side from committing genocide against Muslims.

Even after the war, he and some friends from the Katiba decided that the only way to maintain the homogeneity of Bosniak politics was to push Croats into agitating for more separatist policies. To this end, they conspired to mail bombs to local Croat politicians, but the plot quickly unraveled and Mehmud spent a few years in prison. Yet when I first met him years later, Mehmud's attitude toward the Croats was somewhat different. It was 2010 and Željko Komšić of the avowedly non-nationalist Social Democratic Party had just been re-elected to the country's presidency, whose three seats are constitutionally reserved for a Bosniak, a Serb, and a Croat.[63] Komšić identifies as Croat yet most SDP supporters—and most voters overall—were Bosniaks. This "crossover" voting disrupted the nationalist logic of the Bosnian political system, which assumed—but did not require—that voters would cast ballots only for co-nationals. Critics of this outcome argued that as a result, the presidency now had two members elected on the back of Bosniak votes. Mehmud agreed that effectively depriving Croats of the ability to choose their own nationalist representative on the presidency was not only unjust but also dangerous, as it would only push Croats to ally with Serbs against Bosniaks. Mehmud's complex attitude toward Croats—moral disgust at looting their homes, a desire to live apart from them including through violence, a fear of provoking them—evinced a sensibility that was not reducible to either liberal or socialist logics of multinational coexistence, but rather came out of a tense interplay between Bosniak nationalism and Islamic piety. Mehmud's experience of the war left him determined to be ready should it come again: he became something of a survivalist, intent on teaching his sons how to shoot, hunt, and live in the wild, skills they were eager to show off to me.

While Mehmud embraced a particularly right-wing variant of Bosniak nationalism, Muhsin had more or less dispensed with it altogether by the time I came to know him. During the war, he had been one of the most senior Bosnians in the Katiba. After the war, he finished his university studies and for a number of years held a high-paying job with a European multinational corporation. The first time we met for coffee, he told me, "I would rather have atheism with justice than something called Islam without justice. In the next census, I will not even call myself a Bosniak. I would rather call myself a Turk, or a Yugoslav." For Muhsin, the Ottoman empire and socialist Yugoslavia were the readiest historical examples of just and competent rule in Bosnia. He pointed to the case of his own family, which had much of its land nationalized by the socialist regime but put to good use, such as housing and schools. Moreover, Muhsin said, that system allowed former owners to reclaim any land not used for the stated purposes of seizure. Muhsin's father had started this process just before the war to retrieve a portion of their nationalized lands; after the war, in a time of alleged transition to a market economy, attempts to recover his erstwhile private property were met with derision in government offices. Muhsin's nostalgia for Yugoslavia extended beyond the economy,[64] however, and encompassed even a sense of being in the wider world, of open vistas on the universal:

> With the Yugoslav passport, we could travel to the east and to the west. There was good music, music that was known and respected throughout Europe. . . . I considered myself a civilized man. I could read Latin [script], I could read Cyrillic, and on the weekends I could read Arabic letters in the mosque. I was a civilized man. And now they want to just cut us up [pantomimes scissors in both hands shredding some paper] into something smaller . . . [sits back, exasperated].
>
> Once my little son saw the church here and asked me, "Daddy is our mosque bigger than their church?" I could not believe that he would ask me such a thing. "Our" mosque, "their" church?! I told him, No, these houses of worship are for our people too. If there is a fire there, we should go to help put it out, it is not only for "them." I don't know how he learned such a thing, from his friends, from school, from—

As Muhsin grappled for the right word, I proferred, insipidly, "from this context?" To which he snorted, and spat the words, "Yes, from this context." The sense of frustration for Muhsin as both an individual and as a father was as palpable as the cigarette smoke in the air of the cafe. Like so many others in Bosnia—of all national groups, religions, and attitudes toward piety—Muhsin did not see the nation-state that he had fought for as providing any kind of meaningful path to justice, freedom, prosperity, or any other universal values that it should have brought into place.

DESTINATIONS AND ORIGINS

Beyond offering inclusion in shared terms, universalist projects must present the opportunity to master and even shape those terms as well. In this sense, the Katiba opened up new horizons for some Bosnians desiring to become more than mere "locals." The universalist project did not only ground encounters between peoples, but helped set texts and people into motion too, albeit with effects that could not be foreseen or controlled for.

Just as any number of Bosnians working for Western peacekeepers, bureaucrats, diplomatic missions, and NGOs leveraged their contacts and skills to pursue work, education, trade, or romance in Europe or the US, some Bosnians also used the Katiba to leave. Jihad itself appears to have been the least likely route out, with only a handful of known cases of the unit's Bosnian veterans going on to fight in Chechnya or, a generation later, in Syria.[65] And unlike with the ansar who came to Bosnia, the Bosnians who did travel to Syria included whole families with women and children aiming to live under Islamic State governance.[66] Risks and disappointments were never far, however. Perhaps best-known in this regard is Ibro Delić, a locksmith by trade and veteran of the Katiba who spent just under two months in Haritan, northern Syria, in 2013 before coming home. During his trial for terrorism-related charges in Bosnia, Delić claimed his intention was to see the situation for himself rather than to align with the Islamic State, and that his visit was so short because he quickly grew concerned by the infighting between armed factions.[67]

Scholarships, pilgrimages, and marriages, with the help of savings and luck, played larger roles than jihad in the postwar lives of Bosnians from the Katiba. Jusuf, the teenager who ran away from home, took his first trip abroad thanks to the Katiba, for hajj in the summer of 1995. He started to learn Arabic during the war, and through connections with people who worked for Arab NGOs in Bosnia pulled together scholarships to study in Jordan. There he discovered a broad range of possibilities that existed between the rigidness he had sometimes seen in the Katiba and the compromised traditionalism he perceived in the IZ, and his views on Islam evolved accordingly. As one of his friends from the Katiba who also studied in Jordan put it to me:

> In Bosnia [during the war], you had either the Islam of the IZ or you had a very particular kind of Salafi Islam. But in Jordan you have the Muslim Brothers, the Salafis, including the so-called nonpolitical Salafis [ghayr al-siyāsī], and even anti-Salafis like Hasan al-Saqqaf.[68]
>
> Take the example of Palestine. Because Palestine is nearby and there are so many Palestinians in Jordan, it has been a very important issue and you can see so many different opinions amongst Muslims. Some support peace with Israel, others want to fight Israel, still others think the Palestinians should emigrate from Palestine if they cannot live under Muslim rule. There is a great

> variety [tanawwuʿ] of opinions, Jordan is like a place to *test* [uses the English word] all of them, a laboratory.

Here, the geography of blame in public debates that frequently glosses travel to Arab countries as a "radicalizing" force readily falls apart. Far more interesting here were diverse forms of circulation between Bosnia and the Middle East after the war. For Jusuf, his time abroad changed the course of his life. Before returning home, he met a Palestinian merchant in Amman who encouraged him to set up a perfume store in Bosnia as a way to export some of his own goods. When I knew him, Jusuf owned several shops and sometimes made money as a tour guide for wealthy Gulf Arab visitors as well, not an unusual combination in an economy where many people combine different kinds of formal and informal work.

Then there were those who never returned to Bosnia, who "made it," in a sense. Imad el-Misri's Bosnian interpreter—the one who in all likelihood translated *Notions That Must Be Corrected*—moved to the United Arab Emirates and became an Islamic authority in his own right, giving lectures online, including some he says are based on the lessons given in the Katiba. According to rumors, an outstanding warrant for suspected war crimes has kept him from coming home. Kerim, another Bosnian mujahid, came up most frequently in conversations as the most successful. Not only did he study in Jordan, but he also married an Arab woman there. We've never managed to cross paths in person, but the eloquence and subtlety of his written Arabic shines through in the emails we have exchanged. Kerim settled in Kuwait and eventually found work as a muezzin in a mosque, calling Muslims to prayer in a language that may not be his "own" but was chosen by God to deliver His message to all.

Chapter 3

AUTHORITIES

THE MUJAHIDS' TASK WAS A DAUNTING ONE: TO CHARGE UPHILL and seize a fortified Serb position protected by large anti-aircraft weapons pointed downward to repel any infantry advances. Possessing little more than mortars and small arms, they were badly outgunned and expected heavy losses. Under cover of darkness, several hundred mujahids, ansar and Bosnians together, slowly made their way toward their objective, snaking between minefields one carefully snipped tripwire at a time. At the appointed hour, the mujahids charged, steeling themselves for what promised to be a bloody confrontation. Yet the Serbs' guns unexpectedly tilted upward and started firing into the sky instead, even though the Muslims had no aircraft. The fighting ended quickly, in a decisive victory for the jihad. Afterward, the Serb soldiers who had been taken prisoner reportedly said that when the battle started, they had been aiming at horsemen clad in white charging at them from the sky.

Accounts place this event during the battle of Vozuća, in northeast Bosnia, in September 1995.[1] The story harkens to a precedent from the early history of Islam: the intervention of angels on the side of the Muslims at the Battle of Badr, as attested to in the Quran (3:123–125), multiple hadiths, and other texts. It is not only the broad outline of the story that matches, but also the mode of transmission—no one I spoke to ever saw the angels themselves, but instead always made sure to attribute the claims to the Serbs.[2] Miracle accounts like this circulated widely in the jihad and in the media materials produced about it.[3] The most common type tell of fallen martyrs whose bodies remain fragrant and fresh even months after death, often with smiles on their faces (Figure 5). A Palestinian physician recalled an incident from his time working in a hospital during the war: another Palestinian, a mujahid, was brought in barely alive, guts and blood spilling out, and drew his last breath in the operating room. "Everywhere his body went, there was the smell of musk." Another category of miracle involved fortuitous intervention by the elements, which sometimes carried a strong hint of angelic participation, as in the Vozuća story.[4] Mehmud, whom you met in the previous chapter, introduced me one day to an old friend from the Katiba. When I asked about miracles, the friend jogged Mehmud's memory about another mujahid from their town who emerged unscathed after being subjected to a withering barrage of "friendly fire" from close range on a moonless night. These stories were, of course, far from universally accepted. Some jihad veterans I knew, both ansar and Bosnians, dismissed the accounts as simple propaganda. Others were more cautious: they didn't witness any themselves but wouldn't gainsay the claims of fellow mujahids. There was also a general evocation of the Katiba's own specialness as a miracle in itself, the fact that men from so many different races and cultures could organize themselves into an effective fighting force.[5]

Miracles have always had their politics, especially in times of war—indeed, the relationship between the miraculous and violence is in many ways constitutive of authority. While Carl Schmitt famously defined the sovereign as "he who decides on the exception," a further elaboration of his has received somewhat less attention: "The exception in jurisprudence is analogous to the miracle in theology. Only by being aware of this analogy can we appreciate the manner in which the philosophical ideas of the state developed in the last centuries." For Schmitt, sovereignty—the form of authority that characterizes the modern state and relies on a logic of exception—must be understood as a "secularized theological concept" whose roots lie in the notion of God as "omnipotent lawgiver."[6] Sovereignty, however, is only one type of authority among others, and miracles can be understood in terms other than exception. Reading miracles as gratuitous grants of transgressive power from God can reveal a very different form of authority at work in the Bosnian jihad: not a logic of sovereignty, but one of solidarity instead. The mujahids asserted the right of individual Muslims to travel and participate in jihad elsewhere without the permission of any government, in defiance of the international legal order's preference for state-authorized violence. Too often this is glossed as a total rejection of state authority, yet the mujahids upheld this arguably radical principle while developing a pragmatic approach to collaborating with the Bosnian army.

The clearest institutionalization of this authority came with the establishment of the Katiba, which fought in the name of both the Bosnian nation-state and the umma. The Katiba was where most ansar were concentrated in the Bosnian army, as well as the hundreds of locals who joined them. With its multinational composition and considerable autonomy from the chain of command, the Katiba exemplified how a universalist project could develop a logic of solidarity, one that neither venerated sovereignty nor erased it.[7] Returning to the story that opened this chapter, we can discern two different faces of sovereignty at work. In seeking to recapture territory from Serb nationalist forces, the Bosnian army was asserting sovereignty internally (just as their

FIGURE 5. Abu ʿAli from Kuwait was one of the many mujahids who was reported to have smiled after their martyrdom, a common example of a jihad miracle. Source: Azzam Publications.

opponents were seeking to do so through secession). But sovereignty also faces outward, including through membership in an international legal order that confers license to wage war outside one's own borders: in the skies above Bosnia during the battle of Vozuća, there were American, British, French, and other jets under the umbrella of the North Atlantic Treaty Organization (NATO) waging a brief bombing campaign against Serb forces that set the stage for the negotiations to end the war.[8] As a universalist project with a distinctive logic of authority, the jihad transgressed both the internal and external faces of sovereignty. Like those mysterious horsemen floating somewhere between the armies on the ground and NATO's jets in the air, the jihad unfolded violence along a different dimension altogether.

THE GIFT OF MIRACLE

Ansar embarking upon jihad in foreign lands act in the name of the umma but live in a world of nation-states. Thus they must justify traveling to fight without the permission of a national government, be it one's own or in the arena of conflict. In the Bosnian jihad, this was far more concrete and pressing than establishing an Islamic state, although many mujahids supported this latter proposition in general and some were disappointed to learn that it was not atop the agenda.[9] Adopting an Islamic state as a programmatic goal would also have invited potentially debilitating disagreements over the implementation of shariʿa and the constitutionalization of Bosniak nationalism.[10] In any event, according to multiple interviews, the Katiba's leadership emphasized in speeches that the goal was to help Bosnian Muslims defend themselves and that any other agendas or political programs should be left at the door. This was as much about preserving the Katiba from factionalism—as well as potential provocateurs planted by Arab or Western intelligence agencies—as it was about any kind of "moderation." In the jihad, the challenge was how to fight alongside a much larger Bosnian army with very different sensibilities and priorities; authority was less about rule than it was about solidarity.

The question of solidarity largely has been eclipsed by the overwhelming analytical attention devoted to Islamist movements seeking to capture or influence state power in their own countries.[11] This blind spot is part of a larger problem, which is that political theology too often has been understood as political theology *of the state*. To return to a point made earlier, Schmitt's influential account emphasizes God's ability to make miracles happen as the model for the sovereign's power to suspend law through the state of exception. This logic of exception withdraws the extraordinary from the ordinary while remaining in relationship with it: sovereign power possesses violence that can transgress all law but that is *nevertheless always legal*—a paradoxical framing that has generated much commentary.[12]

As flawed as this framework may be, alternatives and critiques largely hew to its state-based contours; the absence of a political theology that can think concretely across state boundaries is striking.[13] For its part, anthropology has a long tradition of showing how miracles can point to forms of authority beyond the state, but it is almost always presented as a residual form of *local* popular power checking the sovereign.[14] Often this power is found in saintly individuals, a tendency stretching at least as far back as Max Weber's formulation of "charismatic authority" as a counterpart to the bureaucratic rationality characterizing the modern state.[15] Bonnie Honig has gone further and sought to flip the vertical relationship Schmitt posits by showing how the miraculous can channel various forms of popular power and even radical democracy.[16] Even the messianic tradition, such as Walter Benjamin's call for a "real state of emergency" to confront fascism, is more helpful for thinking the abolition of the state form as such rather than the possibilities lurking in the interstices between states in the world.[17] Yet for as long as states exist in a larger system, there will always be a need to think about orthogonal relations of violence across borders—neither wars between states nor those pitting states against their own people.

Jihads engaged in solidarity force us to reckon with a political theology that crosses borders in very concrete ways. The document most widely cited as outlining some theory of authority for these jihads comes from the pen of ʿAbd Allah ʿAzzam (1941–1989), identified in the canon of Western terrorism expertise as the "godfather of jihad." Born in Palestine, ʿAzzam earned his doctorate in fiqh from al-Azhar; taught at universities in Amman, Jeddah, and Islamabad; and emerged as a prominent advocate for the Afghan jihad in the Arab world. ʿAzzam established the well-known Services Office [Maktab al-Khadamāt], which sought to coordinate foreign support for the jihad, including humanitarian aid and armed volunteers. Because he worked closely with the young Osama bin Laden, ʿAzzam has often been described—at considerable risk of anachronism—as an intellectual ancestor, or even as a co-founder, of al-Qaʿida.[18]

In 1984, ʿAzzam issued his famous legal opinion, or fatwa, declaring participation in the Afghan jihad to be *fard ʿayn*, an individual duty for every able-bodied Muslim in the world, akin to prayer or fasting during Ramadan.[19] Such obligations should also be capable of fulfillment without permission from any other authority. ʿAzzam and most fiqh scholars agreed that it is fard ʿayn for Muslims to defend against non-Muslim invaders. The *scope* of who the duty falls upon, however, followed a loose notion of localized territorial affiliation.[20] The distinctiveness of ʿAzzam's argument came in expanding this circle of obligation, first to Muslims in neighboring countries and then to the umma entire if the invaders are not repelled. The gaps in his reasoning as to how such an enormous undertaking could practically come to fruition did not escape the notice of critics.[21] Thus, although it employs the language of obligation, ʿAzzam's fatwa is perhaps instead better understood in context as conferring license, a way for Muslims to justify joining the jihad when other ties would have held them back. Traditional jurisprudence specified that when jihad is fard ʿayn, even a debtor, child, or wife can participate without taking leave of their creditor, parent, or husband, respectively. ʿAzzam sought to reason analogically from this doctrine to include rulers as well.[22] In effect, ʿAzzam was rejecting one of the core claims of the international legal order, namely that only states have the right to wage war.

Yet while ʿAzzam's fatwa empowered individuals over states by allowing them to participate in transnational acts of violence, this did not mean he rejected the state system altogether, as is often presumed. ʿAzzam operated according to a logic of solidarity, maintaining a resolutely localized sense of authority in the Afghan jihad—a struggle that sought control of a state *within* the international legal order and openly aligned with members of that order, not least the United States.[23] ʿAzzam wanted to support, rather than displace, the Afghan mujahideen factions; he attempted to mediate disputes between them; and he favored channeling ansar to join them rather than creating a separate force.[24] In other contemporary jihads, too, ansar invariably fight in cooperation with some local groups that themselves ultimately seek state authority and must come to terms with the state order. In the 1990s, even al-Qaʿida, the archetypal "global terrorist network," understood its status as guests in Afghanistan and always recognized the authority of the Taliban, however insincere they may have been.[25] Two decades later, the self-declared Islamic State claimed to erase what it called the "Sykes-Picot borders" separating Iraq and Syria, but also contemplated a future of diplomatic relations in the world system.[26] The jihad in Bosnia took this logic to its ultimate limit, as one of the few transnational jihads in which ansar were aligned with a recognized nation-state member of the international community.

Reconciling ʿAzzam's radically individualized notion of jihad with his support for local factions seeking statehood requires situating the fatwa in a broader theology. And for this, it may help to turn to the mystical realm. For ʿAzzam's first book about Afghanistan was a treatise on jihad miracles, *Signs of the Merciful One in the Afghan Jihad*, which was reprinted and translated in numerous editions and languages.[27] For the mujahids I have spoken to in nearly a dozen countries, it was ʿAzzam's miracle stories, not his juristic output, that resonated most widely.[28] This was especially the case in Bosnia, where the fiqh manual distributed by the Katiba adhered to a more traditional analysis of fard ʿayn in jihad without ʿAzzam's expansive theory of obligation—after all, there was little practical need to convince Bosnians that foreign Muslims were obligated to join their fight.[29]

Signs of the Merciful One combines historical and political analysis of the jihad in Afghanistan, narrations of miracles very similar to those mentioned from Bosnia, and reflections on the nature of miracles themselves. The Arabic term for the type of miracles we have been discussing so far is *karama* (plural: *karamat*), a word that also can mean dignity or honor and is etymologically linked to notions of generosity.[30] This aspect of gratuitousness is important: karamat may be a way for God to boost people's faith or morale, but they are not the means through which battles are won or lost. The existence of karamat is indisputable but should not cause people to drift from trust in God [*al-tawakkul*] to complacency [*al-tawākul*]. And the lack of such phenomena should never be held against someone in assessing their piety or worth.[31] Moreover, karamat are also only a subset of the acts that transgress the customary order of things, so care must be taken to distinguish them from miracles wrought by prophets on the one hand and magic on the other.[32] Comparisons to the former would suggest dangerous pretensions, to the latter charlatanism. For all of these reasons, such extraordinary occurrences should be spoken of with caution.[33]

ʿAzzam's political theology contrasts with Schmitt's notion of miracle as the model for sovereign exception in three important ways. First, while sovereign miracle stands in for centralized power exercised by a ruler, jihad miracles are more dispersed: there is no worldly "he who decides," no individual who can summon this power at will. If sovereignty, to borrow Ernst Kantorowicz's classic formulation, imagines the king as having at once two bodies—a mortal body natural and an immortal body politic—the political theology of these jihads is expressed in karamat whose appearance may be granted through some mujahid bodies or none at all.[34] Second, karamat transgress the existing order of things without purporting to preserve the old order or establish a new one, so they are free of sovereignty's anxiety to reconcile rule and exception.[35] In crossing borders for jihad, ansar defied sovereigns without necessarily seeking to replace them; whether fighting against recognized governments as in 1980s Afghanistan or alongside them as in 1990s Bosnia, their attitude toward state sovereignty was contingent and pragmatic. Third and finally, karamat do not exhaust the category of the miraculous. The sovereign state tries to bring the power of the miraculous to earth and harness it as a weapon, forever unstable; in contrast, the jihad lets the miraculous be, treating it as a potentiality that can suddenly condense in the atmosphere like the flying horsemen of Vozuća, disrupting the order of things as a sign of God's favor. Similarly, this political theology is rooted in only one of many possible readings of Islamic traditions.[36] The existence of jihad miracles leaves ample room for multiple authorities to claim to embody Islam and to collaborate with each other.

When read together, ʿAzzam's fatwa on jihad and his work on miracles can help us sketch a political theology that is dispersed, transgressive, and nonexhaustive: that, in short, can provide a justification for fighting in the shadow of a nation-state system, in the space between rulers and the rebels who wish to replace them. In Bosnia, the most significant institutionalization of this notion of authority came with the Katiba—how the mujahids exercised and navigated authority in that space is the matter to which we shall now turn.

JIHAD UNDER TWO FLAGS

The Katiba was officially established in August 1993 as an autonomous unit within the Bosnian army consolidating most of the ansar with a roughly equal number of Bosnian volunteers.[37] Of the Bosnians, about half came from either the Zenica or Travnik areas. The unit's administrative headquarters was in Zenica, with its primary base camps around the village of Mehurići. It was subordinated to the 3rd Corps and operated according to broad strategic goals set by the high command. In the words of Muhsin from

Chapter 2, one of the Bosnians who helped establish the unit, it fought under "two flags": that of the umma and that of the recognized nation-state of Bosnia-Herzegovina. The Katiba's iconography reflected this dual commitment: in publicity materials distributed abroad, its logo was a black flag emblazoned with the monotheistic creed of Islam, "There is no god but God and Muhammad is his Prophet," fluttering over a map of Bosnia. Yet in its everyday correspondence with the army, the Katiba used stamps and seals with Bosnian army insignia. The Katiba chose its own leadership and raised funds abroad, although it appears to have procured armaments locally. The unit's rules enjoined regular prayer and banned alcohol, fornication, pork, swearing, and—unlike other units denominated as Muslim, such as the 7th Muslim Brigade—smoking. In place of a conventional military hierarchy, the Katiba made decisions through a consultative body [majlis al-shūrā] comprising senior mujahids. Bosnian recruits had to complete approximately forty days of Islamic education as a prerequisite to military training, which the next chapter will discuss in greater detail.

The Katiba may have been the largest and most visible of the configurations of ansar fighting in Bosnia, but it was not the only one. There were also smaller groups: the best known was led by Abu al-Zubayr from the Saudi city of al-Ha'il. Abu al-Zubayr's group consisted of several dozen mujahids from Saudi Arabia and other Gulf countries, as well as people the Katiba turned away or kicked out. There were very few Bosnians. It was based in villages north of Zenica, with subgroups near Željezno Polje, Travnik, and Tuzla that were attached to different local Bosnian army units. This group was less regimented than the Katiba—mujahids were freer to stay in the villages with Bosnian families and did not have to submit to a rigorous schedule. Many of these men were coming from the Afghan jihad and were accustomed to more decentralized and informal arrangements. Yet whenever the Katiba launched major operations they would show up and participate.[38] In contrast to these bands of foreigners, there were individual ansar serving in various army units as mascots of solidarity from the umma.[39] The 4th Muslim Light Brigade, discussed in the previous chapter, included about a dozen Arabs, of whom three were killed in battle.[40] Its leader, the preacher Muderis—who was fluent in Arabic, studied at al-Azhar, and was one of the many who told me about the karama of Vozuća—explained to me that since

Konjic was on the road from the Croatian port of Split to Sarajevo, he would occasionally meet Arabs traveling for jihad or aid work, or both, and some stayed with him.

Neither Abu al-Zubayr's militias nor the individuals embedded in Bosnian army units like that of Muderis were organized enough to present an alternative to the logic of state sovereignty. It was in Travnik, where Abu ʿAbd al-ʿAziz and his men linked up with the Muslim Forces, that the model for what would later become the Katiba emerged: a fighting unit with comparable numbers of Bosnians and ansar, which would include a regime of Salafi-oriented religious education for Bosnians.[41] This arrangement articulated a form of authority for a universalist project which sought to evaluate and critique Bosnian practices and particularities but not to erase them. This logic is neatly illustrated in a pamphlet signed by Abu ʿAbd al-ʿAziz directing Arab volunteers on how to join the Muslim Forces, which is worth reproducing at length:

> In the name of God the most merciful and compassionate
>
> Program for the journey to Bosnia-Herzegovina
>
> Before arriving in Bosnia-Herzegovina, it is necessary to attend to the following matters:
>
> 1. Devotion to God Almighty, inside and out
> 2. Adherence to the Book of God and the sunna of his Prophet (Peace Be Upon Him), according to the program of the righteous predecessors [al-salaf al-ṣāliḥ]
> 3. Good knowledge [maʿrifa] of the conditions of the country
> 4. Good knowledge of the customs and traditions [al-ʿādāt wal-taqālīd] of this state and the neighboring states
> 5. Psychological and mental readiness to confront existing strife
> 6. Not getting into party matters [al-umūr al-ḥizbiyya] and various groups [jamāʿāt]
> 7. Buy tickets and make reservations on an airline to the Austrian capital Vienna after getting a visa only for Austria.

8. Contact one of the Brothers in Zagreb to arrange your reception, by phone or fax: [number] or through [name and telephone number].

9. In case you cannot contact anyone or there is no one to receive you, do not get irritated. Head to [location] in Zagreb by bus and call from there.

10. In Zagreb there is a house for greeting, receiving, and seeing people off.

11. It is preferable to have heavy winter clothes and high-top boots.

12. It is preferable to carry German currency (German marks)

13. For those who are prepared to drive, please obtain an international driver's license from one of the tourism companies in the Kingdom [of Saudi Arabia]

God grants success
Your Brother,
Mahmud Bahadhiq (Abu ʿAbd al-ʿAziz)[42]

The order of these points is instructive. Abu ʿAbd al-ʿAziz begins with the most important requirement and the one broadest in scope, namely devotion to God. The second point telescopes rapidly from the general call to heed the Quran to the much more specific indexing of Salafi doctrine, which is nevertheless framed in broader terms—described as the way of the early Muslims [al-salaf al-ṣāliḥ]. From there, he proceeds to highlight the importance of local conditions, customs [ʿādāt], and mores, but the value attached to them is neutral. Then, and only then, can the practical details be attended to. He calls for "devotion" and "adherence" to general Islamic precepts, but only "knowledge" of local conditions and customs. The attitude toward the local—and, by extension, to Bosnian sovereignty—is necessarily an ambivalent one: for universalist projects such as the Bosnian jihad, the local is construed as an object of *both* critique and respect. By speaking generally of conditions, customs, and traditions, the local—whether glossed as nationalism, state sovereignty, or anything else—is neither presupposed nor precluded, but merely encompassed in a universalist project, awaiting further evaluation and reinscription according to higher orders.

The Katiba followed this logic. The unit sought to assure supporters abroad that it was formed "under the army in organizational matters [al-umūr al-niẓāmiyya] but proclaimed upon its foundation absolute loyalty to God, His Prophet (Peace Be Upon Him), and His book and refuses to appeal to any order or traditions outside the provisions of the shariʿa."[43] Its public statements never referred to "sovereignty" [sayyāda] and instead described its relationship with the army as one of "partnership and independent administration" [al-mushāraka wal-idāra al-mustaqilla].[44] The Katiba made clear that its accession to state authority in Bosnia was a solely pragmatic matter—this was important because many of its members had participated in jihads elsewhere *against* recognized states and could very well do so again in the future. The Katiba argued that participation in the Bosnian jihad did not require authorization from any government, as explained in its newsletter:

> Astonishingly, there are many doubts raised around the jihad today, such as that combat and jihad are only permitted with a duly empowered [mumakkan] amir or imam. Most scholars hold the view that jihad is not impeded by the absence of an authorized imam or amir. Whether he exists or not, this does not mean the suspension of jihad while waiting for an imam or amir.[45]

The choice of terms here repeatedly evoked worldly and spiritual authority—amir and imam, respectively. States claiming both forms of leadership, such as the kingdom of Saudi Arabia, were put on notice: failure to act would be no reason to bar other Muslims from doing so on their own. They could and—in the case of the Katiba, did—choose their own leaders and would make their own decisions.

SACRIFICE AND STATEHOOD

A series of failed and bloody attempts to break the siege of Sarajevo near the town of Ilijaš over the autumn and winter of 1992 resulted in recriminations between the ansar and the Bosnian army. This is a helpful place to explore the collaborative relationship that evolved between the two. For despite all their public veneration of martyrdom, the ansar felt that they were being used by the Bosnian army as cannon fodder and they were not happy about it. It seems obtuse to point out that the celebration of wartime sacrifice in jihad does not equal a willy-nilly embrace of death, but the widespread association of contemporary jihads with suicide operations demands such a clarification.[46] In various press interviews, Abu ʿAbd al-ʿAziz bragged about one effort, in which he claimed fifty-five ansar mujahids fought and eight were killed, including Abu Muhammad al-Fatih, a member of the Bahraini royal family.[47] He also spoke publicly of poor coordination between the Bosnian territorial militias and the Muslim Forces that left his men dangerously exposed during battle.[48] In late December, the Muslim Forces, now reorganized as the 7th Muslim Brigade, made another attempt at Ilijaš to alleviate the pressure on Sarajevo. The mujahids broke through enemy lines without sufficient backup, only to find themselves forced to withdraw under withering counterattack from Serb artillery. Those killed included the Egyptian commander as well as his Bahraini deputy.[49] Another Bahraini wounded in the incident accused the Bosnians of poor planning and lack of preparation, quipping, "This isn't an attack, this is suicide. Death awaits us above."[50]

From the perspective of the Bosnian military leadership, however, the problem was that the mujahids disobeyed orders and had dashed too far ahead of the rest of the army.[51] Throughout the war, other units complained about "the Arabs" as undisciplined, uncooperative, and dangerous. Ansar mujahids reportedly attempted to burn abandoned Croat homes in the village of Guča Gora in 1993 and vandalized Catholic and Orthodox cemeteries.[52] There were also stories of Arabs threatening or harassing members of the Bosnian army, be they non-Muslims or Muslims deemed impious.[53] While criminal acts and breakdowns in discipline were hardly limited to ansar or religious Bosnian Muslims, such incidents became loaded with additional significance, as expressions of a dangerous underlying fundamentalism.[54] Yet notwithstanding handwringing over the mujahids' alleged unruliness, Bosnian generals valued them as shock troops—it was precisely their reputation as religious fanatics that served a useful purpose in demoralizing the enemy.[55]

The creation of the Katiba satisfied many agendas at once. For the army, subordinating the mujahids to centralized authority was key to strengthening its control over territory and population. For Bosnians who had joined the ansar, it was a welcome opportunity to regularize their legal status and avert possible charges of draft dodging or desertion from other army units. The Katiba also provided an address for assigning—or better yet, deflecting—responsibility for foreigners alleged to have committed atrocities or infractions. As one Bosnian member of the Katiba explained to the Hague tribunal, "People were not familiar with the fact that there were different [ansar] groups and the relationships between them, so it was very simple to say, for any of them, that this was an Arab from the El Mujahedin Detachment, when actually it was not the case."[56] After the murder of a British aid worker in January 1994, the Katiba issued a letter providing an alibi for a Yemeni and a Palestinian arrested in connection with the incident while also attesting that the third suspect, a Saudi, had left the unit months earlier and was not under its responsibility.[57]

Consolidation into a single unit also enabled the mujahids to negotiate more effectively with the Bosnian army. Fadhil the Iraqi, whom you read about in the opening of this book, stressed in a conversation with me, "Nobody forced anything on the Katiba. They were free to refuse operations, and they did refuse operations. For example, the army wanted the Katiba to try to lift the siege of Sarajevo. But that would have been a suicide mission!"[58] In the winter of 1994, the mujahids balked at the army command's request to fight in the Mt. Ozren area. Instead, the Katiba had the campaign pushed back to 1995, deploying near Zavidovići for operations aimed at ultimately connecting Tuzla and Zenica by capturing Doboj. The objectives included seizing a number of hilltops occupied by Serb forces that other Bosnian army units had been unable to capture. Months of painstaking reconnaissance followed: ansar and Bosnian accounts tell of famous field commanders such as al-Muʿtazz Billah from Egypt and Abu ʿAbd Allah from Libya scouting out Serb positions on foot, at times from only meters away. Especially important in light of the Ilijaš debacle was constructing secondary roads to facilitate evacuation of the wounded from the front lines. A publicity video produced by the Katiba featured mujahids in raincoats cutting down trees for this task.[59] For the mujahids, such planning and care spelled the difference between seeking martyrdom and mere suicide, or between tawakkul and tawakul.

Perhaps most important, the Katiba was entrusted with training and overseeing regular Bosnian army units in battle.[60] According to Abu Hamza, the Katiba was keen to ensure that it would not be abandoned in case something went wrong: if the mujahids were to break through Serb lines, they would need reinforcements to follow and hold that territory. Several dozen mujahids, Bosnians as well as ansar like Abu Hamza who could speak the local language, were dispatched to conduct religious training in the neighboring units to strengthen their motivation and morale and to build trust.[61] The commander of one of these units described this as "religious training and the bonding of our troops with the people . . . of Arabic origin."[62] At least a dozen men left their units to join the Katiba.[63] Others were less enthused: there were complaints that the mujahids had insulted the Bosnian state, President Izetbegović, and chief mufti Mustafa Cerić, and sought to kill Croats and Serbs serving in the Bosnian army. Apparently the remarks came about during an argument over the Katiba's attempts to enforce their notorious smoking ban, one of their least popular practices.[64] Despite these tensions, the Katiba largely achieved its objectives over the course of three battles—the second, and probably the bloodiest in terms of casualties among the mujahids, was later dubbed "Operation Karama"—culminating in the September 1995 action at Vozuća. In these engagements, the Katiba led the charge, but with hundreds of soldiers from other units among their ranks and following behind.[65] For a brief moment just before the end of the war, the Katiba basked in the sense of having successfully become a vanguard of a universalism larger than itself.

IN A WORLD OF SOVEREIGNS

The Katiba invoked an authority beyond the Bosnian state whose concrete manifestations were the ideas, men, and money brought to the field of jihad. While these broader networks may have crystallized the sense of working for the umma rather than a single state, they were still very much enmeshed in other states and the state system as a whole. The jihad's universalism operated through—and not despite—these concrete transnational ties. This can be seen at the level of the leadership as well as in the difficulties faced by ordinary fighters.

One recurring source of tension for the Katiba arose from the difference between its largely Egyptian and Northern African leaders and its main financial backers from the Gulf states. Some clarification about the role of Gulf donors may be helpful here, as prevailing discussions tend to treat them as uniform actors whose money and ideology flow effortlessly into the minds of locals. While reminiscing about these old politics one day, Abu Hamza from Syria conceded that the Egyptians tended to dominate the Katiba. But he hastened to point out that the mujahids had to maintain their independence from Gulf money too. "The Saudis, they are a little"—Abu Hamza paused while searching for the right adjective—"dull [balīd]. They think that money acts by itself. They had a Bedouin mentality [ʿaqliyya badawiyya]. For example, just because they have American employees in their companies, they think they control the Americans and not the other way around." He described how donors would arrive and open suitcases full of cash ("so much that your eyes would jump out"), only for the Katiba's amir, Abu al-Maʿali, to rebuff the offer if he felt there were too many strings attached.

The Saudis, for their part, were already somewhat lukewarm on supporting volunteers going to fight in Bosnia, since some prominent veterans of the Afghan jihad—especially Osama bin Laden—were emerging as regime critics around this time.[66] The House of Saud was very supportive of the Bosnian Muslim cause in general and described it using the language of jihad. But the task of encouraging Saudis to *join* the fighting themselves actually fell to dissidents such as Salman al-ʿAwda, one of the major figureheads of the Awakening [Ṣaḥwa] movement.[67] Support for direct participation in the jihad was more open in smaller Gulf states, especially Kuwait, whose main Salafi charity, the Heritage Society, had various ties to the Katiba that will be addressed in greater detail in the Interlude. The Heritage Society's magazine praised the Katiba and published articles about miracles in the Bosnian jihad.[68] Commitment to supporting an overseas jihad, however, was also perfectly compatible with participating in the structures of the Kuwaiti state.[69] Kuwait's Salafi movement was the first in the Arab world to contest parliamentary elections, and its identification with the regime only increased in the aftermath of the 1990–1991 Iraqi occupation.[70]

While the Saudis and Kuwaitis may have differed in their attitudes toward supporting jihad in Bosnia, they shared a vigorous opposition to jihad against their friends, especially Egypt and the United States. Rumors began to spread that the Katiba's Egyptian leaders were members of the Islamic Group, one of the armed groups locked in a low-level war with the Mubarak regime at that time and accused in the 1993 bombing of the World Trade Center in New York. Kuwait's Salafis had little sympathy for organizations like the Islamic Group; the Heritage Society's magazine avoided using the term *jihad* for events in Egypt, instead describing them merely as "violence." Some of the Heritage Society's leading figures were wealthy, US-educated, and embedded in elite family networks with no interest in fomenting the kind of armed rebellion then taking place in Egypt and Algeria.[71] Thus a crisis erupted in 1995 between the Katiba and some of its financial backers in the Gulf, leading to a suspension in donations.[72]

The Katiba appears to have engaged in considerable damage control efforts around the accusation. In March 1995, Abu al-Maʿali along with five members of the Katiba from the Gulf signed an open letter in response to "talk and misconceptions." It rejected the accusation that the Katiba was dominated by a particular political line—a reference to the Islamic Group—and refuted allegations that mujahids from the Gulf were marginalized by listing those holding various leadership positions. On the point of cooperating with Bosnian "communists," the Katiba claimed that they had obtained a fatwa from the prominent Saudi Salafi scholar Ibn ʿUthaymin endorsing the decision to work with the Bosnian army.[73] A week later, Anwar Shaʿban followed up with a personal appeal to one of the Heritage Society's leaders strenuously denying any membership in the Islamic Group and implicitly criticizing its tactics.[74] Although he believed that conditions under Mubarak did justify revolt, "what happened in Egypt is not in the interests of Islam." Shaʿban offered to suspend his relationship with the Katiba if that would satisfy the critics.[75]

The constraint of state politics outside Bosnia was felt not just at the level of donors but in the experiences of ordinary mujahids coming to join the fight. Many ansar hailed from states that criminalized unauthorized participation in overseas wars. Although willing to hand over passports and other identity documents to the Katiba's secretariat for safekeeping, they resisted demands to identify themselves directly to the Bosnian state, lest word get back to their own governments. For the army, this ambiguous relationship prompted anxieties about its ability to "know" the Katiba as it did its other army units—through the everyday circulation of paperwork in certain sets of shared social contexts and relationships. For their part, ansar dealt with the issue of legibility by using kunyas to identify themselves. A *kunya* is an everyday Arabic naming convention that uses the terms *abu* (father) for men or *umm* (mother) for women, generally to denote a lineal affiliation. There are also kunyas referring to well-known figures in Islamic history, such as Abu Dujana. In contexts of clandestine work, use of kunyas is widespread as a security precaution, often in conjunction with a relational adjective, or *nisba*, that usually indicates place of origin or nationality. Hence, "Abu ʿAbd Allah al-Libi" suggests someone whose son is named ʿAbd Allah and who hails from Libya.[76] Kunyas are convenient because they are portable between different contexts of jihad but are also disposable: unlike a legal name fixed in state identity documents, kunyas can be readily changed if one wishes.

Kunyas were the primary basis of identification within the unit as well as in published materials. Years after the jihad, ex-mujahids I interviewed would often give me a blank stare when I asked them about an individual using a legal name but vivid recollections would spill forth if I asked about the same people by kunya.

The Katiba's personnel records reflect the different concerns among mujahids about making oneself legible to the state. For Bosnians who wished to ensure that they were accounted for and not treated as deserters, data are generally accurate and complete. They are listed by full name (including father's name), with place and date of birth, identification number, and date of induction into the unit. For ansar, the story is quite different: almost all of them are listed as kunyas or other nicknames. The lack of legal names, however, did not make these lists completely fraudulent or useless. After all, kunyas served to identify mujahids to each other and as a form of socially contextualized knowledge could be traced back to individuals with legal names. Nor did their attempt to circumvent state surveillance signal a utopian erasure of all national categories, since most of the mujahids paired their kunya with a nisba based on citizenship ["al-Amriki," "al-Fransi"].[77] Moreover, by the end of the war, ansar in the Katiba may have been listed under kunyas or even false names, but they were nevertheless assigned a unique military identification number. Use of kunyas was a technology of universalist practice that allowed the mujahids to exercise transnational mobility in the name of broader community as well as respond to the state's demand that they perform legibility by hiding in plain sight before its gaze.

BY ANY OTHER NAME

On a cloudy winter day the week before the record-breaking blizzard of January 2012 that would leave much of the country drowning in snow, I visited Zavidovići with Jusuf, the Bosniak perfume vendor introduced in the previous chapter. Due to the bitter cold, the town center was mostly empty but we had an appointment with someone eager to meet with me: Senad, an old friend of Jusuf's from the Katiba. During the war, Senad served in the Katiba's small daʿwa unit that went out to proselytize throughout the army. Of the dozen or so Bosnians I knew who had served in the Katiba, Senad was the only one who still looked the part of a "Wahhabi," with his long beard and clean-shaven upper lip. Senad kept one arm solemnly clutched across his chest while carrying a small duffel bag full of Islamic pamphlets. Between eating kebabs [ćevapčići] and catching glimpses of a televised football match, Jusuf and Senad got into an argument. It was friendly and they were both soft-spoken men, but the disagreement was vigorous and neither was giving ground. None of this was a surprise: Jusuf had warned me that Senad was still living in the "time of the war" and that they had different views. Their dispute concerned "the Arabs," as they called them, and their relations with Bosnian Muslims. For Senad, they could do no wrong. He told me that any mistakes made in daʿwa such as harassing nonpracticing Muslims were the fault of overzealous Bosnians who had only recently discovered such ideas of Islam, and that the Arabs had counseled them to be more gradual and inviting. Jusuf sharply disagreed and said the Arabs were not always good guests, that like other guests they should have asked permission before embarking on daʿwa. Later, in the car, Jusuf shook his head in dismay at people like Senad who saw the Arabs only as angels. Jusuf's own time studying in Arab countries had exposed him to a far broader range of experiences with both Islam and Arabs than he had seen in Bosnia. "If you go to Saudi Arabia, you see how bad things are," he said. "In a country like Saudi Arabia, street cleaners are treated so badly that people would rather kill themselves than take such a job."

Despite their differences, both men were deeply invested in protecting the Katiba's reputation, especially after the trial of the wartime commander of the Bosnian army, Rasim Delić, in the Hague. The key legal question was Delić's responsibility for the Katiba's crimes, the most notorious being the execution of fifty-two Bosnian Serb prisoners in September 1995 after the battle of Vozuća.[78] Delić did not deny that the Katiba had committed atrocities, but argued that he had not been in a position to prevent or punish them; to this end, his lawyers portrayed the Katiba as something of an undisciplined rogue unit beyond the control of the Bosnian army. This was part of a broader sense of embarrassment among Bosniak nationalists over the mujahids. For example, a regimental history by the 7th Muslim Brigade, in which some of the ansar served before the establishment of the Katiba, omits mention of any foreign volunteers.[79] It is the same for a book profiling recipients of the Bosnian army's highest decoration, the Golden Lily.[80] Jusuf and Senad felt that in the process they—the Bosnians who constituted the majority of the Katiba—had been unfairly maligned as somehow less loyal or nationalist.

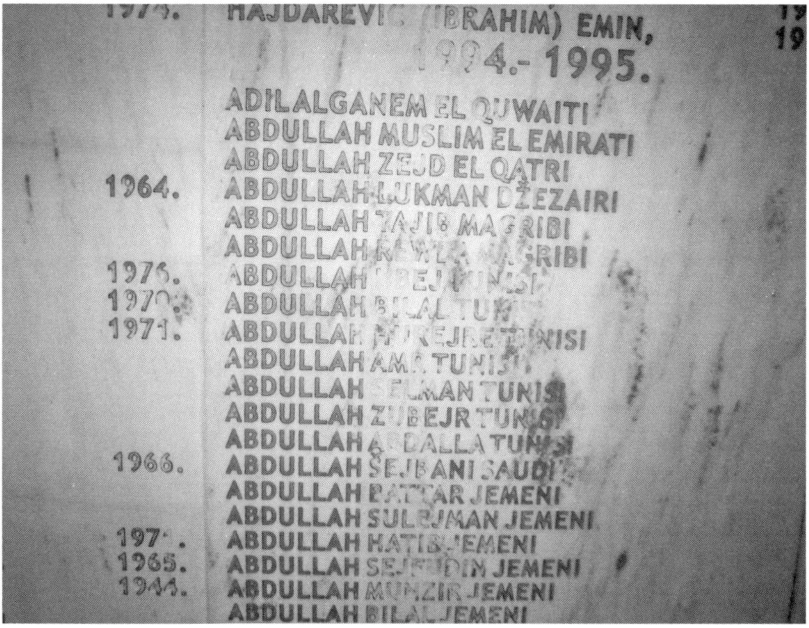

FIGURES 6 AND 7. The municipal war monument in Zavidovići is unusual for including ansar mujahids, each given the appellation "Abdullah." Photos by author.

Jusuf and Senad decided to show me the nearby municipal war monument before the sun set. About one hundred meters from the restaurant, atop a mound of grass in the town center, stands a gently curving stone wall engraved with the names of war martyrs from the area, military and civilian, in gold leaf (Figures 6 and 7). There are over one thousand names, arrayed across some twenty columns. Set off to the right-hand side are the ansar. The small act of not erasing the ansar from a war monument was all the more striking at a time when many Bosniaks living in the shadow of the Global War on Terror were seeking to distance their cause from the foreign volunteers.[81] That it was undertaken by a small municipality rather than a state-level entity may have made the difference: it was lower profile and less likely to attract international attention.

The mujahids are marked on the monument by kunyas rather than legal names. But not exactly kunyas, either. In each name, the kinship term *Abu* was replaced with "Abdullah," or "God's servant" in Arabic: so Abdullah Muhammad instead of Abu Muhammad, and so on. From the perspective of Arabic grammar and naming practices, the substitution was somewhat curious: it turned, for example, "Muhammad's father" to "Muhammad, servant of God." Yet Senad explained that for some reason, the local authorities thought that this formulation "sounded better."[82] When I saw these names, I was immediately reminded of the personnel rosters that the Katiba had submitted to the army: kunyas that would identify the mujahids to each other but it was hoped would mean little or nothing to outsiders. The monikers on this monument, however, took names meant to conceal and instead used them to induct the ansar into a public space of commemoration. And at the same time, they traded the kinship logic of the kunya for a devotional label emphasizing a broader community of faith—one that could never be contained, defined, or inscribed by a single sovereign.

Chapter 4

GROUNDINGS

IT WAS ABOUT HALF PAST TWO IN THE AFTERNOON WHEN AYMAN the Syrian and I arrived at the cemetery outside the village of Livade in northern Bosnia-Herzegovina. It was a day with bright gray skies during the gradual turning of winter to spring in 2010. With his long Salafi beard, amiable demeanor, fluency in the Bosnian language, and willingness to speak publicly, Ayman was frequently sought out by journalists and researchers interested in the topic of jihad. That day he picked me up in Zenica and drove north past Zavidovići up a set of narrow, winding roads. As usual he was very chatty, his rapid-fire sentences interspersed with bouts of laughter. Ayman explained that the poor eating habits of his hurried youth were catching up with him in the form of diabetes and high blood pressure. When I asked if he exercised at all, he laughed even more loudly than before and said emphatically, *Nula!* [zero, as in not at all]—switching from Arabic to Bosnian. But this long drive was in a way taking us back to the more active days of Ayman's youth, specifically the 1995 campaign against the Bosnian Serb forces in the Mt. Ozren area. Our conversation about the war was cut short as we suddenly reached a clearing on a hilltop. From here, the views were striking—the nearby slopes that ringed the horizon were so steep and foreboding that they appeared like barricades of wood and soil. Imagining them through Ayman's tales as teeming with enemy snipers and artillery in snow-covered years past made them seem even more daunting. We got out of Ayman's beat-up old sedan and slipped into the nearby cemetery through an impromptu latch gate. Ayman murmured the greeting "al-salamu ʿalaykum" under his breath.

Arranged in two rows, there were thirty-nine graves for fallen mujahids, easily recognizable by their distinctive style: each had two small, white, cylindrical markers, one of which, on the lower side of the slope, was painted green at the top (Figure 8). This manner of burial was largely unknown in Bosnia at the start of the war. It is associated with the Salafi orientation within Islam, which finds upright headstones to be uncomfortably reminiscent of idols or other objects of veneration. The villagers buried their dead here as well, using the more typical Bosnian Muslim *nišan*—an upright stone marker engraved with name and dates of birth and death, sometimes with a top carved in the form of a cap or turban.[1]

One might be tempted to read the disparate styles of the Salafi headstones and Bosnian nišans as part of a clash between a fundamentalist Arabian Islam and its moderate Bosnian counterpart. But the relationship between the

FIGURE 8. Ayman at the mujahids' cemetery in Livade. Photo by author.

markers in the grass and the bodies underneath is never straightforward nor unchanging, for cemeteries are also sites of contestation. A few years earlier, Abu ʿAli from Morocco and I had visited Mehurići, the village that served as a base for Arab mujahids from the early days of the war. The graveyard there, also used by both locals and mujahids, is more informal than the one in Livade. Some of the headstones, however, bear the names of Bosnians from the Katiba whose families replaced the original Salafi grave markers with nišans instead.[2] Such a change would have likely gone against the wishes of the buried men and are a reminder that for many Bosnians, the decision to join the jihad strained ties with parents and siblings. Or it might simply reflect a personal preference: the family of a Turkish martyr came all the way from Germany to proudly retrace their son's footsteps—yet still placed a nišan over his grave at Livade.[3]

This chapter will explore how mujahids on the ground processed the differences between them in the name of a universalist project unfolding in Bosnia. While outsiders may decry its commitment to Salafism as narrow and exclusionary, the jihad celebrated itself as a site of encounter between Muslims of different races, nationalities, doctrinal positions, and classes. Its amir, Abu al-Maʿali, illustrated this point in an interview he gave to a Bosnian army newspaper:

> What brought together souls from Herzegovina, Krajina, Zenica, Sarajevo, Bugojno, or Višegrad with the souls of the Black man from Gambia or Yemen, or the half-blood [melez] from Algeria or Pakistan—that is Islam. That is why the brotherly relations [bratski odnosi] among the mujahids are of a cosmopolitan character [kosmopolitskog karaktera]. Some Serbs and Croats who have accepted Islam, too, fight in the mujahid ranks.[4]

In this passage, mujahids from diverse municipalities and regions in Bosnia are brought face to face with and potentially complement a spectrum of dark-skinned races. The whiteness of the Bosnians is only indirectly referenced: the Algerian and Pakistani, as "half-bloods," are posited halfway between them and the "Black man," a category which includes not only the Gambian but the Yemeni as well.[5] Abu al-Maʿali's mention of a Gambian was not purely hypothetical: he was in all likelihood referring to the respected mujahid in charge of the Katiba's armory.[6] Hence, Blackness was deployed as non-Arab to exemplify universality while also being subsumed by the category of Arabness.[7] Blackness in particular was also shaped by global structures of white supremacy emanating from the West: Mahdi, the Jamaican-British convert whose story appeared in the Introduction, often found himself interpellated by Gulf Arabs through media stereotypes of African Americans as gangsters.[8] Arab is treated here as a linguistic and cultural category more than a racial one and an implicit baseline that enables the "cosmopolitan character" of Islam, one potentially open to people of all hues. This imaginary of diversity was a central part of the jihad's appeal for participants, bringing to life a notion of a worldwide umma comprising a fifth of humanity and holding out a message of salvation to the rest, even notionally Serbs and Croats.

But the processing of differences was also a concrete organizational and political challenge. To process differences was neither to resolve them into commonality nor to take them as given and fixed—it was, rather, treating them in a way that staged a scene of equality based on certain shared terms of reference.[9] Among other things, Salafi burial practices demonstrate a stark vision of human equality before the divine. Too often universalisms are understood as given sets of ideas that are then imported or imposed into particular contexts, with greater or lesser degrees of success. With contemporary jihads, the name often given to this content is Salafism, which then provides the terms for subsequent explanation and debate. In contrast, this chapter moves the question of difference from the margins to the center of the story. While liberal universalisms manage difference under rubrics such as diversity and multiculturalism, the jihad stressed instead the cultivation of virtues, the creation of kinship bonds, and the founding of a new community. These practices—which fit the Salafi label poorly, if at all—enabled the ansar, along with their Bosnian companions, kin, and some critics to forge a common space for cooperation and contestation under the conditions of the war and in its aftermath.

Like all universalisms, the jihad produced its own exclusions and inequalities, both explicit and implicit. And while it certainly did not live up to its lofty rhetoric, the jihad nevertheless refracted existing social cleavages in distinctive and perhaps unexpected ways, especially at the intersection of race, religion, gender, and wealth. In global hierarchies of race, the structural benefits Bosniaks accrued from whiteness were partially offset by the perception that they were less authentically Muslim than Arabs.[10] And in terms of material conditions, the category of Arab was strikingly bimodal: those coming from the Gulf were seen as rich, the rest as poorer than even the Bosnians. These overlapping dynamics unfolded in different ways along axes of gender. For Bosnian mujahids, relations with Arab ansar were rooted in the idiom of brotherhood, a form of male bonding in which feminine traits such as tenderness and care were publicly celebrated. For Bosnian women, the primary relationship with ansar was marriage, in which racialized sexual desires dovetailed with perceptions of piety and material considerations. An Arab sleeping in trenches alongside Bosnian soldiers or seeking a woman's hand in marriage could be a needy immigrant with nowhere else to go or a fabulously wealthy jihad tourist—and the length of his beard would provide few clues as to which.

DEFINING DIFFERENCE

Universalisms must translate ideals directed at all of humanity into reality in the face of lived differences. These ideals, the specific idioms of universalism, can be drawn from any number of cultural resources in the world; they are crucial for the definition of universalisms, but they are not universalisms themselves. Conceptually distinguishing universalist projects from their dominant idioms—in this case, a Salafi one—is crucial. To understand this jihad as an effect of something called "Salafism" is misleading for many reasons, one of them being that the word itself has a deeply unstable referent.

The noun *Salafism* ties together a cluster of concepts and practices loosely and unhelpfully labeled by outsiders as "purist," "literalist," or "conservative" and treated as a sect, ideology, or social movement.[11] These include a creedal emphasis on God's indivisible oneness, a doctrinal focus on textual narratives of Prophetic tradition over other genres of scholarship, and a canon that heavily praises the writings of Taqi al-Din Ahmad ibn Taymiyya (1263–1328) and Muhammad ibn ʿAbd al-Wahhab (1702–1792). Salafis are often critical of Sufis and suspicious of how their veneration of saintly men considered friends of God can resemble or encourage polytheism.[12] Salafis are associated with distinctive dress and grooming practices such as long beards and short trousers for men and niqabs for women. Most important for this discussion, however, Salafism lacks any inherent political content: Salafis have all sorts of different relationships with the state and—like the general populations to which they belong—exhibit no demonstrable proclivity toward violence as a single group. And even when Salafis are engaged in violence, they do so as part of a wide variety of political projects: as discussed in the previous chapter, Salafi donors in Kuwait could enthusiastically support jihad against Serbs and Croats in Bosnia and oppose it against the ruling regime in Egypt without any obvious ideological inconsistency.

Nevertheless, a major strand of the terrorism expert subculture has taken to speaking of "jihadi Salafism" or "Salafi jihadism" as concepts to identify a locus of threat without producing much insight. Doctrinal approaches in search of a coherent canon have tended to focus on texts endorsing violence against Muslim rulers deemed apostates, arguably the most controversial definition of jihad from a fiqh perspective. Yet such a narrow definition excludes a great many self-proclaimed Salafis writing about and participating in jihad, including many of those who fought in Bosnia and even the "godfather of jihad," ʿAbd Allah ʿAzzam.[13] This approach sets up an untenable opposition between Salafi jihadis and Salafis who merely happen to do jihad.[14] On the other hand, there are approaches that look at practices instead of doctrine in an attempt to describe a distinctive "jihadi culture." This school compiles descriptive laundry lists of behaviors, from prayer to poetry, that are also widespread among Muslims who do not participate in jihad. This not only lacks much conceptual utility—other than debunking simplistic notions of jihadis as insincere Muslims—it ultimately underwrites state logics of profiling.[15] Both the doctrinal and practice-based approaches to jihadology merely refine the general problem of anti-Muslim animus: liberal injunctions against demonizing all Muslims converge with the security state's hunger for more precise profiling and targeting guidelines by agreeing that the culprit is Salafism. This discourse takes up the old racist canard, "Most Muslims aren't terrorists, but most terrorists are Muslims" and substitutes the narrower term *Salafi* for *Muslim*.

In recent decades, anthropologists have sought to push back against popular and expert discourses on jihadism in a variety of ways. A handful have studied jihads or other situations in which Muslims have taken up arms in the name of Islam, although these typically have been conflicts with a national focus and have not examined foreign volunteers.[16] The most prevalent approach has been to insist that studying topics unrelated to political violence while highlighting "ordinary" Muslims is itself a kind of antidote.[17] However otherwise salutary such approaches are, they still effectively cede the analytical ground of jihadism to the state and its adjutant-scribes. Moving from the rejection of essentialism, some anthropologists have turned their critical faculties to the Global War on Terror itself. The most far-reaching interrogation has come from Talal Asad, who has demonstrated that the fascination with the figure of the suicide bomber in the West "tell[s] us more about liberal assumptions of religious subjectivities and political violence than they do about what is ostensibly being explained."[18] Asad has skillfully shown how concepts such as just war and terrorism shape debates in which Western state violence is assumed to be normatively superior and critiqued in a way that only allows it to be *calibrated*, while other forms of violence tend to be *dismissed* as illegitimate per se. By sketching the genealogy of regnant categories for thinking about violence in the Global War on Terror context, Asad's work challenges their legitimacy, both analytically and politically.[19] In this respect, his critique is useful, necessary, and important. Instead of the pluralist appeal to the state that ultimately is reducible to *Please make sure you kill only the right people*, Asad interrogates empire and raises the question, *Who are you to decide that your killing is legitimate?*

Asad's critique of state power extends to contemporary Islamist movements as well for their focus on the "modern project of a state that is no different in essence from any modern state."[20] The state's expansionary tendencies, demand for absolute loyalty, and monopolization of violence render it suspect as a vehicle for actualizing any moral vision. Similarly, Asad slams those engaged in war against the United States in the name of Islam insofar as they reproduce state logics: "Like their state opponents, terrorists are modern, ideological and ruthless."[21] Asad's arguments helpfully restore the coevalness of jihad groups, but it is striking that even he continues to use the term *terrorist* after doing so much to demonstrate the worthlessness of the concept.[22] I mention this not to nitpick over terminology, but to point to the need for a way to think seriously about jihad on its own terms, and not simply as a demonic Other of the liberal state or a pale imitator of it.[23]

Examining the practice of universalism provides a way to move beyond this problem of alterity—either Muslims are radically Other or Muslims are basically the same as Us—to instead treat the regulation of difference itself as the object of study. Salafism is relevant for understanding the Bosnian jihad not because the latter was a violent project but insofar as it was a universalist one. The dominant idioms of public discourse within the jihad were arguably Salafi, but many of its participants were only superficially initiated into Salafi doctrine or were skeptical of it, and a few members of the Katiba were even members of Sufi orders. Many of the practices we will see in this chapter were by no means particular to Salafis in any event. Taking an allegedly "jihadi" segment of Salafism as the main category of analysis reflects the state's obsession—What *kind* of Muslims should we fear?—while skipping past a more basic question: how could this activity of jihad credibly bring together Muslims of such different backgrounds? It is obvious that the jihad drew from the enormous ocean of historically sedimented concepts, institutions, practices, genres, and tropes that come together under the sign of Islam; what requires understanding is not the jihad's "Islamicness" or lack thereof, but rather how the jihad performed the work of universalism, of processing difference. Thinking ethnographically about universalism can provide a framework that is capacious enough to ground concepts of Islam and violence in relation to one another without reductively shackling them together.

We can see this by stepping back and widening the frame beyond the mujahid graves to encompass how they were approached and discussed. Abu ʿAli, who guided me through the Mehurići cemetery, never used the adjective *Salafi* to describe this style of burial, instead referring only to "ahl al-sunna," short for "people of the tradition and the community" [ahl al-sunna wal-jamāʿa], the label from which the Sunni branch of Islam derives its name. Yet across the considerable variation of Sunni burial practices around the world, the position Abu ʿAli ascribed to the ahl al-sunna is clearly in the minority. Moreover, Abu ʿAli hastened to add that "improper" burials with erect headstones are the norm in his home country, Morocco. Here, Abu ʿAli was arguing for the probity of a position on the basis of it being properly Islamic, without using doctrinal, national, or racial labels such as Salafi or Arab. This is unsurprising: those called Salafis often distance themselves from the term, preferring to think of themselves as people of the tradition and the community or simply Muslims. This is not some kind of dissimulation, nor is it merely the Salafi rejection of established schools of Islamic jurisprudence in favor of an ideal of believers having unmediated relationships with texts. Rather, this generalized discomfort with the particularizing effects of labeling can be usefully thought of as an assertion of the right to define the terms of a universalist project, to set standards for oneself and for others. The content of Salafi norms—in this case, the idea that people should be buried in a certain way—is helpful not as an etiology of violence, but for revealing a structure of argumentation around difference. Abu ʿAli was not avoiding disagreement as much as he was staking a broader claim to defining what a Muslim should be. For Abu ʿAli to ascribe an outlier among burial styles to Sunni Islam writ large requires no more gall than an international lawyer proclaiming the existence of new rights in the name of humanity out of thin air. And in recognizing that Muslims in Morocco are not necessarily better adherents to Islam than in Bosnia, he was not unlike do-gooding Westerners who readily concede shortcomings in their own societies as a way of reaffirming adherence to a higher set of standards or ideals—ones that they also happen to assume authority in defining.

VIRTUE OVER CULTURE

One day in the summer of 2011, I visited Fadhil, the Iraqi whose story opened this book, in his flat in Zenica. After years of detention without charge in the immigration center, he had recently been shifted to house arrest, permitted to leave for only one hour a day in order to sign in at a local police station. We were talking about his days in the jihad, and he mentioned that because he spoke both Arabic and Bosnian, his duties included interpreting for al-Muʿtazz Billah, one of the Katiba's military commanders, whom he described as an "excellent mujahid."[24] I asked Fadhil what traits made for a good mujahid, and he thought about it for a moment, before reflecting,

> A good mujahid, first, always has a smile on his face. Second, he must have wisdom [ḥikma]. He should be beloved by people. Of course, courageous too. [But] wisdom and the manner of approaching people are very important. . . . It is important to persuade people so that they become convinced on their own that an action is right. You can't just force this on people.

This notion of good manners and pleasantness—*always having a smile on one's face*—in cultivating an authority based on persuasion rather than coercion was prevalent in the public discourse of the jihad as well.[25] These were part of a broader set of dispositions that emphasized qualities not conventionally associated with soldiering or even masculinity, such as calmness, humility, and leniency. Taken together, these virtues, or *akhlaq*, drew from long traditions of refinement and courtesy in Islam, starting with traits attributed to the Prophet Muhammad.[26] The term *akhlaq* is often translated in English as "morals" or "ethics"; I have chosen to render it as "virtues," whose Latin root, *vir* ("man") helpfully draws attention to the gendered dimensions of debates around ethics and politics in the anthropology of Islam. Whereas these debates have focused on the "agency" of Muslim women or its putative absence, the challenge here concerns the masculinized subject of the mujahid, who instead presents the problem of agency as a dangerous excess.[27] Yet the models of masculine virtue of mujahids in many cases do not appear to be conventionally masculine at all.

One of the most widely cited paragons of akhlaq was Abu al-Harith, the Libyan physician who was amir of the Katiba until late 1993. Descriptions of Abu al-Harith I have come across from Arabs, Bosnians, and non-Muslims consistently stress his quiet and polite demeanor, which also informed his sharp political instincts and deftness with diplomacy. One Bosnian mujahid captured many of these attitudes: "He was the best of men. He did not speak much, but his akhlaq were excellent." Abu Hamza from Syria said, "Abu al-Harith was much beloved by all the Bosnians, at all levels, from the officials to ordinary people. His way of dealing with people was very open and consensus-driven. He would try to persuade people and hear them out." Comparing Abu al-Harith to his successor, the Algerian Abu al-Maʿali, he noted, "You loved Abu al-Maʿali out of fear, you loved Abu al-Harith out of love. Abu al-Maʿali worked with control, Abu al-Harith with akhlaq."[28] Abu al-Harith's akhlaq also provided a basis for interactions with non-Muslims, including with some enemies. For example, a Croat officer kidnapped by the mujahids for the purposes of a prisoner exchange said,

> He was very polite, looked like a diplomat. He was a foreigner. He was very civilised. He asked me whether I was beaten. Then I said that I was kicked only once. . . . He wanted to know what was the date when this was done. And then he told me that it was not according to the Islam [*sic*] teachings to beat prisoners, that this shouldn't be done.[29]

A German army officer who negotiated the prisoner exchange with Abu al-Harith similarly described him as "very well educated in his behaviour, very polite."[30] The surprise embedded in these statements likely reveals the speakers' own prejudices, but also reflects the variety of unlikely sources attesting to Abu al-Harith's behavior. And the gendered aspect of these virtues did not escape notice: Nedžad Latić, an aide to the Bosnian president Alija Izetbegović, recalled that Abu al-Harith had gentle hands, thin fingers, and a voice like a dove, with the "only thing masculine about him being his long beard."[31]

Martial prowess, physical courage, and obedience to authority were of course celebrated in mujahid hagiographies—but note how Fadhil's list of vaunted traits mentioned courage almost as an afterthought. Extolled far more often are the somewhat unmasculine traits of intense meekness and humility in social interactions, especially interpersonal disputes with other Muslims. To take one particularly striking example, we can turn to Abu Muʿadh, the first person who came to mind when I asked Fadhil to name some examples of model mujahids.[32] Abu Muʿadh, a Kuwaiti veteran of the Afghan jihad, was made a leader in the Katiba due to his "superlative virtues [akhlāq fāḍila] and jovial smile, without any affect or pretense. He was courageous and intrepid, meek and modest." Abu Muʿadh "was like a mother to the mujahids. He would console this one, settle in [yuʿawwid] that one, advise this other, look after the comfort of yet another, until Bosnians loved him most of all the ansar mujahids." He interpreted dreams and would appear in the visions of mujahids as far away as Afghanistan years after his death.[33] These traits were praised in a story about the time he attempted to solicit donations for jihad from a wealthy but impatient merchant in Kuwait:

> [Abu Muʿadh] said: "May I speak with you a moment, please?" The merchant replied: "Let's go, hurry up." So he told him about the situation of the Muslims [in Bosnia] and the horrors and misfortunes he had beholden: the killing of old people and children, the rape of women, murder and dispossession, and so forth. Then, suddenly, the merchant responded by spitting in his face with nothing but contempt. He said: "I don't have free time for you or your Bosnians."
>
> Abu Muʿadh, may God's mercy be upon him, replied only with kindness [bil-luṭf] and said: "This spittle in my face is for me, but for your brothers over there, what will you give?" These words stirred the soul of the merchant and he said: "Forgive me, ask whatever you want."[34]

The power to persuade, to defuse tensions—with words that stir the soul—was especially valued in the Katiba, where volunteers from around the world were told to leave behind any preexisting ties they may have had with other organizations, parties, or movements. In praising a fallen Libyan mujahid—one remembered for welcoming his brothers with a "warm heart and a tender bosom [al-ṣadr al-ḥanūn]"—the Katiba's newsletter cited his taciturn nature and quoted the Prophet's words: "I guarantee a house on the outskirts of paradise to him who avoids quarreling even when in the right."[35]

Virtues are both innate and cultivated. They provide a foundation upon which other forms of social interaction, including the acquisition of proper knowledge, are based.[36] These notions of virtue circulate widely in the Muslim world and are by no means the exclusive property of Salafis, but here were a medium through which to process cultural and other differences for very specific ends. The work of instilling these virtues, at least among the Bosnians, fell to a thirty-to-forty-day course that was a prerequisite for any military training or involvement in armed activities. As one graduate explained to journalists, the jihad "was not only fighting—it was also an education. A new soldier had to get an education, both religious and military, he wasn't just sent straight to the front."[37] Many Bosnians had transferred from or simply abandoned other units in the army, drawn to the Katiba's reputation for piety and military effectiveness; this enthusiasm, however, had to be molded in ways deemed appropriate by the Katiba's leadership. The course was a "factory for virtue" in which one undertook "character improvement" [taḥassun al-khulq]. The school was a matter of pride for the unit, advertised in its bulletin:

> The Katiba has taken it upon itself to return the people to the faith, to educate them and restore them to the true Islam, in addition to defending Muslims' honor in Bosnia and liberating their usurped lands. With its formation, the detachment started a shariʿa school during which volunteers study for approximately one month the true doctrine [ʿaqīda], jurisprudence, prophetic biography [sīra], and jurisprudence of jihad, in addition to reading [tilāwa] of Quran and general study of heart-softening devotion [raqāʾiq] and Islamic virtues. In this period, the volunteer is reared through living with his Arab brothers or the Bosnian brothers who preceded him in an atmosphere of brotherhood and commitment. He is raised on the behaviors and ways of dealing with others in Islam and the ethical practices [akhlāqiyyāt] of the believers. Most volunteers graduate only after undergoing a fundamental change.[38]

The course was designed to provide a basic Islamic education for people largely regarded by arriving Arabs—and, perhaps more important, Salafi donors in the Gulf—as lapsed or untrained in their faith after decades of socialism. While Western commentary often views such education as a cover for or inducement to armed activity, the Katiba almost always presented it in the opposite terms, with participation in fighting being a way to bring people into the fold of Salafi Islam. "We do not want a return to the Afghanistan experience, which started with combat, lasted for twelve years, and ended with the expulsion of the Arabs and without the Afghans having learned anything."[39] Ansar were seen in general as not needing such training in Islam, a fact that did not go unnoticed among the Bosnians, although they differed on whether this was something to be criticized or not.[40] Some felt that this was unfair, others argued that those who grew up in the Middle East at least just happened to know more about Islam as a simple, and contingent, fact.

Within the school, the genre of Prophetic biography, or sira, was a core subject. The highlight of the sira curriculum also happened to be perhaps the most important book to have been introduced to Bosnia by the mujahids: *The Sealed Nectar*, by the Indian Ahl-i Hadith scholar Safi al-Rahman Mubarakpuri (1942–2006), discussed in Chapter 2. The final chapter is devoted to recapitulating the Prophet's traits. Mubarakpuri notes that Muhammad "was always friendly, easy-going, and benevolent. He was never sharp-tempered, irate, or angry. He was not loud. He did not reproach. He did not [over]praise. He ignored that which he did not want, and he did not succumb to his passions."[41] Moreover, Mubarakpuri treats humility and calmness not as cultural traits somehow innate to the Arabs, but rather as qualities that are praised precisely because they are not inherent or at least not given as socially widespread. In his analysis of pre-Islamic Arabian society and the reasons that led God to choose it as the site for prophetic revelation, Mubarakpuri lists the virtues valued by the Arabs, including "gentleness and civility" [blagost i uljudnosti]. Such traits were praised in verse, "even though they contrasted on the other hand with bravery and quickness to come to blows."[42] In other words, the Arabs enjoy no cultural monopoly over, advantage in, or even proclivity toward these particular virtues. Instead of a reified "Arabian" Islam being imposed upon Bosnian Islam as a sort of clash of cultures within a clash of civilizations, the reality is more textured and multicentric. In a book by an Indian scholar and appropriated by a multinational group of Arabs for teaching students speaking the language of Bosnia-Herzegovina, we see a vision of virtuous behavior held out to all Muslims as a model for aspirations to be fulfilled, not static Arab cultural descriptions to be emulated by others.

Prophetic virtues were not inculcated solely through text, nor did they exist in a vacuum. The school was also a key site where Bosnians were introduced to the Katiba's strict practice rules, which revolved around bodily regimentation: adherence to the five daily prayers and abstention from alcohol, fornication, pork, swearing, and smoking. Among other things, the rules helped weed out undesirables such as criminals, undisciplined adventurers, and suspected infiltrators from either unsympathetic elements of the Bosnian government or intelligence agencies of Arab states. There was, as in any other disciplinary institution, a fair share of foot-draggers and those who resisted certain rules among Bosnians and ansar alike. The smoking ban—which distinguished the Katiba from the self-denominated "Muslim" units in the Bosnian army—was particularly contentious. Fadhil refused to translate the instruction to the Bosnians and would still smoke at home for a year before eventually changing his mind; one of the trainers, an ex-Pakistan Army man who had settled in the UK, simply ignored the ban altogether. A Bosnian mujahid recalled with a smile another incident in which a Saudi was dictating a "corrected" prayer—one that omitted any reference to Muhammad as "our lord" [mevlana] as potentially undermining monotheism—to a group of Bosnians and made them repeat after him en masse. One of the older Bosnians, either oblivious or resistant to this infantilization, simply kept on with the same old recitation. But for the younger students, there was more enthusiasm for new practices, especially since some saw the Islamic Community [Islamska zajednica, IZ] as ineffective or worse, compromised from decades of co-optation under socialism. There were some material incentives, too: Mehmud, whom you read about in Chapter 2, finished at the top of his class and received 100 Deutschmarks and a beautifully decorated Quran which he showed me in his home. Jusuf the perfume vendor won fourth place in a Quran recitation contest, and the Katiba paid for him to go on hajj in 1995.[43]

One might be tempted to note an elective affinity here between strict regulation of the body for ritual purposes and for military discipline.[44] While this emphasis on teaching about bodily regulation through accessible texts may have converged with the army's needs, the same attitude toward texts could also encourage the questioning of authority figures. For teaching in the Katiba's religious school hardly went uncontested. The head teacher was Imad, whose tract *Notions That Must Be Corrected* was at the center of controversies discussed in Chapter 2. In the school, he had a Bosnian right-hand man and interpreter, Nasir. Several Bosnian mujahids remembered Nasir and Imad developing some differences and felt some pride in Nasir because he seemed to be the most educated among them about Islam and could hold his own with Imad and the other Arabs. In those years, Imad was not yet fluent in the local language, but he knew enough to be able to tell when Nasir was adding things in his interpreting, to his chagrin. The Bosnian students also organized their own study circles, where they sometimes learned things they weren't supposed to. One, Arslan, whose father was a communist party leader in his home town, remembered his surprise at discovering in a Bosnian translation of al-Sayyid Sabiq's *Fiqh al-Sunna* that it was allowed to trim one's beard if it got too long, something that contradicted what he had heard from Imad (and Imad had given them the book, to boot).[45] For Mehmud, the jihad was a time of intense studying, a competition [takmičenje] for who would learn more, but one he experienced as "in the heart. There was no need for Nasir or Imad or anyone to tell us to learn, we would read ourselves." Thus the authority of pedagogical texts based on an explicit promise of verifiability held out a *promise* of mastery that encouraged dispute but also provided some justification for the disparate treatment of Bosnians and Arabs as contingent and not based on some inherent defect.[46]

Here we can return to akhlaq as providing one way of processing the differences that arose between various mujahids. Muhsin, introduced in Chapter 2, who was in charge of personnel issues for the Bosnians in the Katiba, told me about a mujahid from Željezno Polje who wanted to keep praying according to the Hanafi way, which would entail, among other things, touching one's earlobes with the thumbs and crossing one's hands over the stomach. Muhsin prayed in the Hanbali manner encouraged by the Arabs in the Katiba—hands on the chest instead—but nevertheless supported his decision: after all, the Katiba had officially adopted a policy of not endorsing or rejecting any particular madhhab. When the mujahid told Muhsin that

Imad had threatened him with expulsion from the Katiba unless he changed his prayer style, Muhsin became angry: "Imad doesn't have that power, and there is no such rule." Muhsin and Imad took the matter to the amir Abu al-Maʿali, both demanding an end to the ambiguity: an explicit rule either mandating a certain manner of prayer or proclaiming that the style of any recognized madhhab was permissible. Abu al-Maʿali patiently listened to both sides. He gently reiterated that Imad lacked the authority to expel anyone or give ultimatums, but did not impose any new rule. Angered, Imad stormed out of the office, slamming the door shut behind him. Later, Abu al-Maʿali told Muhsin he did not believe the issue of prayer form important enough to warrant expulsion, but that he also did not wish to promulgate a rule that would be rightly perceived as an open rebuke to Imad.

Consistent with prevailing notions of akhlaq in the Katiba, Abu al-Maʿali did not seek to resolve the dispute as much as to process the differences in it. This allowed differences to exist without congealing into rigid identities: just as Mubarakpuri's portrayal of akhlaq relativized Arabness in order to praise a notion of Islam over an ethnic identity, the dispute between Muhsin and Imad did not crystallize into one pitting Arabs against Bosnians as such. Muhsin prayed in the same way Imad did, while Abu al-Maʿali sympathized with the Bosnians. There were, of course, higher stakes attached to the importance of akhlaq in matters of persuasion and dealing with disputes: the Katiba was not a conventional army unit with a strictly vertical chain of command. Malcontents could—and did—leave for other units, especially Abu al-Zubayr's less formally organized band of mujahids. Abu al-Maʿali knew that Imad had the ability, so he should desire, to divide the Katiba if he quit and took his allies with him, both Bosnians and ansar. But whether at the level of individual differences or of collective schisms, notions of akhlaq were helpful in the processing that was the everyday work of the jihad as a universalist project.

BROTHERS IN FAITH, BROTHERS IN LAW

Another key site for the processing of differences in the jihad was kinship, whether in the bonds that formed between mujahids or through marriage between Arab men and Bosnian women. Kinship—often metaphorically treated as a basic building block of nationalist or other "autochthonous" forms of belonging—here helped forge bonds and communities across differences of nation and race instead. As in the discussion of akhlaq, Islamic idioms of kinship did not create smooth, harmonious ties but rather provided terms in which tensions and disputes could be grounded and processed. But kinship in the jihad—as well as among those sympathetic to it, including some aid workers and proselytizers who did not fight—could also strain ties with other family members who did not share their vision of piety. The mediation of these latter tensions underscores that universalist projects are embedded in everyday contexts, with sometimes surprising outcomes.

The first form of kinship, albeit "fictive," was brotherhood [ukhuwwa], an idiom commonly used among pious Muslims everywhere. Mujahids also refer to each other as "brothers"—more often than "friends" and never as "colleagues"—and also use the label for those who they feel are part of a common orientation of piety, regardless of whether they fight. Brotherhood was the idiom for particular kinds of homosocial intimacy that was only intensified on the front line, in the base camp, and at prayer anywhere. If the virtues of care discussed earlier such as tenderness were valued among the mujahids, it was within the framework of brotherhood that they were allowed to come to maximum fruition as love. One audiocassette testimony by British mujahids mentions two Saudi companions who were so close that upon their arrival, "all the mujahidin soon came to know about the love between Abu Sayf and Abu Hamad." During a battle at the village of Bijelo Bučje, they were both struck down and buried together in a single grave. The narrator likens this to an incident during the early years of Islam in which martyred companions were buried together wrapped in a single garment, quoting the prophet Muhammad's declaration that "They loved each other in this world and they shall love each other in the next."[47] The anecdote of joint burials in a single shroud is also referenced in *The Sealed Nectar*: "They buried two or three [martyrs] in each grave and would wrap two together in one garment (blanket, sheet, etc.). . . . So they buried ʿAbd Allah bin ʿAmr bin Haram and ʿAmr bin al-Jamuh in the same grave [mezar] because they were great friends [veliki prijatelji]."[48] The original Arabic goes further and explicitly refers to the "love" [maḥabba] between the two.[49]

The expression of such intense homosocial intimacy among the mujahids contrasted sharply with the machismo elsewhere in the army that Bosnian mujahids associated with sinful behavior. Some readers may also find this affection at odds with their expectations about militaries, pious Muslims, or both, but anyone familiar with social life in the Middle East or South Asia would unlikely be surprised.[50] Ismail Royer, the white American convert who joined the jihad, recalled unconsciously carrying these practices back to the United States, only to arouse suspicions even from Muslim friends living there about his sexual orientation. But this love between mujahid brothers catches the eye here because the forms it takes are both marked as part of Islam—including its Salafi orientations—but also hardly exclusive or reducible to it. Instead of glossing them as "jihadi," it is more fruitful to examine how they make a universalist practice possible.

The idiom of brotherhood was often mediated through material objects, especially when ansar came from wealthier countries with consumer goods that caught the eye of Bosnians.[51] We can see this with Abu ʿUmayr, a Saudi veteran of the Afghan jihad who arrived in Bosnia around 1994:

> The night before the battle he started giving out his belongings—his money, his clothes, whatever he owned—to the guys [shabāb]. He said to his brothers: "I smell a wonderful fragrance, is one of you using some kind of perfume?" They denied it. They searched and brought forth all the fragrances they had [and asked him]: "Is this the one you are smelling?" They went through all of them and he said: "No, it's different, indeed more wonderful."
>
> Before the battle he told his Bosnian friend [ṣāḥib] Derviš: "Tomorrow after the operation, I have a special surprise, inshallah." He went quiet and told the guys that if he were to be killed, that his Casio watch would go to Derviš the Bosnian.
>
> The day of the battle came and he could smell the wonderful fragrance that clung to him. The battle started: the mujahids advanced and seized the first mountain, but the Bosnians did not manage to advance from the other direction, so the Arab mujahids and their companions were besieged between two mountain peaks. Abu ʿUmayr turned around and smiled a strange and amazing smile filled with joy and delight as a bullet entered straight into his heart and he fell dead, inshallah martyred. The mujahids regrouped and pulled back.
>
> And what of Abu ʿUmayr's friend? Derviš the Bosnian asked: "Where is Abu ʿUmayr?" They pulled out his watch and said: "This is the surprise that Abu ʿUmayr promised you. He's been killed." Derviš fell to his knees and wept like a child. They all cried over his departure, but that is what God almighty willed.[52]

The story of Abu ʿUmayr the Saudi, his Bosnian brother Derviš, and the Casio watch features common themes of mujahid hagiography, including fragrant odors, premonition of death, and the bequest of personal objects as a way to signify ties of affection. The friendly coveting of material goods wasn't always well-received, of course. Mahdi, the Jamaican-British convert who made an appearance in the introduction to this book, recalled his irritation at being asked by a Bosnian for his boots if he were to be martyred, thinking to himself sourly, "You're quite the liberty taker, aren't you?"

The bond between Abu ʿUmayr and Derviš is also noteworthy because Bosnian mujahids as individuals do not feature very prominently in published martyr hagiographies and ansar memoirs. Language barriers made for communication challenges, but the struggles to overcome them could provide their own form of endearment as well. Most communication was done in a mixture of elementary Arabic, Bosnian, English, and hand gestures. They developed a common simplified patois, a mélange of Arabic and the local language, with some English and Italian mixed in. One example of such a sentence I was given comprehensibly concatenated Arabic terms (here boldfaced) and Bosnian ones (in italics): "**aḥmar** *traka armija* **jabha shimāl** *ruka*" [**red** *armbands* for the *army* on the **front line's left**-*hand* side]. Abu Hamza wistfully reminisced about the "very beautiful phenomenon" of a basic language of mutual comprehension [lughat al-tafāhum], in which certain specific terms from one language or another would become widely shared, such as *manjeria* for lunch (from Italian *mangiare* for food). Some of the Bosnians took on Arabic nicknames deemed more "Islamic," especially if their names were unfamiliar to the Arabs or difficult to pronounce. Names of individuals with specific roles also became metonymous for places associated with those roles: "Abu al-Harith" came to refer to the clinic, for example, after the Katiba's physician and erstwhile commander.

The mujahids who arrived early in the war tended to learn more of the local language than those who came later. Many were trapped and unable to travel due to the war between the Croats and Bosnian Muslims that raged for much of 1993 and were scattered as individuals or in small groups among Bosnians. After the 1994 Washington Agreement restored Croat-Muslim cooperation, routes to the outside world reopened and the number of arriving mujahids increased dramatically. Many of these were from the Gulf and were participating in jihad on a seasonal basis during holidays from work or study. With larger numbers of ansar, it became possible to organize combat groups along language lines to facilitate communication, although this also had a tendency to reduce the opportunities for mixing with Bosnians. One Bosnian complained that the Arabs had their own "nationalism" [nacionalnosti] and liked to keep to themselves. "They lacked trust in the Bosnians' ability to do things; for certain tasks, such as guarding a warehouse or tracking its inventory, they would sometimes give the job to an Arab with no education or experience over a more qualified Bosnian." The other Bosnians I spoke to, however, all had several Arabs they fondly recalled for their willingness to reach across barriers of race and nationality.

Perhaps most important for linguistic and cultural immersion, however, was marriage to local women. One of the key paths through which Arabs met their future wives was Bosnian mujahids introducing them to their own sisters. Several of the mujahids you have read about in this book came to know their wives in this way, including Ayman the Syrian. Abu al-Harith from Libya, the commander renowned for his politeness, also married a woman with three brothers in the Katiba: one of them was Nasir, Imad's interpreter and junior lecturer in the Katiba's religious school. Thus brothers in faith [ikhwa fillāh] were sometimes also brothers-in-law, as homosocial intimacies could help give rise to an archetypal heterosexual bond: marriage. Sisters were introducing each other to different Arab fighters and aid workers as well, and indeed may have even played a more active role in making such arrangements.

The sisters of fellow mujahids were but one source of spouses. Other mujahids married widows, a practice that has the additional virtue of prophetic example, as Muhammad's first wife, Khadija, was also a widow. Abu Hamza married a woman whose first husband was a Bosnian imam murdered by Serb nationalists at the Omarska concentration camp in northwest Bosnia early in the war.[53] Finally, some mujahids married women displaced or expelled from their places of residence, as we saw with Abu ʿAli. These categories were, of course, overlapping: Abu al-Harith's widow, sister to three mujahids, got re-married to an Egyptian mujahid we will meet later. Abu Hamza's wife was both the widow of a Bosnian imam and a refugee in Croatia when they met.

Under the conditions of my fieldwork, it was exceptionally difficult to interview Bosnian women who married Arabs. None of the Arab ex-mujahids introduced me to their wives; a few of the Bosnians from the Katiba did, but usually only in passing, and they often did not speak English or Arabic, while my command of the local language did not allow for discussing such sensitive topics. In the few times when I was able to meet with wives of ex-mujahids, it was often because their husbands were in detention and they perceived me primarily as a human rights worker connected to a local NGO. There were few opportunities to discuss the circumstances under which they married or met their husbands. It was in only one interview, interpreted by a female Libyan-Bosnian friend, that I managed to get a wife's perspective on courtship with mujahids: Latifa, then a teenager in the years after the war, grew up in a small village near Travnik and recalled turning down several suitors, both Bosnian and Arab mujahids, before finally marrying a Tunisian who had spent several years working in Italy beforehand installing heaters. Latifa was hesitant at first:

> When I first met him I said I didn't want to marry him. I didn't feel mature enough or even interested in getting married. The second time he said, "I have been dreaming of you. I dreamed of you for three nights." I asked, "Well, what if *I* wasn't dreaming about *you*?" [laughs] But he was persistent and in the end I agreed.

For Latifa, marriage offered a way out of a boring village life and to escape from a domineering mother: "I never got to get out of my home or see people. I thought that through marriage I could go out and see new people, new society. Nobody told me how all of this was supposed to work." Latifa's main criterion in choosing a husband was one who did not insist on her covering her face. Yet after marrying her husband (who nevertheless expressed a preference for the veil), she found herself trying the practice and taking to it: "I surprised him by putting it on because I liked and wanted it. I didn't want to do it because of someone else, for someone else's sake, but out of my own free will." A decade later, living in a small house on the outskirts of Zenica without any regular source of income and raising two sons alone, Latifa only covered her hair. With her husband detained in the immigration center, she had to do more things for herself and found the veil to be too much of a burden in interacting with society.[54] Latifa's sisters seem to have fared a bit better: an older one wed a Saudi fighter and moved with him to Riyadh, and they all still keep in regular contact, while her younger sister married an Algerian who now works in a mosque in another city in Bosnia. Two other sisters married Bosnian Muslims from Krajina.

While parsing the desires of various individuals is always fraught, I encountered the perception, mostly voiced by the Bosnian mujahids I knew, that a mutual racial exoticization was at work in many of these marriages. Arslan, mentioned earlier, had a sister who married a Kuwaiti aid worker who occasionally fought in the Katiba's operations. During a brief visit back home, the Kuwaiti apparently decided after hearing some lectures from Salafis that fighting alongside the lapsed Muslims in Bosnia could not be properly considered jihad and stuck to his aid work. Shortly after the war, he left and divorced Arslan's sister over the phone, but she soon wed another Kuwaiti, a US-educated software engineer who took her home with him and treated her well. This second husband was a celebrated mujahid killed while fighting against the US invasion of Afghanistan in 2001; when I met Arslan, his sister was still in Kuwait, living alone and working as a teacher at an international school.[55] Here is Arslan's view on the saga:

> For some of the Arabs, it was like an adventure. Some of them were interested in marrying women who were white, with long blond hair, and tall, like my sister. . . . Even a woman who may be considered so-so [niṣf-niṣf] here might be very interesting to them. Also it can be so difficult and expensive to get married in a place like Saudi Arabia because of the dowry [mahr]. I saw when I lived in Jordan how difficult it can be to get married. And in those days especially in Bosnia, Kuwaitis were seen as big important people who had lots of money.

Arslan's narrative evokes how these relationships disentangled and reconfigured conventional hierarchies of race and wealth: Bosnian women were considered desirable through their whiteness, but it was Gulf Arabs who had money and mobility and, for some, an image of spiritual authenticity. Notwithstanding Arslan's emphasis on the economic dimensions, there is evidence that the attraction was mutual and experienced partially through racial difference, not despite it. Muhsin, who discussed with me and his wife many of these cases when I came to their house for dinner, elaborated on the theme of race and attraction, in both its homosocial and heterosexual valences:

> It became a sort of fashion [moda] amongst Bosnian girls in the area to marry Arabs. The Arabs were handsome, with their dark eyes. They were attractive to Bosnian girls. Attractive both sexually and spiritually. There was a big demand from the hearts and the hormones of the Bosnian girls. It's not correct, absolutely not correct, to say that they married for money or on empty stomachs. My wife said that many girls were sexually attracted to Arabs. If they were appealing to us as boys, imagine how it was for those girls!

Bosnian families often opposed the marriage of their daughters to these suspicious foreigners. Latifa's mother was not crazy about the idea at all, or about the other daughters who married Arabs—something that Latifa speculated stemmed from her mother's own experience of having married a Kosovar Albanian. Arslan opposed his sister's first marriage, even as their communist father gave his consent out of respect for her wishes—"Imagine, at the time, I was the one who was praying and observant and my father, who is not at all religious and never prays, insisted that the marriage be allowed to go through!" Even Bosnian mujahids like Muhsin initially faced objections from the families of their future wives. While Bosnian men who joined the Katiba often did so at the risk of antagonizing their own families and in some cases cutting ties with them, it was the women's relationships with the Arabs that exacerbated concerns for all.

The flip side of such romances, however, were the spreading stories of Arabs marrying women and then abandoning them. Such marriages of convenience were a major concern in the jihad for their ability to undermine the moral authority of a universalist project. Marriage to generally wealthier and more mobile citizens of Gulf countries, in particular, carried a greater risk that their wives would be abandoned or, perhaps worse, taken abroad and then cut adrift in an unfamiliar country. The issue also alarmed the nascent Bosnian state, which tasked the Islamic Community in Zenica with collecting information on such marriages.[56] The Katiba was mindful of the impact these behaviors had on its reputation, as described in a message from Anwar Shaʿban to one of the leaders of Egypt's Islamic Group:

> Some youths have taken advantage of [sfruttano] fatwas by Muslim scholars, committing acts of immorality in the application of these fatwas. In particular the fatwa on marriage with divorce in mind [allo scopo di fare il divorzio], as

> has been attributed to ʿAbd al-ʿAziz bin Baz. There are many cases in which a youth married a Bosnian girl for a period of days or months, after which the youth leaves and then sends her a message saying he has repudiated her. These behaviors have distorted the image of [other] mujahid youths who are residing in Bosnia. For this, we ask that you clarify what is wrong and right regarding this matter. . . .[57]

The fatwa Shaʿban mentioned was issued by the chief mufti of Saudi Arabia. It permitted marriage with the secret intent to divorce on the rationale that this would provide students and other travelers in non-Muslim countries a means for regulating the temptation to indulge in extramarital sexual activities.[58] This fatwa was widely criticized, including by many other Salafi scholars, and its use in Bosnia underlined the dangers to the IZ's interpretive monopoly on Islamic law. As mentioned in Chapter 2, the IZ issued a fatwa in December 1993 reaffirming its adherence to the Hanafi madhhab—an opinion that had no system of courts to enforce it.

The question of which madhhab would apply was especially important in the issue of consent for marriage. In many cases, Arab men wished to wed Bosnian women and girls, but their fathers objected. In response, some Arabs would cite the dominant position in the Hanafi school that women may marry as long as they are mentally competent, of age, and free from coercion; their fathers' agreement was not required. One Bosnian imam I interviewed, Halil Mehtić, decried this behavior as "selective" since the position of the Hanbali madhhab, which many Arab Salafis held to, requires the consent of the woman's guardian.[59] At the same time, Bosnian fathers demanding the right to refuse on their daughters' behalf were themselves implicitly repudiating the Hanafi position propagated by the IZ, to say nothing of the state's own civil marriage laws.

The Katiba was in a dilemma: endorsing the IZ's attempts to make Hanafi law the sole school of jurisprudence for Bosnian Muslims would offend Salafi sensibilities and indirectly support the very type of nationalist divisions between Muslims that the unit repudiated. Yet the Katiba was also anxious not to antagonize the IZ or Bosnian Muslims further. In response, the Katiba dodged the doctrinal question of which madhhab to uphold and instead sought to exercise more control over the mujahids under its command. Starting in 1994, the Katiba took several steps to curtail "immoral" marriage practices:

first, speeches from senior mujahids reminding everyone that their purpose in Bosnia was jihad, not marriage. Then, the Katiba adopted a rule requiring any ansar mujahid to spend six months in Bosnia before marrying a local woman.[60] This would allow time for others to vet their character and suitability for marriage. Finally, Abu al-Maʿali decided to require the consent of both the woman's parents and the Katiba's command. When I asked Muhsin for any example of this policy being tested, he telephoned his wife at home, who reminded him of a "girl" (he did not specify her age) whose parents forbade her from marrying a mujahid suitor.[61] The Katiba received information that the girl's father had consented only under threat, so Abu al-Maʿali called him in and told him to report anyone who exerted any pressure on them. The two never wed. Muhsin also acknowledged that the policy may not necessarily have been grounded in a strong fiqh doctrinal argument: "It's true that this is not based in shariʿa rules. But shariʿa is both rules and principles. What's important is the good." The Katiba's attempts to regulate marriage with the local population represented an improvisational response to a practical legal challenge: it sought to accommodate the IZ's concerns without endorsing its quasi-nationalist project of interpretive authority. At the same time, the Katiba did not explicitly base its position in Islamic legal doctrine. Instead, it relied on its authority as a military unit informed by appeals to both Islamic and national legitimacy.

FROM KINSHIP TO COMMUNITY

As Ayman and I left the Livade mujahids' cemetery, he noticed the season's first sprouting of violets [ljubičice] and picked a handful to bring home to his wife. Across the road, three older women with handkerchiefs on their heads sitting on the balcony of a house waved at us. Ayman waved back and shouted warm greetings in turn. They invited us in for coffee but he politely demurred. We got into the car and he explained that he didn't feel comfortable accepting the women's invitation, especially if their men were absent. A few kilometers later, Ayman stopped to chat with a local man, an old friend from the army days, while two darker-skinned boys gathered around the car to look on.

Further down the road, we arrived in the village of Bočinja and drank coffee with some locals as they took a break from fixing a tractor engine. Ayman pointed to one and joked that he was the biggest terrorist of them all, because his beard was the longest. In October 1995, the Katiba had seized Bočinja as war booty, reportedly painting numbers on the homes abandoned by their Serb owners, making an inventory of the goods inside, and bringing livestock to graze in the nearby fields.[62] At the war's end, the Katiba was disbanded and most of the ansar left, but several dozen mujahids—Arabs and Bosnians—settled in Bočinja with their wives and children, forming a community, or džemat. It was an attempt to collectively live in accordance with proper Islam and also to sustain the sense of community they had found in the jihad. It was also, as Ayman emphasized to me, a place to settle for people who had nowhere else to go: Arabs with no abode, often married to women who had themselves been ethnically cleansed from their homes. The džemat enforced rules of religious practice similar to those in the Katiba: no drinking, no smoking, and so on. Niqab was commonly worn by the women. The community held its own prayers and religious classes, outside the supervision of the IZ. It had its own clinic and radio station, organized collective street-cleanings, and experimented in various forms of shared land cultivation. The few Serb families remaining in the village remained on alert, and those displaced by the mujahids agitated for the return of their homes. Neighborhood disputes and provocations—Muslims disturbing Serbs with the sound of the call to prayer, Serbs roasting pigs on open spits in front of the mosque during prayer time, Muslims angrily throwing the pigs into the nearby river—were cast by media as clashes of civilizations in miniature.[63] By the time of my visit, most of the Muslims had left and things had settled into the kind of cold indifference and discomfort that has become common throughout Bosnia since the war.

Quite a few of the people you have read about here spent time in Bočinja, though most were a bit reticent in discussing life there. Imad was again the self-styled authority on all things Islamic. Abu al-Maʿali remained a key figure until he left for Afghanistan in 2000, under pressure from the Bosnian state. Abu Hamza and Ayman emerged during this period as the unofficial spokesmen of the džemat, hosting journalists and other visitors, even allowing a documentary film to be made by a Bosnian television station.[64] Arslan the son of the communist official lived there for a few months, but resented how Bosnians seemed always to be taking orders from Arabs and never the other way around. He recalled watching with frustration as one of his compatriots, an experienced potato farmer, had to defer to an Arab who seemed to know nothing about the task. There were dramas and tragedies, too: an Egyptian mujahid and his wife, a white German convert, were unable to conceive children. He married a second woman, the widow of another mujahid, and things spiraled downward; the two wives were seen once arguing in the street, and the first one returned to Germany, where she wrote a tell-all memoir.[65] Abu Shahid, a Tunisian drill instructor from the Katiba, died while swimming in a nearby river; his wife married another Tunisian mujahid. The children from those marriages were the two boys whose curiosity drove them to Ayman and me as we stopped outside of Livade.

In the formation of new multiracial families and even a community centered on Bočinja, the former mujahids sought to carve out spaces where they could live as they pleased, but this did not mean forsaking the outside world in its entirety. Though often treated simply as a microcosm of the nation, family could also generate transnational connections, as the erstwhile ansar remained embedded in multiple kinship networks with varying orientations toward Islamic practice.[66] The first time I visited Abu Hamza's house in Sarajevo after he was placed in the immigrant detention center, I met his six children, of whom the oldest three were from his wife's first marriage to the slain imam. As we talked about their father's health and his indefinite captivity in a mix of English, Arabic, and Bosnian, they also showed me several albums filled with family photographs, many taken while they lived in Bočinja. One of the pictures stood out: in it, Abu Hamza is sporting a long black beard, wearing a spotless white robe (thawb) and sitting on a couch next to a bald clean-shaven white man in trousers and a pink button-up shirt: his wife's brother, on a visit from Austria. Most of her family emigrated to Switzerland after Abu Hamza's Bosnian father-in-law was released from the Omarska concentration camp. These photographs seemed to depict a "typical" European experience: sitting at home or on holiday, no headscarves or other religious symbols in evidence. One of Abu Hamza's daughters explained that although she and her siblings pray regularly (and that all the sisters wear hijab) and the Swiss branch of the family does not, each side is still fond of the other and differences in religious practice are not much discussed. Close-knit families spanning multiple borders while encompassing different attitudes toward the practice of faith are extremely common, yet they are largely overlooked in narratives of radicalization, which assume that mujahids' families must either be appalled by their actions or somehow complicit.[67] But more important for the analysis here, we see that although part of the family has like many Bosnians become "diasporic" by migrating abroad, it is the branch that stayed in the country that is nevertheless seen as embracing "foreign" practices. The dichotomy between foreign and local Muslims tends to ignore the ties of kinship that remix these categories, at most regarding Bosnian wives as victims or fools. Just as with the questions over how to bury Bosnian mujahids—whether with Salafi markers, Hanafi nišans, or perhaps both—differences are never solidified nor extinguished, but continuously mediated and processed as long as they share a common ground.

Within and beyond Bočinja, however, the džemat began to flounder soon after the war's end. Some of the Katiba's resources—especially its cars—were "privatized" to help set up small businesses specializing in things like butchery and lumber, run by some of the brothers who stayed behind. They had names such as al-Karama and Bedr Bosna, reminders of the Katiba's most important battles. On the nonprofit side, various organizations were set up to continue the spirit of Salafi-inspired awakening that started during the war, including the Active Islamic Youth and its magazine, *SAFF*. All were loosely part of a common džemat, but disputes soon broke out over control and money, both between and among Bosnians and Arabs. People I knew were far less keen to talk about their experiences working in these firms and quitting them than about the jihad itself; recriminations were still fresh.

By the summer of 2000, little of this would matter any more. That was when NATO peacekeepers showed up in Bočinja and started to evict the former mujahids and their families in order to return the houses to their Serb owners. Universalism is like a rainbow: even when one can see it, one cannot grasp it or make out exactly where it ends. With the end of the jihad, these families still had universalist ideals in the broad sense, but they were no longer exercising violence across borders; they were, rather, chafing against the state in the way that so many others do, especially in a place like Bosnia where the state remained very much in question after the war. A few members of the džemat managed to purchase the homes they were living in from the Serb owners and stay—those were the ones Ayman and I met during our visit to the village. But most scattered, giving way to a universalism speaking in liberal idioms and bristling with tanks. Over the next two decades, pressures would only increase

EXCHANGING ARABS

IN THE LATE AFTERNOON ON MAY 17, 1993, AN UNUSUAL RENDEZVOUS took place in Zenica, between the city's football stadium and the Hotel Internacional near the banks of the river Bosna. Over a hundred onlookers—children playing in the street, adults on the way home from work—gathered around two convoys (Figure 9). The first comprised ordinary-looking vans, jeeps, sedans, and a flatbed truck with a double-barreled machine gun mounted on the back. They carried men in camouflage, many wearing masks. Facing them were armored vehicles from the British battalion of the UN Protection Force (UNPROFOR), painted white. Abu al-Harith, the Libyan physician and informal leader of these mujahids, darted about with a hand radio. After several tense hours of waiting, another UN vehicle arrived and out of the back jumped Wahy al-Din, the mujahids' military commander. After him followed about a dozen men, most dressed in sweat suits, haggard but overjoyed. They embraced the fighters awaiting them; one jumped up and down, another began to prostrate in prayer. They piled into the vans and their entire convoy drove away, horns honking and guns firing in celebration. Some of the onlookers cheered and waved. The mujahids had successfully completed their first and only prisoner exchange of the war, trading thirteen Muslims for six Croats seized to secure their release, including Živko Totić, a colonel in the HVO militia.[1]

For the men released on that day, the swap was the culmination of a months-long saga. All passable land routes from the outside world ran through Croatia or parts of Bosnia controlled by Bosnian Croat forces. From early in the war, nonwhite Muslim travelers—primarily of Middle Eastern or South Asian origin, be they mujahids, aid workers, others, and those who fell into more than one of those categories—came under suspicion at checkpoints, especially those run by the HVO. Harassment, interrogation, robbery, and beatings often ensued, as well as, in some cases, captivity.[2] The men released in the prisoner exchange were glossed as mujahids and as "Arabs," even though they included two Bosnians, a Turk, and a Pakistani, and at least some of them were aid workers.[3] In the spring of 1993, the ansar around Mehurići, who would later found the Katiba, made numerous appeals to the Bosnian army to seek the release of these Brothers and even offered to pay a ransom, but to no avail. The HVO and the Bosnian army were by then fighting throughout much of the country, so the latter could no longer serve as a helpful intermediary with the Croats. Therefore the mujahids took matters into their own hands. Wahy al-Din and al-Muʿtazz Billah picked a few dozen ansar and Bosnians and began preparing a raid to seize hostages who could be traded

FIGURE 9. Prisoner exchange between the mujahids and the HVO in Zenica with the mediation of UN peacekeepers, May 1993. Source: International Criminal Tribunal for ex-Yugoslavia.

for the captive Brothers. They ambushed Totić while he was driving to work one morning; his four bodyguards were killed in the firefight but he was taken unharmed. Several days later, Abu al-Harith walked into the Hotel Internacional, then being used as local headquarters for the European Community Monitoring Mission (ECMM), and delivered two copies of a letter, in English and German. It demanded the release of all foreigners in HVO prisons, but instead of addressing the Croats, it spoke to the bodies that collectively call themselves the International Community. "We have tried many times through your agencies and other responsible organisations to release [foreign Muslims] but without any response. So there was no other way left after that only to take those leaders as hostages and to exchange." [4] Once the mujahids invited themselves to the bargaining table, things went somewhat more smoothly. As a video produced by British mujahids put it, "There was a great uproar [over Totić's capture] and the disbelieving United Nations moved quickly now, attaching high priority to the issue." ECMM, UNPROFOR, and the International Committee of the Red Cross all participated in the logistics of the exchange. The mujahids' victory thus lay not only in securing the release of the captives but in forcing the International Community to negotiate with them. "It was a historic event, which will never be forgotten," the video crowed.[5] Humanity's representatives and humanity's enemies shared a stage and shook hands, a scene of dialogue made possible through violence.

This interlude is a pivot point in our larger story. Until now we have been contemplating the vistas opened up by looking at a phenomenon like the jihad in Bosnia as a universalist project. After this interlude, the perspective will shift to situating this universalism in relation to other more powerful ones and in thinking about what happens at the limits of universalism. Just as it has done with the jihad, this book will in the chapters that follow turn to examining better-known universalisms—socialist Non-Alignment, United Nations peacekeeping, and the Global War on Terror—from below in ways that illuminate the transregional social worlds sustaining them. And we will see how these universalisms, in their diverse encounters with the jihad, have spurred a particular racialization of Muslim mobility as threat. This interlude will introduce some of these themes with a consideration and a reminder. Looking backward at the story so far, we can clarify how to think about those who seem radically excluded from this universalist project. And looking forward, it is important to recall once again how universalist projects can emerge out of shifting histories of migration and difference. Or, to put it in terms of the story above: what does it mean to exchange something with enemies who place themselves outside of a universalist project, and what does it mean for that something—or someone—to become exchangeable in the first place? The interlude will show how the mujahids understood the prisoner exchange as part of an ongoing relationship with non-Muslims, contrary to the presumption that they are capable only of enmity. And it will trace how the terms *Arab* and *mujahid* became synonyms, indexing a loose notion of Muslim travelers who were racially distinctive from Bosnians and engaged in activities considered both religious and inescapably worldly: fighting and relief work.

§

Universalism has a necessarily ambivalent relationship with violence: a message directed at all of humanity must regard itself as self-evidently compelling enough not to require coercion, yet valuable enough to preserve and defend by force. Universalisms will produce regimes both to justify that violence and to tame it: as a result, they are more than capable of their share of atrocity.[6] The Katiba appealed to shariʿa in regulating the use of violence, even if like nearly all armies it betrayed those commitments in practice.[7] This occurred most notoriously with the massacres of twenty-four Croat civilians at Bikoši in June 1993 and of fifty-two captured Serb soldiers after the September 1995 battle of Vozuća.[8] The near-total preoccupation with these war crimes in public discussions of the jihad, however, reinforces a presumption that the relationship between the mujahids and non-Muslims in Bosnia can only be one of radical alterity and implacable hostility. In the documentary and testimonial evidence gathered by the Hague tribunal about the May 1993 prisoner exchange, Croats and Internationals alike narrate the ansar as a mysterious presence, erupting out of nowhere with their dark skin and strange tongues and just as quickly fading away. For the HVO in particular, the less said about the swap, the better. From its perspective, the exchange is a settling of accounts, a wiping clean of the slate that allows the two parties to walk away from each other free and clear. For prisoner exchanges imply *parity*, a recognition in spite of itself, which is why they become so charged and fraught when struggles are asymmetric, and especially when racialized. They are humbling for the strong and heartening for the weak, who may not achieve legitimacy but can sneak into its shadow.[9]

For the mujahids, however, the exchange was something else: not a one-off, but a first step to establish ongoing relationships with both counterparties and mediators.[10] The day after the swap was completed, Abu al-Harith visited his European interlocutors again to thank them for their work in successfully concluding the negotiations.[11] And surveillance reports on the Katiba record contacts with Totić two years later, when the mujahids sought his help in securing the release of other ansar in HVO custody. For Abu al-Maʿali, this made sense because Totić had "been with us [on bio kod nas]."[12] Ayman told me that as one of the Katiba's interpreters, he was tasked with making the overture:

> When the Katiba was trying to find ways to get some of the captured Arabs out, Abu al-Maʿali thought of contacting Totić since we had treated him well and maybe he'd be interested in helping. The person on the other end of the line asked who was calling, so I said it was "a friend" so as not to scare them. When Totić finally got on the phone, I explained that we wanted his help. He seemed totally shocked and flustered that I was calling him. He promised to look into it but whenever I called back after that I never got through to anyone or they said it was the wrong number.

Bosnian army archival documents suggest that relations between Totić and the Katiba might have been more involved than this anecdote lets on.[13] While the mujahids used Ayman to cultivate Totić as a potential ally, the Bosnian army saw Ayman as a possible spy for the Croats, due to his language skills and his years living in Rijeka—allegations which he has consistently and vehemently denied. Whatever the exact nature of these contacts, it is clear that the mujahids at the very least continued to see a connection with Totić that outlasted the experience of captivity and exchange.

Such notions of ongoing relation took a wrong turn a few months after the successful prisoner swap. We know less about these incidents because some of the key archival documents and witness testimony remain sealed, so we can only rely on the narrative put forth by the judges in the Hague tribunal. In October 1993, five mujahids fell into the hands of the HVO at Novi Travnik, including Wahy al-Din, the Katiba's military commander. A few weeks later, an Egyptian, Abu Jaʿfar, kidnapped some Croat civilians in Travnik in the hopes of forcing another prisoner exchange. By this time the Katiba had been established and the Bosnian army was pressuring it to release the captives and to cease acting on its own in these matters. After a few days, a British officer serving with UNPROFOR visited the Katiba in Mehurići to deliver a video showing that the captured mujahids were actually dead; only one Bosnian Brother remained in custody.[14] The mujahids indicated that they were likely to release the remaining Croats in their custody and apparently did so soon thereafter.[15] Yet the next day, five more civilians were abducted in Travnik. They were taken to the Katiba's camp at Orašac and beaten severely. One was decapitated. Abu al-Harith reportedly told the army that the abductions were an unauthorized initiative from Abu Jaʿfar and promised to give up the remaining captives. After more pleas and threats from the Bosnian army, the hostages were eventually released.[16] Veterans of the Katiba have since distanced themselves from Abu Jaʿfar; many described him to me as a troublemaker, and Abu al-Maʿali told journalists after the war that he had been expelled as a result of the kidnapping.[17]

This turn from attempted prisoner swap to grisly execution highlights how thin the line can be between the logic of exchange and that of an eye for an eye. But it is also important to bear in mind that Abu Jaʿfar did not erupt into this narrative of raiding and killing from nowhere. He was himself imprisoned by the HVO and was one of those released in the May 1993 deal.[18] Abu Jaʿfar had also quickly adapted himself to local conditions. He arrived early in the war, married a Bosnian woman, and interacted extensively with the locals. As one mujahid put it, "Abu Jaʿfar was in Travnik day and night. . . . He would admit the volunteers coming to Travnik. He was familiar with every corner. He knew Croats, Serbs, Muslims."[19] While the details of this incident may forever remain murky, we can at least understand it through metaphors of relation rather than alienation, of equivalence rather than dehumanization. Revenge may be brutal, but this should not distract us from the fact that it is often grounded in a broader network of expectations and ties, all of which tend to be elided in narratives of radical alterity.

§

Exchanges, of course, do more than open up the possibility of relationships between the parties: they also create an equivalence between the very things—or in this case, people—being traded. The thirteen men freed by the mujahids in May 1993 hailed from Algeria, Tunisia, Pakistan, Egypt, Kuwait, Saudi Arabia, Bosnia, Qatar, and Turkey. And it remains stubbornly unclear what the foreigners were actually doing in Bosnia to begin with. Three of them—two Tunisians and an Algerian—were described in a démarche from the Bosnian army to the HVO as working for humanitarian organizations. In a subsequent missive, the 7th Muslim Brigade referred to the same trio as "foreign citizens who are members of [the Bosnian army], i.e. volunteers serving in our unit."[20] Muslim charitable activity, especially of the transnational variety, has been a major focus of surveillance and suspicion around the world since 2001.[21] But here we see that the categories of mujahid and aid worker were not mutually exclusive. As another letter from the Bosnian army to the HVO explained, "The majority of [foreign] volunteers joined the armed resistance against the aggressor, and a certain number of them were involved in providing humanitarian, medical, and all other forms of aid needed."[22]

Perhaps no one embodied the very public compatibility of these two forms of solidarity better than Kulayb al-Mutayri (Abu ʿAli) from Kuwait.[23] A former military officer and veteran of the resistance to the 1990–1991 Iraqi occupation, he was killed by a landmine in Vitez a few months after being released in the May 1993 swap. Al-Mutayri also worked with the Heritage Society, distributing aid and giving religious instruction. As al-Mutayri was the first Kuwaiti martyr in Bosnia, his death was widely reported back home, and Alija Izetbegović reportedly promised to call on his family should he ever visit the country.[24] For men like al-Mutayri, charity and combat were merely two different ways of supporting Bosnia's Muslims. There were, of course, mujahids who ridiculed aid workers dabbling in jihad as weekend warriors, and aid workers who had no interest in joining the fighting. But regardless of personal choices, the distinction between the humanitarian and the military—a product of long histories of state formation and the rise of regular armies—is at best blurry and historically contingent, not a self-evident or eternal truth.[25]

The alleged nexus between aid work and jihad has been a persistent concern for security regimes: in cases of detainees held at Guantánamo, for example, it came up so frequently that the US military simply decided that for a foreign Muslim in Afghanistan, claiming to be an aid worker was itself to be considered evidence of membership in al-Qaʿida.[26] Yet the opposite phenomenon, of humanitarians pretending to be soldiers, was also possible: one Kuwaiti who did relief work in Bosnia and was later held at Guantánamo claimed that he had been falsely enrolled in the Katiba's records as a way of obtaining Bosnian citizenship.[27] This ambiguity is not merely reducible to anti-Muslim paranoia on the one hand and the operational realities of clandestine armed work on the other: what ties these two activities together is how they are both commonly understood as driven by values—religious, ideological, ethical—that are counterposed against labor as interest-maximizing activity.

The question of whether to classify traveling Muslims as altruists or terrorists, however, overlooks the fact that both jihad and aid work arise out of histories of migration and many of these men came to Bosnia not only as helpers but also as supplicants. Such considerations of survival and sustenance tend to go unnoticed when one imagines aid workers as ethically committed subjects who are healthy, well-fed, and hold desirable passports.[28] This omission becomes even more glaring when we move from the stories of the relatively wealthy Gulf Arabs, like the Kuwaiti Kulayb al-Mutayri, to look at people coming from elsewhere. One such story came out in my conversations with Hasan, a burly and friendly Algerian I first met in Sarajevo's immigrant detention center. Hasan's story, with its gaps and discrepancies, cuts across so many of the standard categories of global problems: he was at various points in his life a humanitarian, a militant, a refugee, a migrant worker, an aid recipient, and a victim of human rights violations.[29] When we first met, Hasan was fighting to get his Bosnian citizenship back, part of a struggle that will be taken up in Chapter 7. He was later released from the center, but without any clear resolution to his legal status. We continued to meet once in a while for coffee in malls around Sarajevo, often with a friend of his who had returned from years of captivity in Guantánamo.[30] Hasan was in those days making ends meet by fixing computers and by therapeutic blood cupping, with many Serb and Croat customers.[31]

Hasan learned blood cupping while in Saudi Arabia. He first arrived there in the early 1990s on pilgrimage after finishing his university degree in Algeria. During this time, civil war broke out in his home country so Hasan took a job with an Islamic NGO in Jeddah, which sent him to teach in a secondary school in Peshawar, Pakistan. At that time, Islamic solidarity with Afghanistan was rapidly undergoing a shift from an international *cause célèbre* to a source of threat, and Pakistani authorities started cracking down on Arabs in Peshawar. Although he was on a one-year contract to work in Peshawar, Hasan had to change plans and quickly returned to Saudi Arabia. For months, he stayed illegally in the country, working in the "gray market" peddling perfumes and other small consumer items. He eventually found a job with what would later become the Saudi High Committee (SHC) for Bosnia-Herzegovina. The SHC was officially established by a royal decree in June 1992 and run largely under the sponsorship of Prince Salman bin 'Abd al-'Aziz, then the longtime governor of Riyadh.[32] It reflected an effort to centralize fundraising for Bosnia under one roof after the Afghanistan experience, and to do so from Riyadh (which experienced a building boom in the 1980s) instead of Jeddah, the more cosmopolitan port city that hosted the older pan-Islamic organizations sponsored by the Saudi state.[33] Over the course of the following decade, the SHC would effectively become the lead Saudi government agency in Bosnia-Herzegovina, channeling $US448 million in aid between 1993 and 2000. The SHC operated at both the public and the private levels: 30 percent of its money came from the Saudi royal treasury, the rest from private donations. Of the funds distributed to Bosnia, half went to the government directly for everything from winter equipment for the army to refugee aid, building schools and mosques, even leasing the premises of the Bosnian embassy in Riyadh.[34]

Hasan arrived in Croatia and after a few weeks was dispatched to help open an SHC branch office in Zenica. He would work as an accountant, drawing on the economics degree he had earned from the University of Algiers. In his group were three others: a Moroccan who had studied in the US and was an office administrator; a Palestinian logistics specialist who would manage the aid warehouses; and a Saudi who would be the head of the office. They set out from Split in June 1992. On the way to Zenica, they stopped in Konjic for several days, where they met Muderis, the preacher and militia commander who made an appearance in Chapter 2. Muderis warmly welcomed the aid workers and was able to fluently converse with them in Arabic, having studied at al-Azhar in Cairo. After leaving Konjic, Hasan and his group reached Zenica. They set about with the sundry tasks of setting up an NGO: renting a house, hiring lawyers to register their office, and so on. "But soon there started a salary problem. We didn't expect to be paid on time during the first three or four months but then they started paying us less than 30 percent of what had been agreed—except for the Saudi office head. So the three of us non-Saudis quit."

The pay dispute here was hardly unusual; the Arabs I knew in Bosnia who had experience working with foreign Islamic NGOs continuously groused about their wages and fretted over their job security, exhibiting little but contempt for the Gulfies who had lorded over them. In practice, the SHC appears to have hired Saudis exclusively for top managerial positions in its offices throughout the Balkans; Arabs from other countries, especially North Africa and the Levant, did much of the administrative and programmatic work; Bosnians were often loaders, guards, cleaners—a caste system of labor not unfamiliar to anyone who has been to Saudi Arabia or its Gulf neighbors, with the unusual twist that the lowest rung of the ladder was occupied by people who happen to be white. A detailed wartime survey of Islamic NGOs in Tuzla compiled by Bosnian secret police bears this out: the director and deputy director of the SHC's office were Saudis, the other four foreign employees were Jordanian, Syrian, Algerian, and Lebanese, three of whom had come to Yugoslavia as students before the war; the Heritage Society employed a Palestinian and a Jordanian who were long-term Bosnian residents, as well as an Egyptian; the two local employees of the International Islamic Relief Organization (another major Saudi-sponsored agency) were also Palestinian and Jordanian.[35]

After quitting his SHC job, Hasan joined the Zenica office of the Heritage Society. Of the various foreign Islamic NGOs in Bosnia at the time, the Heritage Society was one of the most active on the ground, especially in Zenica, Travnik, and Visoko. As we saw in Chapter 2, there was considerable overlap between the Heritage Society's daʿwa activities and those of the Katiba, especially through Imad el-Misri and his publication of *Notions That Must Be Corrected*. Fragmentary evidence suggests that the Heritage Society was also a major channel for Kuwaiti charitable funds to reach the jihad.[36] The Heritage Society provided food supplies directly to the Katiba, likely alongside assistance to other Bosnian army units and civil institutions.[37] Hasan joined the Heritage Society office as an accountant, dispensing cash to employees and needy families. But he left soon thereafter because they wanted to pay him at the rate for local employees, which he deemed too low for his needs.

As a recently arrived single foreign man with no prospect in sight of returning home, Hasan would likely have been unable to rely on the familial and other social networks that Bosnians used to share resources and alleviate burdens in the wartime environment. Archival documents, however, also suggest that Hasan and his companions had a stint in the Katiba—this is something I never had an opportunity to address with him, however, so I will leave it here as a reminder of the murkiness of categories of mobility during the war, as migrants moved between jihad and aid work.[38]

Having left two successive jobs with relief organizations and with further travel threatened by the deteriorating situation between Croats and Bosniaks, Hasan had seemingly limited options: "So I went back to Konjic and joined Muderis. I remembered him as a good man I met on my way to Zenica. At first, I was his guest but then I became part of the group of Arabs around him, in part because he spoke Arabic." His Palestinian and Moroccan friends from the SHC came along later. Drawing from his experience, contacts, and language skills, Hasan worked with Muderis as a coordinator [munassiq] and liaised with foreign Islamic NGOs to obtain supplies such as children's clothing, soap, and the like. These charities did not exclude the Bosnian army from its definition of humanitarian relief or aid. It seems that not only could fighters become aid workers, they could also become aid recipients. In any event, he had come full circle: Hasan moved from an NGO that provided the army with food to an army unit that requested food from NGOs. It was also an upgrade in status by moving to a less powerful patron.

When I pointed out that he had quit other jobs because of salary disputes and now found himself in a situation where he was being paid nothing at all, Hasan smiled. "Look, when I was in Bosnia I wanted to get something financially, but I also wanted to help the people there. The Saudis working in the SHC Zagreb office didn't even want to come to Bosnia! And then they started paying us less than a third of what was promised!" The issue was one of fairness and keeping one's word—better to work for free as a mujahid without an expectation of salary than to be cheated out of duly promised compensation. In both instances, the work was for the good of God and fellow Muslims alike.[39] In a conflict zone, armies and aid groups were among the few institutions that could provide protection and a sense of purpose—this was especially the case for migrants like Hasan, who had few other ways of settling in under conditions of war. Being attached to the army carried other material benefits. It meant steady access to food and even uniforms, which in some instances could get one more easily through a checkpoint. The anxiety over the misuse of aid as a cover for "terrorism" misses the numerous factors pulling in the opposite direction, that encourage the appearance of affiliation with armed forces for reasons unrelated to a desire to fight. In Bosnia, there were possibly as many Arab aid workers pretending to be soldiers as there were mujahids pretending to be humanitarians.

The wartime vulnerabilities associated with being seen as a racially distinct nonwhite Muslim were especially apparent on the roads. One day in September 1994, Muderis sent Hasan to Zenica to request some food supplies from the SHC. It was a routine assignment: although the trip involved crossing through HVO territory, the Washington Agreement had been signed earlier that year, more or less patching up relations between Bosnian Muslims and Croats to focus on their common Serb enemy. After a day of passing through various HVO checkpoints without incident, Hasan and the three Arabs he was traveling with—including the Palestinian and Moroccan companions who were with him in the SHC—were run off the road and arrested.[40] At the HVO prison in Kiseljak, they were beaten, interrogated, and subjected to the freezing cold weather. One day, Hasan overheard the warden saying to a visiting official that the Arabs were being held in order to exchange for Croats in Zenica. Every time the Red Cross came to visit, Hasan and his companions were hidden away; one time, they were taken into the forest near the prison, blindfolded, handcuffed, and made to kneel with guns to their heads so that they wouldn't make any noise. In early 1995, they were transferred to Kaonik, where conditions improved slightly and they were visited by the Red Cross. They were eventually put on trial for "illegally" entering the self-declared Bosnian Croat republic without a visa, sentenced to several years in prison, and fined 2,600 Deutschmarks—exactly the amount of cash that had been confiscated from them during their arrest, Hasan noted wryly. During this time, the Katiba made various efforts to secure their release. As mentioned earlier, they tried to reach out to their old "guest," Živko Totić, for help. They also offered to pay a ransom, apparently to no avail.[41]

Hasan and his fellow captives were eventually shifted again, this time to the Mostar jail. One day, they were put into a van along with several other

Arabs they had never met and taken to an old wooden bridge near the village of Potoci for a prisoner exchange with the Bosnian army.[42] Representatives from the UN, the Red Cross, and the European Community were all there. The war was now over, but tensions were high and trust was low. Neither side wanted to release their captives first, so instead one car from each met at the midway point of the bridge. Hasan and the other Arabs, along with a Bosniak pilot, walked free in exchange for four Croats and a foreign volunteer who fought alongside the HVO. It was an illustrious group: Hasan's Moroccan companion in these travails, Abu Ahmad, was killed in a 2005 shootout with Saudi security services, who accused him of membership in al-Qaʿida. His wife, who hailed from Konjic, and their children would remain stranded in Saudi Arabia for nearly two more years before returning home.[43] The foreign volunteer on the other side was Jackie Arklöv, a half-German and half-Liberian raised in Sweden, a bullied biracial child who embraced neo-Nazism. Several years after his return to Sweden, Arklöv killed two police officers during a car chase and was sent to prison.[44]

After his release, Hasan focused on starting his family—he had married a Bosnian woman and their first child had been born while he was in prison. He received Bosnian citizenship and went back to working for a Kuwaiti aid organization until the end of 1997. Hasan then found a job with a company in Qatar and started traveling back and forth to make preparations to move his wife and children to the Gulf. But back in Algeria, the civil war continued to rage, and pulled in his natal family. Hasan's father and brother were arrested by the security services and told that he was in the mountains with terrorist groups. His new employers in Qatar warned him not to come back after receiving a tip that the Qatari authorities would arrest him and send him back to Algeria. In 1998, having already invested time and money to relocate his family to Qatar, Hasan was back in Bosnia starting over, working for the Kuwaitis once again. In marked contrast to the image of the globe-trotting cosmopolitan aid worker, Hasan found himself a humanitarian by compulsion: as an Arab in Bosnia, it seemed to be one of the few stable livelihoods left open to him. But it was one that also placed him under constant suspicion. During one of his trips back from a project in Kosovo in 2003, Hasan was arrested by the Bosnian authorities on an INTERPOL notice. On this occasion, the Algerians wanted him extradited to face death sentences handed down in absentia. “Every day I thank the Croats for arresting me,” Hasan recalled with a smile—for the crimes he was accused of took place while had been held captive by the HVO. He could not have asked for a better alibi. Hasan presented to the Bosnian judge the documents detailing his time in custody and walked free.

On that day, however, Hasan was surprised to run into a familiar face: the Arabic-Bosnian interpreter in the courtroom, a Palestinian named Tawfiq. It was their second meeting ever. Their first had been six years earlier in the van leaving the Mostar jail on the way to the prisoner exchange in which they were both released, for Tawfiq had also been a prisoner of the HVO. It is to his story that we shall now turn.

Part II

OTHER UNIVERSALISMS

Chapter 5

NON-ALIGNMENT

IN FEBRUARY 1996, JUST A FEW WEEKS AFTER THE OFFICIAL END of the war, Tawfiq was working as an interpreter for an international Islamic charity. One day he was driving to Sarajevo with several other Arabs, university students and United Nations employees, shopping for some difficult-to-find goods. They were pulled over at a checkpoint run by the Bosnian Croat HVO militia near Kreševo, in central Bosnia. Tawfiq's protestations of innocence to the Croat militiamen, delivered fluently in their shared language, had little effect. The Arabs were taken to a jail in Kiseljak, a nearby town. Several days later, they were trotted out and paraded before a group of local journalists as "captured mujahideen." The treaty ending the war had required the departure of all foreign volunteer fighters, and these men were presented as unlawfully hiding in the country to pursue nefarious goals. A photograph from the event appeared in the news: it showed four tired-looking men sitting together, with nothing to suggest Muslimness other than their dark skin and the ominous caption, "Under the guise of humanitarian workers hide a substantial number of mujahids."[1]

One of the group was released within days at the behest of the UN, but Tawfiq and the others languished in prison for months, repeatedly beaten and forced to clean the barracks where they were held. Visiting delegates from the International Committee of the Red Cross labeled them as prisoners of war, despite their having never been soldiers or fighters. Bosnian Croat authorities attempted to prosecute some of the men for war crimes, but the case went nowhere. Finally, after six months, the trio was set free in the prisoner exchange at Potoci with Hasan the Algerian described in the Interlude. Tawfiq and his traveling companions promptly filed lawsuits in the Human Rights Chamber of Bosnia-Herzegovina for false arrest and mistreatment, and won.[2]

Being imprisoned as a jihad fighter was not something Tawfiq had ever expected. His father came to Yugoslavia from Halhul, near Hebron in the Israeli-occupied West Bank, in the 1960s to study engineering. In those days, educational travel to eastern Europe was not an uncommon route for Palestinians and students from the more socialist-leaning Arab republics. Yugoslavia was particularly attractive due to its leadership in the Non-Aligned Movement (NAM), a bloc of states that sought to carve a third way between the Cold War superpowers of the United States and the Soviet Union. Tawfiq's father married a Yugoslav woman and got a job with a state engineering firm; the family moved between projects in Jordan, Libya, and Iraq. These experiences allowed Tawfiq to become trilingual—in Arabic, Serbo-Croatian, and English—and even to complete high school in Jerusalem, near the Jaffa Gate of the Old City. Tawfiq moved back to Yugoslavia for university, and then the war began. Telling his life story to me over cigarettes in a Sarajevo cafe-bar fifteen years after his ordeal in HVO captivity, Tawfiq scoffed at the idea of being labeled a mujahid: he drew a sharp distinction between the Arabs coming during the socialist era whom he described as not particularly observant and the mujahids who arrived later. "Those people," he said with disdain, referring to the latter, "I don't relate to them *at all*."

In tracing racialized notions of Arabs as interloper fanatics embodying a threatening and mobile Islam, we have stumbled across another universalism: Non-Alignment, as it was experienced through the collapse of Yugoslavia and its aftermath. Just as this book has approached the Bosnian jihad as a universalism unfolding in a specific place and time rather than jihad as a general phenomenon, so too does it focus on the mobilities engendered and shaped by Non-Alignment rather than a global circulating idiom. Like the jihad, Non-Alignment provided a way for people of various nationalities and races to come together in the name of a vision for humanity while dealing with difference. If the jihad in Bosnia spoke in an idiom that was Islamic in general while often Salafi in particular, Non-Alignment espoused a broad Cold War neutralism as well as Yugoslavia's specific brand of socialism. But there were also major structural differences that defy any isomorphic comparison or easy analogy: the jihad was an ephemeral product of the war, while Non-Alignment in Yugoslavia was a state-driven project that lasted for several decades. Non-Alignment was explicitly internationalist, while previous chapters have shown how the jihad sought to legitimize violence outside the logic of the nation-state. Hence, comparison can be only one mode of thinking about these two universalisms together.

One of the most prominent and prevalent everyday expressions of Non-Alignment in ex-Yugoslavia was the presence of foreign students, many of whom came from Arab countries. By following circuits of educational travel—the ones that produced Tawfiq's family and many others—this chapter situates the jihad in relation to Non-Alignment by comparing, connecting, and counterposing them. First, this chapter explores Non-Alignment as a transregional site of social encounters rather than purely as a state-based internationalism—in this sense, it resonates with the approach to the jihad taken in Chapter 1. Second, it highlights the unexpected overlaps between Non-Alignment and the jihad by telling the stories of those who participated in both, namely Arab students who played a crucial role in various pan-Islamic efforts during the war thanks to their language skills and local ties. Third, this chapter follows how the war implicitly discredited Non-Alignment, thereby repolarizing racial categories alongside nationalist ones: as Yugoslavs came to identify first and foremost as Serbs, Croats, and Bosniaks instead, the perception of Arabs rapidly shifted from symbols of socialist solidarity to bearers of a rootless Muslimness—as Tawfiq found to his misfortune on the day he was presented to the media as a mujahid.

More broadly, this chapter argues that usefully thinking about Islam and socialism together requires working across different scales of analysis in ways that a carefully wrought ethnographic conception of universalism can offer. In the decades since the collapse of state socialist regimes throughout most of the world and the purported inexorability of neoliberal capitalism, there has been a resurgent interest—whether desirous or fearful—in alternatives to the regime of There Is No Alternative. One variation of this has been the trope of Islam as successor to communism in posing an existential threat to liberalism, capital, the West. Another response has been the nostalgia for various universalisms that have spoken in idioms of the left—quickly followed by nostalgia's eager killjoy companion, dismissal. Yet we must be wary of flattening categories such as Islam and socialism into things that can be readily compared and contrasted, or personified as fighting each other or aligning against others.[3] Both of these categories encompass multitudes of different idioms that have informed distinctive universalisms: Marxist-Leninism, Maoism, Third Worldism, Tricontinentalism, Afro-Asian solidarity, pan-Arabism, and pan-Africanism were not simply items to be chosen off a menu, but were at times engaged in intense competition and conflict. And just as many different universalisms could speak in socialist idioms, any number of different socialist trajectories could inflect the same universalism—even a decidedly nonsocialist one like the jihad. Perhaps the Katiba's most celebrated battlefield achievement came from Soviet rather than Yugoslav Third Worldism: the capture of a T-55 tank by a mujahid who had served in communist South Yemen's army and learned to drive such a vehicle while training in Cuba.[4] If universalisms can be approached as lived projects—and not simply as civilizations or ideologies writ large—then they must emerge from somewhere tangible and be apprehended through the experiences of those enmeshed in them. And one must on occasion reckon with the prospect of their mortality.

SHADES OF SOLIDARITY

Like the jihad, Non-Alignment as a universalism can be usefully understood by moving away from grand ideological pronouncements and examining the transregional circuits that helped constitute its everyday existence. At stake in these pages is not so much writing a proper social history of Non-Alignment—an important task for future scholarship—as it is reconstructing some sense of this world from those who lived through its collapse and aftermath in Bosnia. The collective memory of Non-Aligned connections was very much part of the Yugo-nostalgia that persisted in spite of, or perhaps because of, the dynamics of nationalist violence in the 1990s and 2000s. For many Bosnians I knew, Non-Alignment came up in reminiscences of Muammar al-Qaddafi and Saddam Hussein as familiar faces on state television; in memories of relatives and friends working abroad; and, of course, through a sense of lost mobility. Until December 2010, Bosnian citizens needed visas to enter the European Union, a sharp contrast from the days of the iconic Yugoslav red passport [crveni pasoš] that enabled sojourns to both east and west during the later Cold War.[5] There were also fond memories of seeing Arabs, Africans, and Asians on the streets of Belgrade, Zagreb, and other Yugoslav cities as emblems of a lost cosmopolitan world. Because socialist Yugoslavia was a labor-exporting country and did not have a recent history of ruling colonies abroad, such educational travel from the Third World was the primary means of accessing a sense of the racial diversity that characterized the more "advanced" West. While the historical record makes clear that prejudice and racist harassment were also part of this experience, this hardly ever came up in my conversations with Arabs and Bosnians reflecting on that era years later.[6] "Those were the days of solidarity between Tito and Arafat, so people were kind to the Arab students," recalled a Muslim Sarajevan librarian I met when I mentioned my research to him, who had himself studied in South Asia. "Some people thought of them as exotic and handsome. And especially for some of the Muslim families here in Sarajevo, there was some appeal in that."[7] Kamal, a Syrian I knew, first arrived in Yugoslavia in 1983 after having turned down a scholarship in West Germany because he did not want to go to a capitalist country. In Belgrade, he rented a room from a Serb family with whom he got along very well and was wistful about those early days: "People were very friendly, they had a sort of affection for Arabs. Those were the days of the Non-Aligned Movement. Maybe people had positive images of Tito and his friendship with Nasser. They also had a lot of sympathy for the Palestinian people as a people fighting for self-determination. And at the time I didn't know or care about the differences between Serbs or Croats, everyone seemed to be Yugoslav."

As a gathering of states, the NAM was notionally committed to avoiding entanglement in the camps of the Cold War superpowers. Non-Alignment provided Yugoslavia access to badly needed alliances and diplomatic capital after the country was expelled from the Soviet camp in 1948. It was officially launched at a 1961 conference in Belgrade but emerged against a complex backdrop of competing agendas among postcolonial and other smaller states, including the 1955 Asian-African conference at Bandung (in which Yugoslavia did not participate) and the 1956 Brioni declaration, issued by Josip Broz Tito, Gamal Abdelnasser, and Jawaharlal Nehru.[8] The NAM encompassed the majority of the world's nation-states—including, paradoxically, many that were very much aligned with the United States or the Soviet Union. While this heterogeneity may have undermined the NAM's ability to act as a force in world politics, it also contributed to a sense of universality that proved especially fortuitous for Yugoslavia. Long before the Balkans became an object of concern for liberal humanitarians and pan-Islamic activists alike in the 1990s, Yugoslavia was a significant actor on the world stage in its own right through its prominence in the NAM. And Yugoslavia arguably had even more at stake than did other major players. Unlike India, Yugoslavia could lay no claim to world power status; and unlike Egypt, with its pan-Arabist and pan-Africanist horizons, it could not seek leadership of a wider regional formation.[9] Moreover, as an industrialized European state, Yugoslavia did not comfortably fit within Afro-Asian or Third Worldist molds.[10] Non-Alignment provided a structuring logic not only for Yugoslav foreign policy but in helping Yugoslavs make sense of their distinctive role in the world; it was a key part of the state's ideological legitimation, alongside Brotherhood and Unity as an overarching principle for managing nationalism and worker self-management as the cornerstone of a market-oriented socialist economy.[11]

In the Middle East in particular, Non-Aligned Yugoslavia had strong relationships with Arab republics such as Egypt, Iraq, Syria, and Libya. All of these states shared an emphasis, to varying degrees, on centralized authority with long-serving "big men"—Tito, Saddam, Asad, Qaddafi—at the helm. Non-Alignment provided a framework (or, some might suggest, a cover) for economic ties, especially in extractive industries, infrastructure, and arms.[12] In the early decades, Egypt was probably Yugoslavia's most important partner in the region: Tito and Nasser enjoyed a close personal bond and met over twenty times. By the 1980s, Egypt arguably was eclipsed by Iraq as Yugoslavia's closest Arab ally. Some sixteen thousand Yugoslav experts worked on major construction projects there, from Baghdad's iconic Babylon Hotel to underground bunkers and arms factories. In the first half of the 1980s, Iraq alone accounted for 70 percent of all Yugoslav military exports, exceeding $US5 billion in value.[13]

As Tawfiq's story reminds us, Non-Alignment for many in Yugoslavia and around the world gave rise to new experiences, encounters, families, and lives away from the limelight of grandiose summits and important delegations that have dominated written histories.[14] Not only did thousands of Yugoslavs work in the newly decolonized countries, but students came from many of those same places to universities in Belgrade, Zagreb, Sarajevo, and other cities. As early as 1960, citizens of Arab countries—especially Algeria, Sudan, Iraq, Egypt, and Syria—constituted half of the foreign student population.[15] They appear overwhelmingly to have been single men. Despite limited opportunities to learn Serbo-Croatian in the Middle East (as opposed to English, French, or Russian), Yugoslavia was an appealing destination for several reasons. It did not demand visas for citizens of many Arab states and provided numerous scholarships; even without such aid, the country was not unaffordable for some middle-class families, especially from countries such as Iraq during the oil-boom years of the 1970s. One of the best-known examples of this phenomenon was the Saudi-Iraqi novelist ʿAbd al-Rahman Munif, author of the *Cities of Salt* quintet and a leading figure in twentieth-century Arabic letters. Munif completed his doctorate in petroleum economics at Belgrade University on a Baʿath party scholarship between 1958 and 1961.[16]

While most Arab students like Munif returned home or migrated elsewhere, some married local women of various backgrounds and stayed in the country and its successor states. A few, like Tawfiq's father, found employment in Yugoslav companies working in the Middle East, thereby shuttling between the two regions. The extent to which these Arabs constitute a self-identified community or diaspora remains unclear.[17] Yet individual Arab immigrants in ex-Yugoslavia have stood out in public life. Youssef Hajir, a Palestinian surgeon born in Haifa, became well-known as the director of a clinic in the frontline Sarajevo neighborhood of Dobrinja during the war. He published a memoir about his experiences working in the emergency room.[18] Nabil Naser, another Palestinian physician, ran in the 2010 parliamentary elections on a ticket led by media tycoon Fahrudin Radončić. In Croatia, two half-Palestinian brothers, Anas and Ahmad Sharbini, are famous professional footballers. The world that Non-Aligment and its mobilities made possible was also by no means an exclusively Arab or Muslim one: a Christian Ghanaian physician, Benjamin Markin, well-known for his work in a Mostar hospital during the war, later served as independent Bosnia's first ambassador to Japan; another Ghanaian doctor, Peter Bossman, was elected mayor of the Slovenian city of Piran in 2010.

Notwithstanding the pervasiveness of this nostalgia for the cosmopolitan and congenial aspects of Non-Alignment in Bosnia—and indeed, in many parts of the world—the Arabs I knew from places such as Syria and Iraq were suspended between a collapse of that universalism from both ends, with their homelands and adopted countries having descended into war. Unlike the jihad, Non-Alignment was an explicitly internationalist form of universalism: it presupposed and valorized nation-state projects, developing in an era when the nation-state came to be seen more and more broadly as the universally optimal framework for organizing political life. National categories were not given, but were being actively remade in this history, in connection with ethnic and sectarian ones. An important, if underappreciated, parallel between these Arab republics and Yugoslavia was their embrace of identities that did not fit squarely within a one-nation-one-state mold, promising a kind of capaciousness even while nevertheless enacting significant violence against those who did not conform to them. Arabness [ʿurūba] provided an important regional banner for anticolonial solidarity linking multiple nation-states but left the place of non-Arabs such as Berbers and Kurds unclear. The Yugoslav project, in contrast, sought to aggregate multiple south Slav peoples under a single state, but in doing so also systematically marginalized non-Slav populations, most egregiously Albanians and Roma.

In my fieldwork, Bosnians and Arabs alike could indulge in nostalgia without waving away the force of contemporary nationalist and sectarian categories. Kamal presented himself as a minority within a minority, being a Sunni Arab hailing from an area of Syria dominated by Ismaili Shiʿa: his critique of the Syrian state was very much tied up with a sectarian analysis that saw the regime as favoring various minorities over Sunni Arabs. Fadhil the Iraqi, whose story opened this book, also viewed things in his homeland in sectarian terms. In this regard, he would sometimes reflect on the bloody fates of his two homelands of Iraq and Yugoslavia-cum-Bosnia, the country of his birth and the one where he has spent most of his life. Fadhil's analysis of sectarian violence in Iraq resonated with his discussion of national or ethnic differences in Bosnia: they once mattered little in everyday life, yet now they framed politics in a way that made any alternatives inconceivable. One day, Fadhil explained how there had always been envy and resentments of groups in Iraq, especially the Shiʿa, and it had long predated Saddam's rule: "It was like a cart perched on top of a hill, ready to slide down at any moment." At the same time, it was the Americans who "brought" the idea of sectarianism to Iraq by constantly stressing Shiʿa grievances even though they knew very well that Shiʿa were well-represented in the ranks of the Baʿath party. Fadhil emphasized that sectarian tensions were deeply rooted and long-standing, even as he also blamed the United States for instigating sectarian conflict. He was perfectly capable of subscribing to the two dominant scholarly theories of "ethnic conflict," namely the primordialist and the instrumentalist, at once.

When I asked Fadhil about histories of coexistence between different sects and ethnic groups in Iraq, he smiled and explained his family tree. He identified as a Sunni Arab. But his paternal grandfather was a Shiʿi from Najaf and his maternal grandmother was a Kurd from Sulaymaniyya. One paternal uncle is married to a Kurdish woman, whose daughters had married Kurds, Turkmen, and Shiʿa; Fadhil had a brother and a sister, each married to Turkmen. Many ex-Yugoslavs could boast similarly complex family trees and would also affirm that the reality of intermarriage and other forms of sociality across such differences did not render sectarian categories any less relevant. When I asked him in 2011 to compare violence in the two countries, Fadhil responded, "Believe me, what the Shiʿa did would put the Serbs to shame. The Serbs would line people up and shoot them, one by one." He pantomimed firing a pistol and made a shooting noise: *ṭukh, ṭukh, ṭukh*. "The Shiʿa, they would torture people in the most horrible ways imaginable. Using drills on their kneecaps. Burning them alive. Dipping them in nitric acid. Putting them in ovens alive. Horrible, horrible forms of torture. I saw a video on YouTube of them covering someone with petrol and then lighting a match to burn them alive." For Fadhil, the afterlife of Non-Alignment was two different countries both wracked by civil conflict, comparable only through a bleak assessment of techniques of brutalization: not a yearning for the old days of socialism, but a sense that *even* the horrors of the Bosnian war paled in comparison to the bloodletting in Iraq a decade later.

While Non-Alignment may have staged encounters between national subjects, people understood as Yugoslav and Arab, the individuals involved were also more than those things, parts of disparate identities and projects that cut against national categories. As we saw in Chapter 1, the jihad as a universalism drew from and wove together many different strands of migration into a single canvas; Non-Alignment instead was imagined as a quilt stitching together patches already made, but which when torn apart would bleed from all sorts of unexpected places.

FROM VANGUARDS TO EXILES

Perhaps more productive than simply comparing the jihad and Non-Alignment as two universalisms on vastly different scales would be to examine their areas of overlap and the individuals who moved between them. The wars of Yugoslav succession are often framed as a transition from Brotherhood and Unity to a clash of civilizations: Bosnian Muslims mobilized their co-religionists in the Middle East, while Serbs drew from their Orthodox brethren, from Greece to Russia. This narrative, however, all too hastily erases Non-Alignment's own pan-Islamic legacies. The Serb nationalists who inherited the remnants of the Yugoslav state may have been ethnically cleansing Muslims in Bosnia, but they also drew on long-standing ties with majority-Muslim states in NAM like Iraq, Syria, and Libya to counteract Bosnian diplomatic outreach. In the "New World Order" of the 1990s, these states were especially keen to join Yugoslavia in pushing back on US-led interventionism and found themselves labeled as "rogue states" as a result. Before the invasion that led to his overthrow, Saddam Hussein even took the precaution of sending nineteen fighter jets to Serbia to keep them from being destroyed by the US military.[19]

It would be easy to read these alignments as dovetailing legacies of Yugoslav and Arab socialisms, and this would not be entirely wrong. But discourses of pan-Islamic solidarity played a role in the creation of these Non-Aligned ties as well. In Yugoslavia, Non-Alignment gave Muslim elites a way of identifying with both the socialist state and the umma at once. High-profile Yugoslav Muslim diplomats like the brothers Nijaz and Faik Dizdarević served in various Middle Eastern capitals.[20] Yugoslavia's Islamic Community also participated in outreach to majority-Muslim countries, projecting an image of socialist tolerance for religious practices in an attempt to draw a favorable contrast with the Soviet bloc.[21] This was, to be sure, a version of pan-Islamic unity that left many Muslim nationalists in Yugoslavia and Islamist movements in Arab countries out in the cold. Yet the mobilities fostered by Non-Alignment also inadvertently allowed these more marginal movements to connect as well. As a result, it was citizens of Arab NAM countries who ended up as crucial intermediaries in pan-Islamic organizing when the war broke out. As the universalist project of Non-Alignment lost its institutional framings and its ideological purchase, it nevertheless shaped what came later in surprising ways: the ties it fostered between states served nationalist projects of anti-Muslim violence, while the social worlds it created facilitated the organization of different forms of pan-Islamic activism, including the jihad. Such were the curious afterlives of this universalism.

In the eyes of pan-Islamic activists arriving in ex-Yugoslavia during the war—be they fighters or aid workers—Arab students were a natural choice to work as interpreters, guides, and advisors on local context.[22] Some became (or already were) actively devout in their commitment to Islam, others were not. On a more prosaic level, transnational Islamic NGOs were also an important source of livelihood for Arabs whose studies (and stipends) were disrupted by the war. As a half-Palestinian, half-Bosnian, Tawfiq would have been an especially strong candidate for interpreter jobs, but many more recently arrived Arab students also joined this line of work. In the early months of the war, Gulf-based Islamic aid organizations relied heavily on "local" Arabs not only as interpreters, but to handle many of their operations. The Saudi High Committee's first office in the region was opened by a Syrian physician who had studied in Croatia and would later serve as deputy director. The Services Office—the infamous Peshawar-based Arab NGO that had channeled foreign mujahids to the Afghan jihad—also set up a short-lived Zagreb presence; its first two employees were Algerian and Sudanese students.[23] The Katiba, too, had its handful of local Arabs, some as mujahids and others as merely paid employees who manned the front desk and answered phones for a salary.

The Kuwaiti Salafi magazine *al-Furqan* extolled the role of these Arabs in linking Bosnia to the Muslim world, reveling in the irony of how students considered the crème de la crème of socialist Arab countries transformed into "soldiers of Islam" when faced with the atrocities there.[24] And indeed, even at its height, Non-Alignment was always more than a simple celebration of socialist solidarity. When Arab students came to Yugoslavia, politics from home tended to follow. In the late 1950s, clashes broke out in Belgrade between Iraqis on the one hand and Egyptians and Syrians (then citizens of a United Arabic Republic) on the other, leading the Yugoslav authorities to house them in separate neighborhoods.[25] The Arab student activist scene in Yugoslavia included some Islamists as well, trying to make do with the space between both home and host regimes that were skeptical of or hostile toward their politics.[26]

Perhaps the most notable figure in the overlap between Non-Alignment and pan-Islamic activism from below was Elfatih Ali Hassanein, who came to Belgrade from Sudan for medical school in 1964. Hassanein hailed from a nationalist family and was part of a generation raised in consciousness of Third Worldist solidarity—his younger brother, Sukarno, was named after the Indonesian leader who hosted the Bandung conference.[27] But Elfatih Hassanein was also a dedicated member of the Sudanese Muslim Brotherhood from its early years in the political wilderness and sought to make the best use of the opportunities afforded by travel for his activism. He founded an underground organization for Arab Islamist students throughout eastern Europe and also developed ties with Muslim nationalists in Yugoslavia, forging a decades-long friendship with Alija Izetbegović. His memoirs recount the day-to-day challenges faced by many Arab students in Yugoslavia in adapting to food and weather; identifying and avoiding racist teachers and students; and adjusting to socializing with women outside of the family and to homesickness.[28] But they also chronicle his early adventures in political organizing. He faced off with the Sudanese ambassador—a communist army officer whose love of alcohol is luridly highlighted in the memoir—and boycotted the visit to Yugoslavia by Sudanese president Gaafar Nimeiry.[29] Throughout his time in Yugoslavia, Hassanein shrewdly exploited the opportunities available to him: in Sudanese student association elections, he built alliances with independents against communists; he made sure the Union of Muslim Students in Eastern Europe held its conferences in Yugoslavia, taking advantage of the country's relative lenience toward Islam compared to the Soviet bloc.[30] Hassanein went on to further medical training in Vienna and found employment at a hospital in Abu Dhabi. But after Izetbegović and other Bosnian Muslim nationalists were put on trial in 1983, Hassanein resigned from his job and returned to Vienna to resume his organizing. With his brother Sukarno and others, he founded an NGO in Vienna, the Third World Relief Agency (TWRA)—a name they deliberately chose for its apparently non-Muslim nature.[31] When the war in Bosnia broke out, Hassanein used the

TWRA to help the Bosnian government procure supplies; he also served as one of Izetbegović's key advisors on relations with the broader Muslim world and provided commentary to both Bosniak nationalist and Arab Muslim Brotherhood audiences.[32]

As Izetbegović's most prominent Arab collaborator, Hassanein figures prominently in journalistic narratives about Bosnia in global Islamic conspiracies. In particular, the TWRA was accused of involvement in violating the UN arms embargo on ex-Yugoslavia, money laundering, and other illicit activities.[33] Whatever the merit of these allegations, Hassanein's ties to the Arab mujahids seem to have been somewhat distant. His name does not surface in the surveillance reports on the Katiba I have seen nor in my interviews with mujahids. In his memoirs, Hassanein writes that he did not support calling for volunteers to fight in Bosnia; at most, he favored having a small number of foreigners come in order to share their experience and knowledge and to build ties with Islamist movements around the world. Moreover, the Katiba's Salafi tilt was unlikely to be very appealing to Hassanein, who is also a prominent Sufi.[34] Hassanein's most important connection to the jihad actually came several years after the war, when he arranged for Abu al-Ma'ali, the last amir of the Katiba, to leave the former mujahids' village in Bočinja and fly to Malaysia.[35] The United States had been pressuring Izetbegović to get rid of the Algerian mujahid and even suspended a military aid program to Bosnia in 1999. Hassanein leveraged his contacts in Islamist political parties and embassies in Bosnia, Turkey, and Malaysia to help his old friend Izetbegović quietly remove this embarrassing presence. While conspiracy theorists may identify Hassanein as a shadowy jihadist mastermind, it seems more likely that this was an instance in which a state-oriented Muslim Brotherhood network helped clean up the remnants of a non-state Salafi-inflected one.

Hassanein benefited as the steady ascent of Islamists to state power back home in Sudan enabled him to be a player in the inter-state arena, complete with a diplomatic passport. In contrast, Syrian Muslim Brotherhood supporters in Yugoslavia were in a far more precarious stance in the shadow of state power, with the memories of the 1982 Hama massacre still fresh. In the 1980s, every Yugoslav city with Syrian students had its own branch of the Syrian Ba'ath party keeping a close eye, especially on those sponsored through government scholarships. As a top scorer in Syria's national university entrance exams, Kamal found himself involuntarily enrolled in the party. Abu Hamza claimed that when seventeen of the twenty-one students in Rijeka voted against Hafez al-Assad in one of his periodic "re-elections," the embassy sent an official that same day to give them a talking-to. And as Yugoslavia came apart, Serb nationalists using anti-Muslim rhetoric openly embraced states such as Syria, citing a shared struggle against Islamists. For Syrian Islamists in Yugoslavia, the convergence between the enemies in front of them and those back home was becoming clearer than ever.

Abu Hamza and Ayman, whom you have read about throughout this book, came to the jihad through this Non-Alignment trajectory. Both were middle-class Sunni Arabs from Syria; Abu Hamza's father was an army officer, and a relatively pro-US one at that, while Ayman's was a civil servant. Abu Hamza was in his youth a quiet supporter of the Muslim Brothers, especially after the uprising and massacre in Hama. Both came to Yugoslavia to study medicine in the 1980s. Both worked as interpreters with aid organizations during the war before devoting themselves full time to jihad, where they were also translators. Such intermediary work could also be informal and occasional, especially in areas where bilingualism was in short supply. A decade after the war, they both still reveled in their ability to straddle the two worlds—of embodying Salafism with their long beards while also speaking fluently in the local language and idioms. Abu Hamza studied in Belgrade and Ayman in Zagreb, so they would tease each other as "Četnik" and "Ustaša"—pejorative terms for Serb and Croat nationalists, respectively. One day, when I met with them in a restaurant to discuss their legal woes, Abu Hamza and Ayman enthusiastically introduced me to palačinka, a local crêpe-like delicacy. The sight of a Chinese man and two bearded Arabs speaking loudly in a foreign language and gesticulating over a dessert plate aroused noticeable curiosity and discomfort from onlookers. Ayman, ever the jokester—both when I knew him and in the recollection of Bosnians who hadn't seen him since the days of the war—loved to play on stereotypes of language, race, and culture and referred to me endearingly (I think) as "Bruce Lee." One of his favorites, conveyed in Arabic: "How do you say 'Montenegrin' in Chinese? Lian chu ga!" The punchline was a play on the local term *lijenčuga* (lazybones), combining the clichéd onomatopoeic rendering of Mandarin prevalent among tonally impaired languages with a nod to the regional stereotyping of Montenegrins as indolent.

Having come to Yugoslavia through Non-Alignment and then joined the jihad, Abu Hamza and Ayman were trapped in the interstices between multiple universalist projects and doubly exposed in the era of the Global War on Terror. By having chosen to participate in jihad, they were at chronic risk of deportation but could also never safely return home as long as the Baʿath regime remained in power. They moved through one universalism, embraced another, and as we will see in Chapter 7, found themselves in the crosshairs of a third. But as Tawfiq's story reminds us, the racialization of Arabs as terrorists in Bosnia did not start after 2001—and this is one last legacy of Non-Alignment that must be explored.

FROM GUESTS TO STRANGERS

One thing universalist projects do is provide a way of processing differences, including race. And when such processes are suddenly disrupted or cease, then race can take on new significations. The Non-Alignment project celebrated racial diversity as a sign of universality, even as it did little to challenge global hierarchies of race and unsurprisingly recapitulated various notions of nonwhite backwardness.[36] The war witnessed a violent repolarization of these racial categories: Arabs in particular quickly went from being tokens of socialist cosmopolitanism and solidarity to undercover jihadis, signs of a globally threatening Islam.[37]

The repolarization of racial categories here intersected with the resurgence of nationalist ones. In the logic of nationalism, Serbs and Croats have historically denied or downplayed Bosniak claims to nationhood. But they also relentlessly presented themselves as defenders of the West against a threatening Islam—here, they were complementing nationalist logics in a regional struggle with racial logics operating on a global scale. Specifically, there were two distinct axes of racialization at work: the precarious whiteness of Balkan peoples on the one hand and the racialization of Muslims as foreign, dangerous, and rootless on the other.[38] Serb and Croat nationalists resisted their own racialization as backward, not-quite-white Balkan subjects by drawing a contrast with Bosniaks as racially Muslim and hence threatening to the West. Yet such efforts were complicated by the way that the racialization of Islam tends to construe Muslims as *other than* white: being phenotypically and linguistically indistinguishable from Serbs and Croats, white Bosniaks only presented as Muslim when they took on gendered signs of bodily comportment, such as veils and headscarves for women or beards for men. Indeed, warnings of the dangers posed by "white Muslims" with the ability to evade conventional racial profiling techniques signal this assumed contradiction between whiteness and Islam.[39]

In this context, the racialization of Arabs as paradigmatically Muslim—including and especially as nonwhite—played a distinctive role in the war.[40] The existence of Arab fighters and aid workers could be used to further the racialization of Bosniaks as Muslim. Thus the sites of encounter through which the jihad as universalist project processed difference—such as fighting alongside Bosnian men or marrying women—would in the eyes of Serb and Croat nationalisms support their claims that notwithstanding their whiteness Bosniaks should be racialized as Muslim. The Bosnian Croat officials who paraded Tawfiq and his traveling companions as "mujahids" needed their *manifest* nonwhiteness as Arabs to demonstrate Bosniaks' *latent* nonwhiteness as Muslims. And for those Bosniaks seeking to prove that they could be authentically both Muslim and European, Arabness served as a repository to locate all of the negative aspects of Islam from which they wished to dissociate themselves. Thus the racialization of Arabness as the sign of threatening Islam could serve the interests of all three major nationalist projects in Bosnia.

We can follow this process with Nadir, who came to Yugoslavia from Gaza, Palestine, in 1983 for medical school. The first time he told me his story was during a visit to his apartment on the outskirts of Sarajevo in 2007. Like others, he used the Arabic word *ghurba*—foreignness, alienation—to describe the difficulty of his early days in Yugoslavia. Although obtaining a visa had been straightforward, Nadir struggled with language, weather, and mores; he only wanted to return to Palestine, to eat his mother's food. One of his brothers, who had studied in Egypt and worked in Saudi Arabia and Australia, told him, "You have to complete your studies. Ghurba is hard. Be a man and achieve your goals." Little did Nadir know, he would make his home in this country and return to Gaza only a few times; in our Arabic conversations, he would routinely grasp for words and find only their Serbo-Croat equivalents, or mix the two, once describing a "counter-attack" as a "kontra-ʿamaliyya."

After coursework in Belgrade, Niš, and Novi Sad, Nadir moved to Banja Luka, in Bosnia, for further medical training in 1988. Banja Luka suited Nadir, who prefers medium-sized cities like Sarajevo and Gaza; Belgrade had been too big for him. Two years later, he married a local Muslim woman. Like all the other Arabs I know from this period, he had colleagues and friends of all backgrounds and regarded them as Yugoslavs first. As the country began to come apart, one of Nadir's Serb friends assured him, "Yes, you're Muslim, but we see you as an Arab, not like *those* Muslims," referring to Bosnian Muslims. However tentative this reassurance, his marriage to a Bosniak woman made it irrelevant.[41] On May 22, 1992—"the date is engraved [manqūsh] into my memory"—Nadir and his wife were expelled from Banja Luka along with a group of other Bosnian Muslims as part of the ethnic cleansing of the city by Serb nationalists. A Serb friend and fellow medical trainee, Sasha, was the one who came and told him it was time to go. Nadir thought Sasha was joking, until catching a glimpse of the pistol in his hand. Nadir and his wife could pack a few clothes but had to leave their furniture and other possessions. "The thing I was saddest about was my medical books." Their group was placed on a plane and flown to a military airport near Belgrade.

Serbia turned out to be the easiest part of Nadir and his wife's extended exile. Nadir still had Arab friends there from his studies and was able to stay with them for several months. Within Serbia itself, there was no large-scale ethnic cleansing at the time and the two could go about their daily lives, albeit with great caution.[42] Nadir was determined to return to Bosnia to complete his studies and earn his diploma. He and his wife navigated the evolving borders of southeast Europe as they made their way to newly independent Croatia via Hungary. Their attempts to enter Croatia encountered a strange objection: Nadir as a stateless Palestinian was permitted due to Non-Aligned ties, but his wife needed a visa for an area that barely a year before was part of the country of her birth. Nadir attributed this to her wearing a hijab, as well as the fact that she was from Banja Luka (now a Serb-controlled city). After a month of waiting, they befriended an Egyptian UK citizen working for an international charity, who gave them a ride to Zagreb in his official car. They crossed the border in the early morning, with the border guards sleepily waving them through.

Nadir and his wife moved to Split: he found a job with a British Muslim charity, she with a Saudi one. By this time it was early 1993, and access to most of Bosnia was cut off by the Muslim-Croat war. When there was a lull in the fighting, Nadir seized the first opportunity he could to return, at the head of a twenty-two-truck aid convoy. The convoy members were predominantly Bosnian Muslims and he was the only Arab. Before reaching Travnik, they encountered a surprise HVO checkpoint.

> They stopped the convoy and started checking us and I caught their attention. They asked, "Who are you?" I showed them papers explaining that I was the head of the convoy and a humanitarian worker. Then they told me to get out of the truck. My heart dropped to my feet like this [points to his feet: zayy hayk]. I was terrified and wondered what would happen to me. It was the blackest moment that I've ever lived. They told the convoy to move along and that I would come later, but thank God the drivers refused. They said, "He's the head of the convoy, we aren't moving without him." I am so thankful for this.

The HVO soldiers took Nadir to a shipping container by the side of the road to await further instructions on his fate. They told him, "You're an Arab, you must be a mujahid." Nader looked on in terror as they read his details into the phone and awaited a response. After two hours, there was a call back. It was the Croatian army—which had considerable sway over the HVO—announcing that he was cleared to travel. The soldiers suddenly became friendly and even wished him a happy iftar, as it was Ramadan. "Eventually we arrived in Zenica. Believe me, it was like arriving at the American dream [Waṣalt ilā al-*American dream*, wallāhi]. Freedom!"

Nadir's roadside encounter with the HVO—with a single phone call potentially separating him from the fate suffered by Tawfiq, or worse—illustrates the precariousness that Arabs experienced during the war as perceptions toward them shifted. In the course of less than a year, as people in the land began to see themselves as Serbs, Croats, or Muslims first, Nadir found himself transformed from a Non-Alignment guest to a mere "Arab" and presumed mujahid. His wife experienced a different set of restrictions on her mobility for wearing hijab. Between the mass expulsion of Bosniaks from Banja Luka and the singular profiling as an Arab during the encounter at the HVO checkpoint, Nadir was exposed to two distinct logics of violence. Either could just as easily have ended for him with a bullet to the head. The glossing of Arab aid workers as potential jihad fighters would soon become routine: in 1999, Nadir was held and questioned at the Croatian border for three hours while en route to a humanitarian mission in Kosovo. At that point, when they asked if he knew Osama bin Laden, he simply laughed in resignation at the absurdity.

A few years after our initial conversations, Nadir and his wife visited Banja Luka for the first time since their expulsion. "Banja Luka is very different now," he noted. "Before, people there were accustomed to foreigners walking around, but now you have so many recent arrivals from the villages. When they see someone who looks different or is dark-skinned, they stare at you like this"—Nadir craned his neck and widened his eyes in an expression of mock amazement. During the visit they mostly moved around by car rather than on foot, as Nadir's wife was anxious about being harassed for her hijab. I asked him if he had any interest in reconnecting with old friends and colleagues in the city. Nadir's reply was typical of many Bosnians of different nationalities who lived through the war:

> You remember my friend Sasha I mentioned to you? These people turned on us. And it's all so different now, we didn't recognize any of the names on the wall in the hospital except for the older ones who were teaching when we were studying there. I remember one Serb doctor who was sad when we left. He told us, "I don't want you to think that all of us Serbs are like this." But he's passed away.

The resigned bitterness in Nadir's voice toward ex-colleagues and former friends—as well as the lament for "good" individuals from the "other" side who have since departed—signals his assimilation to a local context redefined along nationalist lines. But his lament over Banja Luka's postwar provinciality points to the loss of broader horizons previously marked by Non-Alignment. Once merely a regional city in Non-Aligned Yugoslavia, Banja Luka is now the ersatz capital of a statelet for Serbs within an "internationalized" Bosnia, a status promotion of sorts in nationalist terms; but for Nadir, who once reveled in the city's modest scale, the opposite is the case. As a darker-skinned man born on distant Mediterranean shores who tamed his ghurba in a strange region, Nadir pitied nationalist subjects for their insularity: "In 2008 we were stuck in a traffic jam on the road near Kotor Varoš. There was an older man by the side of the road who saw my wife in her hijab and made a slashing motion across his throat. Idiot! [Yā ghabī!] What year is this? This is 2008, it's not 1992! The war is over! We are living in the *third millennium!* Ugh, *such* a backwards mentality."

BROTHERHOOD AND UNITY, ON OTHER SHORES

In April 1999, NATO warplanes bombed Serbia's Interior Ministry in Belgrade, which was then ethnically cleansing Albanians from Kosovo. Among the losses were archival records on solidarity with Non-Aligned countries—a fitting capstone, perhaps, for a near-decade in which this universalist project was eroded from so many different directions.[43] The world that Non-Alignment shaped, of course, has not entirely disappeared, just as socialism continues to mark aspects of life in ex-Yugoslavia. The 2011 Libyan uprising brought the persistence of these ties into public view. Thousands of workers fled the fighting and returned to the ex-Yugoslav states, whose governments worried about the fate of their multibillion Euro contracts in a post-Qaddafi dispensation. But fighting wasn't bad for all businesses, as rumors spread of veterans of the Yugoslav wars working as mercenaries. The patchy media reports, speculative as they are, suggested a familiar hierarchy of racialized labor: white South African special forces for Qaddafi's personal security detail, while officers from ex-Yugoslavia commanded predominantly Black foot soldiers.[44] Racialized notions of labor and fighting came to the fore in a curious mirror image of what happened to Arabs in wartime Bosnia: although Black men—depicted as "African mercenaries"—were the primary target of racialized roundups and executions, Slavs also became objects of suspicion.[45] The new authorities in Tripoli detained five Serbs, suspecting them of being mercenaries, whereas they claimed to be civilian road workers. One correspondent for a Zagreb newspaper was told of there being Serbian and Croatian nationals among a group of alleged mercenaries executed by rebels in Misrata—"very well," snickered one online commenter, "Brotherhood and Unity reign again between Serbs and Croats, at least in Libya."[46]

In both cases, the long-running decay of larger projects—socialist Brotherhood and Unity between Yugoslavs, Non-Alignment solidarity between Yugoslavs and Arabs—left little else to legitimize either the pursuit of profit or the taking up of arms. It also made the rapid reconfiguration of alliances somehow more plausible: Libya's tentative rapprochement with the West quickly collapsed into the familiar dynamic of humanitarian war and regime change, with jihad groups going from shared enemy to useful ally, if only briefly. In 2004, the CIA kidnapped Abdelhakim Belhadj, a veteran of the Afghan jihad, and delivered him to Libya for interrogation and torture. By 2011, Belhadj found himself leading victorious rebels into Tripoli under NATO air cover.[47] In the musical chairs of shifting allegiances and identifications, the imaginaries of Non-Alignment survived mainly as irony, nostalgia, or sometimes a mix of both. Media stories described Qaddafi's wife, Safiyya Farkash, as a Croat from Mostar whom the Libyan ruler met while studying at the Yugoslav Air Force Academy in that city.[48] For former Yugoslavs with memories of an era in which Qaddafi was a regular feature of the daily news and once rode a horse into a packed Belgrade stadium, this kind of transregional figurative kinship did not seem entirely implausible. Especially when you consider that Farkaš is also a Hungarian name ("wolf") carried by some families that now identify as Croat. Alas, it was never so. Qaddafi's wife was actually born in al-Bayda', in eastern Libya, and belongs to the Baraʿsa tribe, and the Brother Leader never studied in Yugoslavia. To the best of our knowledge, at least.

Chapter 6

PEACEKEEPING

IN FEBRUARY 1995, A STRIKING REPORT CROSSED THE DESK OF the Bosnian army's intelligence command coming from the 1st Corps, which was responsible for the defense of the capital. Declared a "safe area" by the United Nations Security Council, Sarajevo was about to enter its third consecutive year under siege by the heavy artillery of the Bosnian Serb forces perched atop the hills that ringed the city. The world's attention was transfixed by media images of civilians dodging sniper fire on the way to fetch water or collect humanitarian aid. Blue-helmeted soldiers from the UN Protection Force (UNPROFOR)—soon to be the largest UN peacekeeping operation in history—played gatekeepers to this urban prison, patrolling its sole official transit point, the international airport. The dispatch came from a "reliable source"—likely a Bosnian employee of the UN—about a meeting that took place in the vicinity of UNPROFOR headquarters in the Nedžarići neighborhood. The source claimed to have met with a captain in the Jordanian army serving as an UNPROFOR military observer in Vogošća, a northern suburb of Sarajevo under Serb control.[1] The captain was searching for his brother Salah, who had joined one of the mujahidin units. He had heard that Salah had been injured, was treated abroad, and now had returned to continue the fight. The captain was hoping the Bosnian army could find his brother and offered his help to them in exchange.

Given his access to Serb-controlled areas, the captain's proposal was not to be dismissed lightly. Bosnian army intelligence commenced efforts to trace Salah within days.

I don't know if the captain ever found his brother. But Salah's real name jumped out at me from the page, because I had encountered him before, in other documents and in other people's stories. Salah was from a Bedouin family living on the outskirts of Amman. He studied architecture in Italy, was an important member of the Katiba, and had been decorated with the highest award in the Bosnian army, the Golden Lily. He married a woman from Zenica and after the war settled in the Salafi commune in Bočinja. Salah got a job with a Kuwaiti NGO and designed mosques and prayer rooms for Bosnian military bases and offices. He and his family returned to Jordan in the early 2000s.[2] I reached out to Salah through some mutual contacts during a visit to Amman in 2016, but after a few promising signals he ultimately declined an interview.

In the eyes of some, the contrast between these two kin, Salah and the captain, could not be greater. One was risking his life on behalf of humanity, serving the International Community under the blue flag of the United Nations; the other was part of a motley band of armed fanatics implacably opposed to all forms of peaceful coexistence between faiths and nations. The story of the mujahid and peacekeeper brothers, however, also provides a useful starting point for moving away from this stark narrative. The brothers shared more than common bloodlines, of course. They were both in a foreign country engaged in projects that were justified in terms directed at all of humanity, and part of forces bearing arms. And both projects were enmeshed in negotiating various compromises with the locals they encountered.

This chapter will take up another universalism and its relationship to the jihad in Bosnia, this time peacekeeping. Like Non-Alignment, peacekeeping is an internationalist form of universalism—but unlike Non-Alignment, peacekeeping has a military dimension that requires it to engage more directly with questions of violence. This chapter will map the convergences and conflicts between mujahids and peacekeepers and the respective universalisms they worked to realize, by situating them in the common history of empires and diasporas that has unfolded over previous chapters. We will see how the umma and the International Community are better understood as banners that can be raised by different actors under various circumstances rather than strict ideological categories. An ethnographically grounded and conceptually supple approach to universalism shows that far from representing clashing civilizations or even competing ones, mujahids and peacekeepers were rather like Salah and the captain: kin grown distant under different flags who might have had trouble recognizing each other if they found themselves face-to-face, kin grown distant who might have been startled to find that their paths had crossed again.

The approach developed in this chapter does more than help situate the jihad in Bosnia in relation to peacekeeping: it also points to a different way of thinking about peacekeeping altogether. UN peacekeeping operations constitute one of the largest extraterritorial deployments of military forces in the world today—second only to those of the United States—and the Bosnia crisis was a crucial episode in the development of this practice at the dawn of the post–Cold War era. Yet for too long, peacekeeping has been regarded through its own language of justification, an idiom that loosely and selectively cobbles together notions of international peace and security, humanitarianism, democracy promotion, and others. The logic of internationalism—which treats the state as the basic unit for the macro scale and the presumed backdrop for individual behavior on the micro scale, obscures much of the social reality of peacekeeping: namely, that it is also a space of encounter that remakes racial, ethnic, national, and other forms of difference, and that it often does so in ways deeply rooted in histories of empire and diaspora.

BLACK BEARDS AND BLUE HELMETS

As a universalist project in Bosnia, peacekeeping was beset by confusion between shifting and conflicting goals, each of which also raised questions about the use of force: to act as impartial referee between warring sides or to impose a political settlement; to merely facilitate the delivery of humanitarian aid or to actively protect it; to deter mass atrocities or to prevent them. Easier than identifying a coherent program or set of ideas is to understand that this universalism acted in the name of something called the International Community and manifested in the presence of people known simply as "Internationals." Over the past quarter-century, there has been a vigorous and wide-ranging debate over these universalisms in war zones around the world.[3] Internationals have no rigidly bounded body of membership: some, such as employees of intergovernmental organizations, enjoy formal immunity from local legal processes while others may receive various benefits from association with the right kinds of foreignness. Internationals are predominantly Western and white but—and this is important—not exclusively so. Some fall into categories of both local and International if allowed to by some combination of passport, education, or language skills. The existence of Internationals in distinct, even segregated, social spaces has been a notable aspect of life in Bosnia as well as in other "conflict zones" from the 1990s onward.[4] A voluminous literature has emerged on the challenges facing such interventions and how to improve them, while some scholars have been even more openly critical of these interventions, analogizing them to colonialism.[5] Yet no matter how sharp the disagreements in these debates, their parameters have largely played out with Internationals and locals as the protagonists. Other categories of actors have fallen out of these debates and eluded scholarly attention: Chinese businessmen, migrants and refugees from the Global South trying to reach western Europe, and, of course, Muslim fighters and aid workers coming in the name of the umma. Internationals in the Balkans and other zones of intervention have often registered the presence of transnational Muslim activists as a threatening one.[6]

In the decades since the end of the Cold War, the notion of the International Community as an actor that can be invoked—even with a sense of irony or skepticism—has crystallized not only as a cornerstone of diplomatic speech but also in manifold sectors of activity, such as development, relief, human rights, democracy, security, and so on. Unlike its more pointed predecessor, "the Free World"—which gestured to the putatively unfree Communist bloc—the International Community enjoys more pervasive, if anodyne, pretensions to universality. It is dominated by "the West" (an only slightly less unstable category) but not reducible to it. This is akin to how the jihad referenced the umma as its horizon of belonging, envisioning the inclusion of humanity through the teleology of conversion, the hope that one day all people will accept Islam. One may argue, of course, that the International Community is still a more universal category than the umma, since the former already includes all of humanity through the mechanism of (near-)universal state membership in the UN whereas the latter only includes self-identified Muslims. But this distinction is dubious at best: it is not at all clear that the proportion of people in the world who identify with the International Community is necessarily greater than the proportion of those who accept Islam and its basic tenets of faith. In other words, universalisms are best understood in terms of the scope of their claims and their ability to normalize those claims among others—*not* whether those claims are scrupulously adhered to.

As we saw in Chapter 3, the jihad in Bosnia drew its authority for violence from outside the state system and sought to supplement it through a logic of solidarity. In contrast, the various and confused theories of authority justifying the peacekeeping project in Bosnia were all ultimately based on resolutions of the UN Security Council. The Security Council's ability to make such proclamations stems from the organization's charter, which itself is a treaty signed by most of the world's states. Thus, according to this reasoning, the use of violence by peacekeepers is a function ultimately delegated by the International Community to a small group of states.[7] This principle of sovereign delegation is also grounded in firm political realities and material relations: peacekeeping is carried out using state military forces "on loan" to international organizations but ultimately accountable to their own national capitals. As a result, the terms of this delegation are unclear and deeply fraught: the authority to use violence was restricted to patrolling a "no fly" zone over the country and to self-defense in the six cities and towns designated as "safe areas"—but not necessarily to protecting the safe areas themselves.[8]

The primary *institutional manifestation* of peacekeeping was UNPROFOR, the largest peacekeeping force in the history of the United Nations.[9] At its peak, UNPROFOR had nearly forty thousand troops from dozens of countries.[10] UNPROFOR consisted of units and personnel loaned by national armies and managed by the UN's Department of Peacekeeping Operations. At the same time, individual national governments could withdraw their contingents at will and retained exclusive authority to discipline their own personnel. And while most UN peacekeeping operations had been led by neutral or non-aligned states, UNPROFOR was dominated by western European powers, especially Britain and France.[11] This reflected both the conflict's European location and the sudden disappearance of the need for Cold War balancing. And UNPROFOR was not alone: in the skies above, NATO was tasked with patrolling the no-fly zone and, toward the end of the war, bombing in support of the blue-helmeted peacekeepers.[12] Like UNPROFOR, NATO operated under a UN mandate, but it retained a separate operational chain of command to its Brussels headquarters. This gave rise to the awkward and widely criticized "dual key" arrangement whereby any use of force by NATO required the consent of both the UN secretary general and the NATO commander. As a result, units from the same national military forces were operating under different command arrangements: for example, British troops on the ground serving with UNPROFOR answered to UN headquarters, while British air force pilots flying above were commanded by NATO in Brussels. This convoluted structure served US interests, affording Washington enormous influence over peacekeeping without having to place its forces under even nominal UN management.

In contrast to this constellation of interlocking alliances, the jihad's institutional structures were relatively streamlined, as described in Chapter 3: mujahids in Bosnia all served under the aegis of a single state, whether in the Katiba, with Abu al-Zubayr's group, or as individuals in regular army units. The Katiba represented about as many nationalities as did the peacekeepers of UNPROFOR, but it was far smaller and nimbler.

THE OTHER "MUSLIM FOREIGN FIGHTERS"

One day in the summer of 2007, while walking through the city park in Tuzla, in northeast Bosnia, I came across a simple obelisk, no more than two meters tall (Figure 10). It was a monument dedicated to United Nations peacekeepers. Displayed most prominently on its face was the crest of the Pakistan Army's Punjab Regiment, whose storied 17th battalion served in Tuzla with UNPROFOR under the designation PAKBAT-2 in 1994–1995. Beneath the crest was a row of equally sized flags of Pakistan, Bosnia-Herzegovina, and the United Nations, and then inscriptions in English and Bosnian extolling the battalion's efforts.[13] The dried remains of several bouquets sat at the foot of the obelisk, likely left over from the visit earlier that year by Pakistan's military ruler, General Pervez Musharraf. The monument is but one reminder of the peacekeepers from majority-Muslim countries who made up over a quarter of UNPROFOR's total ranks.[14] Pakistani contingents deployed in Vareš and Tuzla; Turks in Zenica; Egyptians in Sarajevo; Bangladeshis in Bihać; and Malaysians in Konjic. Across the border in Croatia, Jordanian units patrolled cease-fire lines and an Indonesian medical battalion also served. Throughout former Yugoslavia, Muslim peacekeepers under the flag of the UN far outnumbered foreign Muslims who fought in the jihad. Yet their presence is among the many things that are occluded if we read the jihad and peacekeeping as stand-ins for Islam and the West, respectively. These peacekeepers were part of a universalism that spoke in the idioms of the International Community but invoked pan-Islam alongside it as well.

FIGURE 10. Monument to Pakistani UN peacekeepers, Tuzla. Photo by author.

While UNPROFOR's leadership was European, it relied heavily on troops from poor countries, especially as the war dragged on and the force's mandate expanded. And the global color line runs through peacekeeping more broadly, with troops from the Global South performing much of the labor and assuming much of the risk of managing war at the "periphery" of the international system.[15] As is the case with volunteers joining the jihad, Western commentators have regarded poor, nonwhite peacekeepers with suspicion, wondering what could possibly make them willing to travel to war zones in distant countries. A variety of reasons have been adduced: for governments to accrue diplomatic capital through participating in multilateral institutions, for armies to acquire real-world experience overseas, for officers and soldiers to journey someplace exotic and to receive extra pay.[16] These explanations are fine as far as they go, but this backdrop of puzzlement marks the space where the appeals of universalism are summarily dismissed, leaving only a rhetoric of pure idealism and a reality of crass materialism as the inevitable and all too convenient refutation. If the jihad is negative universalism that is the opposite of the peacekeeping project, then peacekeepers from the Global South represent a kind of internal deficiency, always the first to be suspected of corruption, incompetence, or other malfeasance. This was even more so the case in the anomalous situation of ex-Yugoslavia, which inverted the typical racial hierarchies of white peacekeepers policing nonwhite natives.[17] What is often overlooked, if not denied, is that peacekeepers from poor countries are also capable of seeking meaningful participation in universalist projects, and indeed can invoke the universal in more than one register.

This is where, once again, histories of diaspora and empire can help place different invocations of the universal in a common history. The monument in Tuzla is a reminder that Pakistan was the fourth-largest contributor of troops to UNPROFOR, with more peacekeepers inside Bosnia than any other majority-Muslim country.[18] Pakistan and India are perennially among the leading participants in UN peacekeeping operations around the world, as well as among those who have lost the most soldiers. Both countries have together deployed over a quarter-million soldiers overseas on UN missions.[19] The immediate political reasons for these undertakings varied: for India, it stemmed from a commitment to Non-Alignment in the 1950s and

1960s, whereas for Pakistan the shift came later in part to keep the army away from domestic politics.[20] But their ability to participate in peacekeeping is rooted in a shared history in what was once the largest all-volunteer military in the world: Britain's Indian Army. While empires everywhere have sought ways to recruit natives to police their own lands, the British in India were particularly successful in raising a force that could also be sent to fight all over the world, one comparable in size to its own metropolitan army. To this day, regiments on both sides of the 1947 partition lines maintain a strong sense of historical continuity dating back to the colonial era through national wars and peacekeeping deployments, proudly recounting their campaigns across South and Southeast Asia, Africa, Europe, and the Middle East.[21] The accumulated experience of overseas deployments in the service of the empire across vastly different climates in cooperation with Anglophone forces gave the armies of India and Pakistan a ready interoperability with peacekeeping.

Nearly a decade after first stumbling across the PAKBAT-2 monument in Tuzla, I finally met the battalion's leadership. Qasim Qureshi commanded PAKBAT-2, and his deputy, Jamal Zia, had paid for the monument. Both happily reminisced about their experiences in Bosnia when I visited them in the tidy housing colonies for retired army officers and civil servants that sit on the outskirts of Lahore. They eagerly reminded me of the illustrious history of their unit, 17 Punjab—called the Haidris, after Pakistan's highest military decoration, the Nishan-e-Haider.[22] They traced the unit's origins back to 1818, when the princely state of Bhopal raised a contingent for service to the East India company—native troops funded by a local potentate but placed under British command. In different iterations, the unit served multiple tours on the northwest frontier with Afghanistan. It also fought and bled in both World Wars, from France to Italy, from north Africa to Iraq to Ethiopia. During partition, the unit was allocated to Pakistan, where it went on to fight against India in the wars of 1948, 1965, and 1971.[23] Qureshi was the son of a top army general himself and attended an elite military prep school before entering Pakistan Military Academy; Zia grew up in the garrison city of Rawalpindi, his father an army contractor. Both men spent the bulk of their army careers in the Haidris, including stints studying or being seconded abroad, and went on to prestigious postings: Qureshi coordinated relief efforts for the 2005 earthquake in Kashmir and after retiring as a major-general he was ambassador to

Sri Lanka and served in the Strategic Plans Division, the secretive body that oversees the country's nuclear assets; Zia finished as a brigadier and ran the Inter-Services Intelligence in Punjab province.

Qureshi and Zia recounted the prejudices and expectations their mission faced for coming from a majority-Muslim country. The UN bureaucracy and Western officers in UNPROFOR were skeptical of the intentions and competence of the Pakistanis.[24] On the ground, all sides expected them to favor the Bosnian Muslims—even the Bosnian Muslims themselves. Qureshi and Zia spoke of laboring to ensure that they lived up to all the standards of professionalism and impartiality befitting a UN peacekeeping operation, while at the same time doing everything possible to act on their sympathy with Bosnian Muslims. They claimed to serve all Bosnians, even sparking complaints from a Bosnian mufti who argued that non-Muslim villages were already receiving more than ample aid from Christian organizations abroad.[25] They also said that they aggressively interpreted their mandate to fire back at Serb forces while escorting aid convoys, drawing a distinction between shooting to kill versus shooting to suppress and deter. Like other units in UNPROFOR, PAKBAT-2 had a significant civil affairs component that acted as a form of cultural diplomacy. The peacekeepers cooperated with NGOs, including Islamic organizations such as the Saudi High Committee, to distribute humanitarian aid, and their engineers worked to repair windows in refugee camps. The battalion set up a Pakistani cultural exhibition.[26] In Qureshi and Zia's recollection, however, one of the services their unit provided that was in greatest demand was circumcisions for Muslim men.

As part of the universalist project of peacekeeping in Bosnia, the Pakistanis stressed their conformity with the mandate promulgated by the United Nations Security Council as well as their comportment with "international" norms such as impartiality and professionalism. At the same time, they saw their work as an act of solidarity with fellow Muslims in Bosnia. The project of peacekeeping had a dominant idiom but had ample space for alternative visions and discourses to exist, in part because internationalism presupposes and relies on nationalism and because peacekeeping itself always enjoyed only the most precarious legitimacy and tenuous coherence. And since Pakistani nationalism is itself imbued with tensions and anxieties over its relationship with broader notions of umma, this unsurprisingly also played out in Bosnia, and sometimes in ways difficult to predict. For while the peacekeepers on the ground were conscious not to transgress their limited mandate, Pakistan's military was more than happy to let audiences back home think that they were pursuing more muscular forms of intervention. One of the country's most popular television dramas of the 1990s, *Alpha Bravo Charlie*, was sponsored by the military and featured a protagonist serving in Bosnia who charges into combat against the Serbs.[27]

While commitments to the umma had a place in peacekeeping, they could breed suspicions about it as well. We can see this in the experience of the Egyptian battalion that served in Sarajevo throughout most of the war. The mission was covered in the Egyptian media, undoubtedly shoring up the regime's image as a legitimate protector of Muslim interests. It came shortly after Egypt's participation in the 1991 US-led war against Iraq, a divisive decision that exposed the regime to vociferous criticism from Islamists and many others.[28] For a few months before UNPROFOR's leadership was Europeanized, an Egyptian general was responsible for all peacekeepers in Sarajevo, including French and Ukrainian units. The choice of nationalities was a not-so-subtle attempt at "balance" between states labeled as Catholic, Muslim, and Orthodox.[29] Egyptian foreign correspondent—and later editor of *al-Ahram* newspaper—Yehia Ghanem visited Bosnia in 1993 and wrote a memoir fulsomely praising his blue-helmeted compatriots. Ghanem stressed that the Egyptians were second to none in their professionalism, including their European counterparts. He described in vivid detail an ambush that the peacekeepers stumbled into, with an intrepid Egyptian special forces officer charging into a burning armored vehicle to rescue his wounded Canadian colleague. Ghanem also claimed that Philippe Morillon, the French general who led UNPROFOR in Bosnia at the time, kept a personal security detail composed entirely of Egyptians due to their skill and their fidelity.[30]

The Egyptian battalion, of course, also faced problems in its deployment. They complained about the quality of their food, lack of television, not receiving per diems, and the noise from a nearby nightclub. They also had to plead with UNPROFOR headquarters to send money to pay the wages of local Bosnians working with the contingent.[31] Ghanem's rosy account of Egyptian peacekeeping also did not prevent him from penning a scathing indictment of the International Community's actions, especially when carried out by

European states. He wrote about French and Ukrainian peacekeepers extorting hapless Bosnians for their jewelry, their appliances, even (in the case of women) their bodies in exchange for food staples and heating fuel. "At least one could posit geographical or economic motives, religious or historical hatreds, for the [atrocities of the] Serbs; but for these international criminals, what excuse could they possibly have?!"[32] These betrayals were for Ghanem a mere prelude to the January 1993 killing of Bosnian deputy prime minister Hakija Turajlić, who was riding in an UNPROFOR armored vehicle when French peacekeepers opened the hatch and stood by as he was shot to death by Bosnian Serb troops. The Egyptians, on the other hand, were the Bosnian Muslims' only true friends: they spent their off-duty time repairing water and electricity lines, they opened their clinic to the local civilians. For Ghanem, the Egyptians' dedication and humility was not unrelated to Islam, pointing out their "adherence and devotion to religion" [al-iltizām wal-tadayyun].[33]

Whatever the reliability of the details in Ghanem's account, it stands as a helpful exposition of an official discourse that sought to present Egyptian nationalism, participation in the International Community, and Islamic solidarity as not only compatible but even mutually reinforcing. In Ghanem's telling, it is the Egyptians who are faithful to the UN's stated mission and goals and not the corrupt, biased European troops. This was not only a critique of the West but a statement about the importance of Islamic solidarity at a time when the Mubarak regime's legitimacy was vigorously contested by armed Islamist groups—some of whose supporters were also fighting in Bosnia. Needless to say, the ansar do not make an appearance in his account. Only the regime can credibly stand for Islam. In this way, Egypt's participation in UNPROFOR served both internal and external agendas, making use of the ample space that exists under the banners of the International Community and the umma.

State attempts to use participation in peacekeeping in Bosnia to bolster pan-Islamic credentials hardly went uncontested, however. Writing in the Kuwaiti Salafi magazine *al-Furqan*, the Moroccan activist Mustafa Abu Saʿd accused an unnamed Arab state with troops in Sarajevo (which could only be Egypt) of fostering black marketeering of essential staples between Bosnian Muslims and Serbs.[34] The elliptical nature of the criticism made sense in context; only a few years earlier, Egypt had participated in the US-led war to eject Iraq from Kuwait. Kuwait's Salafis were careful not to say anything that could be taken to endorse the armed campaigns waged by the Islamic Group and Islamic Jihad against the Mubarak regime. Abu Sa'd however, did not reject UNPROFOR as such or Egypt's participation in it; instead he merely asked the unnamed government to "replace [the peacekeepers] with better ones, as they are unwelcome from either the Bosnian government or the Muslim people here."[35] He also urged Islamic NGOs in the Balkans to affiliate themselves with the UN so they could avail themselves of resources such as identity documents, insignia decals for vehicles, and even the assistance of the blue helmets. Abu Sa'd illustrated his point with an anecdote: during the fighting in the Croat-Muslim war, Islamic aid organizations in Italy were unable to reach a camp of 3,700 Muslim refugees in Gradac, Croatia. The only way they could go was to work with Caritas, the Catholic charity, which required them to place Caritas insignia on the front of their cars—next to the logos of the Muslim NGO. "We obtained a fatwa from one of the shaykhs in Mecca, who permitted this, since it was the only path to relief for besieged Muslims and to save them from hunger and cold."[36]

The examples above give some sense of how the universalist project of peacekeeping nevertheless allowed spaces for different forms of pan-Islamic solidarity work. It was also the case, however, that one could support multiple universalist projects as well. Peacekeeping and the jihad were distinct insofar as one sought to distribute violence ultimately through states while the other did not, but that hardly meant having to choose between them in practice. Abu Sa'd and the Kuwaiti Salafis who published him knew this all too well. In the pages of the December 1994 issue of *al-Furqan*, he penned two articles that appeared side by side: one was a glowing dispatch describing the achievements of the mujahids' Katiba in Bosnia. The other was a statement calling for Bosnia's full and unconditional incorporation into the European Union.[37]

NEITHER ENEMY NOR ALLY

The jihad and peacekeeping were both universalist projects, but with different structures of antagonism. Peacekeepers had no enemies, properly speaking, and instead set themselves above all the warring factions and accountable to none of them. In contrast, the jihad was engaged in solidarity with the Bosnian Muslims and adopted their enemies and allies as its own, even if it was much less willing to seek the goodwill of the International Community. These two actors—the peacekeepers in a vertical relationship with the locals and the mujahids in an orthogonal one—both disrupted the logic of the other. The peacekeepers tended to see the mujahids as interlopers distinct from the Bosnian Muslims, with no standing to fight on behalf of brethren. For their part, the mujahids dismissed the peacekeepers' proclamations of neutrality and secularism as charades, but they focused on fighting the Serbs and, when appropriate, the Croats as well. The relationship between the mujahids and the peacekeepers was one of agonism rather than enmity: tense and ambiguous, where both cooperation and hostility were possible.[38]

In Zenica, there did not appear to have been any major confrontations with UNPROFOR. From mid-1994 until the end of the war, a Turkish contingent was deployed in the city, and their twenty-four-hour patrols in the predominantly Croat neighborhoods near the Katiba's headquarters helped lower tensions.[39] Instead, one of the most common sites of friction between the blue helmets and the mujahids was on the roads between cities. For both sides, and in different ways, roads were a space of danger and vulnerability. Peacekeepers and mujahids were conspicuously foreign and more likely to take wrong turns into unfriendly spaces. UNPROFOR did not seek to control territory; rather, its mobility was interstitial almost by definition, whether in monitoring cease-fire lines between warring sides or escorting humanitarian aid from one zone to another. To be a peacekeeper was often to find oneself at the mercy of the checkpoints of the varying parties. Mujahids, due to their racialized visibility, also found themselves at their most vulnerable while at checkpoints run by the HVO, as we saw in previous chapters. The UN archives are littered with terse mentions of mysterious "mujahidin" making menacing slashing gestures at Internationals or training their guns on them. In most incidents, one side is driving by the other, as when mujahids reportedly tried to pass Internationals at dangerously high speeds or even run them off the road.[40] In a few cases, mujahids robbed UN military observers and made off with their cars.[41] Tensions escalated into open violence in a handful of incidents, especially with the British. In the summer of 1993, the two sides briefly exchanged fire in central Bosnia. In October 1995, British peacekeepers shot dead a Bosnian mujahid while he was at home with his family recovering from combat injuries.[42] A few days later, the Katiba let loose a rocket over the heads of a British UNPROFOR convoy to send them a message.

While tensions and armed confrontations were also not uncommon with the local warring groups—especially the Bosnian Serb forces, who took peacekeepers hostage on multiple occasions—Internationals nevertheless saw mujahids as a category unto themselves, a kind of shadowy presence hovering in their peripheral vision, recognizable through a combination of racial and sartorial cues.[43] At the same time, the peacekeepers struggled to develop even rudimentary intelligence on these foreigners: their reports exhibited considerable confusion and speculation, conflating various sorts of foreign Muslim actors under the general heading of mujahidin, from Iranian military advisors to NGO workers and proselytizers.[44] The two certainties that emerge from the archive are that peacekeepers knew little about the mujahids, but they knew a mujahid when they saw one. This dynamic could produce moments of uncanny familiarity. Vaughan Kent-Payne, a major in the British army serving in UNPROFOR, expressed this sensation during a tense standoff with mujahids—including "at least three blacks [*sic*], one of whom carried a 64 mm rocket launcher" [45]—at a checkpoint near their base in Mehurići:

> [M]y attention was grabbed by someone suddenly shouting, "Death to the infidels" in English, but not just in English but in a broad Yorkshire accent, which is a region of England which I'm from and where all the soldiers from my battalion are from. And this was very incongruous in the middle of Bosnia to hear a man from a foreign military organisation insulting us, calling us unbelievers in our own language of English . . .
>
> I said to him, "I think we come from the same place. Why don't you go home too." And he then—he then started swearing at me. And I said, "Look, we're all Yorkshire brothers." And he said, "You're definitely not my brother," and then started to insult [the] British and UNPROFOR in general.[46]

The "very incongruous" feeling that Kent-Payne experienced at being insulted by a mujahid not only in his own language but in his own regional accent marks the spot where universalist projects come into contact. The peacekeeper's claim to speak in the name of the universal was being challenged not only directly in the demand that he go home, but also indirectly in being hailed in an accent that reminded him of his own provincial origins. Furthermore, when Kent-Payne tried to pull the mujahid into their shared particularity—"Look, we're all Yorkshire brothers"—he was met with a deflection: "You're definitely not my brother." The mujahid did not deny also being from Yorkshire, but he did reject the invocation of fraternity, as if saying, we may come from the same place and that's fine, because everyone comes from somewhere. But only one of us speaks for the universal, and it's not you.

The uncanniness that emerges from the peacekeeper's account, however, also speaks to the unequal stature of these two universalist projects. For the British peacekeeper, the encounter was the first time he even became aware of mujahids in Bosnia; it is "incongruous" to be challenged by a fellow Yorkshireman because he only expected to find in Bosnia locals and Internationals such as himself. For the mujahids, however, such ignorance was literally impossible: they were marginal actors, and they knew it. In their narratives, the peacekeepers are also peripheral characters; not because they are shadowy and mysterious or unexpected, but because they are not clearly either friend or foe. But there is a deep undercurrent of skepticism and mistrust over their right to speak for the universal, which means they can at best be regarded as a helpful source for supplies, whether through raiding (as with the theft of automobiles) or more dramatic means.

We can see this in one story narrated by ansar involving Abu al-Zubayr. From June 1993 to March 1994, the town of Tešanj in northern Bosnia was jointly besieged by both the Serb and Croat forces, even as those two armies continued to fight against each other elsewhere. One day, a "strange occurrence" [wāqiʿa gharība] took place that demonstrated the extent of God's care for the mujahids. Abu al-Zubayr was sitting on the second floor of his Bosnian in-laws' house thinking deeply about how he could feed his family under the current circumstances. At that moment, a plane flew overhead and dropped a multi-ton load of supplies, which landed directly next to the house. Abu al-Zubayr dashed toward it, broke open the crate, and took all the flour, oil, salt, coffee, and milk that he could, until his wife's family's kitchen was full of food.[47]

Like the other accounts of miraculous events circulating in the jihad, the story is a reminder of God's ultimate authority over man or, in this case, the International Community. Normally, the Internationals hold themselves above (in this case, quite literally) the warring locals, ostensibly serving them according to a set of vaguely defined ideals—neutrality, humanitarianism, and so on—but ultimately unaccountable. In this story, the aircraft of the International Community become mere instruments of God's desire to assist his pious subjects: here, an Arab mujahid and his Bosnian family. Abu al-Zubayr is posited not only as a striving Muslim through his jihad, but as one who is also grounded in the Bosnian context through marriage and his concern for his family's welfare. By highlighting their common faith, intermarriage, and other bonds with locals, mujahids presented themselves as more legitimate advocates of the Bosnian (Muslim) people, more grounded and accountable than the Internationals. While this vision arguably excludes non-Muslims such as Serbs and Croats, the mujahids would argue that the Internationals are no less partial in their actions. In this story, it is precisely this solidarity across difference between Muslims that affords Abu al-Zubayr the authority to contest the arbitration of difference that the Internationals perform when they exclude or marginalize the mujahids. The miracle is the means by which mujahids stake a claim vis-à-vis the Internationals: acting not only as part of a common narrative, but one in which they define the terms instead.

The jihad received more from UNPROFOR than cars and food, however: it also acquired at least one defector. Abdul Manaf Kasmuri, a lieutenant colonel in the Malaysian army, had studied at the UK Royal Military Academy at Sandhurst and earned his commission the year before Vaughan Kent-Payne matriculated there. I met him in the summer of 2018 in Shah Alam, not far from Kuala Lumpur; we had connected rather easily over Facebook a few weeks beforehand. Abdul Manaf (Kasmuri is his father's name, not a family name) had been in the news quite a bit a decade earlier: he spent several years detained without charge under Malaysia's Internal Security Act on suspicion of ties with armed Islamist groups in Indonesia. Abdul Manaf later published a memoir composed in part during his time in internment.[48] Like Abu ʿAbd al-ʿAziz, Abdul Manaf is also on the US Treasury's list of Specially Designated Global Terrorists, so for legal reasons I politely (and unfortunately) ignored his hints that I should help get his memoir translated into English.[49] Abdul Manaf described his background as a comfortable one: he was born in 1955 into a Malay family, his father an independent farmer with a modest amount of land. Abdul Manaf was drawn to soldiering from an early age and completed high school at the Royal Military College outside Kuala Lumpur before going off to Sandhurst. The time in England was challenging and stimulating, and it shaped him deeply; he met his wife, a Malay and Chinese nursing student in London, there as well. After his studies, Abdul Manaf was commissioned into the Royal Malay Regiment. He spent about a decade fighting communist guerrillas, which he described as more arduous and dangerous than anything he saw in Bosnia: in the jungle, you may never know the enemy is there until he's right in front of you, and battles can be won and lost in a matter of seconds.

Abdul Manaf became much more interested in Islam in the 1980s through the publications of Darul Arqam, an Islamic revivalist movement with Sufi leanings whose popularity was growing in Malaysia, to the consternation of the ruling authorities.[50] By the time the Bosnia crisis came around, Abdul Manaf was moved as a human and as a Muslim by the situation there and volunteered to serve in UNPROFOR. Soon after arriving in the autumn of 1993, he witnessed the aftermath of the massacre of Bosnian Muslim civilians by the HVO in the village of Stupni Do. Like many other peacekeepers, Abdul Manaf was aghast at the violence and chafed at the UN bureaucracy and its apparent impotence. Everywhere he went, Abdul Manaf's sense of Cold War professional soldiering followed: he cultivated contacts on all sides of the conflict as a way to gather intelligence and navigate checkpoints, once taking messages from a Serb police officer to her mother who continued to live in Sarajevo—"winning hearts and minds," he quipped, a phrase that largely came into prominence through the history of anticommunist warfare in Malaysia. But his political sympathies were clear: he started facilitating or at least turning a blind eye to arms shipments for the Bosnian Muslims, although he was coy on the details both in his memoirs and in person. When Abdul Manaf returned home months later, suspicions over his activities in Bosnia and possibly his "Islamic" leanings more generally led to him being quietly encouraged to retire from the army.

Nevertheless, Abdul Manaf remained committed to helping Bosnia and decided to return with an NGO. While passing through Zenica, he soon found himself asked to lend his expertise to the Katiba.[51] He now called himself Abu Muhammad the Filipino, concealing his true nationality. Abdul Manaf was no Salafi and had little interest in being told how to practice Islam, but the Katiba eagerly took him on regardless. He played a key role in planning and reconnaissance for the 1995 campaign in the Ozren pocket. Along with Abu ʿAbd Allah from Libya, he braved mine-strewn hillside forests to painstakingly scout out the Serb positions. Nearly two decades after studying tank battles at Sandhurst that did little to prepare him for the jungle warfare he faced at home, Abdul Manaf finally had a classic infantry war to fight, with trenches, clear battle lines, even some artillery. It was during this time that the news came of the massacre at Srebrenica, leading Abdul Manaf to scoff that UNPROFOR should have been called the "UN Propaganda Force" instead.[52] Compared to his own experience as a peacekeeper, Abdul Manaf felt joining the jihad was more meaningful, more practical, and more useful. Yet Abdul Manaf's criticism of UNPROFOR's failures did not translate into a wholesale condemnation of all the peacekeepers or of the West. His recollection of the Stupni Do massacre warmly mentioned the presence of a British friend from Sandhurst; he recalled how another Briton was moved to tears by those events, even though he had been a veteran of the Falklands war. Abdul Manaf described the Dutch peacekeepers at Srebrenica as powerless to stop the Serbs, rather than actively conspiring with them. For Abdul Manaf, the jihad was not so much a rejection of peacekeeping as it was a way to ultimately fulfill goals shared by both universalisms.

FIRST AMONG EQUALS

As the war wound down, the universalist project of the jihad came to an end, while that of peacekeeping was drastically transformed. The peace agreement negotiated in Dayton, Ohio, in November 1995 and signed in Paris the following month preserved Bosnia-Herzegovina as an independent, sovereign, unified state on paper. But it also provided a political and legal framework for the International Community—now firmly led by the United States—to establish a clear overall monopoly on legitimate violence in the country, unlike the narrow and ambiguous mandates of the UN Security Council. UNPROFOR was replaced by the new Implementation Force, or IFOR, which was to be led by NATO instead of the UN and significantly larger—with sixty thousand troops, one-third of them from the United States. While the Security Council blessed the operation, the UN's presence on the ground receded in favor of NATO and the European Union.[53]

Commentators have viewed these developments through the lens of geopolitics or operational efficacy, arguing that the greater organizational focus, clearer political mandate, and, above all, the leadership of the United States cut a sharp contrast with hapless UNPROFOR. But the shift is also useful for thinking about different configurations of universalism under the rubric of the International Community. There was a contraction of multilateralisms at work: if the British and French had been content to use the globalism of the United Nations to organize and legitimize their influence within UNPROFOR, the Americans would do the same to the Europeans through the institutions of Atlanticism, especially NATO. It was the classic style of American hegemony—Washington did not rule other states, it was merely *primus inter pares*, or first among equals. As if to add insult to injury, some UNPROFOR units stayed on and became part of IFOR, simply exchanging their UN colors and insignia for NATO ones. This was true of troops from non-NATO countries as well, such as Egypt, Jordan, Pakistan, and even erstwhile great power adversary Russia. Peacekeeping in Bosnia shifted from attempting to manage and contain the war to a project of state-building and governance.

The Dayton accords also imposed a new constitution on Bosnia that combined logics of nation and state in a manner as parodic as it was grisly. Fifty-one percent of the territory was designated the Federation of Bosnia-Herzegovina, controlled by Bosniaks and Croats, while the rest became Republika Srpska (Figure 11).[54] The country has three presidents and at least as many prime ministers, in accordance with institutions divided along nationalist lines. This dysfunctional structure only encouraged further Euro-American management of political affairs, as concentrated in the Office of the High Representative, a position created to oversee the civilian aspects of implementing Dayton.[55] The High Representative, always from an EU country with a US deputy, has the power to impose legislation and sack elected officials.[56] Over time, stewardship of the post-Dayton regime largely shifted from Washington to Brussels, just as the 2004 departure of US forces left leadership of the remaining peacekeepers in EU hands. Although the US has continued to wield decisive influence—especially on issues it prioritizes—Bosnia's future has been tied much more closely to the

EU, though not necessarily as a potential member. Notwithstanding distant promises of eventual integration, in practice Bosnia-Herzegovina became a semi-formal EU periphery state.

Dayton ushered in the end of the jihad, as well. Before agreeing to send troops to Bosnia, the United States was keen to expel foreign Islamic elements that it deemed unfriendly. While it was a sideshow in the much larger issues to be settled at the end of the war, Washington insisted on it.[57] The primary concern was Iran and Hizballah.[58] But the Sunni ansar were marked as well.[59] The agreement therefore included a provision requiring the withdrawal of "all foreign Forces, including international advisors, freedom fighters, trainers, [and] volunteers" within thirty days. The same provision, however, specifically exempted UN and NATO-led peacekeepers and police.[60] This simultaneous

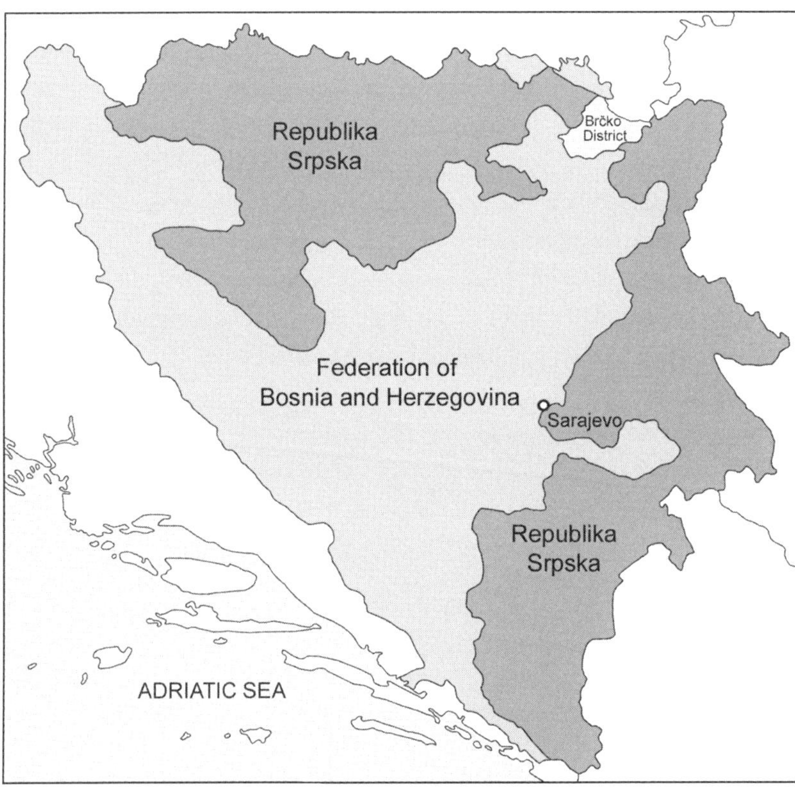

FIGURE 11. Bosnia's "soft partition" under the Dayton Agreement. Map by Dale Mertes.

gesture of exclusion and exemption is perhaps the starkest example of how a universalist project arbitrates on difference: here, intervention explicitly codes difference as "foreign" in order to separate mujahids and Bosnians, while coding its own foreignness to Bosnia as merely the distance between the universal and the particular.[61]

In the weeks between the conclusion of the Dayton negotiations and the arrival of US troops, Washington pressured Izetbegović to expel the mujahids and the Iranians.[62] On December 8, 1995, a NATO advance team traveled to Zenica and quizzed Bosnian officials about the Katiba, including its personnel, equipment, and tasks. Shortly thereafter, a delegation from the Katiba—Abu al-Maʿali, Anwar Shaʿban, and Ayman as interpreter—met Rasim Delić and Izetbegović himself. The mujahids were told that the Katiba would be dissolved soon in accordance with US wishes and that preparations would have to begin for evacuating them. On December 12, Delić issued an order disbanding the Katiba.[63] The edict also came in a more corporeal form. Two days later, while the Dayton agreement was formally signed in Paris, five mujahids were killed in an ambush near an HVO checkpoint, including Anwar Shaʿban and Abu al-Harith. The attack was a surprise, since the Croats and Bosnian army had been in a truce for nearly two years, leading everyone with whom I have spoken to believe that it was sponsored by the US. There was apparently no investigation, nor even a demand for one from the Bosnian side.

The Katiba convened a special meeting, one attended by almost everyone. At this point, many of the leading authority figures were gone. There was some debate over what to do. Like almost every other party to the conflict, the mujahids mustered little enthusiasm for Dayton. Moreover, some wanted revenge for the murder of the five brothers, but the army would not permit it. Some argued that the Katiba could best serve the Bosnian Muslims by delaying their departure, as giving in immediately would only invite pressure for further concessions; others feared what would happen to the ansar mujahids in particular if they surrendered their arms.[64] By the various accounts I have collected, such proposals to resist, strike back, or otherwise continue the jihad were outvoted. There was no use in opposing an agreement the Bosnians themselves had signed and starting a conflict with the people they came to help protect. The word went out to the Katiba's networks of contacts and supporters. One fax to London intercepted by the Bosnian army explained, "We are finished here and don't want to be in prison like the Arabs in Pakistan.... Bosnia is finished ... this peace is final."[65]

The evacuation of the ansar was coordinated between Bosnia and Croatia, with the mediation of the US. During one of our long drives, Ayman told me that most of the mujahids left in a convoy of buses that proceeded from Zenica westward to Jajce and then Bihać, where they were housed in an old military base. From there they were taken, individually or in small groups, to Zagreb to fly wherever they wanted. The US managed to arrange for many of the mujahids to be photographed and fingerprinted as well.[66] A hundred or so stayed on, naturalizing and marrying Bosnian women, including those who settled in Bočinja. Bosnia was no longer a point of convergence, but a point of departure: the ansar moved on to become migrants, students, pilgrims, and refugees once more. Some returned home to pursue ordinary lives, others went out in search of new jihads, in Chechnya, east Africa, Afghanistan, or elsewhere. Over the coming years and no matter where they were, many would find themselves hunted.

Chapter 7

THE GLOBAL WAR ON TERROR

> You decide to take a taxi up there and every cabbie asks you where it is, because they DO NOT KNOW. And how would they know, when leading to the Center is a gravel path through a part of the forest, that one would never imagine ends at some state institution flying the flag of the European Union? There are actually three barracks, and the grounds are enclosed by a five-meter-high steel structure. Even from outside you can tell that it is sooooo cold in there, since a shack is a shack, and you can't catch any glimmer of warmth, or anything that tells you this is a place where human beings live.[1]

ABU HAMZA'S CHILDREN WERE RIGHT: THE TAXI DRIVER DID NOT know how to get to the immigration detention center in Lukavica, a neighborhood on the outskirts of Sarajevo that was allocated to Republika Srpska after the war. Each time we stopped for directions, I thought of this letter I had received from them a few weeks earlier and the sense it conveyed of heading into a strange and unwelcoming land on the other side of a nationalist boundary dividing the city. In the wooded hills behind the Slavija football club stadium, there was an old Yugoslav army barracks housing Serb refugees, its walls adorned with a spray-painted cross surrounded by four S'es in Cyrillic, a nationalist slogan—"Samo sloga Srbina spasava" (Only unity saves the Serbs). Just up the path beyond the barracks stood the detention center, surrounded by black metal fences. Two of the buildings were simple white-walled one-story structures, the third was the permanent facility: two stories of concrete covered with pastel colors, still unfinished and unoccupied. The fence, which also enclosed a small exercise yard with a basketball hoop, was not yet complete either. A dozen or so uniformed guards milled about. Over the main gate flew the flags of both Bosnia and the European Union, a reminder of the €1.2 million grant from Brussels that helped fund construction of the facility.[2]

The Lukavica site was the centerpiece of an emergent apparatus for controlling migration in one of the many areas being reorganized into a buffer zone around the EU. Once part of a Non-Aligned state that sought to bridge east and west, Bosnia-Herzegovina by the late 2000s was enlisted to man the ramparts of fortress Europe. However, at that time the country's first immigration prison wasn't holding migrants caught crossing the border, but six Arabs who were all long-term residents with Bosnian wives and children. All were being held without criminal charges and instead labeled as "threats to national security" on the basis of secret evidence, and all had been on hunger strike for the past few weeks. Over the course of my subsequent visits, there would be steady progress in the center's construction: the path up the hill would be paved over, the fence completed, and the permanent building brought into use. The facility was officially inaugurated in the autumn of 2009, over a year after the arrival of the first detainee, who happened to be Abu Hamza.

My visits began just before the official opening; I came as an unpaid volunteer with the Helsinki Committee for Human Rights in Bosnia-Herzegovina, a local NGO. I had proposed to the Helsinki Committee that I visit and monitor the conditions there and the detainees' cases in light of the hunger strike, since I already knew some of them, spoke Arabic, and had some background working for human rights organizations. They readily agreed. I had with me a bag of pears and bottled water, as Abu Hamza's children told me the hunger strikers would accept food from visitors. After handing over my phone and passport at the gate, I was escorted into one of the prefabricated buildings and sat in a sparsely furnished room near the entrance: there was a radiator, a small square table and a slightly longer rectangular one, a few chairs. The guards brought Abu Hamza a few moments later. He wore a bright orange jalabiyya and a baseball cap. Emblazoned on both was the word BOSNATANAMO in black letters. Although tired and having lost considerable weight from the hunger strike, he seemed in decent spirits or at least happy to receive a visitor. The guard left us alone in the room together. I presented Abu Hamza with the food and water, which he accepted and put to one side. He also had a gift ready for me, one that he described as expensive, since he considered me dear to him (using the same Arabic word for both expensive and dear, ghālī): a bottle of perfume from Saudi Arabia. He took my left hand and placed one drop on it to demonstrate the fragrance's potency. With the exchange of gifts completed—mine, an ambiguous gesture of solidarity with prisoners, his a token of a particular kind of masculinized piety—he started to brief me on the health of the hunger strikers and the status of their cases. Each had lost their Bosnian citizenship and was slated for deportation to their countries of origin. At various points in the conversation, we wandered into talking about his experiences in the war.

This immigration prison has come into view in this final chapter, but it has shaped so many of the stories you have already read in this book. When Abu Hamza was quoted in prior chapters, it was often from our conversations in Lukavica; Hasan the Algerian first told me of his sprawling wartime adventures, gaps and all, while there; Ayman drove me to the cemetery in Livade a few months after his release; when I spoke to Latifa about how she met her husband, it was not long after seeing him in Lukavica myself. If this book is an ethnographic history, the prison grounded its ethnographic present. And now this chapter will take up the most powerful universalism of this book, the one that has overshadowed all that has come before it: the Global War on Terror, whose unsightly acronym GWOT will be retained in these pages. It will focus on carceral mobility, the shuttling of captives from one place to another, a global network of circulation whose nodes include Lukavica, Guantánamo Bay, and prisons in Egypt, Syria, and Tunisia. Like Non-Alignment and peacekeeping as they unfolded in Bosnia, GWOT is a universalism operating primarily through national governments. But it also helps illuminate what happens at the limit of universalisms, the refusal to process certain forms of difference. As Raffi Gregorian, a US diplomat serving as the International Community's deputy viceroy of Bosnia, described the Arabs: "They look alien. They talk alien. They act alien. This is a parochial society that has its own approach to Islam, and they don't fit in."[3] Here, Internationals can cast suspicious Arabs as "foreign" to Bosnia while treating their own foreignness as unremarkable and incidental, merely marking the distance between the universal and the particular. GWOT here presents itself not as a war against Islam but as a war to protect Muslim diversity and tolerance. If Carl Schmitt argued that politics was about the ability to distinguish between one's friend and enemy, then speaking in the name of the universal is about making that decision on behalf of others.[4]

GWOT is but one of many universalisms employed in the imperial formations of the United States, of course. But thinking of GWOT as a universalism in the way that this book has done with the jihad also affords a distinct perspective on the role of sovereignty in US empire. Ever since its fashionable reemergence in anthropology and adjacent fields, sovereignty has often been invoked as an abstract category, a synonym for any kind of power or authority. Instead, our attention to how universalism entails the management of differences points to the need to think of sovereignty in plural, rather than singular terms: as not merely authority over a territory or people but membership within a system of multiple states. The details in the story above—from the EU flag over Lukavica to Abu Hamza's sartorial references to Guantánamo, all in a prison run by the national government of Bosnia—are reminders of this fact. Sovereignty is not the domination that the United States asserts over the world; it is, rather, the legal logic that channels, organizes, and legitimizes that domination through the agency of *other* states that are supposed to be independent and equal. Indeed, the campaign to hunt down former mujahids in Bosnia is an ideal case for studying the mechanics of empire, for two reasons: because the Dayton regime formalizes foreign control in ways that most postcolonial states prefer to hide and because secret State Department cables from the time of my fieldwork obtained by the dissident US soldier Chelsea Manning and released by the Wikileaks organization give a contemporaneous glimpse of the more classic forms of behind-the-scenes influence.

A SOVEREIGN UNDERGROUND

For nearly a generation, the Global War on Terror has been a key organizing principle for the world order, driven by the United States as the primary hegemonic power.[5] Cheerleaders and critics of GWOT alike have tended to accept the premise that it represents what Giorgio Agamben has evocatively—if cryptically—called a "global civil war": a state of emergency that is indefinite in duration, geographical scope, and legality, blurring traditional distinctions between war and peace, domestic and foreign, policing and warfare.[6] And the most notorious and enduring symbol of this campaign has been the detention facility at the US naval base in Guantánamo Bay, Cuba, which we can also refer to by its military designation, GTMO. Mainstream critiques, especially from liberal legal advocates, have framed GTMO as aberrational and "un-American," erasing ongoing forms of racialized—and especially anti-Black—carcerality on the geographical mainland of the United States.[7] More far-reaching scholarly analyses that have analyzed GTMO in the context of US empire focus on the specificities of the base's history in the Caribbean region rather than as part of a contemporary formation of global power.[8] Nearly two decades after GTMO received its first detainees from the war in Afghanistan, both the mainstream and more radical debates tend to share three crucial and interrelated limitations: a focus on torture over captivity more broadly; a preoccupation with GTMO in isolation from the network of prisons of which it was only the most visible; and a focus on litigation in US courts, even though this network is designed to evade their jurisdiction.[9] These limitations allowed GTMO to more easily fade from public attention in favor of debates over drone warfare, buttressing a false narrative that as GWOT normalized, the focus of violence moved from detention to killing.

Close attention to empire, especially as something that can be grasped ethnographically, requires starting with a central dilemma in the shaping of US foreign policy for at least the past century: how to reconcile unequal power relations with the commitment to recognizing the formal juridical equality of independent nation-states. This problematic was at its most intense during the Cold War, when the weakness of the older European empires and the competitive threat posed by the Soviet Union converged with decolonization struggles. Within this framework, international institutions, bilateral agreements, financial instruments, military alliances, arms deals, and development aid emerged as the weapons of choice for securing the dependency of nominally independent states. The result was what Kwame Nkrumah called "neo-colonialism," or "the worst form of imperialism. For those who practise it, it means power without responsibility and for those who suffer from it, it means exploitation without redress."[10] GWOT builds on the structures of Cold War hegemony but departs from them in crucial ways. It marked a shift away from a struggle against a specific ideology of communism advanced by a state adversary and toward a war against an emotion—terror—embodied in amorphous and largely invisible groups and individuals.[11] GWOT continues the long-standing reliance on client states while adding another layer: an open exercise of war powers untethered to any sovereignty but that of the United States, directed against "nations, organizations, or persons" deemed by the president to be enemies.[12] The overlaps, resonances, and frictions between these different forms of sovereignty are where empire is most visible to the ethnographic gaze.

GTMO is thus only one node in a global network of carceral circulation. The best-known locations were managed by the US military—GTMO, Abu Ghraib and Camp Bucca in Iraq, Bagram in Afghanistan—and there were the secret CIA-run "black sites" in Romania, Poland, Thailand, and elsewhere. But most facilities do not operate under the flag of the United States—indeed, GWOT in this respect should be thought of more as a set of practices that activate and make short-term use of certain spaces as sites of captivity, including hotel rooms and private planes.[13] Let us think of this as a kind of sovereign underground: a network of sites, practices, technologies, and discourses that is transnational in nature. Parts are above ground and visible, and others are not; but it is altogether shaped by the US imperative of pursuing its goals through the framework of client-state sovereignties—or, on occasion, nonstate militias and rebel forces—whenever possible so as to minimize responsibilities and costs.[14] This network demands empirical investigation from the bottom up and in cross-sections, in terms of the interlocking juridical structures at work linking the US to its client states and, as important, its client states to each other.

The famous case of the six Algerians taken from Bosnia to GTMO has often stood as an example of GWOT's terrifyingly global scope because they were detained far from the recognized battlefield of Afghanistan. But what has escaped widespread notice is that they were sent to Cuba only after the Algerian government declined to accept custody.[15] At around the same time, several Egyptians and Jordanians were forcibly repatriated as suspected terrorists—including Imad el-Misri, who was reportedly tortured upon arrival in Egypt and spent seven years in prison.[16] These deportations were also orchestrated by the United States, but attracted little attention and were merely seen as routine administrative matters of immigration law.[17] The disparate destinations for detention is perhaps best explained by reference to the transnational structures of security collaboration under US hegemony. While Algeria cooperated broadly with the US in GWOT, the incredibly close operational relationships enjoyed by the CIA and its Egyptian counterparts made the latter an especially willing and trusted proxy jailer. An important episode in this relationship played out during the Bosnian war: in September 1995, the CIA oversaw the abduction of Talʿat Fu'ad al-Qasimi, a leader of the Islamic Group, while he was traveling through Croatia on his way to visit the Katiba. Al-Qasimi was never heard from again, most likely shipped back to Egypt and executed.[18] It was the first known case of "extraordinary rendition," the US practice of seizing individuals abroad and sending them to third countries for detention, interrogation, and torture. Indeed, the small number of Egyptians held in GTMO overall compared to other Arab nationalities—a fact that has also received virtually no attention—suggests that many of them were sent directly home from Afghanistan or Pakistan.

With the broader sovereign underground in mind, it becomes possible to appreciate GTMO's special place in it anew. For it *was* an aberration of sorts: not in the liberal sense of being a prison outside the law, but in being one whose extreme public visibility precluded the kind of flexibility and discretion on which GWOT captivity practices ordinarily thrive.[19] The turn to using GTMO in all likelihood signified a momentary crisis of confidence in late 2001 when the US was unsure about the reliability of its partners: after all, most of the 9/11 hijackers had come from a trusted ally, Saudi Arabia. And in Afghanistan, captives held by US forces and their local allies at the Qalaʿ-e-Jangi fort rose up, killed a CIA officer, and resisted for a week before being crushed through aerial bombardment. But this panic soon passed and transfers to GTMO largely stopped by 2003. It was the older pattern of arms-length detention through local clients that has endured and continued to sustain GWOT. During the 2006 invasion of Somalia, Ethiopian forces seized and rendered over one hundred foreign Muslims of various nationalities. Later on, the CIA was able to work in the country directly, using the facilities of local militia.[20] A decade later, the United Arab Emirates and its own proxy armed groups in southern Yemen opened detention centers in which US personnel have also worked.[21] And as the self-declared Islamic State in Iraq and Syria (ISIS) lost territory in 2017 and 2018, thousands were held in internment camps in eastern Syria run by Kurdish forces under the watchful eye of US commandos—including many European Muslims whose governments openly expressed a preference that they be killed rather than returned home.[22] These sites have enabled the US to warehouse, interrogate, and dispose of thousands of more people with far greater flexibility and far less scrutiny than at GTMO.

The GWOT captivity practices described above also depend heavily on separating local Muslims from foreign ones and treating the latter as worthy of special mistreatment. This move is a consummately universalist one: deciding which differences are contingent and which are absolute, in sifting Good Muslim from Bad Muslim. Circling back to Bosnia and its place in carceral networks beyond its ties with GTMO, we can see this dynamic at work at various moments, even in situations not obviously connected to GWOT. In the years since the war, the International Community has been frequently criticized, not so much for bringing a new form of colonialism to Bosnia, but for being only half-hearted and disengaged in its efforts to corral the bickering nationalist parties. The result has been a cycle of dependency: locals engage in dysfunctional politics, Internationals are forced to intervene, locals are then disempowered again. Yet whenever the situation of any foreign Muslim deemed to be suspicious came up, Internationals acted with unusual decisiveness. The International Community initially struggled to reverse the effects of ethnic cleansing and to encourage refugees to return home often to areas where they would be part of a vulnerable minority. NATO staunchly refused to get involved—until the time came to break up the community of jihad veterans in Bočinja. In July 2000, US troops descended on the village, and the Arabs quietly left the homes, which were then mostly returned to their former Serb owners.[23] Several years later, the first person prosecuted for war crimes by the newly established State Court of Bosnia-Herzegovina was an Iraqi—not a mujahid, but a merchant living in Travnik from the days of Non-Alignment accused of helping Abu Jaʿfar when he abducted Croat civilians in October 1993 in the incident described in the Interlude.[24] Time and again, Arabs were constitutive outsiders: acting against them was one of the very few things Serbs, Croats, Bosniaks, and Internationals could all agree on. They were a foreign threat of concern to other foreigners. This story unfolded on an even larger scale and at greater length in struggles over citizenship and the very definition of foreignness in Bosnia.

THE REMAINDER OF CITIZENSHIP

The weeks after 9/11 were in Bosnia, as in many other places, a time of hasty decisions. On October 5, Imad was stripped of his Bosnian citizenship and deported to Egypt the next day.[25] A month later, authorities canceled dozens more citizenships held by Arabs, a move that was reversed by courts on appeal. Finally, in early January 2002, police transferring the Algerian Six to the airport for handover to US forces—in defiance of an order from a local court—faced angry protesters. The deportations were later deemed unlawful, and the public outcry over these moves was among the many factors that cost the ruling Social Democratic Party half of its seats in the lower house of the national legislature during elections later that year. Henceforth, attempts to connect Bosnia to GWOT networks of captivity would have to be more careful and legalistic—although with procedural safeguards that were far weaker than, for example, those enjoyed even by accused war criminals.

The first step in rendering suspicious Arabs deportable was removing their Bosnian citizenship. Under a wartime law, foreigners in the army could obtain citizenship nearly automatically; up to seven or eight hundred "Afro-Asians" did so either through this provision or by marriage to Bosnian women.[26] In late 2005, the Bosnian parliament passed a set of amendments that revived and gave sweeping new powers to the special State Commission for the Review of Naturalization Decisions of Foreign Citizens, charged with reviewing all cases dating to independence in 1992 and up to 2006. The amendments empowered the State Commission to cancel naturalizations in cases for which "regulations in force in the territory of Bosnia and Herzegovina at the time of the naturalisation had not been applied."[27] In effect, citizenship could be withdrawn if any procedural irregularity was discovered, regardless of its gravity or intent, or even whether the individual involved was at fault—a broader standard than perhaps in any other country in the world.[28] The State Commission conducted its reviews in secret, and the amendments further gutted the appeal procedures. Notably, denationalization was not permitted if it would result in statelessness; in other words, the preservation of another, presumably "original," citizenship was crucial as an address for future deportation.

Fadhil the Iraqi's case demonstrated the effect of these new powers. According to the State Commission, his citizenship was revoked because he allegedly held two different Bosnian naturalization certificates. Fadhil explained that his first naturalization certificate used his father's name as the last name, following his Iraqi passport. The second one was issued a month later using a tribal name [laqab] instead, because that was on his Bosnian marriage certificate and army papers. This kind of confusion was unsurprising because in Iraq last names based on a nuclear family unit are not universal: everyone knew the country's erstwhile ruler as Saddam Hussein (after his father) not Saddam al-Tikriti (after the tribe). And because both documents had the same naturalization number, Fadhil therefore assumed that the second certificate simply superseded the previous one. I watched Fadhil explain this bureaucratic mishap to an unsympathetic human rights lawyer in Lukavica one day, only to be berated for not knowing the proper procedures. She agreed that Fadhil was not intentionally deceiving anyone—after all, why would a man who lived in the same place with the same family for several decades forge different citizenship documents with the same naturalization number?—but the second certificate should have clearly indicated that it was canceling out the previous one. Although Fadhil had recently obtained certification from an Iraqi embassy that the names on the two documents were indeed referring to the same person, the lawyer was unmoved. Fadhil found decades of his bureaucratic existence wiped out, and the lawyer expressed frustration that officials do not respect the rules in issuing paperwork.

The State Commission makes sense less as a purely authoritarian act of suspending the law and more as a proceduralist campaign dictated by powers beyond and above the state. When viewed from up close, states of exception often look more like states of saturation of ordinary bureaucratic procedures, a plenitude of law rather than a hollowing of it.[29] When sovereignty is thought of as multiple but unequal, rather than singular and supreme, it is possible to identify a different kind of discretionary power: not the actions of sovereigns in their own spaces, but the actions of sovereigns *through* the spaces of others. In these situations it may be impossible to tell if a state's actions should be understood on their own terms or as dictated by an external power—and that may very well be the point.

Again, the Bosnia citizenship case is instructive. By law, the State Commission's nine members included three Internationals: one was a US army officer attached as a legal advisor to NATO headquarters in Sarajevo; another was a British immigration police officer. And despite the State Commission's apparently comprehensive mandate, no one had any doubt that it was primarily aimed at ex-mujahids and other Arabs. In a classified cable, the US embassy described reviewing the citizenship of ex-mujahids as a "top USG counter terrorism priorit[y]."[30] The State Commission met behind closed doors and within a few months began mailing out brief decisions—one or two pages each—depriving people of citizenship. Abu Hamza was at the top of the list and was informed shortly after our first meeting in December 2006 that he was no longer a Bosnian citizen. There had been no trial or evidentiary hearing.

Over the course of the next twenty months, Abu Hamza allowed himself to become the test case for the new citizenship law, actively litigating it at every turn even as the courts continuously rubber-stamped the State Commission's decisions. He sought, with varying degrees of success, to enlist more legalistic allies among local and international NGOs. With my own background in human rights issues, I contributed to these efforts in assisting the Helsinki Committee and Human Rights Watch in the preparation of *amicus curiae* briefs. Abu Hamza pleaded his case with anyone who would listen, compiling multivolume books of paperwork—citizenship and immigration documents, school and army records, birth certificates for his children—dating from his arrival in Yugoslavia in the early 1980s, a testament to the sheer facticity of his long-running bureaucratic existence in the country. Nevertheless, the letters continued to arrive informing Arabs that they had lost their citizenships. The names of those who could not be reached by post were published in Bosnia's official gazette, some 660 altogether.

The US continued working behind the scenes to circumvent local opposition. In May 2007, the ambassador complained to Washington that Security Minister Tarik Sadović was attempting to enact a regulation that would exempt those with children in Bosnia from expulsion, "a measure that would render many of the former mujahideen undeportable."[31] Two months later, the newly arrived High Representative Miroslav Lajčák publicly admonished Sadović to carry out "the tough actions needed in this area," in order for the EU to relax its visa requirements for Bosnian citizens.[32] Meanwhile, US embassy officials took to boxing in the recalcitrant Sadović by cultivating direct relationships with the agencies under his nominal control: the embassy even hosted a lunch for security and law enforcement chiefs who openly criticized him.[33] All this time, the embassy was quietly promoting a new immigration law that would establish a detention regime and facilitate deportation, and drawing up a list of several dozen whose expulsion would be a priority.[34] Things took an unexpected turn when, in early 2009, the chairman of the State Commission, Vjekoslav Vuković—also an assistant minister of security in charge of fighting organized crime and corruption—found himself arrested in Croatia in connection with a suspected mob murder there.[35] The State Commission's work ground to a halt, but by that time its main task of denationalizing Arabs was complete.

One of the more bizarre incidents in the public campaign over the issue came in the spring of 2008, while Abu Hamza's appeal was still pending. The entry for Bosnia in the US State Department's annual terrorism report praised the work of the State Commission for, among other things, stripping the citizenship of someone on a UN terrorism list, naming him as "Abu Hamza al-Masri (Imad Al-Hussein)." The real (and very much publicly available) name of the Abu Hamza you have been reading about is indeed Imad al-Husin, but he is Syrian so he is known as Abu Hamza al-Suri, not Abu Hamza al-Masri. Abu Hamza al-Masri is an altogether different person: a notorious Egyptian exile then living in the UK, missing one eye and both hands from an explosion in Afghanistan.[36] Upon discovering this claim, Abu Hamza sent me a furious email demanding to know if it would be possible to sue the US government for libel in its courts. Although there was no obvious legal remedy, he got lucky: international human rights organizations raised the issue, and the State Department took the unusual step of issuing a public correction and apology.[37] Given the importance of documents such as the annual terrorism report in setting public expectations and doling out criticism and praise, the incident underscored the transnational contours of debate over the issue. As with other Bosnians, Abu Hamza was forced to deal with the powers that mattered—not so much the state under which he lived, but the foreign governments behind it—through public statements and the media in lieu of traditional avenues of official appeal and interaction.

Abu Hamza's efforts were not purely focused on litigation, however. He and Ayman formed a group called Ensarije—Bosnian for the adjective for ansar—complete with a website, to mobilize support for their cause and to share the latest information. Here, calling the organization Ensarije seemed almost an invitation to Bosnians to reciprocate the sacrifices rendered during the war. Those veterans who were willing to speak out gave a series of interviews to Bosnian and foreign media to argue their case.[38] Ensarije circulated a photograph of the disabled veteran Abu ʿAli from Morocco, holding his denationalization order in one hand and in the other a sign with a verse written on it that he would quote frequently during our meetings. Loosely translated to preserve the sense of rhyme, it said, "It was all 'Welcome brother' / In time of war / But 'Farewell, brother' / Now that it's no more" [Kada je bio rat / tada bujrum brat / a sada kada nema / rata onda / Allahimanet / brate].

From the beginning, mobilizing people was a challenge. When I first met Abu Hamza, he told me that Ensarije had been denied permission to register as an organization and that many of the Brothers were still reluctant to publicly defend themselves in the manner that he and Ayman did. Nevertheless, a few spirited protests were organized. One of them was held in February 2008 and drew several thousand people, filling the main square in Zenica between the old cinema (then closed for renovation) and the dilapidated socialist-era general department store (Robna kuća). The speakers included an imam, representatives of war veterans' and invalids' groups, Arab ex-mujahids, and their families. The children spoke of their fear of having their fathers taken away. Ayman the Syrian told the crowd that some Bosnian politicians wanted to expel Abu Hamza in the name of the people, "though I am sure this is not in your name, but in their name only. You are against this, and the proof is your gathering here today!" Another speaker, a long-haired man disabled during the war, spoke from his wheelchair: "I have no beard, but I carry in my bosom a human heart, like the heart of Abu Hamza." Two days later, the American embassy reported on the rally in a confidential cable to Washington, promising superiors that they were "working with Bosnian law enforcement agencies to ensure they are making adequate preparations for an eventual deportation of

Abu Hamza."[39] The efforts paid off: in October 2008, the Constitutional Court upheld the decision to revoke Abu Hamza's Bosnian citizenship, and he was taken to the still-incomplete detention center at Lukavica within days.

Abu Hamza and Ensarije were making full use of classic institutions of civil society and liberal citizenship—registering NGOs, holding rallies, filing lawsuits—to call for strengthening the legal category of citizenship. In this sense, they were pointing to a deeper structural problem with the post-Dayton dispensation, namely its elevation of national belonging over state citizenship.[40] The Bosnian constitution stresses political belonging to one of the three constituent peoples: Bosniaks, Serbs, and Croats. Those who do not identify with any of these groups, called "Others," cannot run for the presidency or stand for the upper house of the national legislature.[41] And even members of the constituent peoples are effectively barred from certain elected offices in the two main entities that make up the country, the Federation of Bosnia-Herzegovina and Republika Srpska. In the constitutional arithmetic of the Dayton protectorate—the attempt to balance an equation between three nations, two entities, and one state—Others are an irreducible remainder. Alongside Jews, Roma, Albanians, and recent Chinese immigrants—to say nothing of the offspring of "mixed" marriages—naturalized Arab citizens found themselves caught in the interstices of this structure. And by being placed in the category of "Other" rather than Bosniak, Abu Hamza and the other Arabs had little choice but to demand rigorous standards for arbitrary deprivations of citizenship as well as safeguards against deportation to torture or mistreatment and respect for the sanctity of family rights. GWOT narratives presented the denaturalization campaign as a struggle between an International Community attempting to build a non-nationalist civic state versus foreign Muslims seeking to destroy it. But it was actually those labeled as "foreign fighters" who had the greatest stake in upholding the institution of citizenship in Bosnia.

CIRCULATIONS, INTERRUPTED

Over the course of my visits to the Lukavica detention center, the authorities started supplementing the Arab "security detainees" with newer arrivals, migrants who had recently been caught after crossing the border. These were Arabs, Iranians, Turks, and others, many of whom fled Greece after the 2010 economic crisis. Lukavica not only became a site for Bosnia's role as a buffer state on the edges of the EU, but was also catching migratory movements between its member states as well, highlighting the fractured and uneven geographies of Europe and its boundaries.[42] The security detainees, long tarred as foreigners despite the years they spent in Bosnia, paradoxically became a bridge between the new arrivals and the authorities. Once, when I was sitting with Fadhil in the meeting room in the prefab facility, a guard was performing intake on an Arab, but was struggling to explain the need to remove his belt and sign certain forms. Fadhil interrupted our conversation to walk over and facilitate, an almost automatic gesture of intermediation very much in line with the work that he had done in the Katiba during the war.

Relations with Fadhil, Abu Hamza, and the others who had been living in Bosnia were considerably easier for the guards to manage also thanks to sheer long-term familiarity, even though the deteriorating relations affected all the inmates. Abu Hamza became a sort of dean of the detainees. His "shaykhly" appearance—the very same visual cues that mark him as foreign in the eyes of many Bosnians—earned him some measure of respect and also made him a useful interlocutor with the staff. "You know, non-Arab Muslims [aʿājim] tend to respect shaykhs more than even Arabs do. So with my beard and the way I look there is some respect. When I come to the TV room, one of them will give up his seat for me." Abu Hamza also became a public spokesman for the security detainees, not unlike back in the days of the Bočinja community. His family, especially one of his daughters, was the most active in reaching out to the media, and he would often speak for the group before visiting delegations. During our meetings, he would bring his leather-bound notebook, filled with various scribblings and notes in both the local language and Arabic of ideas for organizations to lobby, people to speak to, human rights reports about conditions in Syria, and so on. Phone numbers, addresses, doodles cluttered the margins. Pursuing separate legal cases about his asylum and residency permit in the Bosnian courts as well as his application before the European Court of Human Rights, Abu Hamza was persistently litigious and hands-on, guiding his lawyers as much as they advised him.[43] Sometimes this made me uncomfortable, especially when he seemed to know more about some of the other detainees' legal cases than they did (they often shared the same lawyer). Our conversations, always conducted in Arabic and frequently without the presence of guards (who seemed bored out of their wits even when sitting in the room with us), meandered between discussing health conditions, his legal cases, and his memories from before prison.

Abu Hamza's family was able to visit him regularly, and indeed it was these kinship ties that were also marked as a source of threat. The Bosnian state has largely adopted discourses of otherness regarding the Muslim family as a locus of practices unnerving to the prevailing order. That it can do so in a country where so many identify as Muslim only testifies to the power of this order. This was spelled out most explicitly as Abu Hamza's case made its way slowly through the European Court of Human Rights. As a transnational forum staggering under the weight of its enormous docket consisting of cases from forty countries submitted in multiple languages, the Court rarely holds hearings in person. Most cases, like Abu Hamza's, are concluded purely on an exchange of papers that must be translated, copied, and circulated among the parties. In response to the points in Abu Hamza's petition on the potential threat to his family rights under the European Convention of Human Rights if deported, the Bosnian government articulated a vision of belonging that is worth quoting at length:

> In particular, without any prejudice, the Respondent Party notes that until to-date the applicant has retained his typically Arabic [*sic*] appearance (manner of clothing, hair style and long beard). Also, his family has accepted and consistently followed his manner of living, based on some very strict and original forms of Islam. This is corroborated by the fact that the applicant's wife is wearing the face cover, [and] although wearing of face cover is not banned in [Bosnia], this fashion of dressing is a rarity and is mainly present among the members of the Arabic ethnic minority in the country. In reference with this, the Respondent Party particularly wishes to point out that Bosnia and Herzegovina is based on a multi-cultural, multi-religious and multiethnic society with a strictly secular political and legal order. However, from the aforementioned circumstances of the case, it is obvious that the wife of the applicant, although a [Bosnian] citizen, has fully accepted the Arabic [*sic*] tradition, culture and customs faithfully followed by her husband, who has never stopped this so that all of the cited circumstances of the case are indicative of

> the conclusion that the applicant has never developed any particular social or cultural links with Bosnia and Herzegovina.[44]

The brief suggests—"without any prejudice," to be sure—that piety practices such as wearing a veil or long beard should be construed as foreign. This marks the gap between notions of diversity—a "multi-cultural, multi-religious, and multiethnic society"—and those of secularism, providing a stark example of how the latter enacts its own exclusions. But here we can place that analysis in a broader logic that also incorporates challenges to the prevailing order, such as that represented by the Bosnian jihad. Note that in the passage quoted above, the submission glosses "strict and original forms of Islam" as "the Arabic tradition." Yet as we saw in Chapter 4, this conflation of culture and Islam is exactly what mujahids as well as many other practicing Muslims worldwide have rejected time and again. The jihad exhibited a tension inherent in any universalist project—including those based on some notion of human rights—insofar as it seeks to incarnate values that are held out to all mankind yet have a particular provenance. Mujahids and other Salafi activists readily conceded that the practices they promoted were not necessarily the norm in Arab countries and should certainly not be seen as "Arab," but rather as "Islamic"—even if they also at times operated under the loose assumption that Arabs generally knew more about Islam than Bosnians. The submission implicitly rejects the universalist aspirations embodied in Abu Hamza's family's choices of bodily presentation to the world by rendering them as another particularity to be managed and removed.

Meanwhile, the human rights groups tended to have less to say about Lukavica, fewer visitors came to the prison, and media coverage receded. The prisoners quietly abandoned the partial hunger strike. Bosnians who had supported the Arabs also seemed to be losing patience or energy. When I first met Jusuf, one of the Bosnian veterans of the Katiba, in 2010 he said that I was the only foreigner he had met who wanted to write about the issue of the Arabs fairly and that it made no sense to criminalize people like Abu Hamza. Nine months later, he asked me why I was still focusing on the Lukavica situation, in light of so many other pressing problems in the world.

On the eve of the October 2010 elections, Abu Hamza's family released a photograph of him in his orange Bosnatanamo garb with a stolid expression on his face alongside the following caption: "After two years in PRISON in the Immigration Center, we have nothing more to say: THE PEOPLE KNOW!" (Figure 12). The last phrase, "the people know" [Narod zna] was also the campaign slogan of the SDA party. It invoked an allegedly self-evident nationalist appeal—"The People" being Bosniaks, who simply "know" that the SDA is the right choice. This open-endedness invited any number of subversions. On "Narod zna!" posters around Sarajevo, for example, one could find plastered a counter-message from the activist group Dosta! [Enough!]: "The people know . . . that we are thieves" [Narod zna . . . da smo lopovi]. In the case of Abu Hamza's family, however, the inversion of the SDA slogan was different, an invocation of debts unpaid to foreign volunteers who participated in the war, an attempt at pricking guilty consciences. This poster turns that which *need* not be said into something that *dare* not be said: it intimates that "The People Know" that the government is betraying the Arabs to the Americans and should do something about it.

This image of the foreign volunteer, cast into oblivion and making a moral claim on the nation for which he fought, into which he married, but to which he may no longer belong, calls to mind a particular figure of exclusion: the enemy as declared by a universalist project such as GWOT. But the image pushes back, too. For Abu Hamza's BOSNATANAMO photo can be read not just as a claim to nationalist belonging, but as a different imagining of how the Bosnian nation and the umma should interrelate: in other words, a different set of terms for universalism. His beard and jalabiyya signal Islamic piety and the solidarity it promises. But the color and writing on his garments gesture to US hegemony and specifically to GTMO. He is implicitly inviting Bosnians to reject the prerogative of the US to determine on their behalf who speaks for the universal and who is a mere foreigner. The photo says to Bosnian Muslims, I'm not a foreign Arab, I'm a fellow Muslim. I am your brother, don't you remember me?

MEN IN THE SHADE

While Abu Hamza and a few other Arabs in Bosnia actively fought their deportations and languished in detention, GWOT continued to acquire and circulate captives around the world. Reda Seyam, the Egyptian with German citizenship

Nakon dvije godine
ZATVORA u
Imigracionom centru mi
nemamo ništa za reći.
NAROD ZNA!
Porodica Imada Al
Husina, Abu Hamze
BOSNATANAMO
BOSNATANAMO

FIGURE 12. Photo of Abu Hamza released by his family to appeal to Bosnian Muslims for support.

whose marital woes in Bočinja were mentioned at the end of Chapter 4, was arrested in Indonesia under suspicion of being connected to the 2002 bombing in Bali. He at least had the relative good fortune of being escorted home by German intelligence to keep him out of CIA hands.[45] Another veteran, who oversaw the fighters' kitchens during the war, was abducted somewhere in Africa and rendered to Egypt. From Bosnia, a few deportations quietly went ahead even before the citizenship cancellations were completed. Badreddine Ferchichi was sent back to Tunisia on September 1, 2006, in an operation that "required virtually no [US government] handholding." Once Ferchichi was home, his jailers reportedly suspended him upside down from the ceiling and beat him; a military tribunal convicted him for the crime of unauthorized enlistment in a foreign army.[46] In late 2007, an Algerian, Atau Mimun, was also deported.[47]

Then in 2010, the uprisings that would become known as the Arab Spring had the side effect of making deportation from Bosnia easier. Latifa's husband was expelled to Tunisia without his family shortly after the revolution on the strength of the argument that with a new regime in place, human rights concerns were no longer an issue. This was especially poignant in the experiences of Zayd from Egypt. Zayd was connected to many of the people who have already appeared in this book: he was married to the widow of Abu al-Harith, which makes him the brother-in-law of Nasir, the self-styled Islamic scholar who was Imad's interpreter during the war. I met Zayd in 2010, shortly after he was declared a threat to national security and detained in Lukavica just before US Secretary of State Hillary Clinton's visit to Bosnia-Herzegovina. It seems that Zayd had been under surveillance for a while, which by itself was unsurprising: he was a veteran of the Katiba and after the war spent some time working in the Kerama company run by the džemat in Bočinja. Zayd had a degree in veterinary medicine in Egypt and was one of the workers in Milan who joined the jihad after encountering Bosnian refugees in Italy and hearing their stories.

Zayd and his family had settled in a cluster of homes set aside for widows and children of war martyrs on the outskirts of Sarajevo, and Zayd did his best to earn a living by peddling various wares. The location was especially convenient, since Zayd's eldest son—the biological son of Abu al-Harith—had won a scholarship to a prestigious high school nearby. And because

Zayd never took Bosnian citizenship, the drama over the State Commission had largely passed him by. But one day, press reports appeared based on anonymous official statements intimating that a suspiciously large sum of money—the rough equivalent of $US24,000—had been wired to his bank account, far beyond what a simple peddler should have. Zayd's explanation was more straightforward: Abu al-Harith's family in Libya had sent the money so Zayd could eventually build a house for his eldest son. Zayd claimed that Abu al-Harith's family had even made a sworn statement to the Bosnian authorities, communicated through the Libyan embassy in Sarajevo, attesting that the money was for lawful ends. The state was unmoved: notwithstanding his immigration status being otherwise proper, Zayd was deported as a threat to national security, after having spent nearly two decades in Bosnia. The same farflung kinship networks that were helping to sustain the family after the jihad had in the end been used to justify their violent disruption by the state.

Zayd landed in Cairo on a plane accompanied by two Bosnian police officers. Unlike with Imad's deportation back in 2001, he was released after only a brief questioning. The regime had apparently "closed the Bosnia file" a few years previously, possibly in light of its successful co-optation of the groups that it fought so bitterly in the 1990s. With Mubarak now gone, participation in the Bosnian war was a distant enough memory not to merit an automatic trip to prison upon return home. But by the same token, Zayd had trouble attracting any interest from the Egyptian human rights groups, and my own efforts to help in this regard also went nowhere.

A month after Zayd was deported to Egypt, I managed to meet him again on a hot summer day in a park in the Alf Maskan neighborhood of Cairo. Zayd had come from his parents' home in al-Mansoura, 120 kilometers away, two days earlier to pick up his wife and children arriving from Sarajevo. Tahrir Square was reoccupied by protesters that month, recreating the atmosphere of the eighteen days of the previous winter that had shaken the world. Elsewhere, things still seemed "normal" on the surface: the park, with its outdoor restaurants and a running track nestled between congested surroundings, was part of the sprawling assemblage of businesses run by the Ministry of Defense. Zayd brought three of his children to the park, who were exhausted by the trip and disoriented by being in Egypt for the first time. Tagging along was another Egyptian from the Katiba who had been expelled from Bosnia with Imad in the months after 9/11. As we strolled in the park, Zayd's son told me in his stumbling Arabic that he kept up ties with the family of his biological father and had visited them in Libya four times, although communications were difficult with war raging in the country. As we sat down at a table, a waiter demanded that we order beverages from him and that the ones we had purchased from a neighboring kiosk were from a separate business. This made Zayd very uncomfortable, as he did not want to buy more overpriced sodas, but also strenuously objected when I tried to pay. The waiter let us sit for a few minutes for free. When he came back, Zayd offered to pay him five Egyptian pounds to leave us alone, but he refused. When we tried to buy only one drink, the waiter balked again since there were five of us. We had to order a minimum of three drinks. Zayd was frustrated, the kids said they didn't want anything, but at the same time it was one of the few shady spots to sit in the park on an oppressively hot day. Eventually we gave in and got two juices and a soda.

The waiter's unsubtle prodding of Zayd and his family reminded me of Palestinian writer and revolutionary Ghassan Kanafani's novella *Men in the Sun*, a famous literary demonstration of the vicissitudes of statelessness. In Kanafani's story, Palestinian refugees seeking work in Kuwait are tragically caught in the interstices of a nation-state system, metaphorically and literally trapped at a border crossing, where they suffocate while hiding in a tanker truck in the stifling desert sun. In a contemporary world order that uses postcolonial sovereignty and citizenship as a form through which to structure unequal powers relations, the dilemma is quite different. This system *does* have a place for such men—their national homes—and can work to put them back there, with violence and at the expense of lives that have become inextricably transnational. Once again, it is worth noting that in the campaign against ex-mujahids in Bosnia, rendering people stateless was not an option: a stateless person can become a burden for the government of the territory in which she finds herself. Rather than being forced to wait at a border, destroyed by the sun in Kanafani's sense, Zayd and others like him find themselves experiencing an inverted relationship between mobility and captivity, rendered home and expected to disappear however uncomfortably into the shadows of "ordinary" national belonging.

Zayd's difficulty in finding a place in the shade only compounded his sense of being out of place in the land of his birth. He no longer had friends, colleagues, or even much in the way of memories. Zayd told me he was in very bad shape [taʿbān jiddan jiddan], upset at the Bosnian authorities, the Egyptian embassy, and his own lawyers for his humiliating experience at Sarajevo airport, when he said he was prevented from submitting an asylum request in front of his family. His only thoughts were to find ways to somehow get back to Bosnia, despite the remoteness of that possibility, and to recover some personal effects that the police had seized from him and never given back. Although his wife and children were going to spend the summer with him in Egypt, the kids' schooling meant that they would have to return to Sarajevo. He didn't know what he was going to do. The day before, as I accompanied him on a visit to a local human rights organization, I asked Zayd if he felt any strangeness [ghurba] in Cairo. He looked at me and replied, "I feel ghurba in all of Egypt."

SPLIT DECISIONS

On February 7, 2012, the European Court of Human Rights in Strasbourg simultaneously decided two cases of men I had come to know over the course of this research. In Abu Hamza's case, the Court decided that returning him to Syria would present an unjustifiable risk of torture or ill-treatment. Furthermore, the Court ruled that immigration detention had to be linked to deportation or a related goal; "national security" by itself was not good enough. Under the Court's ruling, Bosnia could either seek to deport Abu Hamza to another country or release him.[48] For four additional years, Bosnia refused to do either, until a new law limited total detention in Lukavica to eighteen months.[49] After over seven years in captivity, Abu Hamza walked free. When I saw him last in 2018, he was still barred by the authorities from leaving the Sarajevo area but overall in good spirits—at the urging of one of his daughters, a veteran of many marathons, he had taken up bicycling.

As for Fadhil the Iraqi, he lost. Despite the dynamics of his hometown of Kirkuk—caught in a three-way power struggle between Kurds, Sunni Arabs, and Turkmen—the Court opined that "a general situation of violence" was generally not sufficient reason to outlaw deportation, except in extreme cases. Fadhil's lawyers had argued that being repatriated while labeled a security threat would signal to Iraqi authorities that he was a Sunni "jihadist" and put him at risk of ill treatment. But because Fadhil had visited family in Kirkuk in the early years of the US occupation before his Bosnian legal troubles began, the Court reasoned that it would be safe for him to be deported there. After all, the situation in Iraq had improved.[50] Two years later, the emergence to global prominence of ISIS would turn Kirkuk into a frontline city, ruled by Kurdish forces until 2017. Nevertheless, as with Abu Hamza, the Court concluded that Fadhil's imprisonment at Lukavica on the basis of "national security" alone was unlawful. For the sixteen months he spent in detention before the start of deportation proceedings, the Court awarded him some compensation: two thousand Euros.

In both cases, the Court declined to rule on the family rights issues involved: their decades in Bosnia, their wives, children, and grandchildren all counted for very little in the analysis. Abu Hamza and Fadhil were treated as individuals pleading for recognition as potential victims of torture and extralegal detention, and no more. And in their own ways, they remained suspended. Abu Hamza's Bosnian citizenship was never restored, so he remained an unlawful migrant, with no right to work or access to other basic services. A handful of other "security detainees" such as Ayman and Hasan were in a similar situation: they had succeeded in getting the courts to overturn the cancellation of their Bosnian citizenships, but without obtaining any kind of recognized legal status. Most of the others in Lukavica were eventually deported. Fadhil was in a third category. Having been transferred to house arrest earlier, he concluded he had no choice but to flee the country where he had lived for over thirty years. With the two thousand Euros he had been awarded as compensation by the Strasbourg court for the violation of his human rights, Fadhil paid a smuggler to get him to western Europe, where he has sought refuge and stability ever since. Separated from his family, he has frequent panic attacks and nightmares.

Acknowledgments

Acknowledgments in a book are the scholarly equivalent of a bankruptcy process: they are a declaration of debts (and hence an indirect blueprint of assets) and an acceptance of personal responsibility in the hope of redemption, setting the stage for an imposition of order among creditors whose logic is very much open to question.

Thanks go to those who decided, at not inconsiderable risk, to welcome me into their lives: not only those who traveled to Bosnia-Herzegovina, but their families and friends as well. Some are named in this study but a great many more are not. During my time in Bosnia, I also benefited enormously from the hospitality, insight, and criticisms of many people. Those who can be mentioned publicly include Dino Abazović, Ahmet Alibašić, Laura Boushnak, Tarik Bushnak, Srđan Dizdarević, Jasminka Džumhur, Salma Ettarashani, Amira Grahovac, Mladen Grahovac, Vedran Grahovac, Bernard Harbaš, Nada Jačimović-Harbaš, Muhamed Jusić, Dženita Karić, Amar Kasap, Peter Lippman, Andreja Mesarič, Sabina Nikšić, Sabrina Perić, Irfan Subašić, Sadžida Tulić, Sumeja Tulić, and Sarah Wagner. For their help with libraries and archives, I owe thanks to Dragan Golubović, Fatima Kadić-Žutić, and Asim Zubčević. In working on rights issues in Bosnia, Harisa Bačvić, Clive Baldwin, Eva Ottavy, Caroline Ravaud, Luiza Toscane, and Wanda Troszczynska van Genderen were crucial collaborators.

The research and writing of this book were supported by the Wenner-Gren Foundation for Anthropological Research and the American Council of Learned Societies. A Paul & Daisy Soros Fellowship funded much of my legal training. A workshop to discuss a draft of this book was funded by the Center for International Social Science Research and the Department of Anthropology Lichtstern Fund at the University of Chicago. I owe special thanks to Laleh Khalili, Natalie Rothman, Noah Salomon, Nikhil Pal Singh, and Lisa Wedeen for participating in this workshop and improving the manuscript in great measure. Other financial support for this research came from the Columbia University Committee on Global Thought and from the Asia Center, Center for European Studies, Center for Middle Eastern Studies, and Department of Anthropology, all at Harvard University.

Several research assistants helpfully collated, transcribed, and summarized materials in Arabic, Bahasa, Bosnian, Turkish, and Urdu: Francesca Chubb-Confer, Dijana Grahovac, Tesbih Habbal, Patrick Lewis, Branka Stojković-Megrant, Audrey Teo, and Radmila Turanjanin. Ayan Kassim and Nida Paracha also helped to consolidate and collate editorial feedback on the manuscript.

The coming together of this book as a physical object relied on many talents. Omar Khouri created the image on the cover which was inspired by the story that opens the third chapter, in a style inflected by a Silk Road aesthetic that vividly captures the sense of wonder and mischief I have often felt while viewing the jihad through Chinese eyes. Dale Mertes produced the maps inside. I thank them both for their patience, aesthetic vision, and painstaking attention to detail. At Stanford University Press, Kate Wahl has been an early and unfailing supporter of this project, while Jessica Ling and Leah Pennywark ably steered it through the production process.

Aside from those already mentioned, those who cannot be named, or those I have regrettably forgotten to list, a great many people have sustained me over the years with their ideas, mentorship, accountability, hospitality, camaraderie, love, and often some combination thereof. They include my parents as well as Salma Abu Ayyash, Nadia Abu El-Haj, Lila Abu-Lughod, Abdel Halim Abu Samra, Hussein Ali Agrama, Asad Ali Ahmed, Amna Akbar, Michelle Augustine, Cemil Aydın, Anand Balakrishnan, Aslı Bâli, Tarak Barkawi, Orit Bashkin, Adia Benton, Lauren Benton, Naor Ben-Yehoyada, Nadia Ben-Youssef, Sean Brotherton, Samar al-Bulushi, Steven Caton,

Julie Chu, Leandro Couto de Almeida, Shannon Lee Dawdy, Lara Deeb, Alireza Doostdar, Sameera Fazili, Owen Fiss, Katherine Franke, Sarah Fredericks, Aisha Ghani, Maryam Monalisa Gharavi, Michael Gilsenan, Tom Ginsburg, Daragh Grant, Zahra Hayat, Ghenwa Hayek, David Henig, Angie Heo, Engseng Ho, Tarek Ismail, Larisa Jašarević, Ryan Jobson, Paul Kahn, Anjali Kamat, Maryam Kashani, Ramzi Kassem, Devesh Kapur, Nehad Khader, Humayun Khalid, Mona Khalidi, Rashid Khalidi, Mana Kia, Mekhala Krishnamurthy, Larisa Kurtović, Genevieve Lakier, Satyel Larson, Odette Lienau, Mahmood Mamdani, Susan Marks, Joseph Masco, William T. S. Mazzarella, Brinkley Messick, Hope Metcalf, Elham Mireshghi, Rupa Mitra, Katrien Naessens, Aria Nakissa, Natacha Nsabimana, Zuzanna Olszewska, K-Sue Park, Juno Parreñas, Linda Quiquivix, Intisar Rabb, Kareem Rabie, Aziz Rana, Judith Resnick, François Richard, Justin Richland, András Riedlmayer, Lisa Rofel, Sayres Rudy, Diala Shamas, Jim Silk, Shirin Sinnar, Sam Sternin, Ajantha Subramaniam, Kaushik Sunder Rajan, Madiha Tahir, Chris Toensing, Shaira Vadasaria, Sarah Waheed, Joy Wang, Jessica Winegar, Alice Yao, Emrah Yıldız, and Huma Yusuf. These colleagues, comrades, and kin have helped give shape to a place in the world for this book.

Notes

INTRODUCTION

1. Often the first thing one learns about the country is that Bosnia has three dominant nationalities: Serbs (who are of Orthodox background), Croats (who are of Catholic background), and Bosniaks (who are of Muslim background). Muslims made up a plurality of Bosnia's population before the 1992–1995 war and are a slight majority today.

The second thing one should learn is how important it is to unthink many of the assumptions embedded in these categories. Chapter 2 will discuss this in greater detail. For now, it's helpful to keep in mind that the adjective *Bosnian* pertains to the country of Bosnia-Herzegovina or the state identified with it, but it does not refer to a widely recognized nation. So, for example, "Bosnian Serbs" are those who identify with the Serb nation living in Bosnia.

2. *Salafi* is a word that will appear throughout this book and will be discussed more thoroughly in Chapter 4. In the interest of not letting explication stand in the way of argument and narrative, let us say for now that Salafi is perhaps most usefully thought of as an orientation of Islamic creed and practice that tends to be perceived by others as particularly strict and dogmatic. *Wahhabi* is used as a synonym for Salafi, often considered pejorative.

3. Some readers may be familiar with the word *mujahideen*, one of the plural forms of *mujahid*. This term was popularized in (largely favorable) English-language media coverage of Afghans fighting against Soviet forces in the 1980s and used approvingly in speeches by US president Ronald Reagan.

4. The other major alternative category to the citizen-soldier that has returned to prominence in the past quarter-century has been the mercenary. The latter, tethered to some form of state authority and recast as the private military contractor, has enjoyed far greater legitimacy in an era of neoliberal capital. In relation to the citizen-soldier ideal, however, the two figures provoke mirrored anxieties: the volunteer is seen as motivated by an excessive ideological zeal, the mercenary as having no cause other than pecuniary gain. On the broader relationship between state-formation, the organization of violence, and the rise of the citizen-soldier model, see Janice Thomson, *Mercenaries, Pirates, and Sovereigns.*

5. For some time, the discipline of International Relations has been criticized for erasing or marginalizing the thick sets of social relations that shape the interactions between states. "Paradoxically, the core concepts of [International Relations] work to drain international relations of their content! The discipline's object of analysis—the international—becomes a spare space of strategic interaction between [nation-states as] 'pre-existing' entities." Tarak Barkawi and Mark Laffey, "Retrieving the Imperial," 112.

6. Another terminological signpost may be in order here. In this book, *Islamist* movements are those that take the state as a primary locus of activity, one that should conform to and uphold some notion of Islam. *Pan-Islamic* actors are those whose primary concern is solidarity with other Muslim communities throughout the world. One can be a pan-Islamic activist without being an Islamist and vice versa, although there is often considerable overlap between these two positions.

7. Both framings, of course, were shaped by long historical antecedents. "Ethnic conflict" was a new name for an old problem, namely the expulsions, exterminations, and subordinations that were often demanded by the logic of the territorial nation-state. And the specter of Islam—the only major worldwide missionizing religion other than Christianity—as a virus threatening to unite disparate peoples against the West has played its part in many an armed mobilization over the centuries. The two framings are overlapping and mutually reinforcing in any number of conflicts. See, e.g., Mahmood Mamdani, *Saviors and Survivors.*

8. The Socialist Federal Republic of Yugoslavia comprised six constituent republics: Slovenia, Croatia, Bosnia-Herzegovina, Macedonia, Montenegro, and Serbia. After the other republics seceded, Serbia and Montenegro in 1992 christened their union the Federal Republic of Yugoslavia (FRY) and designated it the successor to the former communist state. At the same time, the FRY supported Serb nationalist forces fighting to secede from Croatia and Bosnia. Those wars effectively ended in 1995 with a decisive victory for

the Croatian state (accompanied by mass ethnic cleansing of Serbs from Croatia) and a soft partition in Bosnia along nationalist lines. Separately, ethnic Albanian rebels in Kosovo—an autonomous province within Serbia—waged their own insurgency, leading to a NATO bombing campaign against the FRY in 1999. Kosovo was placed under international governance and unilaterally declared independence in 2008; the legal status of the territory remains unresolved. In 2006, Serbia and Montenegro parted ways.

9. The contemporaneous literature on ethnic cleansing in the 1990s Yugoslav wars is quite immense. For a useful overview of this process in Bosnia and postwar attempts to reverse it, see Gerard Toal and Carl Dahlman, *Bosnia Remade*.

10. It took some twenty years after the collapse of Yugoslavia for full-length ethnographies of Bosnia in English to appear that were *not* about nationalism, the war, or Western intervention. See Larisa Jašarević, *Health and Wealth on the Bosnian Market*; Maple Razsa, *Bastards of Utopia*. For earlier challenges to this trend, see Stef Jansen, "The Privatisation of Home and Hope"; Pamela Ballinger, "Watery Spaces, Globalizing Places."

11. Much of this work was in dialogue with postcolonial theory, especially Edward Said's book *Orientalism*. See Dušan Bjelić and Obrad Savić, *Balkan as Metaphor*; Maria Todorova, *Imagining the Balkans*; Milica Bakić-Hayden, "Nesting Orientalisms." As Catherine Baker has powerfully argued, this literature's bracketing of race is consistent with postcolonial theory's own uneven treatment of race and slavery. See *Race and the Yugoslav Region*.

12. For one corrective to Balkanist anthropology's undertheorized approach to processes of racialization, see Chelsi West Ohueri, "Mapping Race and Belonging in the Margins of Europe."

13. 553 U.S. 723 (2008). Two of the men have published a memoir of their experiences. See Lakhdar Boumediene and Mustafa Ait Idir, *Witnesses of the Unseen*.

14. Cemil Aydın helpfully draws a distinction between the older concept of umma as the community of Muslim believers and "the Muslim world" as a modern geopolitical category that emerged under the globalized white supremacy of nineteenth-century imperialism. "The Muslim world" as a concept thus exists both as a fixture of Western imaginaries as well as a category that Muslim activists could seize upon for their own critiques of imperialism. See *The Idea of the Muslim World*.

15. Writing about Muslim confrontations against Portuguese expansionism in the sixteenth century Indian Ocean, Engseng Ho traces how notions of jihad "emerged out of diasporic Muslim circles, and its expression affords us one view of empire through diasporic eyes . . ." "Empire Through Diasporic Eyes," 222.

16. Comparisons to Palestine and Andalusia were explicit in the titles of Arabic-language books about the war. See, e.g., ʿAbd al-Wahhāb Zaytūn, *al-Būsna wal-Harsak: Filasṭīn ukhrā fī qalb Ūrūbbā*; Muḥammad Muḥammad Amzyān, *al-Būsna wal-Harsak: al-Andalus al-thāniya!*

17. Much of the best scholarship on race and Islam emerges from work on or in conversation with the Black radical tradition and is thereby more squarely planted within the West (even as it challenges the boundaries of that category) than the kinds of encounters charted in this book. See, e.g., Sylvia Chan-Malik, *Being Muslim*; Su'ad Abdul Khabeer, *Muslim Cool*; Hisham Aidi, *Rebel Music*; Sohail Daulatzai, *Black Star, Crescent Moon*; Junaid Rana, *Terrifying Muslims*; Sherman Jackson, *Islam and the Blackamerican*.

18. It is worth noting that foreign volunteers fought on all sides of the war, and this study further contributes to the disproportionate attention given to Muslims. Most of the criticisms of Arab fighters were also in evidence against foreign volunteers on the Croat side, including lack of discipline and mistreating local women. See Nir Arielli, "In Search of Meaning."

19. This conjoined figure of threat—jihadi, Arab, Wahhabi—is a flashpoint in broader debates over piety and the public role of Islam in Bosnia, whose most contentious issues include women's headscarves and the design of new and refurbished mosques. See, e.g., Andreja Mesarič, "Wearing Hijab in Sarajevo"; Emira Ibrahimpašić, "Women Living Islam in Post-War and Post-Socialist Bosnia-Herzegovina"; Azra Akšamija, "Our Mosques Are Us."

20. Here, I follow Roxanne Euben, who treats jihad as a form of meaning-making that is central to understandings of politics rather than outside of it: "[I]n this view jihad endows human struggle to remake a common world with existential weight." Roxanne Euben, "Killing (for) Politics," 10.

21. Faisal Devji has made a similar point, comparing al-Qaʿida to various global humanitarian movements such as those organized around global warming or nuclear dangers. The approach here differs, however, in the purpose of the comparison. Devji insists on placing al-Qaʿida outside the threshold of the political, either because it allegedly lacks a rational means-ends calculus or due to its commitment to the abstract category of humanity over the nation-state. See *Landscapes of the Jihad*, 3–4; *Terrorist in Search of Humanity*, 18–23. The accompanying empirical emphasis on media outputs as reflective surfaces leaves unread the actual histories, relations, dilemmas, and antagonisms of jihad groups—what one might otherwise call their politics. This

perspective short-changes not only jihad groups but the other universalisms Devji compares them to, such as environmental or human rights campaigns, which are also treated as pathologies of globalization.

22. Anna Tsing argues that treating universalism ethnographically requires understanding it "as an aspiration, an always unfinished achievement, rather than the confirmation of a pre-formed law. Then it is possible to notice that universal aspirations must travel across distances and differences, and we can take this travel as an ethnographic object." *Friction*, 7. Tsing's work on universalism, which unfolded in the shadow of debates over globalization and the environment in the 1990s and early 2000s, can be usefully connected to parallel thinking about themes of aspiration and disputation that have recurred in the anthropology of Islam and Muslims. See Naveeda Khan, *Muslim Becoming*; Talal Asad, "The Idea of an Anthropology of Islam," 14–17.

23. Étienne Balibar makes a similar point in cautioning against making any "plea for or against universalism as such" in favor of disentangling the processes and tensions that are inherent to universalisms as actually existing endeavors. "On Universalism."

While Balibar's engagements on the contingencies and multiplicities of universalism are valuable, this book proposes a way of understanding universalisms on a smaller scale that can be more easily approached through empirical research. Otherwise Balibar's concept of universalism risks lapsing into banal anti-essentialism, however, especially when asked about Islam: "Islamic State is a local variant of jihadism, which itself should not be conflated with Muslim fundamentalism in general. And *a fortiori* fundamentalism should not be confused with Islam, which is itself deeply divided between different traditionalisms and varieties of modernism. . . . It is Islamic State that is barbaric, not Islam." Jean Birnbaum, "Etienne Balibar : 'L'universel ne rassemble pas, il divise'," *Le Monde*, September 9, 2017.

24. The authority to make those evaluations and set those standards will always be an object of contestation. Similarly, the extent to which a particular universalism's criteria for evaluating differences is accepted is an empirical question: "[T]he universal does not have any necessary body, any necessary content. Instead, different groups compete to give their particular aims a temporary function of universal representation." Ernesto Laclau, "Universalism, Particularism and the Question of Identity," 90.

25. For a useful collection of essays that ethnographically interrogate the category of humanity in its deployment in various "Western" discourses such as humanitarianism and biomedicine, see Ilana Feldman and Miriam Ticktin, *In the Name of Humanity*.

26. Arguably the most influential overview of international law's colonial dimensions remains Antony Anghie, *Imperialism, Sovereignty, and the Making of International Law.*

In the shadow of such critiques, the persistence of international law as a ubiquitous language for articulating emancipatory demands has occasioned much reflection among legal scholars about universalism in various forms. Sundhya Pahuja, for example, calls attention to the need to study the "operationalisation of universality," or the process by which certain norms become accepted as universal. *Decolonising International Law*, 40–41. Emmanuelle Jouannet has also grappled with the paradoxical relationship linking international law's hegemonic tendencies and its liberatory promises. Interestingly, she uses the example of al-Qaʿida to demonstrate the limitations of any concept of rational discussion as a basis for renewed universality. See "Universalism and Imperialism," 402–3.

27. See, e.g., Charles Henry Alexandrowicz, *The European-African Confrontation*; *An Introduction to the History of the Law of Nations in the East Indies (16th, 17th, and 18th Centuries)*. For a critical appraisal of Alexandrowicz's work, see David Armitage and Jennifer Pitts, "'This Modern Grotius': An Introduction to the Life and Thought of C.H. Alexandrowicz," 21–31.

28. See Carl Schmitt, *The Nomos of the Earth.* From a perspective that seeks to challenge empire and white supremacy, the utility of a Nazi thinker like Schmitt stems precisely (and primarily) from his proximity to liberal modes of reasoning, accompanied by a candor and incisiveness that can come only from the envy of runner-up colonizers.

29. Nevertheless, the move to historicize international legal institutions, including the role of non-Western elites, remains salutary. See, e.g., Mark Mazower, *No Enchanted Palace*; Arnulf Becker-Lorca, *Mestizo International Law.* That Marxist approaches to international law, while generative in their own right, have also yet to systematically engage with social history is perhaps more surprising. See, e.g., China Miéville, *Between Equal Rights*; B. S. Chimni, *International Law and World Order.*

30. Needless to say, international legal institutions have themselves also been the object of anthropological research and have raised questions of universalism similar to those explored here. See, e.g., Kamari Clarke, *Fictions of Justice*; Sally Engle Merry, *Human Rights and Gender Violence*; Annelise Riles, *The Network Inside Out*; "Anthropology, Human Rights, and Legal Knowledge."

31. An empirical approach to universalism can be discerned in the work of a common ancestor of both anthropology and the study of international law, the British jurist and colonial official Henry Sumner Maine (1822–1888). In interrogating the prehistory of international law—which he thought of as most analogous to whatever norms governed relations between kinship units in "primitive societies"—Maine argued against the common conflation of *jus gentium*, or the law of all peoples, and natural law, philosophically derived from principles of nature. Maine explained that for the Romans, *jus gentium* was drawn from practices observed to be prevalent among the various tribes and communities in Italy and used to govern relations with the very large population of foreign residents. *Jus gentium* was merely a technology for managing differences born from necessity, without any kind of transcendent value attached. It was only later, when ancient Greek natural law ideas were combined with this Roman legal tradition, that *jus gentium* began to take on an aspirational dimension that would come to inflect international law much later on. See *Ancient Law*, 41–47.

32. Chinese migration to Bosnia since the 2000s has been an outgrowth of a larger community in Serbia. See Felix Chang, "Myth and Migration"; Gordana Blagojević, "Savremeni stereotipi Srba o Kinezima u Beogradu."

33. Clinics are essentially legal services organizations housed within law schools, meant to provide students with practical experience, such as drafting motions and arguing in court, under the supervision of a licensed attorney. This clinic, formally known as the National Litigation Project (NLP) of the Allard K. Lowenstein International Human Rights clinic at Yale Law School, was highly unusual in being attached to a well-resourced and prestigious law school. NLP grew out of litigation challenging the detention of Haitian asylum seekers at Guantánamo Bay naval base in the early 1990s and was reincarnated during the Global War on Terror to challenge the policies of the George W. Bush administration.

34. We represented Mr. Zuhair in the framework of seeking a writ of *habeas corpus*. The June 2008 Supreme Court decision in *Boumediene* found that Guantánamo detainees had habeas rights, but it left the lower courts to improvise a framework for how to decide such claims, including determining the relevant standards for detention, evidence, and so on.

35. See *Zuhair v. Bush*, 592 F. Supp. 2d 16 (D.D.C. 2008). Guantánamo habeas petitions were litigated in Washington, due to personal jurisdiction over respondents (often the president or the secretary of defense) based in that city.

36. Work on this case required obtaining a security clearance, which entailed waiving many of my privacy rights and undergoing a background investigation comparable to those used for government employees. Defense lawyers in Guantánamo habeas cases typically received "Secret" level clearances. Several million people hold security clearances in the United States, including civil servants, outside contractors, and other individuals.

37. The question of what can or cannot be brought out of secure facilities is one that underscores the fluid and ambiguous nature of government secrecy classifications, especially because most information classified as secret by the government already exists in the public domain. In Joseph Masco's ethnography of the Los Alamos nuclear research facility, a scientist recounts being told that the orange he brought to work for lunch could not be left unsupervised, since regulations deemed any spherical object in the laboratory to be classified. See *The Nuclear Borderlands*, 268.

38. Other legal regimes of secrecy also applied. Much of the unclassified material was nevertheless deemed "protected" by the courts and kept from public release. This is a type of secrecy managed by the judiciary rather than the executive branch. Finally, I am governed by the legal profession's rules on confidentiality governing the attorney-client relationship.

39. The role of *amicus curiae* has evolved over the centuries, from providing a specialized service requested by courts (often knowledge on technical matters) to something more like third-party partisanship. In the contemporary US federal judiciary, the latter function is dominant. See Samuel Krislov, "The Amicus Curiae Brief."

40. See "Expert Opinion on Deprivation of Nationality," submitted by the Helsinki Committee for Human Rights in Bosnia and Herzegovina and the Allard K. Lowenstein International Human Rights Clinic, Yale Law School, as Amici Curiae Supporting Appellant/Applicant Al Husin Imad, Case No. AP 1222/07, Constitutional Court of Bosnia and Herzegovina.

41. See "Written Comments by Human Rights Watch" as amicus supporting applicant Al Husin Imad, application no. 3727/08, European Court of Human Rights, March 1, 2011. The brief was researched and drafted by the following students at the Yale Lowenstein Clinic: Jay Butler, Sally Pei, and Julia Spiegel.

42. See *Imad al Husin*, AP-1222/07 (Const. Ct. Bosn. & Herz. 2008); *Al Husin v. Bosnia and Herzegovina*, 3727/08 (Eur. Ct. H.R. 2012).

43. I submitted an expert report in an asylum case in the United Kingdom related to issues discussed in this book that formed part of the basis for granting the relief requested.

See Decision and Reasons, appeal AA/00537/2016, ¶¶ 51–58 (First-tier Tribunal, UK Immigration and Asylum Chamber, June 7, 2017).

I was also an expert in sentencing proceedings for Talha Ahsan in US District Court in Connecticut. For more on the role of experts in that case, see *USA v. Ahmad and Ahsan*, Sentencing Hearing Transcript 39–41, 3:06–cr-00194–JCH (D.Conn. July 9, 2015), ECF No. 211.

Ahsan's co-defendant, Babar Ahmad, fought in Bosnia and produced much of the early English-language media materials about the jihad. Ahmad also created Azzam.com, one of the first English-language websites supporting transnational jihads. Ironically, Azzam.com would be a major reference for terrorism "experts" unable to read Arabic. I was able to interview Ahmad while he was serving his sentence in federal prison in Pennsylvania and after his return to London.

44. Mohammad-Mahmoud Ould Mohamedou has developed one of the more thoughtful elaborations of al-Qaʿida's strategic logic, attributing it to "a natural development whereby the perceived failure of particular states to act on behalf of populations and their interests has led to the creation of a regional entity seeking to undertake those martial responsibilities globally." *Understanding Al Qaeda*, 36.

45. *Liqāʾ al-yawm*, "Ayman Abū ʿAbd al-Raḥmān: al-mujāhidūn al-ʿArab fil-Būsna," aired September 1, 2000, on al-Jazeera, http://aljazeera.net/programs/pages/64c0194e-9379-4a4b-b9fe-e5cf7016bc75.

46. See Edward Said, "Impossible Histories: Why the Many Islams Cannot Be Simplified," *Harper's*, July 2002; Samuel Huntington, "The Clash of Civilizations?" *Foreign Affairs*, Summer 1993.

47. As Sayres Rudy notes, the Global War on Terror's logic of distinguishing moderate and radical Muslims has "embraced the anti-essentialist heart of [Said's] *Orientalism*" in a way that has sapped the political utility of that book's critiques. Sayres Rudy, "Pros and Cons," 39.

48. See Mahmood Mamdani, *Good Muslim, Bad Muslim*. It should go without saying that various kinds of differences among Muslims—between practicing and nonpracticing, Sufis and Salafis, Arabs and Bosnians, or between the various schools of *fiqh* (Islamic jurisprudence)—do not map directly onto specific political orientations. History is full of more than enough counterexamples to disprove the stereotypes of violent Salafis, pacifist Sufis, and so on.

49. W.E.B. Du Bois, *Black Reconstruction in America*, xliii.

50. For more on the limitations of standard liberal challenges to Islamophobia,

see Azeezah Kanji and S. K. Hussan, "The Problem with Liberal Opposition to Islamophobia," *ROAR Magazine*, Spring 2017.

51. Terror as an instrument of governance has a long and variegated history across different contexts, from the French Revolution to the Jim Crow regime in the southern United States. See, e.g., Verena Erlenbusch-Anderson, *Genealogies of Terrorism*.

CHAPTER 1: MIGRATIONS

1. This vignette is culled from interviews with Abu ʿAbd al-ʿAziz published in Arabic, English, and Serbo-Croatian. See Roman Majetić and Marko Franjić, "Kur'an je moje jedino vojno pravilo," *Globus*, October 16, 1992; Yūsuf ʿAbd al-Raḥmān, "al-Mujāhidūn al-ʿArab ʿalā arḍ al-maʿrika," *al-Anbāʾ*, October 9, 1992; Muḥammad al-Rāshid, "Masʾūl al-mutaṭawwiʿīn al-ʿArab wal-Muslimīn fil-Būsna wal-Harsak fī ḥiwār maʿa *al-Mujtamaʿ*," *al-Mujtamaʿ*, October 6, 1992; Tom Post and Joel Brand, "Help from the Holy Warriors," *Newsweek*, October 5, 1992; Asʿad Ṭaha, "*al-Sharq al-Awsaṭ* tadkhul maqarr qiyādat quwwāt 'al-mujāhidīn al-ʿArab' fil-Būsna," *al-Sharq al-Awsaṭ*, September 10, 1992; Andrew Hogg, "Arabs Join in Bosnia Battle," *The Times*, August 30, 1992.

2. Muḥammad al-Rāshid et al., "Abū ʿAbd al-ʿAzīz masʾūl al-mujāhidīn al-ʿArab fil-Būsna wal-Harsak yataḥaddath ilā *al-Mujtamaʿ*," *al-Mujtamaʿ*, December 29, 1992, 28.

3. In an online interview published around 2002, Abu ʿAbd al-ʿAziz pointedly declined to take up an invitation to criticize pro-Saudi clerics. See "Liqāʾ shabakat Anā Muslim maʿa amīr al-mujāhidīn al-ʿArab—sābiqan—fil-Būsna wal-Harsak," available at http://saaid.net/leqa/8.htm.

4. Perhaps the most widely cited typology of Salafism—a category that will be discussed further in Chapter 4—is Quintan Wiktorowicz's spectrum of "purists, politicos, and jihadis." This formulation renders politics and violence as mutually exclusive, which is to say it treats state violence as normal while conflating all forms of nonstate violence as deviant. "Anatomy of the Salafi Movement."

5. Works that attempt to identify "foreign fighters" or "foreign volunteers" as a distinct category helpfully delink the phenomenon from Islam but tend to focus on motivation (like the search for meaning) and opportunity structures (recruitment through friendship or kin networks), thereby paradoxically highlighting their similarity with state armies. See, e.g., Nir Arielli, *From Byron to bin Laden*; David Malet, *Foreign Fighters*. Without theorizing social and political contexts as properly transnational, however, this approach risks ultimately exchanging methodological nationalism for methodological individualism.

6. Schmitt's concern was that the unmoored mobile partisan would become a tool of international communism. In this respect, his framework still assumes the centrality of state sponsors, regular powers to legitimate the irregular fighters. See *Theory of the Partisan*, 75–76. The perception that jihad fighters reject secular state authority altogether—which will be queried in Chapter 3—represents a distillation of the logic of Schmitt's argument beyond what even he may have anticipated.

7. See Carl Schmitt, *The Nomos of the Earth*, 42–49, 80–85, 152–71.

8. See Malet, 217. To some it might be obvious that the most numerous "foreign fighters" in Iraq were US soldiers. But the lack of self-awareness in this term also helps to illustrate the distinction between difference marked as foreign and the difference that is treated merely as a gap between the universal and the particular. We will return to this question in the final chapter.

9. Illustrative examples of such "boomerang studies" include Thomas Hegghammer, *Jihad in Saudi Arabia*, 38–69, and Bernard Rougier, *Everyday Jihad*. There is an antecedent discourse on "Afghan Arabs" in Arabic-language press stemming from the early 1990s, when veterans of the Afghan jihad were blamed for fomenting insurrection in Egypt and Algeria. The most detailed journalistic accounts of the Egyptian case include Muḥammad Ṣalāḥ, *Waqāʾiʿ sanawāt al-jihād*; Hishām Mubārak, *al-Irhābiyyūn al-qādimūn*; ʿIṣām Dirāz, *al-ʿĀʾidūn min Afghānistān*.

10. The trope is prevalent in the cottage industry of "terrorism expertise" in the Balkans, which uncritically compiles and summarizes media stories that are themselves sensationalist, unsourced, and poorly fact-checked. See, e.g., Lorenzo Vidino, *Al Qaeda in Europe*; Shaul Shay, *Islamic Terror and the Balkans*; John Schindler, *Unholy Terror*; Evan Kohlmann, *Al-Qaida's Jihad in Europe*; Yossef Bodansky, *Some Call It Peace*. There is also an ample literature produced by Croat and Serb nationalists, mostly aiming to smear their Bosniak counterparts with the charge of association with al-Qaʿida or other forms of "radical Islam." See Ivica Mlivončić, *Al Qaida se kalila u Bosni i Hercegovini*; Miroslav Toholj, *"Holy Warriors" and the War in Bosnia and Herzegovina*. Accounts by Bosniak journalists on foreign fighters are generally more nuanced in rejecting this conflation but do little to challenge reductionist and conspiratorial portrayals of the foreign fighters themselves. See Vlado Azinović, *Al-kai'da u Bosni i Hercegovini*; Esad Hećimović, *Garibi*. Political scientists have attempted only preliminary comparative studies of foreign fighter impact on insurgent behavior. See Tiffany Chu and Alex Braithwaite, "The Impact of Foreign Fighters on Civil Conflict Outcomes."

11. While Arabs and other Muslims coming to Bosnia for jihad comfortably accepted the label of ansar, Bosnians were only imperfectly understood as muhajirs. Those who fled or were expelled were often affixed with this label, but most Bosnian mujahids were fighting for the ability to remain in their homes. Muhajir and its variants in other languages (Turkish: *muhacir*, Bosnian: *muhadžir*) also have an important valence in the modern history of the Balkans. The term was applied to the successive waves of Muslims who left in the wake of the gradual contraction of Ottoman territory from the nineteenth century onward. See, e.g., Leyla Amzi-Erdoğdular, "Afterlife of Empire," 55–119; Kemal Karpat, *The Politicization of Islam*, 184–88; Karpat, *Ottoman Population*, 55–59. Needless to say, the historical memory of these events also resonated during the wars of the 1990s. And there were at least a few Bosnian muhadžirs who came back to fight, including in the Katiba.

12. One need not resort to the history of early Islam to challenge Schmitt's attempt to parochialize and tame the partisan: perhaps the most famous partisans of all, the communist-led forces in Yugoslavia during World War II, were resolutely internationalist and included many cadres who gained valuable combat experience in the Spanish Civil War.

13. The relationship between Islam and universalism in this book is ultimately a contingent one: universalisms draw freely and loosely from any number of different idioms whose historical origins and complexities are important but beyond the scope of this book. In contrast to Shahab Ahmed's ambitious and erudite attempt to theorize the category of Islam as such in terms of a hermeneutic process connected to the act of divine revelation—which inevitably raises questions about the boundaries of the concept—the argument here is content with the relative *un*-importance of determining what is or is not Islamic. See Shahab Ahmed, *What Is Islam?: The Importance of Being Islamic*. For the purposes of this book, a universalism speaks in an Islamic idiom if the ideas it is propagating and drawing upon are recognized as Islamic and accepted as binding by the participants in that project.

14. Too often, universalisms are treated simply as sets of ideas whose origins must be explained or whose implementation must be examined. In contrast, an anthropological approach should highlight the processes by which universalisms draw from disparate forms of circulation—be they of ideas, people, or goods—while also recombining and inflecting them with new significance. This combination of movement and transformation echoes Marx's discussion of money as a "universal equivalent": through the medium of exchange, any commodity can become money and money

can become any commodity. Marx also understood this universality to be contingent and historically emergent: for any material to serve as money presupposes social convention (legal and otherwise), and its function as money must be limited in time and space. See Karl Marx, *Capital*, vol. 1, 178–87. The analysis here, however, departs from Marx's reliance on exchange as the telos of circulation: the smoothness with which goods and money are swapped for each other otherwise untouched does not capture the ways the protagonists of this story are transformed by their peregrinations as they come to embrace and embody universalisms.

15. While this chapter's transregional approach is in part an attempt to read Bosnia's relationship with pan-Islam outside of an Ottomanist framing, it is largely consonant with the spirit of scholarship that seeks to tell transregional social histories of the Ottoman empire, including, e.g., David Henig, "Crossing the Bosphorus"; E. Natalie Rothman, *Brokering Empire*; Isa Blumi, *Reinstating the Ottomans*; Malte Fuhrmann, "Down and Out on the Quays of İzmir"; and Fuhrmann, "Vagrants, Prostitutes and Bosnians." See also Dominique Kirchner Reill, *Nationalists Who Feared the Nation.*

16. Although al-Albani did not endorse travel to Bosnia for jihad, the recording of their meeting circulated widely. Nasir al-Bahri (Abu Jandal), a Yemeni raised in Saudi Arabia, cited it as one of his influences for embarking on jihad. After the war, he joined al-Qaʿida and served as a chief bodyguard to Osama bin Laden. See Khālid Ḥammādī, "Tanẓīm al-Qāʿida min dākhil kamā yarwī Abū Jandal (Nāṣir al-Baḥrī) al-ḥāris al-shakhṣī li-bin Lādin (1)," *al-Quds al-ʿArabī*, March 18, 2005, 17.

17. Amīr Ḥamza, *Bosniyā ke ʿArab shuhadāʾ*, 19–20.

18. See 73 Fed. Reg. 31,545 (June 2, 2008); UN News Centre, "Four Pakistani Militants Added to UN Terrorism Sanctions List," December 11, 2008, *UN Daily News* Issue DH/5295.

Decisions to add individuals to the UN terrorism list are made by a committee of states at the request of other states; no actual evidence is reviewed by the committee. See Gavin Sullivan, "Transnational Legal Assemblages and Global Security Law."

19. Emerson was a journalist who dedicated his career to spying on and harassing Muslim organizations in the United States starting in the 1990s and infamously blamed the 1995 bombing in Oklahoma City on Muslims.

20. Kohlmann's potted account of the history of al-Qaʿida erroneously states that the organization's foundation was announced in a "monumental treatise" called "The Solid Base" (al-Qāʿida al-ṣulba) on page 46 of the April 1988 issue of *al-Jihād* magazine. Kohlmann, 9. The article in question—three pages long, so hardly a "monumental

treatise"—does not announce the creation of any new organization or make any mention of global jihad or the United States. Its use of the word *qāʿida* in the headline refers to one of its everyday Arabic meanings, the idea of a "base," in this case referring to the need for a particular type of Islamist vanguard in the specific context of the Afghan jihad. ʿAbd Allāh ʿAzzām, "al-Qāʿida al-ṣulba," *al-Jihād*, April 1988.

Not only does Kohlmann's misunderstanding of the article suggest that he did not read it, but he cites the article's bibliographic data mistakenly—the article appears not on page 46 but on pages 4 *through* 6. The missing hyphen is the telltale clue, for the identical citation error is made in another major text of the terrorism expertise canon, Rohan Gunaratna, *Inside Al Qaeda*. Like Kohlmann, Gunaratna mischaracterizes the article as a "founding document" for al-Qaeda; unlike Kohlmann, he transparently admits that he could not read the article, and instead relied on a translation by Reuven Paz, former head of research for Israel's Shin Bet secret police and later director of the International Policy Institute for Counter-Terrorism. See *Inside Al Qaeda*, 243n1. Whether the misunderstanding of this document stems from Paz's translation or from Gunaratna's interpretation of it is unclear.

In any event, Kohlmann is in good company in plagiarizing Gunaratna's misinterpretation and erroneous citation of ʿAzzam's article. The same trail of mishaps occurs in a document that has had far more impact than Kohlmann's book—the report of the bipartisan National Commission formed to investigate the September 2001 attacks in New York and Washington. See Darryl Li, "Lies, Damned Lies, and Plagiarizing 'Experts'," *Middle East Report*, Fall 2011.

21. See Kohlmann, 15–24. Abu ʿAbd al-ʿAziz is also the subject of a chapter in Daniel Byman, *Road Warriors*, 39–54.

22. It is possible that a different individual named ʿAbd al-Rahman al-Dawsari also fought in Afghanistan, but Kohlmann cites a biographical source on the famous scholar—one that also references his death. See Kohlmann, 31n6.

23. See Marcy Wheeler, "Evan Kohlmann: Garbage In, Garbage Out," *emptywheel*, July 29, 2015, https://www.emptywheel.net/2015/07/29/evan-kohlmann-garbage-in-garbage-out/; Trevor Aaronson, "Doogie Huckster: A Terrorism Expert's Secret Relationship with the FBI," *The Intercept*, July 27, 2015.

24. In his discussion of al-Dosari and elsewhere, Kohlmann relies heavily on a prosecution document in a criminal case (one that itself lacks any sources or other indicia of reliability) without mentioning that it was rejected by the judge. See Kohlmann, 31, 49, 214, 228; see also *U.S. v. Arnaout*, 2003 U.S. Dist. LEXIS 1635 (N.D. Ill. 2003).

25. See, e.g., Byman, 40–41, 273fn3; Stephen Tankel, *Storming the World Stage*, 39, 278fn18; Mohammed Hafez, "Jihad After Iraq," 79; Hegghammer, *Jihad*, 48–51. See also Hegghammer, "Famous Jihadi Red Beards," http://boredjihadi.tumblr.com/post/135442944977/famous-jihadi-red-beards [site deleted, but archived elsewhere].

26. Abu ʿAbd al-ʿAziz's real name appears in Lashkar literature as early as 2002, see, e.g., Muḥammad Ṭāhir Naqqāsh, *Bosniyā ke jihādī maidānoñ meñ*, 191, 205.

27. The Hadrami diaspora is the subject of an extensive literature. See, e.g., Sumit Mandal, *Becoming Arab*; Leif Manger, *The Hadrami Diaspora*; Engseng Ho, *The Graves of Tarim*; Linda Boxberger, *On the Edge of Empire*; Ulrike Freitag and W. G. Clarence-Smith, *Hadhrami Traders, Scholars, and Statesmen*. The Bahadhiqs are a minor Hadrami tribe, but its branches extend also to Mombasa and Surabaya, on opposite sides of the Indian Ocean. See ʿAlī Bākhayyil Bābaṭīn, *Idrāk al-fawt fī dhikr qabāʾil tārīkh Ḥaḍramawt*, 40; Ibrāhīm Aḥmad Maqḥafī, *Mawsūʿat al-alqāb al-Yamaniyya*, Vol. 1, 801.

28. *Holder v. Humanitarian Law Project*, 561 U.S. 1, 24 (2010). In that case, an American NGO found itself exposed to potential criminal liability merely for offering designated terrorist groups training in international humanitarian law. If one subscribes to the notion that the definition of terrorism is nonstate violence against civilians, then it would seem that helping terrorists give up terrorism can itself be a form of supporting terrorism.

29. To be precise: the statute in question, 18 U.S.C. § 2339B, concerns the several dozen "foreign terrorist organizations" (FTOs) declared as such by the State Department, a different category from the Treasury's list of thousands of "Specially Designated Global Terrorists" (SDGTs) that includes individuals like Abu ʿAbd al-ʿAziz. In the context of material support prosecutions, there is no clear standard for determining whether any individual (SDGT or otherwise) is part of an FTO—but in any event, I had no interest in offering myself up as a test case for this question.

30. The Bahadhiq brothers I interviewed had different recollections about their grandfather Ahmad's work in Hyderabad: Khalid believed he joined the military, while Mahmud said he worked as a clerk. One of Ahmad's brothers migrated even further east to the Indonesian island of Java and was buried there.

31. See Boxberger, 190–91.

32. Nita Verma Prasad, "Indian or Arabian?" 200.

33. Muslims were about 10 percent of Hyderabad's population throughout the first half of the twentieth century, of whom Hadramis were a small fraction. The Hyderabad

branch of the Hadrami diaspora in Hyderabad has received less thorough treatment than its counterparts in island southeast Asia, but some of the relevant work includes Seema Alavi, *Muslim Cosmopolitanism in the Age of Empire*, 93–108; Prasad; Leif Manger, "Hadramis in Hyderabad," 410–15; Ṣalāḥ ʿAbd al-Qādir Bakrī, *Tārīkh Ḥaḍramawt al-siyāsī*, Vol. 2, 239–40; Khālid Bāwazīr, *Mawānīʾ sāḥil Ḥaḍramawt*, 73–110; and Omar Khalidi, "The Arabs of Hadramawt, South Yemen in Hyderabad."

34. Having established themselves in 1858, the Quʿaytis were later effectively deputized by the British to create a buffer zone around Aden. For more on the Quʿayti-British relationship, see Boxberger, 183–240; Ho, *Graves of Tarim*, 257–58. The Quʿayti sultanate was abolished by the 1967 advent of the People's Democratic Republic of Yemen.

35. See *Delić* Exhibit 51 for audio of the August 1992 interview with Abu ʿAbd al-ʿAziz conducted by the journalist Andrew Hogg.

36. On India's attempts to expel Arabs from Hyderabad, see Taylor Sherman, "Migration, Citizenship and Belonging in Hyderabad (Deccan), 1946–1956." On the Arabs' claims to British diplomatic protection either as British protected persons or Commonwealth citizens, see Petition of Arab Representatives to Military Governor Maj. Gen. J. N. Chaudhuri, November 7, 1948, UKNA DO/142/441.

37. Wahīb Aḥmad Kābilī, *al-Ḥirafiyyūn fī madīnat Jidda*, 33–51; ʿAbd al-Quddūs Anṣārī, *Tārīkh madīnat Jidda*, 205. Hyderabad's government and ruling monarchs owned numerous properties in the Hijaz in the mid-nineteenth century and helped to finance the construction of the Hijaz railway later on. See Alavi, 192–93, 224; William Ochsenwald, "The Financing of the Hijaz Railroad," 142.

38. See "Muqābala maʿa al-mujāhid al-shaykh Abū ʿAbd al-ʿAzīz (al-juzʾ al-thānī lā yafūtuk)," June 2, 2002, http://www.montada.com/showthread.php?p=899505 [site now password-protected]

39. The modern South Asian Ahl-i Hadith movement emerged in nineteenth century India, based on a rejection of the four major schools of Sunni jurisprudence and most institutional and public forms of Sufism. Despite some apparent affinities with Salafi movements in the Arabian Peninsula there are also significant areas of doctrinal disagreement. For more on this movement and its relationship with the Salafi tendency in the Middle East, see Martin Riexinger, "How Favourable Is Puritan Islam to Modernity?"; Daniel W. Brown, *Rethinking Tradition in Modern Islamic Thought*, 27–32; Barbara Metcalf, *Islamic Revival in British India*, 264–92.

40. To be more precise, the new organization was Markaz-i Daʿwa wal-Irshad (MDI), of which Lashkar was its armed wing. MDI literature describes Abu ʿAbd

al-ʿAziz as a "founding member" [bānī rukn]. Naqqāsh, 88. MDI was later renamed Jamaʿat al-Daʿwa (JD).

41. Because most Ahl-i Hadith groups in Pakistan opposed involvement in armed jihad, Lashkar was unable to recruit from the movement's religious schools, with the result that most of its fighters came from other doctrinal backgrounds. See Samina Yasmeen, *Jihad and Dawah*, 66. For more on JD's transformation into a more broadly based social movement, especially the role of women activists, see Humeira Iqtidar, *Secularizing Islamists?*, 104–20.

42. Some letters from Abu ʿAbd al-ʿAziz's "advance team" in Bosnia describing the situation and their needs are reproduced in Naqqāsh, 113, 141.

43. Amīr Ḥamza, *Qāfilah daʿwat jihād*, 149–50. Lashkar's unsubstantiated claims to having fielded thousands of fighters in Bosnia have been faithfully reproduced by some terrorism experts; see, e.g., Arif Jamal, *Call for Transnational Jihad*, 184–91.

44. Letter from Abu al-Maʿali to the Qatari Waqf minister, March 23, 1995, *Delić* Exhibit 1438 (Italian translation only). In a defensive letter faxed to the Katiba later that year, Abu ʿAbd al-ʿAziz dodged the allegations of publicity-seeking and, in apparent response to questions about his financial probity, provided a detailed enumeration of funds he had raised and disbursed for the jihad—over two million Deutschmarks, in his estimation—closing with an assurance that he would continue to abide by the Katiba's guidance and leadership. See Fax from Abu ʿAbd al-ʿAziz to Abu al-Maʿali, May 6, 1995, *Delić* Exhibit 1436 (Italian translation only).

45. See, e.g., Abū ʿAbd al-ʿAzīz, "Fawā'id min mudhakkirāt amīr al-mujāhidīn fil-Būsna" (2003?), http://www.arabforum.net/vb/showthread.php?threadid=37619 [link now dead but text reposted elsewhere]; "Muqābala maʿa al-mujāhid al-shaykh Abū ʿAbd al-ʿAzīz 20 Rabīʿ al-awwal," June 1, 2002, http://www.montada.com/showthread.php?p=899448 [site now password-protected].

46. Hadrami sayyids were of course also active in the jihad. Arriving in Bosnia around the same time as Abu ʿAbd al-ʿAziz but in a separate group was Muhammad al-Habashi (Abu al-Zubayr al-Madani), also a Saudi citizen descended from the town of Say'un in Hadramawt. Abu al-Zubayr had a distinguished combat record in Afghanistan, having fought at Jaji, as well as in Jalalabad and around Kabul. He was known for reciting poems and anthems and recorded a popular cassette, *Caravans of Martyrs* (Qawāfil al-shuhadā'). Abu al-Zubayr fell in a battle at the Sarajevo airport, a mere seventeen days after arriving in the country. His brother ʿUmar (Abu Usayd) was also esteemed for his anthems and later joined the Katiba; by the 2000s, his

works had developed a considerable online following. Media reports claimed that he joined al-Qaʿida's branch in the Arabian peninsula and went to fight in Syria in 2014. See "Shahīd āl al-bayt fī qalb Ūrūbbā fil-Būsna wal-Harsak al-shahīd Abū al-Zubayr," *al-Jihād*, December 1992; Hamza Hendawi, "In Yemen, a Woman's Life Entangled with Al Qaeda," Associated Press, February 21, 2014.

47. This analysis is indebted to Engseng Ho's account of how diasporic Hadrami sayyids, due to their farflung social networks and religious authority, have played a prominent role in pan-Islamic mobilizations against Western imperial powers across different contexts. See "Empire Through Diasporic Eyes." While the jihad was nourished and sustained by diasporic circulations of the kind represented by Abu ʿAbd al-ʿAziz, its commitment to a broader Islamic idiom required downplaying that very indebtedness. As a universalist project speaking in an Islamic idiom, the Bosnian jihad ultimately had to abjure the kinds of genealogical imaginaries that diasporic formations tend to invoke. This is why Abu ʿAbd al-ʿAziz's Hadrami origins are not considered particularly noteworthy of narration to his audiences (in addition to any resentment at how he may think sayyids, for example, emphasize their origins over their talents).

By positioning diasporas as feeding into universalist projects, this book uses the latter concept to take some of the conceptual burden off the former that it must do elsewhere, especially in the theorization of Black and Jewish diasporas. For example, Brent Hayes Edwards has usefully approached the African diaspora as a site of productive differences and disjunctures across Black internationalisms in tension with its sense as a set of discourses about a myth of origins. See "The Uses of *Diaspora*." For various reasons, invocations of "Muslim diaspora" as a singular category, while real, remain overshadowed by a geographical imaginary of a "Muslim world" with manifold, and often national, diasporas within and beyond it.

48. Naqqāsh, 88. The metaphor of intoxication, of course, also has Sufi resonances notwithstanding the text's Ahl-i Hadith commitments.

49. Aḥmad bin Ḥāzim bin Muḥammad Bek Tawfīq al-Maṣrī, *Tajliyat al-rāya*, 349. The term I have translated as "rubes" is *saʿayida*, the plural form of the adjective for people from Upper Egypt, a part of the country stereotypically associated with poverty and backwardness.

50. The practice of naming using kunyas will be discussed in greater detail in Chapter 3.

51. Excerpts of last testaments left behind by mujahids in Bosnia are reproduced in Mehmet Ali Tekin, *Bosna Şehidlerimiz*, 169; "Awwal shahīd Qaṭarī fil-Būsna," *al-Jihād*, March-April 1994, 46.

52. I have chosen the word *cheer* to render this quote in a more idiomatic manner for English. Abu ʿAli's actual request to his mother was to ululate in joy rather than weep [zaghridī wa-lā tabkī].

53. The turn to North African labor in the 1980s followed a century during which Italy was a net labor exporter, not only to the United States and Argentina but also southward: Libya (through direct colonization), Tunisia, and Egypt. In Cairo and Alexandria in particular, large and at times politically active proletarian populations emerged, composed of Italians, Greeks, and migrants from numerous Ottoman realms that remained well into the era of Nasser. See Ilham Khuri-Makdisi, *The Eastern Mediterranean and the Making of Global Radicalism, 1860–1914*, 146–49; on Italian migration to Egypt and Tunisia, respectively, see Joseph John Viscomi, "Between Italy and Egypt" and Julia Clancy-Smith, *Mediterraneans*.

54. See Elisabetta Zontini, *Transnational Families, Migration and Gender*, 4; Ruba Salih, *Gender in Transnationalism*, 30.

55. See Zontini, 4; Ayman Zohry, "The Migratory Patterns of Egyptians in Italy and France," 15–17; Faïçal Daly, "The Double Passage," 188; Daly, "Tunisian Migrants and Their Experience of Racism in Modesta."

56. See *Delić* Exhibit 1201, 96 (Italian translation only).

57. Karay (often Romanized in Bosnian press as Karaj or Karraj) continued to excite media attention in Tunisia, where he was accused of involvement in terrorist plots. See, e.g., Khadīja Yaḥyāwī, "Khaṭṭaṭa li-ʿamaliyyat Shibba'w min dākhil aswār sijn burj al-rūmī: al-qabḍ ʿalā al-irhābī 'Abū Ḥamza' fī maktab ʿadl ishhād bil-qaṣba," *al-Shurūq*, November 2, 2014. Because he has been the subject of quite extensive and sensationalist coverage, it is worth drawing attention to the few sources where he speaks for himself, including his April 28, 2005 testimony in the *Maktouf* case in the State Court of Bosnia (audio only) and ʿAbd al-Bāqī Khalīfa, "'Abū Ḥamza al-Tūnisī': nādim ʿalā al-taṭawwuʿ lil-qitāl ilā jānib al-Muslimīn," *al-Sharq al-Awsaṭ*, February 13, 2004.

58. As the largest Pakistani city near the border with Afghanistan, Peshawar was the hub for foreign aid efforts, diplomats, and spies from all directions. Nevertheless, it has acquired a reputation in the security literature as a "laboratory" of jihadism. See Rougier, 70–112. For snippets on the community of Arab pan-Islamic activists—aid

workers, journalists, proselytizers, mujahids—who settled in the 1980s and 1990s, see Miṣbāḥ Allāh ʿAbd al-Bāqī, *Ḥaqīqat al-ghazw al-Amrīkī li-Afghānistān*, 78–107; Ahmad Muaffaq Zaidan, *The Afghan Arabs Media at Jihad*, 9–14; Muhammad Amir Rana and Mubasher Bukhari, *Arabs in Afghan Jihad*.

59. For biographical sketches of Shaʿban, see Abdullah Rafi', "Sjećanje na Šehide Bosne," *El-Asr*, September 2008; "Ricordo di Anwar Shaʿban," *Il Messaggerro dell'Islàm*, November-December 1995; Nedžad Latić, "Hrvatska drži Šejha Ebu Talala u zatvoru i traži zemlju koja je voljna da ga primi," *Ljiljan*, November 15, 1995. On patterns of communications between the Katiba, ICI, and the outside world, see, e.g., Fax from Abu ʿUthman al-Kuwayti to Anwar Shaʿban, February 27, 1995, *Delić* Exhibit 1201 (Italian translation only); Fax from Katiba HQ (Zenica) to Abu Amin, ICI Milan, April 12, 1995, *Delić* Exhibit 1388.

60. In the 1970s, the Islamic Group was a broad-based movement with strong support on Egyptian university campuses. Many of its cadres joined the much larger Muslim Brotherhood while others took the remnants of the group in a more confrontational direction, culminating in a low-level insurgency in the 1990s. After its leadership largely was killed or imprisoned, the Islamic Group began the process of renouncing armed struggle. By the time of the 2010 uprisings, it was one of the more pro-regime political formations on the Egyptian scene. For background, see, e.g., Abdullah al-Arian, *Answering the Call*; James Toth, "Islamism in Southern Egypt."

61. The Abu Omar kidnapping, known as the "Imam rapito" affair in Italy, led to the conviction in absentia of twenty-six US citizens. Several Italian security personnel were tried in connection with the case. The European Court of Human Rights found that Italy violated rights of Abu Omar and his wife under the European Convention of Human Rights, both through allowing the abduction to take place as well as in the deficiencies of the subsequent prosecutions. The Court ordered Italy to pay the two of them a combined total of €115,000 in damages and expenses. See *Nasr et Ghali c. Italie*, 44883/09 (Eur. Ct. H.R. 2016).

62. Ḥamad Qaṭarī and Mājid al-Madanī, *Min qiṣaṣ al-shuhadāʾ al-ʿArab fil-Būsna wal-Harsak*.

63. Suvad Hadžić, *U kljunu zelene ptice*, 153.

64. On war wounds and moral economies among disabled African-American gang members and US military veterans, respectively, see Laurence Ralph, *Renegade Dreams*, 119–39; and Zoë H. Wool, *After War*, 97–113. In contrast to both of those cases, Abu ʿAli situates the horizontal relationship of moral debt owed by Bosnian Muslims alongside a

vertical relationship with the divine. In his understanding, it is the incommensurability of the latter that guarantees the rebalancing of the former; such immanence-in-excess can also be thought of as a way for universalist projects to subsume nationalisms within them, as will be explored more in later chapters. On communal building practices in rural Bosnia—especially for homes of hodžas (holy men), who are in a similar relationship of mediated reciprocity with locals—see William Lockwood, *European Moslems*, 108–9.

CHAPTER 2: LOCATIONS

1. It remains unclear if the Heritage Society explicitly authorized or was aware of the book being published in its name. The organization announced that it was printing books to "correct" Bosnian Muslims' dogma, but this usually involved translating texts by prominent Salafi scholars such as ʿAbd al-ʿAziz bin Baz and Muhammad Jamil Zeno. See Khālid al-Muṭawwaʿ, "al-Khurūj min nafaq al-Būsna al-muẓlim (1)," *al-Furqān*, January 1994.

2. Imad el-Misri, *Shvatanja koja trebamo ispraviti*, 2, 9–10, 13.

3. Dervišalija Hodžić, "Samozvani mudžtehid," *Preporod*, March 1995, 21. A mujtahid is an Islamic legal scholar qualified to exercise reasoning independent of otherwise binding authority [ijtihād], such as that claimed by the major schools of Islamic jurisprudence.

4. Furthermore, Latić reminded el-Misri of the importance of customary practices [ʿurf] that do not conflict with shariʿa: he ridiculed the suggestion that Muslims should wear black and grow beards since in Bosnia, those practices are stereotypically associated with Serbs. "Razbijanje Bošnjaka pod plaštom islama," *Ljiljan*, May 3, 1995, 29.

5. Fikret Arnaut, *Mezhebi u Islamu*, 29–30, 60–63.

6. el-Misri, 8.

7. Latić, 29. Others, too, could not resist throwing some of el-Misri's chauvinism back at him: "as with so many times when I tried to learn something from Arab professors, doctors, missionaries, and others about their opinions on preaching the original, most authentic Islam, I felt as I did in my youth when I read pulp [šund] literature: empty and deeply disappointed." Hodžić, 21.

8. According to Jusuf and several other veterans I spoke to, the Katiba eventually created a special unit for those under eighteen that was separated from combat duties, after the army high command issued an order banning the use of child soldiers. For more on the historical emergence and vicissitudes of the international legal category of the child soldier, see Kamari Clarke, *Fictions of Justice*, 89–109.

9. The villages around Bugojno were also the site where William and Yvonne Lockwood conducted some of the first ethnographic studies of Bosnian Muslims by Western scholars. William Lockwood in particular evinced a classically empiricist approach to the question of universalism in his research, which investigated whether marketplace interactions between peasants of different ethnic groups gave rise to other kinds of social bonds. In an equally classic gendered division of labor, his partner, Yvonne Lockwood, worked on folksongs, primarily among women. See William Lockwood, *European Moslems*; Yvonne Lockwood, *Text and Context*.

10. The Ottoman legacy is a necessarily ambivalent one here. On the one hand, much of Salafi discourse is deeply critical of the Ottomans for various reasons, including their indulgence of mystical practices said to conflict with monotheism, such as saint veneration; their adherence to the Hanafi school of jurisprudence, which Salafis reject; and the historical memory of the Ottoman-sponsored war against followers of ibn ʿAbd al-Wahhab in the nineteenth century. At the same time, the Ottomans introduced Islam on a large scale in Bosnia and ruled for centuries, meaning that many signs mobilized by Salafis and others to demonstrate Bosnia's authentically Islamic nature are in some way attributable to the Ottomans. From the other end, Bosnian Muslim discourses on the Arab world also resonate with various forms of Orientalism that were prevalent in the Ottoman empire from the nineteenth century onward. See, e.g., Ussama Makdisi, "Ottoman Orientalism." In any event, we will see in this chapter that the Austro-Hungarian legacy is as relevant to understanding the institutional landscape of Islam in Bosnia as the Ottoman one.

11. Muḥammad Nāsir al-Dīn al-Albānī, *Silsilat al-hudā wal-nūr*. For more on al-Albani's "quietism" in matters of jihad, see Joas Wagemakers, *Salafism in Jordan*, 60–92.

12. The dynamics of nationalism in the region have been subject to extensive commentary in recent decades—so much so that it is arguably the single most dominant theme in studies of the Balkans. These discussions have only rarely been critically approached through the question of secularism, largely due to an assumption that parts of the world that were ruled by socialist regimes left religion behind long ago. Recent scholarship has challenged this focus on nationalism at the expense of religious practice. See, e.g., David Henig and Karolina Bielenin-Lenczowska, "Recasting Anthropological Perspectives on Vernacular Islam in Southeast Europe"; Andreja Mesarič, "'Islamic Cafés' and 'Sharia dating'." The brief overview here is one attempt to answer the provocation by Pamela Ballinger and Kristen Ghodsee calling for genealogies of secularism that take into account

the experience of ex-socialist states in eastern Europe. See "Socialist Secularism." As will be discussed, however, the dynamics outlined here predate the socialist era in important ways.

13. On the debates over Bosnian Muslim nationality during the socialist period, see Brenna Miller, "Faith and Nation"; Husnija Kamberović, "Between Muslimdom, Bosniandom, Yugoslavdom and Bosniakdom"; Sabrina P. Ramet, *The Three Yugoslavias*, 286–95; Wolfgang Höpken, "Yugoslavia's Communists and the Bosnian Muslims." On the "Muslim question" in general, see Edin Hajdarpasic, *Whose Bosnia?*; Fikret Adanır, "The Formation of a Muslim 'Nation' in Bosnia-Hercegovina"; Sabrina P. Ramet, "Primordial Ethnicity or Modern Nationalism"; Ivo Banac, *The National Question in Yugoslavia*, 359–77.

14. The relevant anthropological literature on secularism can be broadly divided into two categories, according to whether Muslims are either the majority of the population or else cast as a minority against a dominant group. For examples of the former, see Hussein Ali Agrama, *Questioning Secularism*; Humeira Iqtidar, *Secularizing Islamists?*; Yael Navaro-Yashin, *Faces of the State*. Studies of Muslim minorities and secularism include Nadia Marzouki, *Islam: An American Religion*; Mayanthi Fernando, *The Republic Unsettled*; John Bowen, *Can Islam Be French?*

15. The centralized administrative body for Islamic affairs in Bosnia was called the Islamic Religious Community (Islamska vjerska zajednica, IVZ) for much of the twentieth century. For the sake of simplicity and at the risk of some anachronism, the name IZ will be used consistently here.

On the early history of the IZ and its roots in Austro-Hungarian rule, see Robert Donia, *Islam Under the Double Eagle*. On later periods, see Adnan Jahić, *Islamska zajednica u Bosni u Hercegovini za vrijeme monarhističke Jugoslavije*; Denis Bećirović, *Islamska zajednica u Bosni i Hercegovini za vrijeme avnojevske Jugoslavije (1945–1953)*. For a brief overview in English of the IZ's institutional development, see Fikret Karčić, "Administration of Islamic Affairs in Bosnia and Herzegovina."

16. This dynamic of nationalist identities defined according to religious categories moving toward territorial projects mirrors in many respects the history of the "Muslim question" in South Asia as well, spawning a series of comparative studies. See Sumantra Bose, *Contested Lands*; Robert Hayden, "Antagonistic Tolerance"; Radha Kumar, *Divide and Fall?* One significant difference, however, is that processes of bureaucratizing the administration of Islamic affairs have tended to be more centralized in the Balkans; there is no body equivalent to the IZ in India, Pakistan, or Bangladesh.

17. This is not to say, however, that "secularizing" processes only began with the Austro-Hungarian occupation. Bosnia was a major site for the Ottoman empire's tanzimat reforms, including the 1859 reorganization of Bosnia's shariʿa courts. See Fikret Karčić, *Šerijatski sudovi u Jugoslaviji 1918–1941*, 20. Indeed, although the Austro-Hungarian empire wished to curb or at least control Bosnia's ties to the Ottoman realm, it also arguably continued many of these earlier reforms. See Leyla Amzi-Erdoğdular, "Afterlife of Empire," 221–33.

18. See Karčić, "Islamic Revival in the Balkans 1970–1992." On secret police surveillance of Bosnian Muslims, including the IZ, see Ivan Brešlić, *Čuvari Jugoslavije*, Vol. 3: Muslimani.

19. See Isa Blumi, "Political Islam Among the Albanians," 3–9; Ger Duijzings, *Religion and the Politics of Identity in Kosovo*, 128–31.

20. On the shifting approaches to Bosnian Muslim nationalism among the Bosnian ulama, see Dunja Larise, "The Islamic Community in Bosnia and Herzegovina and Nation Building by Muslims/Bosniaks in the Western Balkans."

21. The fragmentation of the IZ was also subjected to a logic of nested secession: just as each republic of Yugoslavia that broke away had to contend with its own separatists, the administration of Islamic affairs in Serbia today remains divided between those who recognize the authority of the IZ in Sarajevo and followers of the mufti of Belgrade.

22. Mustafa Cerić, "Fetva broj 2," *Preporod*, December 1993.

23. Enes Karić, "Šerijat s bradom," *Preporod* (*Zenica*), December 1, 1993.

24. For Serb and Croat nationalists, there are historically two ways of refuting Bosnian Muslim nationhood: either to claim that they are simply co-nationals in denial (i.e. Serbs or Croats by nationality who happen to be Muslims by religion) or "Turks," that is to say, as settlers with no place in the region. Edin Hajdarpasic uses the term *(br)other* to signify this "potential of being both 'brother' and 'Other,' containing the fantasy of both complete assimilation and ominous, insurmountable difference—and thus making visible a range of passages between seeming opposites." Hajdarpasic, 16.

25. The oft-proclaimed division between civic, freedom-oriented (read: universalist) and ethnic, blood-and-soil (read: particularist) forms of nationalism has always been suspect. Pheng Cheah has demonstrated that both forms share a Kantian genealogy that posits the nation as an idealized embodiment of freedom precisely because it should be thought of as an organism, that is to say a self-organized autonomous being. See Pheng Cheah, *Spectral Nationality.*

26. The League's outreach efforts to Muslims in Yugoslavia date at least as far back as sending a delegation in 1974. See Muḥammad Ṣafwat al-Saqqā Amīnī, *al-Muslimūn fī Yūghūslāfiyā*. On the Muslim World League's work in Bosnia, including delegations by top officials, see "Potreba saradnje i koordinacije," *Preporod*, March 1995; A. K., "Obećana saradnja i pomoć," *Preporod*, February 1995; Islam Kadić, "'Saudijski narod je jedan od najosjećajnijih naroda koji znaju da saosjećaju sa svojom braćom u nevolji'," *Preporod*, March 1995.

27. On the US stance toward Iranian military aid to Bosnia, see Douglas Jehl, "U.S. Looks Away as Iran Arms Bosnia," *New York Times*, April 15, 1995; John Pomfret, "Iran Ships Explosives to Bosnian Muslims," *Washington Post*, May 13, 1994. According to Jovan Divjak—a Serb general in the Bosnian army—the famous underground tunnel that connected besieged Sarajevo to the outside world was originally suggested by Iranian military advisors. Jovan Divjak and Florence la Bruyère, *Sarajevo, Mon Amour*, 167–68. A member of the Iranian Revolutionary Guard Corps who had earlier fought in the Kurdish regions of Iran and Iraq was also killed by Croat forces while working in Bosnia. See Maryam Barādarān, *R*.

28. Hizballah is a Shiʿi movement, while Bosnian Muslims are overwhelmingly Sunni. Hizballah has acknowledged losing two fighters in Bosnia. One was born in the Lebanese diaspora in Liberia, the other a former student at Belgrade University—patterns of diasporic circulation that mirror those seen among the Sunni mujahids who are the focus of this book. "Shuhadāʾ al-muqāwama al-Islāmiyya fī shahr aylūl 1994," February 4, 2008, available at https://www.moqawama.org/essaydetails.php?eid=6227&cid=301. A prominent Hizballah commander who fought in Bosnia, ʿAli Ahmad Fayyad (Hajj ʿAlaʾ al-Busna), was killed while fighting in Syria in 2016.

29. See Zehra Alispahić and Nedžad Latić, "Braća su vezana dušama," *Ljiljan*, December 14, 1994. Transnational Muslim Brotherhood ties with Bosnia will be discussed in greater detail in Chapter 5.

30. See Ajet Arifi and Dževad Hodžić, "Turska treba bombardirati Beograd," *Ljiljan*, February 1, 1993. The major Turkish Islamic NGO İnsani Yardım Vakfı (often known by the acronym İHH) developed out of solidarity efforts with Bosnia in the early 1990s.

31. In Bosnia, the term *medresa* denotes a high school dedicated to Islamic subjects. All such schools are under the supervision of the IZ. During the socialist era, the only Islamic high school that remained open in Bosnia was the Gazi Husrev Beg medresa in Sarajevo. Today there are six medresas: aside from those in Sarajevo

and Travnik, such schools operate in Mostar, Tuzla, Visoko, and Cazin. Medresas in Serbia (Sandžak) and Croatia are also tied to the IZ.

32. The Austro-Hungarian medresa building stood out for Abu ʿAbd al-ʿAziz so much that he extolled its beauty to al-Albani and expressed sadness over its appropriation for worldly purposes. al-Albānī, *Silsilat al-hudā wal-nūr*. Abu ʿAbd al-ʿAziz was likely unaware that it was designed by a Catholic architect. See Jusuf Mulić, *Elči Ibrahim-Pašina medresa u Travniku (1939–1946)*, 33–34.

33. Ṣalāḥ al-Dīn, "Nastakhdim silāḥ al-takbīr fī ḥarbinā ḍidda al-Ṣirb," *al-Jihād*, February 1993.

34. See "Kutiba ʿalaynā al-jihād wa-bih waḥdah sanuḥarrir al-Būsna," *al-Jihād*, August 1993; "Nidāʾ wa-rajāʾ," *al-Jihād*, October 1992; Muḥammad al-Rāshid, "al-Jaysh al-Islāmī fil-Būsna wal-Harsak," *al-Mujtamaʿ*, September 29, 1992.

35. Aside from several hadith collections, Karalić translated the widely circulated Egyptian mystical text *Interview with a Jinn* into Bosnian. See Muhamed Isa Davud, *Razgovor sa džinom muslimanom*. On the Islamic University in Medina as a nodal point for scholars and students from many different nations, see Michael Farquhar, *Circuits of Faith*.

36. Muhidin Džanko, "'Priručnik islamske etike i bosanskog patriotizma'," *Preporod* (Zenica), February 1, 1993. There is some ambiguity over the Muslim Forces' position on the question of state implementation of shariʿa. For instance, Mahmut Karalić told *al-Jihād* magazine that their first goal was to establish an Islamic state in Bosnia. See Ṣalāḥ al-Dīn, 25. A year later, in an interview with a Bosnian army publication, Karalić insisted that "The Seventh [Muslim Brigade] is fighting for the kind of Bosnia our state leadership has advocated for from the beginning: unique, indivisible, and multinational, even if many think that the Seventh is fighting for a purely Muslim, or even Islamic, state." "Sedma nije imala uzora," *Patriotski List*, December 1994, 13. The theme of establishing an Islamic state is otherwise absent from the contemporaneous materials I have reviewed from the Muslim Forces and 7th Muslim Brigade—including interviews with other Islamist publications in the Arab world—suggesting that the statement to *al-Jihād* may have been intended primarily as an appeal for support from that magazine's readership.

37. Halil Mehtić and Hasan Makić, *Upute Muslimanskom borcu*, 16–17.

38. See Jusuf Ramić, *Bošnjaci na El-Azheru*, 137; Selman Selhanović, "Iman ulazi u naša srca," *Preporod*, September 1995; Salih Smajlović, "Komandant Muderis," *Preporod*, March 1994.

39. See Cornelia K. Sorabji, "Muslim Identity and Islamic Faith in Sarajevo," 171–92. On women and Muslim revivalism in Bosnia since the war, see Andreja Mesarič, "Wearing Hijab in Sarajevo"; Emira Ibrahimpašić, "Women Living Islam in Post-War and Post-Socialist Bosnia-Herzegovina."

40. See Marko Attila Hoare, *How Bosnia Armed.*

41. The less powerful of the two Bosnian Croat militias, the Croatian Defense Organization (HOS), traced its lineage to fascist strands of Croatian nationalism that historically had viewed Bosnian Muslims as "Croats of the Islamic faith." HOS's parent political party, the Croatian Party of Right, supported a Croatia-Bosnia confederation against Serb nationalism under the slogan "Croatia to the Drina, Bosnia-Herzegovina to the Adriatic" [Hrvatska do Drine, Bosna i Hercegovina do Jadrana]. In some parts of Bosnia, HOS units were nearly half Muslim; the extent to which Muslims joined out of actual identification with Croat nationalism versus for more prosaic reasons such as access to arms is a matter for further research. By early 1993, HOS was defeated and largely absorbed by forces allied with Croatian president Franjo Tuđman, who was more inclined to divide Bosnia up between Croatia and Serbia. For more on HOS in the Bosnian war, see Alex Bellamy, *The Formation of Croatian National Identity*, 77–78.

On Islamophilic strands in Croat nationalism more generally, see Nevenko Bartulin, *The Racial Idea in the Independent State of Croatia*, 37–38, 190–94. Such assimilationist tendencies generated their own tensions and contradictions, especially during World War II. See Emily Greble, *Sarajevo, 1941–1945*, 120–29.

42. See Sorabji, 147–48, 153–54.

43. In contrast, the 4th Muslim Light Brigade in Konjic kept Muderis as both a military and spiritual leader.

44. Imad el-Misri apparently took liberties in translation as well. In the translation of a fiqh manual from Arabic that he oversaw, there is an added footnote—presented as if part of the original text—vitiating the stipulation that parental permission is required for embarking on jihad. Compare Ali bin Ferid el-Hindi, *Skraćena zbirka fikhskih propisa*, 158; ʿAlī bin Farīd al-Kashjanwarī al-Hindī, *Mukhtaṣar al-aḥkām al-fiqhiyya*, 208. This change was likely intended to set at ease Bosnians like Jusuf who had joined the Katiba in defiance of their families' wishes.

45. See el-Misri, 36–61.

46. See Saʿīd bin ʿAlī bin Wahf al-Qaḥṭānī, *Ḥiṣn al-Muslim.* Al-Qahtani was a student of bin Baz and earned his doctorate at Imam Muhammad bin Saud Islamic University in Riyadh.

47. The Saudi High Committee subsequently introduced a different "official" translation of *The Fortress of the Muslim*. On disparate uses of this book among Muslims in Kazakhstan, see Wendell Schwab, "How to Pray in Kazakhstan."

48. See Saʿīd bin ʿAlī bin Wahf al-Qaḥṭānī, *al-Dhikr wal-duʿāʾ wal-ʿilāj bil-ruqā min al-kitāb wal-sunna*, 6–7.

49. Nasir al-Din al-Albani was born in 1914 in Shkodra (Shkodër, İşkodra) in what is now Albania, migrated to Damascus as a child, and died in Amman in 1999. ʿAbd al-Qadir al-Arnaʾut was born in 1928 in Istog (Istok), Kosovo, arrived in Syria in 1931, and died in Damascus in 2004. Shuʿayb al-Arnaʾut was born in Damascus in 1928 to a recently arrived Albanian family and died in Amman in 2016. For more on this community, see Muḥammad Mūfākū al-Arnāʾūṭ, "al-Albāniyyūn fī Sūriya wa-dawruhum fil-ḥayāt al-Sūriyya"; ʿAbd al-ʿAzīz al-Sadḥān, *al-Imām al-Albānī*, 14–16; Maḥmūd ʿAbd al-Qādir al-Arnāʾūṭ, *Sīrat al-ʿallāma al-Shaykh ʿAbd al-Qādir al-Arnāʾūṭ, 1347–1425*, 7–58.

50. This analysis of multiple forms of abridgement, copying, quotation, and commentary across the works of al-Qahtani and el-Misri resonates with the rich Bakhtinian method for analyzing Islamic legal texts developed by Brinkley Messick. For Messick, texts such as these are to be understood as cosmopolitan, in the sense that they were intended to circulate and resonate across different geographic contexts. See *Sharīʿa Scripts*, 26–30, 126–29. One can add to this account an attentiveness to transliteration as a specific act of writing, which understandably does not appear in Messick's exclusively Arabic textual universe. Transliteration is crucial for making Islamic texts cosmopolitan, in bringing them to those who cannot comfortably read Arabic script, as was the case for most Bosnian Muslims at the beginning of the war. In the case of the incantations given in *Notions That Must Be Corrected*, transliteration is writing that facilitates bodily inculcation of text through recitation from memory.

51. Mubarakpuri was from a village just outside Mubarakpur, a town in eastern Uttar Pradesh with a long history of home production and whose weaver community was active in the Non-Cooperation movement against the Raj. See Gyanendra Pandey, "'Encounters and Calamities'."

52. Mubarakpuri's first teacher and uncle, ʿAbd al-Samad Rahmani, had assisted in the preparation of a famous anti-Hanafi polemic widely reprinted in the Arab world, *Tuḥfat al-Aḥwadhī*. Mubarakpuri's first books, in Urdu, were tracts against Ahmadis, and he once reportedly spent three days debating doctrinal issues with Barelvi scholars. See Khālid Ḥanīf Ṣiddīqī, *Tarājim-i ʿulamāʾe Ahl-i Ḥadīth*, 149–57.

53. Despite extensive searches in libraries and personal book collections, I have not yet located a copy of the first Bosnian edition of *The Sealed Nectar*, although it is amply referenced in the Katiba's internal correspondence and external materials. See Fax to ICI, December 25, 1994; Fax from Abu al-Maʿali et al. to ICI Milan, March 7, 1995; *Nidāʾ al-Jihād*, April 20, 1995. I am relying here on the second, undated edition published by the Katiba. The book was printed in Travnik in ten thousand copies and is hardbound with a brown cover. The preface to the second edition warns that trafficking in copies of the book has already begun and reminds readers that the book is a gift [poklon] from the Katiba, to be distributed for free. My guess is that this second edition appeared in late 1995 or early 1996. An advertisement placed by the Katiba in a Bosnian army magazine in November of that year refers to the second edition as "at the printing press" [u štampi]. *Patriotski List*, November 1995, 63.

54. See Jasna Šamić, "Les Naqshbandî (plus particulièrement ceux de Visoko) et leur relations avec d'autres ordres Soufis."

55. Translation is another act of writing that may usefully complicate the heuristic contrast that Messick draws between the broad conceptual categories of the library (works with named authors but no named characters, such as legal treatises) and of the archive (documents full of named subjects but composed, copied, and filled out by largely anonymous clerks and scribes, such as contracts). Texts of the library are *authored*; those of the archive are *written*. See Messick, 22–23. In this context, translators are named like authors, but they are expected to recede, make way for, and enable the voices of others, as is the case with writers of documents. Yet translators' own intentions may diverge quite sharply from those that may be shared by authors and readers alike.

56. See *Nidāʾ al-Jihād*, April 20, 1995, 4; *Patriotski List*, November 1995, 63.

57. As it turns out, Mubarakpuri once wrote a brief essay about how particular affinities [intisābāt]—to a tribe, race, nation, and so on—are natural and neither inherently salutary or negative. "Islam is interested in clarifying the extent to which these affinities are either desirable or proscribed." "Ittijāh jāhilī . . . yajib al-qaḍāʾ ʿalayh," *al-Mujāhid*, May 1989, 39. This essay appeared in an Arabic-language magazine published by an Ahl-i Hadith jihad formation that established a short-lived emirate in the Kunar province of eastern Afghanistan.

58. It was often bundled as part of a collection of twenty books, mostly translations from Arabic, that were given to families as a self-contained library of Islamic texts. These included works by al-Nawawi, Muhammad Yasin, ʿAbd al-Majid al-Zindani,

Ibn Kathir, and al-Bukhari. See Ahmet Alibašić, "Traditional and Reformist Islam in Bosnia and Herzegovina," 15; Nedim Haračić, "Porodična biblioteka," *SAFF*, September 1999. SHC will be discussed more extensively in the Interlude.

59. See Bajro Perva and Selman Selhanović, "Prijevodi me obogaćuju i stručno i znanstveno," *Preporod*, May 1, 1997.

60. See Šavki Abu Kalil, *Uzroci pobjede i poraza*.

61. See Aḥmad Bāḥādhiq, "Akhbār min al-Būsna," *al-Ṣirāṭ al-Mustaqīm*, February 1995; Perva and Selhanović.

62. See, e.g., Larisa Kurtović, "What Is a Nationalist?"; Stef Jansen, *Yearnings in the Meantime*; Torsten Kolind, *Post-War Identification*.

63. Bosnia's postwar constitution is an annex to the American-brokered treaty that ended the war. It will be discussed further in Chapters 6 and 7.

64. Yugo-nostalgia will be discussed further in Chapter 5.

65. Almir Tahirović from Novi Travnik, a veteran of the TO, the 7th Muslim Brigade, and the Katiba, was killed in Chechnya in 2000. See Amir Krivokapa and Kemal Baković, "'Volila bih čuti da je poginuo u borbi . . . '," *SAFF*, May 2000.

66. The most careful analysis of this phenomenon available has identified approximately two hundred Bosniaks—both Bosnian citizens and those in the diaspora—who traveled to Syria and Iraq between 2012 and 2015. See Vlado Azinović and Muhamed Jusić, "The New Lure of the Syrian War—The Foreign Fighters' Bosnian Contingent." One cannot conclude that all of these individuals were fighting with Islamic State or any other armed factions, and anecdotal evidence suggests some returned quickly precisely because they were discouraged by the internecine warfare between various groups. Moreover, it is difficult to discern a direct line of causality between the Katiba and this phenomenon, as most of these emigrants are from a younger generation that grew up after the war. By my best count, four Bosnian veterans of the Katiba have been convicted in relation to the Syria conflict; three allegedly traveled and fought, while Husein "Bilal" Bosnić, the erstwhile leader of the Bosnian Salafi community, was prosecuted for inciting others to go. See *BH Prosecutor v. Husein Bosnić*, First-Instance Verdict, S1 2 K 017968 15 K (State Court of Bosn. & Herz. Dec. 14, 2015).

67. See *BH Prosecutor v. Enes Mešić, et al.*, First-Instance Verdict 32, S1 2 K 018891 15 K (State Court of Bosn. & Herz., Oct. 31, 2016). Delić also gave media interviews during this time criticizing Islamic State, arguing, "Muslims need a state, but not like this. We don't need a state built on a foundation of murders." "Ibrahim Delić: Muslimanima treba država, ali ne ovakva," HRT, November 20, 2015.

68. Hasan bin ʿAli al-Saqqaf (1961–) is a prominent Jordanian critic of Salafism. In Bosnia, his work has been translated and widely discussed. See Hasan Ali Sekkaf, *Vehabizam/selefizam*.

CHAPTER 3: AUTHORITIES

1. The incident, although dated to May 1995, appears in a memoir by a Malaysian mujahid, who also recounts stories of the Serbs being afflicted shortly before the battle by sudden bouts of diarrhea and being set upon by snakes. See Abdul Manaf Kasmuri, *Kolonel jihad*, 87–88.

2. The famous chronicle of early Islamic history compiled by al-Tabari includes several accounts of this incident; in one of them, the defeated Abu Sufyan is allegedly overheard saying, "I swear by God, I do not blame our people [for the defeat]. We met white-robed men on piebald horses, between heaven and earth, for which we were no match and which nothing could resist." *The Foundation of the Community*, 68.

3. The most common form of media production about the jihad are martyr hagiographies, which are replete with miracle stories. See Amīr Ḥamza, *Bosniyā ke ʿArab shuhadāʾ*; Ḥamad Qaṭarī and Mājid al-Madanī, *Min qiṣaṣ al-shuhadāʾ al-ʿArab fil-Būsna wal-Harsak*; Azzam Publications, *Under the Shades of Swords*; *In the Hearts of Green Birds*. They were also relayed by word of mouth: in one writeup, a Salafi activist returning to Kuwait from Bosnia told audiences a story about a Bosnian mujahid who not only foretold his own martyrdom but predicted exactly where on his body the enemy's bullet would strike. See Khālid al-Muṭawwaʿ, "al-Khurūj min nafaq al-Būsna al-muẓlim (1)," *al-Furqān*, January 1994.

4. Western commentary on jihad miracles has paid little analytical attention to this strand, focusing instead on martyrdom and presenting the stories as acts of propaganda that are meant to lure potential recruits with stories of heavenly ascension. See, e.g., David Edwards, *Caravan of Martyrs*, 98–105; Meir Hatina, *Martyrdom in Modern Islam*, 185–86; David Cook, *Understanding Jihad*, 153–57. While martyrdom is certainly an important aspect of jihad, the disproportionate and somewhat decontextualized focus on this category also gestures to liberal anxieties over the meaning of sacrifice and political violence. See Talal Asad, *On Suicide Bombing*, 39–50.

5. These stories and the disputes around jihad miracles echoed similar debates in Afghanistan. See Darryl Li, "Taking the Place of Martyrs." For deeper histories of skepticism toward miracle accounts, see Jonathan A. C. Brown, "Faithful Dissenters."

6. Carl Schmitt, *Political Theology*, 1, 36. For Schmitt, the sovereign's authority to adjudicate on the truth of miracle claims was the strongest example of his role as representative of divine authority on earth. See *The Leviathan in the State Theory of Thomas Hobbes*, 53–56.

7. The move here to relativize state sovereignty resonates with recent important ethnographic theorizations of sovereignty stemming from different contexts. Yarimar Bonilla's study of activism in the French overseas department of Guadeloupe highlights labor activists' disillusionment with the telos of national independence and how it generates alternative political visions. See *Non-Sovereign Futures*. In contrast, Audra Simpson's ethnography of Mohawk politics shows how indigenous responses to settler colonial projects of erasure emphasize a claim to sovereignty—indeed, an effort to "proliferate state sovereignty"—that culminates in, among many other practices, the use of passports to cross international borders and, in the 1990 Oka crisis, the resort to arms in defense of land. See *Mohawk Interruptus*, 154. The Bosnian jihad was a more mobile and ephemeral affair: its claim to authority was strongest as an argument for individuals to participate in foreign wars without any government's permission. Beyond that, such as in questions about establishing an Islamic state in Bosnia, its legitimacy was much more fraught.

8. Which is not to say that NATO was providing close air support to Bosnian forces in that battle. The bombing was primarily targeted at Bosnian Serb air defense installations, rather than ground forces. In contrast, NATO's 1999 air war against Yugoslavia included attacks on civilian infrastructure and media facilities, leading to hundreds, if not thousands, of civilian deaths.

9. I have come across only one statement by the Katiba on this issue, in an unsigned column in the unit's official newsletter criticizing nationalism as causing needless war between the Turkish state and Kurdish guerrillas: "We must work with all our strength to establish a state of the caliphate, a state for all Muslims, without nationalism, with no extremism [taʿaṣṣub] except for God and his Messenger, and this is a great duty." *Nidāʾ al-Jihād*, No. 7, April 7, 1995, 3.

10. The vast literature on these questions includes, e.g., Iza Hussin, *The Politics of Islamic Law*; Noah Salomon, *For Love of the Prophet*; Wael Hallaq, *The Impossible State*; Asghar Schirazi, *The Constitution of Iran*; and Hamid Enayat, *Modern Islamic Political Thought*, 69–110.

11. There are cases, of course, in which the overlap between rule and solidarity has been quite extensive, such as the Taliban during its time in power in Afghanistan

and Islamic State in Syria and Iraq. But the prominence of the latter case especially in recent years should not mislead us into hastily conflating the distinct issues at work.

12. In his influential exposition, Giorgio Agamben pushes Schmitt's reading of sovereignty as exception further by dwelling on the relationship between exception and rule, famously arguing that they merge and become indistinguishable. He analyzes exception etymologically:

> The exception is a kind of exclusion. What is excluded from the general rule is an individual case. But the most proper characteristic of the exception is that what is excluded in it is not, on account of being excluded, absolutely without relation to the rule. On the contrary, what is excluded in the exception maintains itself in relation to the rule in the form of the rule's suspension. *The rule applies to the exception in no longer applying, in withdrawing from it.* The state of exception is thus not the chaos that precedes order but rather the situation that results from its suspension. In this sense, the exception is truly, according to its etymological root, *taken outside* (*ex-capere*), and not simply excluded.

The exception is "not . . . absolutely without relation to the rule"—Agamben's turn to a double negative is an attempt to approach that which cannot be grasped directly. *Homo Sacer*, 17–18 (emphasis in original).

13. By critically reading Schmitt's earlier political theology in a transnational context, this analysis presents one possible way of bridging the earlier and later parts of his career. As Schmitt's interests shifted from constitutional to international law (and as he drifted away from Catholicism), the deism that inflected his work on sovereignty gave way to a more pagan mysticism fixated on the natural elements, land and sea especially. See, e.g., *Land and Sea*; *The Nomos of the Earth*.

14. The conscription of saintly authority in the service of state formation is a theme that dates to the early canon of anglophone anthropology, perhaps most notably in E. E. Evans-Pritchard, *The Sanusi of Cyrenaica*. But miracles have long stood out as a messy remainder. In his influential ethnography of Muslim saints in North Africa, Ernest Gellner left the miraculous as something of an afterthought, being unable to integrate it into his structural-functionalist account. His brief discussion of miracles, which comes at the end of a passage on miscellaneous "further services" provided by saints, concludes with an especially pertinent anecdote: "During the fighting in the course of the French conquest, top igurramen (hereditary saints) were held to be magically invulnerable. Crack shots took aim at them, and found their bullets

miraculously deflected." *Saints of the Atlas*, 139; see also 33, 137–38. More recently, Noah Salomon has shown how the category of the miraculous works to challenge state authority by reference to a story about Sudanese Islamist leader Hassan al-Turabi being suddenly afflicted by incontinence after insulting a prominent Sufi shaykh. See *For Love of the Prophet*, 158–72.

15. See Max Weber, "The Sociology of Charismatic Authority." Weber took the older Pauline notion of charisma as a divine favor bestowed upon individuals and transformed it into a type of authority residing in individuals as an immanent trait. For critical evaluations of Weber's use of the concept, see John Potts, *A History of Charisma*, 111–26; Hamid Dabashi, *Authority in Islam*, 33–45. States, of course, remain invested in co-opting saintly power for their own ends in a variety of ways. See, e.g., Angie Heo, *The Political Lives of Saints*; Alireza Doostdar, *The Iranian Metaphysicals*; Katherine Verdery, *The Political Lives of Dead Bodies*.

16. Emphasizing the importance of receptivity to miracles among their intended audiences, Bonnie Honig has argued for a political theology that favors popular power over the sovereign. See "The Miracle of Metaphor."

17. Walter Benjamin, "Theses on the Philosophy of History," 257.

18. ʿAzzam's writings were aimed at encouraging Muslims to travel to Afghanistan to help repel the Soviets. The logic of his argument does not by itself support what later became al-Qaʿida's *casus belli*, namely attacking the US in order to end its support for regimes in the Muslim world deemed to be illegitimate. ʿAzzam's untimely death in 1989 makes it impossible to know how his views might have evolved, although it is worth noting that the family has taken steps to distance his writings from al-Qaʿida. See Muḥammad al-Shāfʿī, "Zawjat al-zaʿīm al-rūḥī lil-'Afghān al-ʿArab': Qatl Masʿūd waṣma kubrā fī tārīkh Bin Lādin," *al-Sharq al-Awsaṭ*, April 28, 2006; Nir Rosen, "Iraq's Jordanian Jihadis," *The New York Times Magazine*, February 19, 2006. Some jihadologists have revised the earlier understanding of a straight line of thought between ʿAzzam and bin Laden. See, e.g., Peter Bergen and Paul Cruickshank, "Revisiting the Early Account of Al Qaeda," 5.

19. The earliest appearance of the fatwa that I have been able to trace was in a publication of the Muslim Brothers in Kuwait. ʿAbd Allāh ʿAzzām, "Jihād al-kāfirīn farḍ ʿayn," *al-Mujtamaʿ*, October 9, 1984. This ruling was expanded and published in book form as *al-Difāʿ ʿan arāḍī al-muslimīn* (*Defense of the Muslim Lands*).

20. ʿAzzam refers to "people of the *balda*," a term that connotes various scales of community, from a town to a country. *Al-difāʿ ʿan arāḍī al-muslimīn*, 23–24.

21. Adnan Zulfiqar notes in his close reading of ʿAzzam's fatwa that "[f]or pre-modern jurists, it would be untenable to expect someone halfway across the globe to be both informed about the conflict in Afghanistan and be expected to perpetually join the frontlines of every conflict involving Muslims. Yet this is precisely how ʿAzzām constructs the legal duty." "Jurisdiction Over *Jihād*," 459. On critiques of the fatwa from other Islamists and Islamic scholars, see, e.g., Thomas Hegghammer, *Jihad in Saudi Arabia*, 41; Muqbil Bin Hādī al-Wādiʿī, *Maqtal al-Shaykh Jamīl al-Raḥmān*, 29. The turn to encouraging travel to fight in Afghanistan without the permission of governments was apparently a source of considerable tension with the Muslim Brothers and led to ʿAzzam being marginalized or, according to some interlocutors in Pakistan who used to work in the Services Office, actually expelled from the movement.

22. See ʿAzzām, *al-Difāʿ ʿan arāḍī al-muslimīn*, 54–61.

23. During the jihad against the Soviets in Afghanistan, the seven major Sunni mujahid factions formed a united front that successfully sought to occupy the county's seat in the Organization of the Islamic Conference. On these and other diplomatic efforts, see Gilles Dorronsoro, *Revolution Unending*, 224–26.

24. None of this is to suggest that ʿAzzam was impartial in his relations with the Afghan mujahideen. In the early years, he was closest to ʿAbd Rabb al-Rasul Sayyaf, leader of one of the weaker factions in terms of popular support but one who was better able to network in the Arab world due to having spent years studying at al-Azhar and learning to speak Arabic fluently—a pattern not unfamiliar in many a solidarity space. On the entanglements between Arab and Afghan mujahids during the 1980s, see Mustafa Hamid and Leah Farrall, *The Arabs at War in Afghanistan*, 75–87; ʿAbd Allāh Anas, *Wilādat al-Afghān al-ʿArab*. Even the best-known early Arab-only military effort during the jihad, the Lion's Den [Ma'sada] base, was originally envisioned by Osama bin Laden as a joint Afghan-Arab effort. See Anne Stenersen, *Al-Qaida in Afghanistan*, 17.

25. On the tensions between the Taliban and al-Qaʿida, see Alex Strick van Linschoten and Felix Kuehn, *An Enemy We Created*.

26. This is drawn from a document made available online by "terrorism experts"—its provenance is unclear and the context for interpretation is missing. See Mabādiʾ fī idārat al-dawla al-Islāmiyya (2014), 19–20, https://www.scribd.com/document/292084330/Islamic-State-blueprint. It is also worth noting that Islamic State's erstwhile area of territorial governance conformed much more closely to the envisioned French sphere of influence under the (never-implemented) Sykes-Picot agreement. See Aslı Bâli, "Sykes-Picot and 'Artificial' States."

27. ʿAbd Allāh ʿAzzām, *Āyāt al-raḥmān fī jihād al-Afghān*, 1st ed. This book has been partially or completely translated into Turkish, Bahasa, English, and Bosnian. See Abdullah Azzam, *Afgan Cihadında Rahman'ın Ayetleri; Dan malaikat pun turun di Afghanistan; The Signs of ar-Rahman in the Jihad of Afghanistan*; and Abdullah Azam, *Allahovi znakovi u Afganistanskom Džihadu*. In contrast, I have found only an English translation of *Defense of the Muslim Lands*.

28. It is worth noting that at the time he wrote *Signs of the Merciful One*, ʿAzzam believed that the jihad in Afghanistan had not yet reached the point of becoming fard ʿayn upon Muslims worldwide. See ʿAzzām, "Jihād al-kāfirīn farḍ ʿayn," 27; *Āyāt al-raḥmān fī jihād al-Afghān*, 2nd ed., 174–75.

29. See Ali bin Ferid el-Hindi, *Skraćena zbirka fikhskih propisa*, 158–59.

30. Karamat are properly understood as gifts bestowed by God upon His friends; the term is also translated as marvel or charisma. The French Thomist and Orientalist Louis Gardet was among those who long ago identified a link between karama and the notion of charisma as divine favor or grace in the epistles of St. Paul. See L. Gardet, "Karāma."

In a very different context, Alain Badiou has noted a "fundamental link between universalism and charisma . . . universalism supposes one be able to think the multiple not as a part, but as in excess of itself, as that which is out of place, as a nomadism of gratuitousness." *Saint Paul*, 77–78. While the jihad did not take up Badiou's notion of redemption and event, both the presence of the ansar and the gratuitousness of the miracle in their political theology also gesture to the importance of "excess in itself" for thinking politics beyond the ontologies of incarnation and the pragmatics of nationalism and sovereignty.

31. See ʿAzzām, *Āyāt al-raḥmān fī jihād al-Afghān*, 2nd ed., 55–56.

32. See ibid., 59–60. The "customary order of things" is the phrase chosen to translate *al-ʿada*, conveying both senses of custom: repetition in the natural world and unwritten rules in human society—another example of the link between mysticism and divine law.

In the long-standing literature in Islam on phenomena that transgress the customary order of things [kharq al-ʿāda], salutary acts include signs that emanate directly from God, like the Quranic revelations [āyāt]; miracles performed by prophets [muʿjizāt]; and karamat, which are for God's saintly friends. On the less savory side are magic and trickery. See Denise Aigle and Catherine Mayeur-Jaouen, "Introduction: Miracle et *karāma*. Une approche comparatiste," 15; Abū Bakr al-Bāqillānī,

Kitāb al-bayān ʿan al-farq bayna al-muʿjizāt wal-karāmāt wal-ḥiyal wal-kihāna wal-siḥr wal-nārinjāt.

33. See ʿAzzām, *Āyāt al-raḥmān fī jihād al-Afghān*, 2nd ed., 55–56. In her work on Nigerian Pentecostalism, Ruth Marshall has also shown how a dispersed everyday sense of the miraculous can give rise to a more ambivalent political theology that neither venerates states nor rejects them. See Ruth Marshall, *Political Spiritualities.*

34. See Ernst Kantorowicz, *The King's Two Bodies.* In this respect, ʿAzzam departs significantly from traditions of Sufi hagiography that have produced much of the writing on the miraculous in Islamic scholarship, for which karamat often act as proofs of saintliness. For ʿAzzam and for the mujahids in Bosnia, the miracles are presented as evidence of collective more than individual righteousness.

35. Hussein Ali Agrama has highlighted the prominence of the literature on juristic tricks [ḥiyal] as one example of how shariʿa operates without the aspiration to or anxiety over completeness and seamlessness that characterize modern legal rationality. See *Questioning Secularism*, 142–44. Again, the link between the legal and the mystical remains: hiyal also refers to man-made trickery, one of the categories that had to be carefully distinguished from sanctioned forms of the miraculous. See al-Bāqillānī, 56–60.

36. One should stress that Islamic political theologies, to the extent such a category is useful, need not counterpose (mystical) saints and (worldly) rulers: notions of kingship in Safavid Iran and Mughal India were modeled on Sufi forms of authority, in which rulers could acquire saint-like reputations for miracle-making. See Azfar Moin, *The Millennial Sovereign.* For some sense of the wide range of political theologies among self-denominated "Islamic" states and political movements today, see Andrew March, "Genealogies of Sovereignty in Islamic Political Theology."

37. See *Delić* trial judgment, ¶¶ 172–9.

38. Abu al-Zubayr's group is far less well-documented than the Katiba. The portrait here is drawn mostly from interviews with the white American convert Ismail Royer, who served in it during the final year of the war, as well as from an anonymously authored memoir circulated online. See Abū al-Shuqarāʾ al-Hindukūshī, *Mudhakkirātī min Kābul ilā Baghdād.* It is worth noting that Abu al-Zubayr and several of his companions also show up in personnel lists of regular army units. See Information on Foreign Citizens, from Džemal Moranjkić, Ass't. Cmdr. for Reinforcement and Personnel, 319th Liberation Brigade to 3rd Corps SVB, 05/4-[incomplete number], October 27, 1995.

39. Individual Arabs served in other Bosnian army units, some of whom were apparently in Yugoslavia from before the war. See *Prosecutor's Office of Bosnia and Herzegovina v. Šefik Alić*, Second Instance Verdict, X-KRŽ-06/294 (State Court of Bosn. & Herz. Jan. 20, 2011); testimony of Ahmad al-Hajj Ahmad, *Maktouf* trial, March 22, 2005; Intelligence Report from Col. Sead Čudić, 1st Corps SVB, to General Staff SVB, 04/8250-1, June 9, 1995.

40. The unit suffered thirty-six fatalities during the war. All of the dead, including the three Arabs, are memorialized on the website of the 4th Muslim Light Brigade's veterans' association. See http://www.cetvrtamuslimanska.com.ba/sehidi/sehidi.html.

41. Of the three hundred or so whose names I found in an undated personnel roster for the Travnik Muslim Forces, about two dozen appear in the Katiba's records later on. Most of the others likely stayed on in the 7th Muslim Brigade.

42. This pamphlet is reproduced in Muḥammad Ṭāhir Naqqāsh, *Bosniyā ke jihādī maidānoñ meñ*, 191.

43. *Nidā' al-Jihād*, No. 6, March 6, 1995.

44. Letter from Abu al-Ma'ali, et al. to Islamic Cultural Institute (Milan), March 7, 1995.

45. *Nidā' al-Jihād*, No. 8, April 11, 1995.

46. It is also worth noting that suicide operations were not a feature of the Bosnian jihad and indeed would have made little sense under conditions of largely static conventional warfare.

47. See Yūsuf 'Abd al-Raḥmān, "Shuhadā' 'Arab fī ma'ārik al-Būsna," *al-Anbā'*, October 9, 1992; Muḥammad al-Rāshid, "Mas'ūl al-mutaṭawwi'īn al-'Arab wal-Muslimīn fil-Būsna wal-Harsak fī ḥiwār ma'a *al-Mujtama'*," *al-Mujtama'*, October 6, 1992. Hamad bin Khalifa Al Khalifa, also known as Abu Muhammad al-Fatih or Abu Khawla, was one of the first Arabs to join the Muslim Forces in Travnik and the first Bahraini killed in the Bosnian jihad. His death was widely reported in Arabic-language media in the Gulf. See Muḥammad Khayr Ramaḍān Yūsuf, *Tatimmat al-a'lām lil-Ziriklī*, Vol. 1, 151; Maḥmūd Ḥāmid Khalīl, "Abū Muḥammad al-Fātiḥ," *al-Mujtama'*, March 2, 1993.

48. See Muḥammad Nāsir al-Dīn al-Albānī, *Silsilat al-hudā wal-nūr*. A Turkish mujahid who fought in those engagements was similarly critical of the Bosnian army's actions. See Mehmet Ali Tekin, *Bosna Şehidlerimiz*, 121–22.

49. For biographical data on those killed at Ilijaš—including an Egyptian, a Bahraini, a Palestinian, two Afghans raised in Germany, and four Turks—see Tekin, 114–16, 130–31; Azzam Publications, *In the Hearts of Green Birds*; "Shuhadā' al-anṣār fil-Būsna wal-Harsak," *al-Jihād*, May 1993.

50. Ali Hamad, *U mreži zla: međunarodni terorizam i "Al-Kaida"*, 151. This recollection appears in the memoir of Ali Hamad, a Bahraini who was later ejected from the Katiba. After the war, Hamad stayed in Bosnia and served time in prison for various crimes, including a bombing in which he was a co-defendant with my client detained at Guantánamo Bay, Ahmad Zuhair (Zuhair was outside of the country during the trial and denies the charges). During his time in prison, Hamad began claiming that he had been sent to Bosnia by Osama bin Laden, in an apparently failed attempt to gain favor with US officials. He was a former brother-in-law to Saber Lahmar, one of the six Algerians sent from Bosnia to Guantánamo. Hamad likely furnished accusations that contributed to Lahmar's false imprisonment in Guantánamo and started openly aligning with Serb nationalists (his memoir was published by the Serb nationalist newspaper *Glas Srpske*).

51. See Report by Ramo Durmiš, Cmdr., First Battalion, 7th Muslim Brigade (undated). The *Hadžihasanović* trial judgment also discusses tensions within the Bosnian army that emerged after this battle. See ¶¶ 531, 629–630. These included an altercation in the summer of 1993 that resulted in the killing of two Arabs who allegedly attempted to assassinate Mahmut Karalić, the spiritual leader of the 7th Muslim Brigade. See Testimony of Halim Husić, *Delić* trial, March 11, 2008, 7430:2-7432:8; Report from SDB Zenica, March 10, 1994.

52. See Official Note by Osman Fuško, 306th Mountain Brigade SVB to 3rd Corps SVB, 03/383-10, August 26, 1993; UNMO Vitez to UNMO Sector HQ SW, Report Investigation of Harassing and Maltreating of Inhabitants of Podbrezjebje [*sic*] (VJ 90 99) by Mujaheddin, July 29, 1994, UNARMS S-1838-0186-0002; Information by Col. Ekrem Alihodžić, Cmdr., 3rd Corps SVB to General Staff SVB, 03/1-217-950, May 26, 1995.

53. See Official Note by Fikret Skejić, 35th Division SVB to 3rd Corps SVB, 03/1-80-16, July 5, 1995; Information by Col. Ekrem Alihodžić, Cmdr., 3rd Corps SVB to General Staff SVB, 03/1-174-154, July 9, 1995.

54. Tension also arose from Bosnians leaving their units to join the Katiba. The 306th Mountain Brigade—which leveled many of the accusations against the ansar in 1993 around Mehurići and Guča Gora—also had to grudgingly give retroactive approval to the "transfer" of forty-three of its troops to the Katiba. Such a large-scale defection was possible in an environment in which the Bosnian army was in many ways still a collection of autonomous local militias. See Information by Halim Husić, Ass't. Cmdr. for Morale, Information & Propaganda, and Religious Affairs, 306th Mountain Brigade to 3rd Corps Morale Department, 04/68-17, May 6, 1993; Approval for Conscript Transfers, Vezir Yusufspahić, Cmdr., 306th Mountain Brigade

to Elmudžahedin Detachment, 05/120-32, September 9, 1993; List of Members of the Unit, Odred Elmudžahedin, 001/93 (undated).

55. The purported fanaticism of the mujahids also helpfully distracted from an inner truth of state sovereignty that defies total rationalization: the capacity to demand sacrifice through violence. See Paul Kahn, *Putting Liberalism in Its Place*, 230–41.

56. Testimony of Protected Witness 9, *Delić* trial, November 15, 2007, 5636:11-15.

57. On the circumstances of the arrest of the three Arabs, see Report by Col. Ramiz Dugalić, Chief, ARBiH 3rd Corps Security Sector, 03/1-76-3, January 29, 1994. Abu al-Harith's handwritten letter is dated January 30, 1994.

58. Fadhil used the literal term *suicide operation* [ʿamaliyya intiḥāriyya], which lacks any positive connotation. When suicide missions are valorized in Arabic they are usually described as "martyrdom-seeking operations" [ʿamaliyyāt istishhādiyya].

59. See Odred Elmudžahedin, *Podsjelovo/Fethul mubin*. See also *Delić* judgment, ¶¶ 383–384.

60. See Testimony of Fuad Zilkić, *Delić* trial, November 9, 2007, 5301:8-22. Hasan Efendić, who commanded the Territorial Defense militia early in the war and later served as military advisor to Izetbegović, described the army's initial misgivings about collaborating with the mujahids but credited them with "long-running and solid preparation," "great courage," and strong logistics. *Mudžahedini u Bosni i Hercegovini—borci ili teroristi*, 164.

61. See also Testimony of Fadil Imamović, *Delić* trial, October 11, 2007, 3972:16-3973:7. Imamović was the chief of security for the 35th Division, which oversaw the area in which the Katiba was deployed.

62. Testimony of Fuad Zilkić, *Delić* trial, November 9, 2007, 5327:7–8.

63. See Report by Maj. Fadil Imamović, Ass't. Cmdr. for Security, 35th Division to 3rd Corps SVB, 03/1-157-499m, August 6, 1995; Order by Gen. Sakib Mahmuljin to El-Mudžahedin Detachment, 05/5-194, August 9, 1995.

64. Some soldiers from the 328th Mountain Brigade who trained with the Katiba in the hopes of gaining new combat skills and boosting their morale complained that the training consisted entirely of "learning the Qur'an and other religious books." Information Report from Col. Ekrem Hadži Alihodžić, Cmdr., 3rd Corps SVB to General Staff SVB, 03/1-174-143-1, July 1, 1995. The commanders of the 328th and the Katiba met to defuse the tensions. See Information by Alihodžić to General Staff SVB, 03/1-174-149-1, July 3, 1995.

65. Bosnian army publications from the period note the Katiba's role as one of the spearheads of the campaign. See Fuad Frtuna, "Kataklizma tvrđave Četništva,"

Patriotski List, October 1995; Adnan Džonlić, "Oslobođen 'Četnički Staljingrad'," *Patriotski List*, October 1995; Spahija Kozlić, "Uništena Laka prnjavorska brigada," *Prva Linija*, August 1, 1995; Adnan Džonlić, "Sijelo na Podsjelovu," *Prva Linija*, June 1995.

66. According to internal correspondence from Abu ʿAbd al-ʿAziz, the Katiba was unable to raise funds in Saudi Arabia. See Letter from Abu ʿAbd al-ʿAziz to Abu al-Maʿali, May 6, 1995 (Italian translation only). Individuals could still travel to participate in jihad or financially assist those who did. One mujahid who departed from Saudi Arabia recounted to a journalist that his trip to Bosnia was funded by a female schoolteacher who gave him $US2,000. See Khālid Ḥammādī, "Tanẓīm al-Qāʿida min dākhil kamā yarwī Abū Jandal (Nāṣir al-Baḥrī) al-ḥāris al-shakhṣī li-bin Lādin (1)," *al-Quds al-ʿArabī*, March 18, 2005.

67. Al-ʿAwda penned a preface to an online book chronicling the stories of ansar martyrs in Bosnia. See Qaṭarī and al-Madanī. Ironically, he had earlier opposed travel to fight in Afghanistan and maintained his rejection of ʿAbd Allah ʿAzzam's position that participation in the jihad was fard ʿayn for every Muslim. See Stéphane Lacroix, *Awakening Islam*, 195–98.

68. See, e.g., Muṣṭafā Abū Saʿd, "al-Būsna wal-Harsak: āmāl wa-jarāḥ," *al-Furqān*, February 1995; al-Muṭawwaʿ; Muṣṭafā Abū Saʿd, "Ayyuhā al-Muslimūn: man li-Muslimī al-Būsna wal-Harsak," *al-Furqān*, November 1994; "Intiṣārāt al-Muslimīn fil-Būsna," *al-Furqān*, August 1993.

69. The Kuwaiti state welcomed Salafi activists into the state system in the early 1980s as a way to capture sectarian energies after the Iranian revolution as well as to create a counterweight to other opposition parties. The Heritage Society was founded in 1981 by Salafis leaving the Muslim Brotherhood-oriented Social Reform Society. See Sāmī Nāṣir al-Khālidī, *al-Aḥzāb al-Islāmiyya al-siyāsiyya fil-Kuwayt*, 223–25.

70. Islamists, both Salafis and the Muslim Brotherhood, played an important role in resistance to the occupation, especially through the country's food cooperatives (essentially state-subsidized grocery stores), whose governing boards they controlled after a series of elections from the 1970s onward. See Pete Moore, *Doing Business in the Middle East*, 90–91; Shafeeq Ghabra, "Voluntary Associations in Kuwait," 213–14.

71. The first chairman of the Heritage Society, Khalid al-Sultan bin Essa, is one of the key figures in a family business that operates in various sectors, including real estate, finance, and construction. He studied in the US and married an American woman and started his political career as a liberal before joining the Salafi current, which he has also represented in the National Assembly. See Falah Abdullah al-Mdaires, *Islamic Extremism in Kuwait*, 33–34; J.R.L. Carter, *Merchant Families of Kuwait*, 101–3.

One of Bin Essa's nephews, Tareq Sami Sultan al-Essa, was a leader of the Heritage Society during the Bosnian war and took over as chairman in 1995. Tareq al-Essa studied engineering at the University of Colorado Boulder and manages a major construction contracting company. See "Meeting with RIHS Chairman: Defensive in Face of Frank Discussion of USG Concerns," Cable from Amb. Richard LeBaron to U.S. State Department, 06KUWAIT251a, January 25, 2006.

72. See Testimony of Protected Witness 9, *Delić* trial, April 17, 2008, 8685:2-19.

73. See Letter from Abu al-Maʿali, et al. to ICI, March 7, 1995. Although Ibn ʿUthaymin's endorsement of the Katiba's approach also came up in various interviews, I have not been able to find a written or recorded fatwa.

74. Anwar Shaʿban came from the Alexandrian school of Salafism, a group that considered the Egyptian regime to be engaged in disbelief (kufr), but not necessarily the individuals working for it. Hence, it managed to steer a line between the Muslim Brotherhood's relatively accommodationist stance and the path of armed confrontation chosen by the Islamic Group from the 1980s onward. For background on Alexandria's Salafi movement, see Richard Gauvain, *Salafi Ritual Purity*, 287; Ṣalāḥ al-Dīn Ḥasan, *al-Salafiyyūn fī Miṣr*, 17–24.

75. Fax from Anwar Shaʿban to Tareq al-Essa, March 15, 1995, *Delić* Exhibit 1201, 62 (Italian translation only). Events escalated even more dramatically in subsequent months. The Islamic Group would be blamed for an attempt on Mubarak's life at the Organization of African Unity summit in Addis Ababa in June and the bombing of the Egyptian embassy in Islamabad in November.

76. As we saw with Abu ʿAli in Chapter 1, mujahids without children sometimes take a kunya after their father's name.

77. The only nationality-based nisba that I have never seen in jihad contexts is "al-Saʿudi"—since this is a state that takes its name from a ruling family, adopting such a nisba would create an awkward and misleading sense of fealty. Citizens of Saudi Arabia are more likely to use nisbas denoting specific regions or cities within the kingdom, such as al-Hijazi, al-Najdi, al-Sharqi, al-Madani, and so on.

Another practice is to take nisbas based on earlier locations of jihad. Some Afghan Arabs, for example, have penned memoirs using nisbas referencing places in Afghanistan, such as "al-Logari" and "al-Qandahari." See Muṣṭafā Bādī, *Afghānistān: iḥtilāl al-dhākira*; Ayman Ṣabrī Faraj, *Dhikrayāt ʿArabī Afghānī*. Similarly, the moniker "Španac" ("Spaniard") was used by some Yugoslav partisans who had fought in the International Brigades, like Fadil Jahić, Žikica Jovanović, and Vladimir Popović.

78. See *Delić* trial judgment, ¶¶ 285–335. War crimes by the mujahids will also be discussed in the Interlude.

79. See Taib Terović, *Sedma*.

80. Bosnians from the Katiba who received the award, however, are acknowledged. See Hasib Mušinbegović et al., *Monografija Zlatni Ljiljani i odlikovani pripadnici Armije R BiH 1992.–1995.*, 39, 88, 250. At least eleven ansar in the 3rd Corps (apparently all members of the Katiba) received the Golden Lily, and at least nine were awarded the second-highest army decoration, the Silver Shield. See Order by Gen. Rasim Delić, 8/2-5638-2, December 23, 1995; Order by Delić, 8/2-5638-3, December 23, 1995. It has been suggested that the awards were given to a randomly chosen set of mujahids to help smooth their departure from Bosnia at the end of the war. See Testimony of Alija Lončarić, *Delić* trial, April 11, 2008, 8424:13-19.

81. The monument was inaugurated in 2008. See Zavidovići municipality press release, "Svečano otvaranje spomen-obilježja," available at https://web.archive.org/web/20170403160555/http://www.zavidovici.ba/index.php/vijesti-i-obavijesti/vijesti-i-obavijesti-2009–g/46–svecano-otvaranje-spomen-obiljezja.

82. Similarly, a Bosnian book profiling some ansar martyrs refers to the Egyptian Husam al-Din, one of the Katiba's military commanders, as "Abdullah Husam el-Masri [the Egyptian]." Almir Kovačević, *Iskre svjetlosti*, 181–82.

CHAPTER 4: GROUNDINGS

1. On Bosnian Muslim debates over the commemoration and burial of war martyrs, see Sarah Wagner, *To Know Where He Lies*, 213–44; Xavier Bougarel, "Death and the Nationalist."

2. Burial patterns for ansar who were not in the Katiba were also more varied. At the Šadrvan mosque in Visoko, for example, a mujahid described as an ex-brigadier in the Egyptian army is buried with a standard Bosnian martyr nišan.

3. Ahmet Şamil Karaoğlu grew up in Stuttgart and served briefly in the German military as a radar operator. He was killed in the July 1995 battle near Vozuća and buried in the mujahids' cemetery near the village of Livade, where his grave was marked by one of the standardized obelisk-shaped martyr nišans used by the Islamic Community since the war. See Mehmet Ali Tekin, *Bosna Şehidlerimiz*, 163–69. A mosque in the city of Reutlingen was named after him.

4. "Mudžahid nikada ne gubi!" *Patriotski List*, October 1995, 23.

5. *Melez*, here translated as "half-blood," is an archaic, if not necessarily pejorative,

Bosnian term often used for terms such as *Mestizo* or *Mulatto*. It is very likely that Abu al-Maʿali spoke to the journalist in Arabic or French rather than in Bosnian, which lends an additional layer of complexity in parsing this curious turn of phrase.

6. This mujahid was vividly remembered as Muhammad from Gambia in many of my interviews, although his archival paper trail raises even more questions. He appears with slightly different names and dates of birth in the Katiba's records and was apparently awarded the army's highest decoration, the Golden Lily. By most accounts, he was killed after the war while fighting in the Ogaden region of Ethiopia. Intriguingly, a Gambian with the same name was also listed on a website commemorating foreign volunteers fighting alongside Croat forces early in the war and reported killed in action in Travnik.

7. Published accounts in Arabic tend not to mention racial distinctions among Arab mujahids, a fact that cannot be disconnected from diverse forms of anti-Blackness in the region. As a result, it was difficult to identify Black Arab mujahids except in cases when photographs were available or if race was mentioned in other sources. One significant example was Abu Khalid, the first Qatari martyr in Bosnia. His death received substantial media coverage in regional media but his being an Afro-Qatari only came up in a biography by British mujahids. Compare, e.g., Muḥammad Khayr Ramaḍān Yūsuf, *Tatimmat al-aʿlām lil-Ziriklī*, Vol. 2, 11–12; and Azzam Publications, *In the Hearts of Green Birds*.

8. On the simultaneous denigration and appropriation of Blackness among Arab and South Asian Muslims in the United States, see Su'ad Abdul Khabeer, *Muslim Cool*, 83–84.

9. This approach draws loose inspiration from Jacques Rancière's notion of politics as the "processing of a wrong" [traitement d'un tort]. For Rancière, any situation of community presents the problem of a gap between the sum of its parts—construed as social classes, ethnic groups, castes, or otherwise—and the ability to speak for it as a whole. This "constitutive wrong or torsion of politics as such" is also what gives rise to the possibility of politics, understood as a paradoxical act of performing the very equality that the regnant order denies. See *Disagreement*, 14, 35; see also "The Cause of the Other."

Needless to say, the case at hand departs markedly from the parameters of Rancière's thought in two important ways. First, the equality of human beings posited in Islam—and the Salafi emphasis on relationships with God unmediated by scholarly hierarchies—cannot be hastily equated with the equality of thinking and speaking subjects imagined by Rancière, at least not without substantial qualification. Second, jihad shows how war in particular can open spaces for the reconfiguration of relationships that makes politics—in the very narrow sense of which he sometimes speaks—possible. This highlights one significant limitation of Rancière's theory of politics, namely his apparent inability to deal with war (especially of the anticolonial variety)—while he classifies the violence of hegemony under the sign of "police," he ignores war as an agonistic relation through which equality is at times asserted by weaker parties whose ability to reason is otherwise dismissed out of hand. See Ayten Gündoğdu, "Disagreeing with Rancière."

10. The perception of Bosnians as being less authentically Muslim stems at least in part from broader processes that treat "Muslim" as a racialized—and nonwhite—category rather than a confessional one. Within the West, whiteness is primarily associated with Islam under the rubric of conversion and marginal to the primary dynamic between descendants of enslaved Africans and more recent immigrants arriving mostly from the Middle East and South Asia. See, e.g., Sylvia Chan-Malik, *Being Muslim*; Abdul Khabeer; Sherman Jackson, *Islam and the Blackamerican*. Because Bosnian Muslims' relationship with Islam is centuries old and serves as the basis for claims to nationhood, they are far more destabilizing to the racialization of Muslims as nonwhite than recent converts. Ismail Royer told me that as a recent white American convert, his interest in Bosnia was originally piqued at discovering people who were "naturally" both white and Muslim, enjoying in his eyes a relative authenticity.

11. Henri Lauzière's work has significantly clarified debates around the use of the term *Salafi*. Lauzière distinguishes older uses of the adjective *Salafi* to describe various theological or jurisprudential doctrines from the emergence of *Salafism* the noun, an all-encompassing method of life [manhaj] from the 1970s onward. Lauzière traces the trajectory of the latter through the works of the Egyptian thinker Mustafa Hilmi (1932–). Ironically, the very emergence of this more expansive notion of the Salafi exists in tension with the desire for purity (be it ritual, theological, or legal) that allegedly characterizes this orientation. See *The Making of Salafism*, 216–27.

12. It should be noted, of course, that the term *Sufism* is also an etic nominalization that brings together and reifies a disparate set of doctrines, practices, and institutions. See Shahzad Bashir, *Sufi Bodies*, 9–11.

13. ʿAzzam's background was in the Muslim Brotherhood, but he also described himself as someone who "has spent more than a quarter century studying God's

religion [dīn] and carrying the Salafi creed [al-ʿaqīda al-salafiyya].” ʿAbd Allāh ʿAzzām, *Āyāt al-raḥmān fī jihād al-Afghān*, 2nd ed., 61.

14. Daniel Lav uses the term *radical* (and, by extension, *Salafi jihadi*) for those who believe that jihad is permissible against ruling regimes in Muslim-majority countries, an issue that he ultimately locates in a theological dispute over whether and when it is possible to declare that rulers are unbelievers. *Radical Islam and the Revival of Medieval Theology*, 11. Joas Wagemakers similarly speaks of “Jihadi-Salafis” as those endorsing armed uprisings against Muslim rulers deemed insufficiently Islamic, even as he acknowledges that Salafis can and at times do support or engage in other forms of jihad—yet he does not address the conceptual problems this raises. *Salafism in Jordan*, 57. Shiraz Maher reserves the term *Salafi-Jihadi* for what he calls “violent-rejectionists” who oppose the nation-state altogether, also while conceding that many Salafis engage in jihad without meeting such a definition. *Salafi-Jihadism*, 11–12. This narrow and indeed idiosyncratic definition does not prevent him from liberally drawing upon such thinkers who arguably do not meet it, including Abu Muhammad al-Maqdisi and Abu Qatada. For a trenchant critique of the Salafi jihadi concept coming from the competing strand of terrorism experts who favor sociological rather than doctrinal approaches, see Thomas Hegghammer, “Jihadi-Salafis or Revolutionaries?”

15. A recent volume purporting to map the concept of “jihadi culture” exemplifies this problem. The contributors catalogue a series of practices labeled as “jihadi” even as they readily acknowledge that the practices are not particular to jihad contexts at all, but rather shared widely among Muslims. See Hegghammer, “Introduction: What Is Jihadi Culture and Why Should We Study It?” 7. Indeed, the volume serves as compelling evidence against the utility of “jihadi culture” as a category.

As is so often the case, culturalism here ultimately reinscribes stale and harmful notions of Muslim essentialism, in two ways. First, although the volume defines “jihadi culture” as everything jihadis do that is not strictly necessary to military endeavors, the contributors end up focusing on nonmilitary practices that they understand to be Islamic, revealing that for them culture is only meaningful if attributable to Islam and insofar as it stands for alterity—regardless of explanatory utility, which the contributors concede is in short supply. Second, the concept underwrites arguments about Muslim authenticity that reflect unexamined assumptions of normative whiteness, allowing the volume’s editor to conclude, for example, “[i]n the eyes of prospective recruits from a conservative religious background, jihadi groups can appear as culturally relatively authentic. This is in contrast to other subcultures, such as the Ku Klux Klan or the skinhead movement, which, culturally speaking, represent complete innovations and sharp breaks from the mainstream." Hegghammer, "Non-Military Practices in Jihadi Groups," 200. The reasoning that allows labeling jihadism a "relatively authentic" expression of Islam but the Ku Klux Klan to be a "complete innovation" in the history of whiteness is, unsurprisingly, assumed rather than explicated.

16. See Thomas M. McKenna, *Muslim Rulers and Rebels*; David Edwards, *Heroes of the Age*; *Before Taliban*; Cabeiri deBergh Robinson, *Body of Victim, Body of Warrior*.

17. The question of "everydayness" relates to broader questions as to whether one's object of anthropological analysis is Islam versus Muslims, and the different dilemmas these approaches pose. For contours of the debate, see Nadia Fadil and Mayanthi Fernando, "Rediscovering the 'Everyday' Muslim"; Samuli Schielke, "Living with Unresolved Difference"; Lara Deeb, "Thinking Piety and the Everyday Together."

18. Talal Asad, *On Suicide Bombing*, 42.

19. All of this follows from Asad's pathbreaking work that rendered secularism legible as an object of analysis. See *Formations of the Secular*. Asad's students, particularly Saba Mahmood, have taken up this line of attack, demonstrating how notions of secularism are deployed to justify and structure US hegemony. See Saba Mahmood, "Secularism, Hermeneutics, and Empire."

20. Talal Asad, "Muhammad Asad Between Religion and Politics," 87. In place of the state as the horizon for political struggle, Asad posits in this essay a politics based on persuasion across differences and on civil disobedience, albeit both arising from embodied and cultivated dispositions. While this proposal has much to commend it, it is difficult to parse how far this approach actually departs from the liberal modes of subjectivity Asad rightly critiques.

21. Asad, "Thinking About Terrorism and Just War," 19.

22. Here there is a gap between Asad's work on violence—which seeks to deconstruct invidious distinctions between liberalism and its Others—and his influence on the anthropology of Islam, which has emphasized the need to think seriously about alternatives to liberalism. See *Genealogies of Religion*. That the most productive anthropological theorizations of Islam have provided so little help in analyzing jihad is less a sign of this literature's inadequacy than a reason to question why it should bear the burden of this explanation in the first place.

23. As Saba Mahmood has observed, "[W]e have few conceptual resources available for analyzing sociopolitical formations that do not take the nation-state and its juridical apparatuses as their main points of reference." *Politics of Piety*, 194. Mahmood's

ethnography of piety practices fleshes out a kind of affective infrastructure for different modes of politics, but the outcomes are necessarily underdetermined and contingent to the point that other bridging notions are necessary to understand concrete instantiations of political action, including those that invoke jihad. Universalism is proposed here as one such bridging concept.

24. The Katiba's military commanders were Egyptians in their twenties, all close companions who fought in the Afghan jihad. Wahy al-Din succeeded Abu ʿAbd al-ʿAziz as leader of the Arab mujahids working with the Muslim Forces. He was reportedly from a village in Beni Suef governorate and had received basic training at a camp of the Islamic Group in Afghanistan. Wahy al-Din was killed in October 1993 during fighting against Croat forces, and his body was reportedly still fresh when returned to the mujahids three months later. Wahy al-Din was succeeded by Husam al-Din, who was killed by a landmine during military operations against Serb forces in the autumn of 1994. Al-Muʿtazz Billah, the third and final military commander of the Katiba, was from Upper Egypt and a university graduate in law. He oversaw the major offensives in the latter half of 1995 and was killed by Serb tank fire during mop-up operations after the September 1995 Vozuća battle. This biographical data was compiled from interviews and a variety of written sources, including *Nushrat al-mujāhidīn*, November 11, 1994; and "Min qiṣaṣ al-shuhadāʾ al-ʿArab: al-Muʿtazz Billāh," available at http://saaid.net/Doat/hamad/58.htm. See also Aḥmad bin Ḥāzim bin Muḥammad Bek Tawfīq al-Maṣrī, *Tajliyat al-rāya*, 356; Almir Kovačević, *Iskre svjetlosti*, 181–82; Azzam Publications, *Under the Shades of Swords*.

25. The magazine *al-Jihād*, founded and edited by ʿAbd Allah ʿAzzam to promote Arab support for the Afghan jihad, included a regular section titled "Akhlaq of Jihad" between 1987 and 1994, emphasizing a single virtue in each issue.

26. *Akhlaq* is a special plural noun derived from *khulq/khuluq*, or innate disposition. The Arabic root connotes creation, especially of the divine variety, as in the phrase "all God's creatures."

27. This literature is too voluminous to be adequately summarized here, but major works include, e.g., Lila Abu-Lughod, *Do Muslim Women Need Saving?*; Joan Wallach Scott, *The Politics of the Veil*; and Mahmood, *Politics of Piety*.

28. Charles Hirschkind has traced how audiocassette sermons circulating in Cairo have also encouraged the cultivation of such virtues as a means in themselves and also as necessary to the effective conduct of daʿwa and, by extension, the moral reform of society. See *The Ethical Soundscape*, 130–33.

29. Testimony of Živko Totić, *Hadžihasanović* trial, February 20, 2004, 3191:20–25, 3192:1. This prisoner exchange will be discussed in greater detail in the Interlude.

30. Testimony of Dieter Schellschmidt, *Hadžihasanović* trial, May 24, 2004, 7908:20–21.

31. "... samo ga je duga brada činila muževnim." Nedžad Latić, *Boja povijesti*, 94.

32. Born ʿAdil Muhammad Salman ʿAbd Allah al-Ghanim in 1962, Abu Muʿadh hailed from al-Fahaheel, an erstwhile fishing community that since has been absorbed into the southern stretches of Kuwait City. He worked for the national oil company, whose headquarters and main refineries are in the nearby town of al-Ahmadi.

Abu Muʿadh was a renowned athlete and, according to one report, had a "good disposition" [ḥasan al-khalq] "Qiṣṣat shahīd fil-zaman al-ṣaʿb," 2001, Bab.com. At some point in the 1980s, he traveled to Afghanistan for jihad, spending time alongside Jamil al-Rahman, the Ahl-i Hadith leader in Kunar province who was frequently at odds with the larger mujahid factions. Abu Muʿadh returned home and participated in resistance to the Iraqi occupation of Kuwait. He first traveled to Bosnia in the summer of 1992, then returned home to raise funds and gather weapons and came again in 1994. Within the Katiba, Abu Muʿadh was a field commander and amir of the Arab mujahids. He was killed by a Serb sniper in July 1995 in the aftermath of Operation Karama. See *Nushrat al-Mujāhidīn*, November 11, 1994, 1; *Nidāʾ al-jihād*, No. 11, June 10, 1995, 7; Azzam Publications, *In the Hearts of Green Birds*; Odred Elmudžahedin, *Podsjelovo/Fethul mubin*.

Abu Muʿadh's death was widely reported in the Kuwaiti press across political affiliations and occasioned a note of condolence from Bosnia's ambassador to the country. "Kalimat al-safīr al-Būsnī fī taʿziya ʿāʾilat al-shahīd al-Kuwaytī ʿĀdil Muḥammad Salmān ʿAbd Allāh al-Ghānim," *al-Qabas*, July 25, 1995. For more biographical data, see Abū al-Shuqarāʾ al-Hindukūshī, *Mudhakkirātī min Kābul ilā Baghdād*, 6:19–20; "Shuhadāʾ al-Kuwayt fil-Būsna," *al-Furqān*, September 1995; "Istishhād Kuwaytī fī maʿārik al-Būsna," *al-Mujtamaʿ*, August 1, 1995; ʿAbd Allāh al-ʿAtīqī, "Kuwaytī yustashhad difāʿan ʿan al-Būsna wal-Harsak fa-hal nakūn mithlahu?" *al-Mujtamaʿ*, August 1, 1995; ʿAbd Allāh al-Najjār, "Istishhād Kuwaytī fil-maʿārik maʿa al-Ṣirb," *al-Waṭan*, July 26, 1995; Ṣabāḥ al-Shammarī, "Qāwama fī Afghānistān wal-Kuwayt wal-Būsna: wa-lam yatamakkan min muqāwamat jādhib al-istishhād," *al-Qabas*, July 25, 1995.

33. See Walīd Muḥammad Ḥājj, *Madhbaḥat al-qalʿa wa-ghayāhib Ghuwāntanāmū*, 16. Dream visions were a recurring aspect of Abu Muʿadh's biography. One close friend recounted how they were sleeping in the sanctuary in Mecca when Abu Muʿadh awoke

and said he had a vision of Muslims calling for help in Bosnia. "Qiṣṣat shahīd fil-zaman al-ṣaʿb." In a video distributed by the Katiba, Abu Muʿadh is seen describing the dream of one of the mujahids, in which a bearded man clothed in white with a white cap on his head recites Surat al-Nasr from the Quran. *Podsjelovo/Fethul mubin.* Similar visions of the prophet have been a recurring feature of Sufi discourses, especially in stories about inspirations for jihad. See Amira Mittermaier, *Dreams That Matter*, 166–67.

34. Ḥamad Qaṭarī and Mājid al-Madanī, *Min qiṣaṣ al-shuhadāʾ al-ʿArab fil-Būsna wal-Harsak.*

35. *Nidāʾ al-Jihād*, June 10, 1995, 8–9. In another biography of this mujahid, Abu ʿAbd Allah from Libya noted that he was "intensely humble" and that a visitor to the front he oversaw "wouldn't be able to make him out as the commander, due to his subservience [tadhallul] to his brothers." Qaṭarī and al-Madanī.

36. See Aria Nakissa, "An Ethical Solution to the Problem of Legal Indeterminacy."

37. Senad Pećanin and Vildana Selimbegović, "Islamski borbi za BiH," *Dani*, January 14, 2000.

38. *Nushrat al-Mujāhidīn*, November 11, 1994, 2–3. A book that purports to summarize and distill the curriculum of the school is Ibrahim Delić, *Akida ehli sunnetu vel džemata.*

39. *Nidāʾ al-Jihād*, April 3, 1995, 5. The interview was with the "brother responsible for daʿwa in the Katiba," which roughly corresponded to Imad's role.

40. The Katiba announced the establishment of a shariʿa course for ansar later in the war, although I have never spoken to anyone who recalled attending it. *Nidāʾ al-Jihād*, No. 10, May 7, 1995, 5.

41. Safijurrahman el-Mubarekfuri, *Er-rahikul-mahtum*, 442. Quotations here are from the Bosnian version unless otherwise stated.

42. Ibid., 51. The original Arabic goes further on this point, calling these virtues "rare" [ʿazīza] amongst the Arabs due to the "abundance" [farṭ] of courage and bellicosity amongst them. Ṣafī al-Raḥmān al-Mubārakfūrī, *al-Raḥīq al-makhtūm*, 53.

43. In April 1995, the Katiba held a Quran recitation contest with twenty-five Bosnian mujahid contestants and gave cash prizes to six of them. See *Nidāʾ al-Jihād*, No. 9, April 20, 1995, 4.

44. See, e.g., Joseph Massad, *Colonial Effects*, 148–62; Michel Foucault, *Discipline and Punish*, 363–64; Marcel Mauss, "Techniques of the Body," 71–72.

45. Al-Sayyid Sabiq (1915–2000) was an Azhar-educated shariʿa scholar from a village in the Nile Delta and a member of the Muslim Brothers. Part of the exodus of

Muslim Brother activists to Saudi Arabia in the 1950s, he taught at King ʿAbd al-ʿAziz and Umm al-Qura universities before returning to Egypt. Saba Mahmood found that *Fiqh al-Sunna* was also widely used in the women's mosque movement where she conducted fieldwork. See *Politics of Piety*, 80–81.

46. In his ethnography of Salafis in the Bale province of Ethiopia, Terje Østebø posits that illiteracy among a local Muslim population can facilitate Salafi proselytization due to the latter's association with textual authority. See *Localising Salafism*, 38–40. In my fieldwork conversations, there was a sense that low levels of literacy in Afghanistan kept locals in the thrall of local Hanafi authorities whereas the relatively more-educated Bosnians were able to absorb and adopt Salafi texts much more quickly. Abu ʿAbd al-ʿAziz also made this observation in his discussion with al-Albani. See Muḥammad Nāsir al-Dīn al-Albānī, *Silsilat al-hudā wal-nūr*.

47. Azzam Publications, *In the Hearts of Green Birds*.

48. el-Mubarekfuri, *Er-rahikul-mahtum*, 249–50.

49. al-Mubārakfūrī, *al-Raḥīq al-makhtūm*, 314.

50. For a parallel on the homosocial dimensions of brotherhood in the context of jointly buried soldiers, see Alan Bray's study of the history of friendship in England, which opens with an anecdote about a grave in Istanbul of two Crusader knights explicitly designed in the style of a matrimonial tomb. Bray marshals considerable evidence pointing to the overlap between certain socially recognized forms of homosocial and heterosocial intimacy: for example, he demonstrates that the word *wedding* once referred not only to heterosexual matrimony but also to various covenants of friendship between people of the same gender. Putting aside the considerable differences between contemporary jihads and the Crusades, Bray's analysis usefully reminds us that interrogating homosocial intimacy solely in terms of carnality—to focus on whether or not homosociality was a marker of homoeroticism—is too limiting; it should instead be viewed in broader frameworks of kinship and friendship. See *The Friend*, 13–25, 97.

51. The Prophet Muhammad also established a sort of "brotherhood" system pairing needy Meccan emigrants with specific ansar. See Fred Donner, *The Early Islamic Conquests*, 352.

52. Qaṭarī and al-Madanī.

53. A biography of Hamid Softić, the murdered imam, can be found in Muharem Omerdić, *Imami šehidi*, 101.

54. On pious Bosnian Muslim women's fears of adverse social reactions to wearing

headscarves, see Andreja Mesarič, "Wearing Hijab in Sarajevo," 20; Emira Ibrahimpašić, "Women Living Islam in Post-War and Post-Socialist Bosnia-Herzegovina," 249–51, 267–76. For those like Latifa who covered her face, the stigma was even greater.

55. See "Tarjīḥ wafāt al-Kuwaytī Ḥamad ʿAlī Muḥammad al-Sulaymān fī Afghānistān," *KUNA*, December 26, 2001.

56. See Information report by Col. Ekrem Alihodžić, Chief, 3rd Corps SVB to General Staff SVB, 7-1/29-516 (as received), June 7, 1995.

57. Fax from Anwar Shaʿban to Abu Talal, December 25, 1994, *Delić* exhibit 1201 (Italian translation only).

58. See Madawi al-Rasheed, *A Most Masculine State*, 128. The fatwa had come up in discussions of this issue in the Afghan jihad as well. Abu ʿAbd al-ʿAziz mentioned it while recounting to al-Albani the story of a mujahid who without his authorization married a Bosnian girl for only one night, causing him much embarrassment. "I don't want a problem like in Peshawar when some Arabs married and then fled, or divorced on their way to the airport!" al-Albānī, *Silsilat al-hudā wal-nūr*.

59. The Hanbali school is dominant in Saudi Arabia and some parts of the Gulf, and Salafis often follow Hanbali rulings; hence the interlocutor in question called it "the Arabs' madhhab." One of the tenets of Salafi thought, however, is to reject binding adherence to the major schools of jurisprudence. Due to genealogical links and overlaps between Hanbali and Salafi jurisprudential thought, Salafis have at times been accused (and have accused each other) of being crypto-Hanbalis. See Stéphane Lacroix, *Awakening Islam*, 84–86.

60. See also Testimony of Ayman Awad, *Delić* trial, February 9, 2008, 155:4–13.

61. On marriage and especially elopements in rural Bosnia, including those involving people under age eighteen, see Tone Bringa, *Being Muslim the Bosnian Way*, 105–6.

62. See Information Report from Sr. Capt. Hamdija Šljuka, Chief, 35th Division SVB to 3rd Corps SVB, 03/1-80-29a, October 24, 1995.

63. See, e.g., Alenko Zornija, "Mudžahedini pozivaju Srbe da prijeđu na islam," *Zagreb vjesnik*, September 28, 2003; Terry Boyd and Ivana Avramovic, "Fundamentalist Mujahideen Attract Speculation, Fear in Bosnia," *Stars & Stripes*, April 16, 2002; ʿAbd al-Bāqī Khalīfa, "Abnāʾ al-Ṣirb yuraddidūna al-adhān fī Būtshīnā," *al-Sharq al-Awsaṭ*, October 5, 2001.

64. See Jasmin Duraković, "Neka bude."

65. See Doris Glück, *Mundtot: Ich war die Frau eines Gotteskriegers*.

66. A productive contrast can be drawn here between transnational jihads

and locally circumscribed ones. In Cabeiri deBergh Robinson's ethnography of Kashmiri mujahids, marriage and jihad are incompatible. "In Pakistani communities, becoming a fully recognized mujāhid involves renouncing family ties, especially reproductive relations. A mujāhid cannot be a husband or a father. . . . The announcement of a Pakistani mujāhid's formal entrance into a tanzīm is publicized as a wedding and the contract he signs is called a nikah, an Islamic marriage contract. . . . In effect, the mujāhid is transformed into a living shahīd through symbolic exclusion from the social bonds that motivate human emotions and desire." *Body of Victim, Body of Warrior*, 220. This likely arises from the need to separate mujahids from social bonds that might otherwise impede their commitment to jihad (or serve as pressure points susceptible to the state), whereas recently arrived outsiders such as Arabs in Bosnia needed more, rather than less, embedding in local social relations.

67. On the maintenance of kinship ties in the face of sustained ideological differences between Tunisians traveling for jihad and their families back home, see Alyssa Miller, "Kin-Work in a Time of Jihad."

INTERLUDE: EXCHANGING ARABS

1. Also taken were four other HVO officers and two journalists. This sketch of the May 1993 prisoner exchange relies primarily on materials from the *Hadžihasanović* trial at the ICTY. See, e.g., Report from Dieter Schellschmidt, ECMM Zenica to ECMM HQ, May 19, 1993; Testimony of Dieter Schellschmidt, *Hadžihasanović* trial, May 24, 2004, 7909:17–7911:25. The Arab mujahids documented the exchange in a video titled *Bāriqat amal* (A Ray of Hope); some photographs are also collected in *Hadžihasanović*, Exhibit DH 182. Interviews with two mujahids who participated in the swap also informed this narrative.

2. Two of the men released in this exchange anonymously published their account in the magazine of the Heritage Society. They described beatings, forced labor to dig trenches, being used as human shields, and other abuses. "Qiṣaṣ wāqiʿiyya: iʿtidāʾāt al-Kurūwāt ʿalā lijān al-ighātha," *al-Furqān*, June 1994.

Other Muslim detainees remained in HVO custody after this incident. See, e.g., Message from Victor Andreev, UNPROFOR Civil Affairs Kiseljak to Cedric Thornberry, UNPROFOR Director of Civil Affairs, August 18, 1993, UNARMS S-1837-0063-0002 (on French citizens and residents); Message from Emma Shitakha, UNPROFOR Civil Affairs Zagreb to Victor Andreev, UNPROFOR Civil Affairs Kiseljak, July 15, 1993,

UNARMS S-1837-0063-0001 (on employees of the Pakistani Edhi foundation held by HVO).

3. *Hadžihasanović* judgment, ¶¶ 500 ("mujahedin prisoners"), 510 ("Arab prisoners"), 512 ("Arab fighters").

4. *Hadžihasanović* Exhibit P. 109. Two Bosnian Muslim drivers who had been arrested while working alongside the foreign captives were also released in the exchange, although it is unclear if their freedom was explicitly demanded by the mujahids. The men do not appear in subsequent personnel lists of the Katiba, lending some support to the hypothesis that they were civilians working for aid organizations.

5. *Hadžihasanović* Exhibit P. 482, 23–24.

6. Political violence under the sign of jihad is often associated with a disregard for legal norms and purportedly universal values, especially the distinction between combatants and civilians. Jihad is thought to have no law or, if it does, a law (shariʿa) that is radically at odds with other values, especially those embedded in universalisms that may be more familiar to you that speak in the idiom of international law.

There have been several different scholarly responses to this challenge, each salutary in their own way. Some have shown how groups can adopt legal codes and institutions to regulate their use of violence. See Antonio Giustozzi, "The Taliban's 'Military Courts'"; Muhammad Munir, "The Layha for the Mujahideen." Others have sought to demonstrate the fundamental compatibility between Islamic legal norms and international law, be it to challenge caricatures of shariʿa or as part of attempts to reform it, or both. See Nahed Samour, "Modernized Islamic International Law Concepts as a Third World Approach to International Law"; Niaz Shah, *Self-Defense in Islamic and International Law.* And of course, there is scholarship reminding us that even the categories through which international law speaks in the name of the universal are historically contingent and complicit in all manner of imperial violence. See Frédéric Mégret, "From 'Savages' to 'Unlawful Combatants'"; Helen M. Kinsella, "Gendering Grotius"; Antony Anghie, *Imperialism, Sovereignty, and the Making of International Law.* These three responses can be respectively (if crudely) understood as, Yes, jihad has its own law, and one that is like "ours" in significant part; Jihad's law is actually our law by another name; Whatever jihad is, "our" law is actually the problem.

7. The Katiba included in its training for Bosnian recruits basic rules for the conduct of warfare that were broadly consistent with international humanitarian law, including a prohibition on killing noncombatant women, children, the elderly, and clerical figures. Its interpretation of fiqh differed in one major respect, by permitting

the execution of prisoners of war. See Ali bin Ferid el-Hindi, *Skraćena zbirka fikhskih propisa*, 158–60. For more on the genesis of this rule in early Islamic legal history, see Lena Salaymeh, *The Beginnings of Islamic Law*, 43–83.

8. See *Hadžihasanović* trial judgment, ¶¶ 1116–1127; *Delić* trial judgment, ¶¶ 295–307.

9. Between roughly equal parties, exchanges are often done on a "one for one" basis, with attention to equivalencies of rank or other status. This presented issues, for example, during the US Civil War, when the Confederacy—which had achieved quasi-recognition from foreign powers such as England and France and could therefore negotiate with the Union on a rough basis of parity—refused to include Black soldiers in prisoner exchanges. See John Fabian Witt, *Lincoln's Code*, 245–53.

10. On economies of captive exchange and redemption—and attendant legal regimes—at the edges of the early modern Muslim world, especially the Mediterranean and Black Sea frontiers, see, e.g., Joshua White, *Piracy and Law in the Ottoman Mediterranean*; Kathryn Miller, "Reflections on Reciprocity"; Wolfgang Kaiser, *Le commerce des captifs*; Will Smiley, *From Slaves to Prisoners of War*. For a far-reaching analysis of how economies of captive exchange gave rise to new forms of kinship and group belonging in the territories that now lie along the United States-Mexico border, see James Brooks, *Captives and Cousins*.

11. See Testimony of Dieter Schellschmidt, *Hadžihasanović* trial, May 24, 2004, 7912:1–3.

12. This quote appears in a summary of Bosnian secret police wiretaps on the Katiba. Report from SDB Zenica Dept. 6, 2/5/95-1, June 22, 1995.

13. The reliability of these reports is difficult to ascertain. See Report from SDB Zenica, April 21, 1994, 2 (possible error in report date); *Delić* Exhibit 1123 English translation, 2 (pages do not match corresponding Bosnian language version).

14. See 1 PWO MILINFOSUM No. 173, October 18, 1993, 1.

15. See ECMM Humanitarian Activity Report No. 42, October 17–23, 1993, ¶ 68.

16. This sketch is drawn from the *Hadžihasanović* trial judgment, ¶¶ 1360–1390. The captive who was beheaded, Dragan Popović, had a Serb father and a Croat mother, but was generally identified as a Serb due to his first name. Id. fn. 3161.

17. See Ezher Beganović and Kemal Baković, "Nismo činili ratne zločine!" *SAFF*, July 8, 2005, 23.

18. See Report from Ahmet Adilović, Deputy Commander for Morale, Information, and Religious Affairs, 7th Muslim Brigade to Commission for Talks with HVO Representatives, 622/93, April 12, 1993.

19. Testimony of Kamal Karaj, *Maktouf* trial, April 28, 2005 (audio only).

20. Report from Ahmet Adilović, Deputy Commander for Morale, Information, and Religious Affairs, 7th Muslim Brigade to Commission for Talks with HVO Representatives, 622/93, April 12, 1993. See also Letter from Enver Hadžihasanović, Commander, ARBiH 3rd Corps to Croat Community of Herceg-Bosna, 02/33-507, February 16, 1993.

21. Scholarship on transnational Muslim charities includes Jérôme Bellion-Jourdan and Jonathan Benthall, *The Charitable Crescent*; Marie Juul Petersen, *For Humanity or for the Umma?*; Jonathan Benthall and Robert Lacey, *Gulf Charities and Islamic Philanthropy in the "Age of Terror" and Beyond.*

22. Letter from Enver Hadžihasanović, Commander, ARBiH 3rd Corps to Tihomir Blaškić, HVO, 01/1020–1, April 2, 1993. The following year, an Algerian was stopped by the HVO on the road near Žepče, arrested, and beaten unconscious. He was described as both an employee of the NGO Benevolence International Foundation and a member of the Bosnian army's 207th Mountain Brigade. See Report by Ramiz Dugalić, 3rd Corps SVB, 03/1-272-30, October 1, 1994.

23. I will refer to al-Mutayri by his surname rather than by his kunya to avoid confusion with Abu ʿAli the Moroccan from Chapter 1.

24. The Heritage Society emphasized al-Mutayri's aid activities. See, e.g., Khālid al-Muṭawwaʿ, "al-Khurūj min nafaq al-Būsna al-muẓlim (2)," *al-Furqān*, February 1994; "Shuhadāʾ al-Kuwayt fīl-Būsna," *al-Furqān*, September 1995. Accounts from the mujahids claim he was killed in combat. See Ḥamad Qaṭarī and Mājid al-Madanī, *Min qiṣaṣ al-shuhadāʾ al-ʿArab fīl-Būsna wal-Harsak*; Azzam Publications, *In the Hearts of Green Birds.* For mainstream media obituaries, see Muḥammad Khayr Ramaḍān Yūsuf, *Tatimmat al-aʿlām lil-Ziriklī*, Vol. 1, 24–25; and Jār Allāh Ḥasan al-Jār Allāh, "Man huwa safīrunā fīl-Būsna?" *al-Qabas*, October 3, 1995.

25. On the rise of these distinctions, see Helen M. Kinsella, *The Image Before the Weapon.*

26. "Travel to Afghanistan for charity reasons or to teach or study Islam is a known Al-Qaida/extremist cover story without credence." Joint Task Force-Guantánamo, "Assessment of Afghanistan Travels and Islamic Duties as They Pertain to Interrogation," August 4, 2004, available at https://wikileaks.org/gitmo/cover_story_assessment.html.

27. For more on this case, see Darryl Li, "Jihad in a World of Sovereigns," 389–90.

28. The anthropology of humanitarianism, human rights, and development has tended to focus on questions of moral sentiment, ethics, mobility, cosmopolitanism,

and various forms of privilege. This work has raised serious critical questions about the assumptions and practice of humanitarianism, but it tends to reproduce a strict dichotomy between mobile, privileged Westerners and parochial, disempowered locals. In these analyses, Western aid workers tend to be either very highly paid compared to local populations or volunteers; in either scenario, the degree of privilege involved tends to shift writing away from an analysis of interests to a critique of excess instead. See, e.g., Liisa Malkki, *The Need to Help*, 23–75, 165–97; Peter Redfield, *Life in Crisis*; Didier Fassin, *Humanitarian Reason*; Jeffrey Jackson, *The Globalizers*. For one exception to this trend, see Adia Benton, "African Expatriates and Race in the Anthropology of Humanitarianism."

29. The memoirs of two of the Algerians sent from Bosnia to Guantánamo also reflect these dynamics of how pressures of mobility—including the war in Algeria—pushed them toward working for Islamic NGOs. See Lakhdar Boumediene and Mustafa Ait Idir, *Witnesses of the Unseen*.

30. This friend was one of the plaintiffs in the landmark US Supreme Court case, *Boumediene v. Bush*. For more on his experiences, see Darryl Li, "From Exception to Empire."

31. Hasan was one of several Arabs I met or heard about who made a side living through Islamic healing practices such as blood-cupping [al-ḥijāma] or treatment using pieces of paper with Quranic text [al-ʿilāj bil-qurʾān]. The trope of the Arab as traveling healer continues to resonate in the region; during my fieldwork in 2011, a Moroccan healer, Mekki Torabi, drew enormous crowds for days at the Zetra Olympic Hall in Sarajevo—although Hasan and the other healers I knew consider Torabi a charlatan and would balk at the comparison. On Torabi and the broader popularity of Islamic healing practices in Bosnia, see Larisa Jašarević, *Health and Wealth on the Bosnian Market*, 260–66; "Interplanetary Present."

32. Salman ascended to the throne in 2015 and two years later elevated his son Muhammad bin Salman to a variety of high-level roles that allowed him to become *de facto* ruler of the kingdom.

33. Jeddah was home to the International Islamic Relief Organization (IIRO, known in Bosnia as IGASA), the charitable affiliate of the Saudi-sponsored Muslim World League. The SHC made use of IIRO facilities in the Balkans in the early months of the war while it was still being established.

34. This sketch of the SHC, an organization that has been the subject of much controversy and speculation, derives from several primary source documents. On the

SHC's basic structure, role, and expenditures, see Decl. of Saud bin Mohammad al-Roshood, *In re: Terrorist Attacks on September 11, 2001*, 03-MD-01570-GBD-FM (S.D.N.Y. June 25, 2004), ECF No. 262-3. The SHC's own published materials include detailed lists of donors and expenditures. See Ziyād Ṣāliḥ Hadhlūl and Muḥammad ʿAbd Allāh al-Ḥumayḍī, *al-Qiṣṣa al-kāmila lil-dawr al-Saʿūdī fil-Būsna wal-Harsak*; *Najznačajnija dostignuća Visokog saudijskog komiteta za pomoć narodu Bosne i Hercegovine od oktobra 1993. god. do kraja 1998. god.*

35. Report by SDB Tuzla to SDB Administration Sarajevo, November 10, 1995. It is worth noting that the Heritage Society also employed Abu Jaʿfar the Egyptian in its Zenica office. See Fuad Kovač, "Ostat ćemo u Bosni dok bude potrebno," *Ljiljan*, January 10, 1996.

36. According to the Italian translation of one letter faxed to ICI, all funds raised in Kuwait for the Katiba were deposited in an account to be dispersed according to Abu al-Maʿali's wishes. See Fax from Abu ʿAbd al-ʿAziz to Abu al-Maʿali, May 6, 1995, *Delić* Exhibit 1436.

37. In 1995, the head of the Heritage Society's Zenica office and Abu al-Maʿali discussed the loan of fifty tons of flour to the Katiba. See Information Report from Col. Ekrem Alihodžić, 3rd Corps SVB to General Staff SVB, 03/1-174-65-1, April 24, 1995; SDB Zenica, 13/8/95-1, April 14, 1995. This employee also once represented the Katiba in negotiations with Abu al-Zubayr's group over the fate of supplies taken from a warehouse in Travnik by a disgruntled mujahid after his expulsion from the unit. See Fax from Abu al-Harith to ICI Milan, March 30, 1995, *Delić* Exhibit 1201 (Italian translation only).

38. A list of non-Bosnians who left the Katiba signed by Abu al-Harith on February 9, 1994, includes Hasan and his traveling companions and indicates that they joined the small group of freelance mujahids based in the village of Bistričak, north of Zenica.

39. Amira Mittermaier has argued for thinking of Islamic charitable giving as motivated by divine duty ("for God"), "disrupting both the liberal conceit of compassion *and* the neoliberal imperative of self-help." *Giving to God*, 4 (emphasis in original). This is an important intervention but it is also worth noting that Mittermaier's research focuses on *volunteers* who operate from an assumed background of some material security. In the case discussed here of Muslim employees of transnational organizations living far from kinship and other social networks, concerns over livelihood were necessarily foregrounded alongside spiritual ones.

40. The HVO appears to have embarked on a series of arrests of Arabs at checkpoints around this time. See Information Report by Col. Ramiz Dugalić, Chief, 3rd Corps SVB, 03/1-272-30, October 1, 1994.

41. See Letter from Abu al-Maʿali to Father Ivo Kramar, March 8, 1995 (offering to trade information about missing Croats for their release). An SDB wiretap on the Katiba refers to a conversation about attempts to ransom four Arabs in the custody of the HVO, likely referring to this group. See SDB Zenica Section 6, 2/81/95-1, June 25, 1995.

42. See "U Potocima razimijenjeni zatočenici," *Hrvatska Riječ*, August 10, 1996.

43. Abu Ahmad was born Yunus Muhammad Ibrahim al-Hayyari and was granted Bosnian citizenship in 1996. According to media reports, he and his family moved to Saudi Arabia for hajj in 2001 and overstayed their visas. His Bosnian citizenship was posthumously revoked. See Službeni Glasnik, No. 24, April 3, 2007; ʿAbd al-Qādir Muḥammad, "Ghumūḍ yaliff maṣīr zawjat al-Ḥayyārī wa-ṭiflatih," *al-Sharq al-Awsaṭ*, July 4, 2005.

44. While serving a prison sentence for this murder, Arklöv was also convicted for acts committed in Bosnia, in the country's first trial for crimes under international law. See *Prosecutor v. Jackie Arklöv*, Case no. B 4084-04 (Stockholm Dist. Ct. Dec. 18, 2006); Mark Klamberg, "International Criminal Law in Swedish Courts."

CHAPTER 5: NON-ALIGNMENT

1. Marko Herceg, "Postdaytonski politički sudar sa stvarnošću," *Hrvatska Riječ*, February 24, 1996, 7.

2. This narrative draws from an investigation by the Bosnia-Herzegovina Human Rights Ombudsman, summarized in the two cases of the Bosnia-Herzegovina Human Rights Chamber that arose from this incident. See *Samy Hermas v. The Federation of Bosnia and Herzegovina*, CH/97/45 (Hum. Rts. Chamber Bosn. & Herz. 1998); *H.R. and Mohamed Momani v. The Federation of Bosnia and Herzegovina*, CH/98/946 (Hum. Rts. Chamber Bosn. & Herz. 1999). The respondent (the Federation of Bosnia-Herzegovina, which absorbed the wartime Croat civil authorities) did not contest the merits of these cases.

3. One of the more important anthropological considerations of convergences between Islam and socialism in the region is Kristen Ghodsee's ethnography of Islamic revivalism among Bulgarian Pomaks. When the author moves from the nuanced renderings of her interlocutors' understandings of Islam to general comparative statements about Islam and Marxism as ideological projects, the shift in analytical scale raises issues of reification. Hence it becomes possible to assert that "Islam is closer to

capitalism than it is to Marxism. Both Islam and capitalism privilege private property and the particular forms of heteronormative, monogamous gender arrangements that it requires. . . . Islam offers no critique of the relations of production. It is relatively silent on the questions of exploitation among and between Muslims." *Muslim Lives in Eastern Europe*, 199.

4. This mujahid, Abu Hudhayfa al-Battar, was killed in a mortar attack in July 1995. This account of his life draws from multiple interviews (including a Brother who held him as he lay dying), the Katiba's personnel records, and hagiographies. See Ḥamad Qaṭarī and Mājid al-Madanī, *Min qiṣaṣ al-shuhadāʾ al-ʿArab fil-Būsna wal-Harsak*; Azzam Publications, *In the Hearts of Green Birds*; Nedim Haračić, "Mudžahidski safovi," *Patriotski List*, November-December 1995.

5. See Stef Jansen, "After the Red Passport"; Ljubica Spaskovska, *The Last Yugoslav Generation*, 127–32. Scholarship on Yugo-nostalgia has understandably focused on consumerism and the welfare state, with less attention to Non-Alignment. See Breda Luthar and Maruša Pušnik, *Remembering Utopia*. On post-socialist nostalgia in other contexts, see Alexei Yurchak, *Everything Was Forever, Until It Was No More*; Kristen Ghodsee, *The Left Side of History*.

6. In the 1950s and 1960s, racial tensions were reportedly exacerbated by the fact that the Yugoslav government gave higher stipends to foreign students than to its own. See Dragomir Bondžić, *Misao bez pasoša*, 272–73, 284–85. For similar issues among students from Africa more broadly, see Nemanja Radonjić, "A Socialist Shaping of the Postcolonial Elite." For more on Non-Alignment, Yugoslavia, and race in general, see Catherine Baker, *Race and the Yugoslav Region*, 107–16.

Throughout the socialist world, regimes struggled to balance their ideological commitments to antiracism with the everyday prejudices faced by nonwhite students. The East German case has probably received the most scholarly attention. See, e.g., Sara Pugach, "African Students and the Politics of Race and Gender in the German Democratic Republic"; Young-Sun Hong, *Cold War Germany, the Third World, and the Global Humanitarian Regime*, 200–14; Damian Henry Tone Mac Con Uladh, "Guests of the Socialist Nation?" 40–65, 183–214. On Arab countries at Moscow's Communist University for Toilers of the East in the 1930s, see Masha Kirasirova, "The Eastern International," 110–251.

7. Foreign Muslim students reportedly received a somewhat better reception in Sarajevo in the 1960s as well. See Milorad Lazić, "Neki problemi stranih studenata na jugoslovenskim univerzitetima," 70–71.

8. On the historiographic messiness around the Bandung conference and subsequent imaginings of Non-Alignment, anticolonial solidarity, and race, see Robert Vitalis, "The Midnight Ride of Kwame Nkrumah and Other Fables of Bandung (Bandoong)."

9. This was not for lack of trying. Before turning to Non-Alignment, Tito's security strategy was based on the 1953 Balkan Pact, linking it to Turkey and Greece as an indirect affiliation with NATO without the provocation to the Soviets that formally joining the Atlantic alliance would entail. The Balkan Pact soon fell apart for a number of reasons, including Greek-Turkish tensions over Cyprus. See Rinna Kullaa, *Non-Alignment and Its Origins in Cold War Europe*, 88–104.

10. The People's Republic of China in particular emphasized Afro-Asian and Third Worldist framings to implicitly exclude eastern European states deemed "white." See Dragan Bogetić, "Sukob Titovog koncepta univerzalizma i Sukarnog koncepta regionalizma na Samitu nesvrstanih u Kairu 1964," 103–4; Jeffrey James Byrne, *Mecca of Revolution*, 213–14. For their part, Yugoslav authors in Africa during the socialist era frequently embraced antiracist critiques of colonialism, even as they recapitulated stereotypes of civilizational backwardness. See Nemanja Radonjić, "'From Kragujevac to Kilimanjaro'."

11. The Non-Aligned Movement still exists and includes two-thirds of the world's nation-states. None of the ex-Yugoslav republics are still members, however: Serbia and Bosnia-Herzegovina are observers.

12. In the decade after the wars of Yugoslav succession, scholars in Serbia and Croatia turned with renewed interest to relations with the Arab world during the Cold War. See Vladimir Petrović, *Jugoslovenska stupa na Bliski Istok*; Aleksandar Životić, *Jugoslavija i Suecka kriza*; Tvrtko Jakovina, *Treća strana Hladnog rata*.

13. See Jakovina, "Yugoslavia on the International Scene"; Vladimir Kulić, "Building the Non-Aligned Babel"; Jovan Matović, *Vojni poslovi Jugoslavije i svet XX veka*, 369–73, 378.

14. Much of the scholarship on Non-Alignment focuses either on relations between states or the cultural solidarities of prominent writers and intellectuals. See, e.g., Vijay Prashad, *The Darker Nations*; Nataša Mišković, Harald Fischer-Tiné, and Nada Boškovska, *The Non-Aligned Movement and the Cold War*.

15. See Bondžić, *Misao bez pasoša*, 263. In the 1950s and early 1960s, the Yugoslav state prioritized scholarships for Algerians as a form of support for the struggle against French settler-colonialism. See Alvin Rubinstein, *Yugoslavia and the Nonaligned*

World, 87–88. For more on Yugoslav-Algerian relations, see Ljubodrag Dimić and Dragan Bogetić, "La Yougoslavie et l'Algérie."

Educational travel from Yugoslavia to the Arab world was less common but also significant. Haris Silajdžić, who served as Bosnia's wartime foreign minister and prime minister, studied Arabic in Libya in the 1960s and later worked as an Arabic lecturer.

16. Munif reportedly began his shift to exploring literary modes of expression during those years; decades later, he would reminisce about visiting Travnik and recognizing the city's major features, thanks to his familiarity with the vivid descriptions penned by the Yugoslav Nobel literature laureate Ivo Andrić. See Māhir Jarrār, *ʿAbd al-Raḥmān Munīf wal-ʿIrāq*, 28–29; Muḥammad Mūfākū al-Arnāʾūṭ, "al-Sanawāt al-Yūghūslāfiyya li-ʿAbd al-Raḥmān Munīf," *al-Mustaqbal*, March 15, 2004; ʿAbd al-Raḥmān Munīf, "Taqdīm: Īvū Andrītsh wa-ḥikāyāt min al-Būsna."

17. In Slovenia at least, there have been Arab cultural associations. See Maja Lamberger Khatib, "Social Networks Among Arabs in Slovenia."

18. See Youssef Hajir, *Bolnica Dobrinja: monografija*.

19. See Rod Nordland, "Fighter Jets, Remnants of Iraq's Air Force, Are Found to Be in Serbia," *New York Times*, August 31, 2009.

20. During his time as ambassador to Algeria, Nijaz Dizdarević developed a close relationship with the country's first president, Ahmed Ben Bella. See Byrne, *Mecca of Revolution*, 165–66, 203–5. Another brother, Raif, served as Yugoslavia's foreign minister and later as chairman of the country's presidency.

21. See Aydın Babuna, "Bosnian Muslims During the Cold War," 193–97.

22. In contrast, UN peacekeeping troops in need of English-speaking interpreters were able to hire from a far broader pool of locals, often language teachers or educated professionals such as engineers. See Catherine Baker, "Opening the Black Box."

23. An Algerian who was recruited from Peshawar to work in the Services Office's Zagreb branch described it as a small operation focused on aid activities that closed within a few months. In my interviews and in archival materials, the organization is never mentioned as a significant actor, either in terms of aid or military activities. The Services Office's own publications included a few obituaries of Arab mujahids in Bosnia but made no mention of the Katiba. The overall evidence suggests that its involvement in the Bosnian jihad was minimal, likely due to the more general waning of its influence after the 1989 assassination of its founder, ʿAbd Allah ʿAzzam.

24. Muṣṭafā Abū Saʿd, "Khawāṭir sāʾiḥ fī arḍ al-Balqān," *al-Furqān*, January 1995. This author called them "ḥamzat al-waṣl," an Arabic grammatical term referring to

the version of alif (the first letter of the alphabet) that is elided between words. The metaphor evokes a seamless connection.

25. See Bondžić, *Misao bez pasoša*, 277. The Yugoslav state was also keen to restrict foreign students' political activities, lest they embarrass the regime. See Lazić, "Neki problemi stranih studenata," 72. On efforts to control the activism of Afro-Asian students in Cold War Germany, see Quinn Slobodian, "Bandung in Divided Germany."

26. A Moroccan book on the Bosnia crisis claimed that Non-Aligned cooperation included collaboration against Islamist movements: "In killing and torturing the Islamic movement in Egypt—a movement which was itself an inspiration for the Muslim Youth movement in Bosnia—Gamal Abdelnasser was influenced by Marshal Tito's innovation of methods. The two leaders met more than four times per year to trade 'advice' and 'expertise.'" Muḥammad Muḥammad Amzyān, *al-Būsna wal-Harsak: al-Andalus al-thāniya!*, 67.

27. See al-Fātiḥ ʿAlī Ḥasanayn, *Mawsūʿat al-usar al-Maghāribiyya wa-ansābihā fil-Sūdān*, vol. 1, 76–77, 105–11.

28. See al-Ḥasanayn, *Jisr ʿalā nahr al-Dirīnā*, 9–41.

29. At the time, Nimeiry's sympathies were further to the left; in later decades, he would pursue a rapprochement with Islamists. Ironically, it was this ambassador's brother, Hassan Hussein Osman, who would later lead communist army offices in an abortive 1975 coup attempt against Nimeiry. See ibid., 63–65.

30. Soviet-Yugoslav differences mattered in more direct ways as well. According to Hassanein, Naim Hadžiabdić, the head of Yugoslavia's Islamic Community, had demanded his expulsion, only to be rebuffed by the security services because Sudanese Islamists had been alone among foreign students' groups in Yugoslavia to stand with Tito's condemnation of the 1968 Soviet invasion of Czechoslovakia. See al-Ḥasanayn, *Jisr ʿalā nahr al-Dirīnā*, 42–43, 95–103, 115–24.

31. See al-Fātiḥ ʿAlī Ḥasanayn, *Fakhāmat al-raʾīs ʿAlī ʿIzzat Bayqawfīj ka-mā lā yaʿrifuhu al-nās*, 241–45.

32. See, e.g., Fahira Fejzić, "'Amerikanci i Nijemci traže da Austrija promijeni politiku podrške Bosni!'," *Ljiljan*, November 8, 1995; al-Fātiḥ ʿAlī Ḥasanayn, "Raʾīs jumhūriyyat al-Būsna wal-Harsak yashraḥ abʿād azmat Yūghūslafiyā," *al-Mujtamaʿ*, January 19, 1992; Asʿad Ṭaha, "Ḥiwār ḥawla mustaqbal al-Muslimīn fī Ūrūbbā al-sharqiyya maʿa raʾīs rābiṭat al-aqalliyyāt al-Muslima," *al-Mujtamaʿ*, June 19, 1990. Hassanein also developed a longtime friendship with the future Turkish Islamist prime minister and

president Recep Tayyip Erdoğan, who sent a plane to transport Hassanein to Turkey for medical treatment in 2018.

33. See John Pomfret, "How Bosnia's Muslims Dodged Arms Embargo," *Washington Post*, September 22, 1996. Hassanein discusses allegations that he violated UN sanctions in *Fakhāmat al-raʾīs ʿAlī ʿIzzat Bayqawfīj ka-mā lā yaʿrifuhu al-nās*, 286–95.

34. In a biography he penned of the Moroccan Berber Sufi jurist Ahmad al-Zarruq, Hassanein also mentions growing up among many Sufi notables. See *Lamaʿān al-burūq fī sīrat mawlānā Aḥmad Zarrūq*, 10.

35. I was able to corroborate Hassanein's role in this episode with a veteran from the Katiba who met Abu al-Maʿali during his stay in Malaysia. See also Ḥasanayn, *Fakhāmat al-raʾīs ʿAlī ʿIzzat Bayqawfīj ka-mā lā yaʿrifuhu al-nās*, 44–51; *Qiṣṣat ḥarb al-Būsna wal-Harsak*, 339–43.

36. See Jelena Subotić and Srđan Vučetić, "Performing Solidarity."

37. Damani Partridge has tracked a similarly dramatic shift in the fortunes of nonwhite migrants to the former East Germany after the fall of the Berlin Wall. See *Hypersexuality and Headscarves*, 58–65. On the anthropology of race, and specifically Blackness, in the former Soviet Union, see Kesha Fikes and Alaina Lemon, "African Presence in Former Soviet Spaces."

38. On the precarious whiteness of ex-Yugoslavs, see Baker, *Race and the Yugoslav Region*, 170–76. On the construction of Muslims as a racial category as opposed to a confessional one—a process that also subsumes and erases disparate forms of racial, national, and ethnic difference among Muslims—see Junaid Rana, *Terrifying Muslims*; Leti Volpp, "The Citizen and the Terrorist."

39. William Kole, "Terrorists May be Recruiting 'White Muslims' in Balkans," *Associated Press*, April 17, 2006.

40. The obviousness with which Arabs were considered not white is of course also historically contingent. In many other places and times, whiteness and Arabness have also overlapped. See, e.g., Sarah Gualtieri, *Between Arab and White*; Nadine Naber and Amaney Jamal, *Race and Arab Americans Before and After 9/11*.

41. It seems possible that Nadir might have been spared if he had not been married to a Bosnian Muslim woman; a Somali physician who had lived in the city since 1982 managed to stay throughout the war. See Rešad Salihović, "Živim za dan kad će se u Banju Luku vratiti moji prijatelji," *Ljiljan*, August 20, 1997.

42. The sort of systematic violent expulsion denoted by the term *ethnic cleansing* generally did not take place within Serbia itself during the Bosnia war, but was rather

part of a project to create homogeneous areas within parts of Bosnia that could then secede and perhaps be annexed to Serbia. See James Ron, *Frontiers and Ghettos*.

43. See "Fondovi uništeni tokom NATO bombardovanja 1999. godine," Arhiv Jugoslavije, available at http://www.arhivyu.gov.rs/active/sr-latin/home/glavna_navigacija /arhivska_gradja/fondovi_i_zbirke/fondovi_unisteni_tokom_nato_bombardo vanja_1999_godine.html.

44. See Jovo Martinovic, "Gaddafi's Fleeing Mercenaries Describe Collapse of the Regime," *Time*, August 24, 2011.

45. The implicit contrast between "Libyan" and "African"—as if Libya wasn't already part of Africa—signals a construction of Arabness situated in global notions of anti-Blackness. See Jemima Pierre, "Race in Africa Today."

46. Hassan Haidar Diab, "Ubijeni Hrvatski plaćenici u Misrati!," *Večernji List*, September 12, 2011.

47. Belhadj was a leader in the Libyan Islamic Fighting Group (al-Jamāʿa al-Islāmiyya al-Muqātila fī Lībyā), which the regime largely defeated in the 1990s. He and his wife, Fatima Bouchar, were kidnapped by the CIA in Malaysia. See Laura Pitter, "Delivered into Enemy Hands," 91–101.

48. See Ante Božić, "Moamer el Gadafi je oženjen Hrvaticom," *Hrvatska i Svijet Online* 2010.

CHAPTER 6: PEACEKEEPING

1. During the course of the war, over 15,300 Jordanians served in UNPROFOR, mostly in Croatia. A small special forces unit was inside Bosnia-Herzegovina, embedded in the French battalion. A total of 15 percent of the Jordanian military at the time rotated through UNPROFOR. See ʿĪd Kāmil al-Rawḍān, *ʿAmaliyyāt quwwāt al-umam al-muttaḥida li-ḥifẓ al-salām*, 18; Ghazi al-Tayyeb, "Jordanian Participation in PKO & Future Outlook," 56.

2. On the captain's visit and subsequent follow-up, see Memo from Col. Sead Cudić, 1st Corps SVB to General Staff SVB, 04/6408-01, February 20, 1995; Memo from Brig. Gen. Jusuf Jašarević, General Staff SVB to Commands of 3rd and 7th Corps, 7-1/15-141, February 24, 1995; Memo from Ramiz Dugalić, 7th Corps SVB to General Staff SVB, 03/1-1-69/95 (with handwritten notation, most likely added by recipients: "We have no response from the 3rd Corps"). Salah appears under his real name with consistent dates of birth in several of the official lists compiled by the Katiba; see List of Members of Elmudžahedin Detachment from Col. Hajrudin Humo to 3rd Corps SVB,

05/4-1028, May 7, 1995, and List of Members of Elmudžahedin Detachment signed by Gen. Sakib Mahmuljin, 05/6-409-20, February 26, 1996. This suggests that he married or intended to stay in the country well before the war's end; he was reportedly registered at a Sarajevo address while living in Bočinja. For his receipt of the Golden Lily, see Order signed by ARBiH commander Rasim Delić, 8/2-5638-2, December 23, 1995. It is also worth noting that the captain and Salah may have been first cousins rather than brothers.

3. Ethnographic studies of Internationals in Bosnia and their work processes and lifestyles include Andrew Gilbert, "From Humanitarianism to Humanitarianization"; Mojca Vah Jevšnik, *Building Peace for a Living*; Kimberley Coles, *Democratic Designs*, 59–112. For ethnographies of peacekeeping further afield, see Ilana Feldman, *Police Encounters*, 120–43; Robert Rubinstein, *Peacekeeping Under Fire*; Eyal Ben-Ari and Efrat Elron, "Blue Helmets and White Armor."

4. Internationals have also prominently figured in films from ex-Yugoslavia about the war. Emir Kusturica's well-known but intensely controversial film *Underground* (*Podzemlje*, 1995), depicts Black Francophone peacekeepers escorting around a war profiteer as Yugoslavia falls apart in a deployment of racialized difference to underscore the perceived depravity of the UN's actions. Other films featuring Internationals in key roles include Danis Tanović's *No Man's Land* (*Ničija zemlja*, 2001) and Pjer Žalica's *The Fire Is Burning* (*Gori vatra*, 2003).

5. For studies of Euro-American governance in Bosnia, see Andrew Gilbert, "The Limits of Foreign Authority"; Adam Moore, *Peacebuilding in Practice*; Alex Jeffrey, *The Improvised State*; Paula Pickering, *Peacebuilding in the Balkans*; David Chandler, *Bosnia*; Gerald Knaus and Felix Martin, "Travails of the European Raj." An earlier wave of critical scholarship on Western intervention in the Balkans emerged from the constructivist school of international relations theory. David Campbell, *National Deconstruction*; François Debrix, *Re-Envisioning Peacekeeping*, 135–70.

6. One ethnographic study of Internationals in Kosovo captures this sense of menace quite nicely: "it seems that many people in rural areas refuse to speak about the help they received from Islamic organisations. [A Western NGO worker] shared with me that researching the Islamic influence in the rural areas is not only impossible due to refusal of people to speak about it, but it is also dangerous. And she gave me a warning look with a clearly recognisable undertone of conspiracy." Vah Jevšnik, 81. Other Internationals have been more self-aware as to the parallels. Writing about Afghanistan in the late 1990s, Barnett Rubin described al-Qaʿida as constituting "in

effect an alternative international community to the official one." *The Fragmentation of Afghanistan*, xv–xvi. For an early attempt to understand this phenomenon—one outsider's perspective on other outsiders—see also Barnett Rubin, "Arab Islamists in Afghanistan."

7. This is a radically simplified account of prevailing justifications, not a summary of complex doctrinal debates or a substitute for theoretical accounts of how legitimacy is produced as a social reality in international law. For an example of the latter, see, e.g., Ian Hurd, *After Anarchy*.

8. The Security Council declared Sarajevo, Srebrenica, Bihać, Žepa, Goražde, and Tuzla to be "safe areas" in Resolution 824 ¶ 3 (May 6, 1993). It authorized UNPROFOR units in the safe areas to use force in self-defense—but not to protect the safe areas themselves. UN Security Council Resolution 836 ¶¶ 5, 9 (June 4, 1993).

9. Separate from peacekeepers but often conflated with them were unarmed military personnel charged with monitoring the situation on the ground and who often were engaged in disparate forms of mediation. UNPROFOR had several hundred such military observers. There was also the European Community Monitor Mission (ECMM), which consisted of dozens of observers stationed throughout Bosnia and Croatia. For the sake of simplicity, my usage of the term *peacekeeper* here will also cover observers.

10. See *The Blue Helmets*, 745–47. UNPROFOR's scope and mandate evolved as part of the International Community's shifting responses to the wars. Its initial purpose was to facilitate an end to the war in Croatia by patrolling the cease-fire lines between the Croatian army and Serb nationalist forces in Krajina and eastern Slavonia. UNPROFOR set up its headquarters in neighboring Bosnia, just as war was spreading to that country. The force's mandate accordingly expanded to include Bosnia, which would eventually dominate its agenda. UNPROFOR also grew to include a small force in the ex-Yugoslav republic of Macedonia.

In March 1995, the Bosnian, Croatian, and Macedonian branches of UNPROFOR were split into three separate operations, with the Bosnian branch retaining the name.

11. UNPROFOR's first commander was an Indian general, Satish Nambiar. The choice of an officer from a major Non-Aligned country reflected the approach to peacekeeping that was prevalent during the Cold War. But having an Indian general commanding European troops in a European war would not do; he was quickly sidelined and his successors were all western European. Nambiar would go on to criticize NATO's 1999 war on Yugoslavia, citing the importance of Non-Aligned ties between

Delhi and Belgrade. See Satish Nambiar, "Reflections on the Yugoslav Wars"; "India: An Uneasy Precedent."

12. NATO's authority to use violence to enforce the no-fly zone stems from UN Security Council Resolution 816 ¶4 (March 31, 1993). Its mandate to bomb in support of UNPROFOR units in the "safe areas" came in UN Security Council Resolution 836 ¶10 (June 4, 1993).

13. The monument was rebuilt nearby in the Cipelići neighborhood in 2012 due to a redesign of the Tuzla city park.

14. See Benjamin Zyla, *Sharing the Burden?*, 109–10; William Durch and James Schear, "Faultlines," 239.

15. Philip Cunliffe has argued that contemporary peacekeeping should be understood as part of an "imperial multilateralism" that is more decentralized, diffuse, and liberal than older forms of empire. See *Legions of Peace*.

16. Prior to 2014, the UN reimbursed troop-contributing countries at a flat rate for peacekeeping personnel. Throughout the 1990s, the amount was approximately $US1,000 per person per month—considerably higher than the salaries for military personnel from most poor countries. Individual governments could then decide whether and how to augment compensation for their personnel.

17. On racial hierarchies in encounters between peacekeeping forces and local populations, see Paul Higate and Marsha Henry, *Insecure Spaces*; Sherene Razack, *Dark Threats and White Knights*.

18. Jordan's overall contribution to UNPROFOR was larger, but the bulk of its troops were in Croatia, where armed hostilities were not active for most of the war.

19. See Inam-ur-Rahman Malik, "Pakistan," 204; Dipankar Banerjee, "India," 224.

20. Prior to the late Cold War, Pakistan's two significant peacekeeping missions were in Congo and Irian Jaya (now Western New Guinea), both in the early 1960s. See Kabilan Krishnasamy, "Pakistan's Peacekeeping Experiences"; see also Hira Khan, "Pakistan Army as Peacekeepers." In Pakistan's case, however, peacekeeping also afforded extensive opportunities for civil and relief work that augmented its sense of omnicompetence (some might say contempt) in the face of civilian governance back home.

21. At the moment that UN peacekeepers were effectively acting as gatekeepers for the siege in Sarajevo, the novelist and anthropologist Amitav Ghosh made an appeal to scholars to study such gatekeepers, one that has gone largely unheeded. In his plenary speech to the 1994 meeting of the Society for Cultural Anthropology,

Ghosh shared some observations about UN peacekeepers in Cambodia. Invoking the specter of native reservations in North America and southern Africa, Ghosh warned, "The very institution that was (and is) so eagerly embraced by the peoples of the colonized world, as the embodiment of liberty, will become, effectively, the instrument of their containment." "The Global Reservation," 431–32. Ghosh's later work on the British Indian army in novels such as *The Glass Palace* (2000) and *Flood of Fire* (2015)—which gave to broader audiences some sense of the army's global history in imperial warfare—can be seen as one important step in reconstructing the colonial genealogies of the contemporary peacekeeping endeavor.

22. One of Pakistan's most venerated war martyrs, Maj. Raja Aziz Bhatti, was from 17 Punjab and the only recipient of the Nishan-e-Haider from the 1965 war with India.

23. The first troops were supplied by the Nawab of Bhopal, but soon thereafter the British decided to "draw the personnel from the robust fighting classes of northern India instead of recruiting locally," mostly Punjabis of different faith communities. *Historical Record of the 4th Battalion 16th Punjab Regiment*, 3; see also S. Haider Abbas Rizvi, *Veteran Campaigners*.

24. While Director-General of Military Operations, Pervez Musharraf visited Bosnia to prepare the deployment of Pakistani peacekeepers and recalled "that many Europeans were not eager to have a Pakistani force 'intruding' in their domain of influence." Pervez Musharraf, *In the Line of Fire*, 76.

25. The other Pakistani unit in UNPROFOR, PAKBAT-1 in Vareš, found itself continuously accused by both the Bosnian Croats and Muslims of bias. In fall 1994, PAKBAT-1 allowed a Croat school to be opened in Daštansko, a village in the buffer zone that separated Croat and Muslim forces. After Bosnian authorities protested the move, PAKBAT troops attempted to close the school down, eliciting protests from the Croat side as well and leading to months of protracted negotiations and tensions between the parties. See, generally, UNARMS S-1837-0209-0011.

26. See Message from PAKBAT-2 to Deputy Force Commander, UNPROFOR HQ, November 22, 1994, UNARMS S-1838-0603-0001.

27. Pakistan's military, of course, is hardly alone in using peacekeeping to promote its public image. The Hollywood film *Black Hawk Down* (2001), about US commandos fighting in Somalia, also benefited from Pentagon assistance. And as Pakistani army men never fail to point out, their own role in rescuing their American counterparts was conspicuously absent from the cinematic depiction.

28. See Gehad Auda, "An Uncertain Response."

29. The Egyptian general, Hussein Ali Abdel-Razek, was replaced as Sarajevo sector commander by his French counterpart, Marcel Valentin, who described him as "a disillusioned Egyptian who took little interest in his mission." Valentin accused the Egyptians of always staying in their barracks and failing to develop strong relations with the locals, even the Muslims. "The results obtained in carrying out the missions could only have happened thanks to the competence and availability of the French pillar of this multinational force." But of course. Emmanuelle Dancourt, *Général Valentin*, 50, 57.

30. Yaḥyā Ghānim, *Kuntu hunāka . . . yawmiyyāt murāsil ḥarbī fil-Būsna*, 275–80.

31. See Message from EGYBATT to UNPROFOR Sarajevo HQ, December 4, 1993, UNARMS S-1838-0542-0004; EGYBATT to UNPROFOR Sarajevo HQ, June 6, 1994; June 9, 1994, UNARMS S-0138-0542-0001; EGYBATT to UNPROFOR Zagreb HQ, August 22, 1995, UNARMS S-1838-0539-0002; EGYBATT to UNPF Zagreb HQ, September 16, 1995, UNARMS S-1838-0539-0002.

32. Ghānim, 113.

33. Ibid., 276.

34. On peacekeepers and war economies in Bosnia, see Peter Andreas, *Blue Helmets and Black Markets*.

35. Muṣṭafā Abū Saʿd, "Khawāṭir sāʾiḥ fī arḍ al-Balqān," *al-Furqān*, January 1995.

36. Ibid.

37. See Muṣṭafā Abū Saʿd, "Min ajl iḥlāl al-salām fil-Būsna wal-Harsak," *al-Furqān*, December 1994; "Min intiṣārāt al-mujāhidīn," *al-Furqān*, December 1994.

38. For an analysis of similar questions in the pre-2001 days of proto-jihadology, see Brynjar Lia, "Islamist Perceptions of the United Nations and Its Peacekeeping Missions."

39. The archival sources leave unclear the extent to which Zenica's Croats were harassed by mujahids or left out of fear, but in any event several families reportedly returned to their homes after the Turkish peacekeepers arrived. See Craig Jenness, CAO Zenica/Žepče to Victor Andreev, CAC BHC Sarajevo, Situation Report, October 6, 1994, 4, UNARMS S-1837-0059-0004; see also Jenness to Colm Murphy, A/CAC BHC Sarajevo, Situation Report, October 20, 1994, 4 (same folder).

The Turks faced suspicions that their presence was part of an attempt to establish a neo-Ottoman sphere of influence. They were especially anxious to respond to reports in Serb media accusing them of assisting the Bosnians with arms and personnel; the first reconstruction project they were assigned was for an Orthodox

Church, which they interpreted as a deliberately calculated test of their neutrality. See Message from TURKBAT to Sector South West HQ, August 30, 1994, UNARMS S-1838-0627-0005; Oya Akgönenç, "Türk Tugayı Bosna-Hersek'te," *Silahlı Kuvvetler Dergisi*, July 1997, 43.

40. One such incident, in which mujahids reportedly rammed an UNPROFOR Land Rover from behind while attempting to pass it, was attributed to their "fatalistic religion." SSW Daily MILINFOSUM from UNPROFOR MILINFO Cell Gornji Vakuf, August 13, 1994, UNARMS S-1838-0389-0002. See also ECMM Humanitarian Activity Report No 28/94, July 18, 1994, UNARMS S-1837-0157-0001.

41. See, e.g., ECMM Daily Monitoring Activity Report No. 9553, October 21, 1993, UNARMS S-1837-0156-0001; DSR from UNPROFOR UNMO HQ BH to UNPROFOR HQ BH Command, July 15, 1993, UNARMS S-1838-0100-0004; ECMM Daily Monitoring Activity Report No. 9455, June 28, 1993, UNARMS S-1837-0155-0003.

42. See death certificate by Maj. Muhamed Begagić, Garrison Command, 3rd Corps, 11/04-2-1714, November 30, 1995; Esad Hećimović, "Prijeti li sukob mudžahida i Britanaca u srednjoj Bosni?" *Ljiljan*, November 15, 1995.

43. UN Military Observers discerned the presence of mujahids in Guča Gora on the basis of their "peculiar/distinctive head shape," since "most [Military Observers] on the team can immediately recognise mujahadeen arising from previous encounters in this area and on other mission [*sic*]." Daily Sitrep UNMO SSW, August 18, 1994, UNARMS S-1838-0175-0006. In another incident, they "saw two armed mujageddin [*sic*] of Arabian origin" at a Bosnian army base. UNMO HQ Sector SW DSR, July 24, 1994, UNARMS S-1838-0175-0006.

44. According to an intelligence briefing prepared by a British officer in UNPROFOR, "there is a strong likelihood that the Mujahadin are instrumental in increasing the influence of countries such as Iran." "Mujahidin within Sector SW," UNPROFOR Military Information Branch Gornji Vakuf to Headquarters Zagreb, May 24, 1994, UNARMS S-1838-0389-0004. Another analysis asserts that most mujahids "have their religious roots amongst the more fundamentalist Shia sect, whilst the majority of Bosnian Moslems are of the more tolerant, pro-western Sunni." Mujahidin in the ABiH, MILINFO Cel, BH Command Sector SW Gornji Vakuf to UNPROFOR HQ, March 28, 1995, UNARMS S-1838-0397-0004.

45. Vaughan Kent-Payne, *Bosnia Warriors*, 96.

46. Testimony of Vaughan Kent-Payne, *Hadžihasanović* trial, March 22, 2004, 4786:18–24, 4801:1–5.

While settling Bočinja in October 1995, the Katiba also set up checkpoints at the village, leading to a tense encounter with UNPROFOR personnel, who were eventually allowed to pass. See Information Report from Sr. Capt. Hamdija Šljuka, Chief, 35th Division SVB to 3rd Corps SVB, 03/1-80-29a, October 24, 1995; Official Note from Šljuka to 3rd Corps SVB, 03/1-277-1458-2, October 27, 1995.

47. See Ḥamad Qaṭarī and Mājid al-Madanī, *Min qiṣaṣ al-shuhadāʾ al-ʿArab fil-Būsna wal-Harsak*. The narrative describes this as a United Nations plane, but the humanitarian airdrops in Bosnia were overwhelmingly carried out by the US military, with some French and German participation. See A. Martin Lidy, David Arthur, James Kunder, and Samuel Packer, "Bosnia Air Drop Study."

48. See Abdul Manaf Kasmuri, *Kolonel jihad*.

49. See 69 Fed. Reg. 30, 479 (May 24, 2004). Concerns over translation are not purely hypothetical: in 2012, Tarek Mehanna, an Egyptian-American, was convicted of material support for terrorism, partially based on translations he carried out for a jihad-themed website. Mehanna's translations were deemed to be rendering a service to al-Qaʿida, even though no evidence was adduced that the translated text was produced by al-Qaʿida or that al-Qaʿida oversaw the website or the translation. See *United States v. Mehanna*, 735 F.3rd 32 (1st Cir. 2013), *cert. denied* 135 S. Ct. 49 (2014).

50. Darul Arqam combined the teachings of the Awrad Muhammadiyya Sufi order with a modernist bent that emphasized developing economic autonomy, and much of its support was from the growing Malay middle classes. It eventually came to be seen as a threat by the ruling United Malays National Organization party and was outlawed in 1994. See Ahmad Fauzi bin Abdul Hamid, "Islamic Resurgence in the Periphery."

51. The NGO Abdul Manaf traveled with was part of Angkatan Belia Islam Malaysia (ABIM), the largest and most politically active Islamist organization in the country. One of its co-founders was Anwar Ibrahim, the former deputy prime minister.

52. Abdul Manaf Kasmuri, 92.

53. UN Security Council Resolution 1031 (December 15, 1995) welcomed the Dayton agreement and IFOR's deployment to Bosnia.

54. In addition, the Brčko district theoretically belongs to both the Federation and the RS, but is governed separately by the Office of the High Representative.

55. See General Framework Agreement for Peace in Bosnia-Herzegovina, Bosn. & Herz.-Croat.-Yugo., December 14, 1995, 33 I.L.M. 75, 89, Annex 10.

56. Use of the High Representative's "Bonn powers" has declined markedly since 2010.

57. The chief US negotiator, Richard Holbrooke, recalled in his memoirs that "With NATO forces about to arrive in Bosnia, we could not tolerate the continued presence of these people." *To End a War*, 320.

58. See, e.g., Possible Terrorist Threats to US Forces in the Balkans, CIA DCI Counterterrorist Center, November 22, 1995, WJCPL C05917478. The memoirs of CIA officers who worked in wartime Bosnia refer in passing to surveillance on "the Arab Mujahidin" but otherwise only discuss actions against suspected operatives of the Lebanese Hizballah. Robert Baer and Dana Baer, *The Company We Keep*, 4.

59. Anwar Shaʿban in particular had attracted attention at the highest levels of the US government by this point. He was described in a classified briefing paper as "a key Islamic Group terrorist . . . highly likely to attack U.S. citizens." Dealing with the Terrorist Threat to U.S. Forces, National Security Council, December 4, 1995, WJCPL C05962603.

60. General Framework Agreement for Peace, Annex 1-A, art. III.

61. See Li, "A Universal Enemy?"

62. See Memorandum for the President by National Security Advisor Anthony Lake, December 7, 1995, WJCPL C05740371; Summary of Conclusions of Principals Committee Meeting on Bosnia, National Security Council, December 5, 1995, WJCPL C05962599.

63. See Information Report by Agan Haseljić, Chief, ARBiH 3rd Corps SVB to ARBiH General Staff SVB, 03/1-60-4-4, December 11, 1995; Disbandment of the Elmudžahedin Detachment by Gen. Rasim Delić, ARBiH Commander, 4/43-96, December 12, 1995.

64. Abu Hamza al-Masri, the infamous Egyptian preacher and mujahid who lived for decades in the UK, was one of those who opposed disbanding the Katiba. See Kamīl al-Ṭawīl, "'Abū Ḥamza al-Miṣrī' yarwī lil-Ḥayāt qiṣṣat al-intiqāl ilā Brīṭānyā wal-'tawba' . . . thumma 'al-hijra' ilā Afghānistān wal-Būsna wa-'inqādh Khaṭṭāb'," *al-Ḥayāt*, December 2001. Al-Masri arrived in the late stages of the jihad, had acquired a negative reputation for divisiveness, and was ejected from the unit. He will feature in our story again in the next chapter.

65. Report by Col. Agan Haseljić, Chief, 3rd Corps SVB, to General Staff SVB, 03/1-60-44, December 20, 1995.

66. INTERPOL databases contain photographs and fingerprints of some of the departing ansar, labeled, curiously enough, as "Mujahedeen Freedom Fighters." See, e.g., *United States v. Ahmed al-Darbi*, Stipulation of Fact, Enclosure 1 (U.S. Mil. Comm. GTMO Dec. 20, 2013). Several dossiers of detainees held at Guantánamo

published by Wikileaks also describe "pocket litter" of Arab mujahids entering Croatia from Bosnia in January 1996, a trajectory and timing consistent with the evacuation. These claims are sourced to CIA cables (marked by the prefix TD-314) from 2002 and 2003. See, e.g., Joint Task Force-Guantánamo, Detainee Assessment Briefs for ISN 434, February 8, 2008, 11; ISN 168, November 4, 2007, 9; ISN 57, February 3, 2006, 5; ISN 53, April 15, 2007, 7; ISN 5, October 25, 2007, 12; ISN 261, July 28, 2006, 6. In any of these sources, it is unclear if the information originated with Croatian authorities, US intelligence, or some other entity.

CHAPTER 7: THE GLOBAL WAR ON TERROR

1. "TO JE SVE ŠTO MI MOŽEMO—OSMJEHNUTI SE SA ZADOVOLJSTVOM JER SMO MU PORODICA," Statement from the Husin-Softić family, October 6, 2009.

2. See "Handover Ceremony of the EU Funded Reception Centre for Irregular Migrants in BiH," Delegation of the European Union to Bosnia and Herzegovina, November 20, 2009.

3. Jonathan Finer, "In Bosnia, Former Fighters Face Expulsion," *Washington Post*, September 4, 2007. As we have seen throughout this book, diasporic histories can shed light on national policies in disparate ways. Gregorian's father, Vartan, is an Armenian born in Tabriz and schooled in Lebanon. After moving to the US, he became a scholar of the Middle East—among his books is *Islam: A Mosaic, Not a Monolith*—and later a prominent figure in the world of liberal foundations, having served as president of Brown University, the New York Public Library, and the Carnegie Corporation. His son, Raffi, represents a diasporic sensibility repackaged as a consummate product of the US defense establishment. The younger Gregorian served in a variety of State Department and NATO positions, was a naval reserve officer, and earned a PhD from the School of Advanced International Studies at Johns Hopkins with a dissertation on questions of colonial soldiering. See Raffi Gregorian, *The British Army, the Gurkhas and Cold War Strategy in the Far East, 1947–1954*.

4. See Carl Schmitt, *The Concept of the Political*, 26.

5. While GWOT is primarily seen as a response to the 9/11 attacks, the logic of a globalized counterinsurgency was in place at least from the mid-1990s and included US efforts to expel ansar mujahids from Bosnia at the end of the war.

6. Agamben's turn to "global civil war" in the aftermath of the September 2001 attacks represents an attempt to scale up his arguments about the state of exception with a characteristic disinterest in thinking about race and empire. For example,

Agamben suggests that the US is "ignoring international law externally and producing a permanent state of exception internally"—as if international law requires none of the critical interrogation that Agamben brings to bear on, say, constitutionalism. See *State of Exception*, 85; see also *Stasis*, 1–24. Critical geographers have picked up on Agamben's curious lack of attention to international law and empire. See, e.g., Derek Gregory, "The Black Flag."

Agamben seems unsure as to whether he thinks GWOT is one giant state of exception on a planetary scale or simply that every state is sliding into its own permanent state of emergency without anything important happening in the spaces between them. The former scenario without further elaboration risks uncritically treating the world political system as a macrocosm of the nation-state. The latter is as believable as ever but has nothing to do with creating a "global civil war" properly speaking—more important, showing the result of convergence between domestic states of exception does not capture the overall architecture of the system. For helpful illustrations of these two different ways of scaling up the notion of emergency or exception, see Kim Lane Scheppele, "The International State of Emergency"; Stein Tønnesson, "A 'Global Civil War'?" In a way, this is a juridical mirror image to the conundrum animating the first half of this study: how to speak about pan-Islamic solidarity beyond the models of "lumping" and "splitting."

7. This was most common in debates over the fate of GTMO detainees, in which liberals and conservatives tended to agree that federal courts represent a "gold standard" of justice, notwithstanding their important role in a system of racialized captivity with no equal in the world. While one can certainly understand a tactical preference for these courts over the military commissions at GTMO, the liberal embrace of this rhetoric was both offensive on its own terms and also self-defeating: it ultimately reinforced notions of American exceptionalism and beneficence that leave little room for mounting serious challenges to GWOT. For one attempt to remedy this disconnect, see Sohail Daulatzai, "Protect ya Neck."

8. US colonialism in Cuba and Haiti—especially the base's use to detain migrants from these two countries—has been the most common reference point for understanding GTMO's colonial entailments. See, e.g., A. Naomi Paik, *Rightlessness*; Jana Lipman, *Guantánamo*.

9. For one important exception to this trend, see Laleh Khalili, *Time in the Shadows*.

10. Kwame Nkrumah, *Neo-Colonialism*, xi. The US predilection for exercising hegemony through independent states is part of a continuum of indirect rule practices

pursued by other imperial powers. The British empire, for example, maintained a broad spectrum of colonial forms that included nominally independent states.

11. "This new concept of terror maintains the minute-to-minute threat made familiar by decades of Cold War nuclear culture, but it is different in that it is an open-ended concept, one that links hugely diverse kinds of threats . . . and treats them all as equally imminent, equally catastrophic." Joseph Masco, *The Theater of Operations*, 19.

12. Authorization for Use of Military Force, Public Law 107-40, 115 Stat. 224 (2001). Congressional authorizations of military action since the Cold War have been framed in terms of implementing UN resolutions, fulfilling defense commitments to allies, or engaging in other kinds of policing or reprisal actions that do not imply the full parity that war does.

13. See Bruce O'Neill, "Of Camps, Gulags, and Extraordinary Renditions."

14. The US is of course not unique in maintaining such farflung carceral networks. The British, for example, used practices of banishment and confinement throughout their empire, including nominally independent client states, in order to exploit jurisdictional ambiguities. See Khalili, 65–73.

15. See *Hadž Boudellaa et al. v. Bosnia and Herzegovina and Federation of Bosnia and Herzegovina* ¶¶ 51–52, CH/02/8679 (Hum. Rts. Chamber Bosn. & Herz. 2002). Interestingly, the Bosnian government informed a senior Algerian intelligence officer of their suspicions about the men even before the arrests. See id., ¶ 50.

16. David Petraeus, a senior officer in the NATO-led peacekeeping force in Bosnia who would later rise to prominence as a battlefield general in Iraq, saw this as a career-defining moment. He supervised the abduction and rendition of an Egyptian resident of Germany and a Jordanian citizen, an incident that would later spark a parliamentary inquiry in Germany. See Press Release, Bundestag, Kanzleramt war über den Fall Khafagy Informiert, July 17, 2009; Paula Broadwell and Vernon Loeb, *All In*, 51–52; Majdī Saʿīd, "Fī ḍiyāfat Muslimī Almānyā," *Islamonline.net*, August 1, 2006.

On Imad el-Misri's torture in Egypt, see Amnesty International, "Egypt: No Protection—Systematic Torture Continues," 13–14.

17. See *Eslam Durmo v. Federation of Bosnia and Herzegovina* ¶¶ 58, 121, CH/02/9842 (Hum. Rts. Chamber Bosn. & Herz. 2003).

18. See Thomas Kellogg and Hossam El-Hamalawy, "Black Hole," 19–21; Muḥammad Ṣalāḥ, *Waqāʾiʿ sanawāt al-jihād*, 144–49.

19. From an imperial management perspective, burdensome constraints on the management of GTMO do not come only from the courts or the media. A statute passed

in 2014 requires the Pentagon to provide Congress with thirty days' notice of any detainee transfers from the prison, giving ample opportunity for various forms of grandstanding against any release. See Pub. L. No. 113-76, div. C, title VIII, § 8111 (Jan. 17, 2014). This requirement is one more reason why national security elites tend to view the prison as a millstone more than a resource; it is worth noting that no additional detainees were sent to GTMO even after the 2018 executive order that formalized President Barack Obama's failure to close the prison. See Exec. Order No. 13, 823—Protecting America Through Lawful Detention of Terrorists, 83 Fed. Reg. 4,831 (Jan. 30, 2018).

20. See, e.g., Muslim Human Rights Forum, "Horn of Terror"; Jeremy Scahill, "The CIA's Secret Sites in Somalia," *The Nation*, August 1–8, 2011.

21. See Maggie Michael, "In Yemen's Secret Prisons, UAE Tortures and US Interrogates," Associated Press, June 22, 2017.

22. See Charlie Savage, "As ISIS Fighters Fill Syrian Jails, Nations Fear They'll Come Home," *New York Times*, July 19, 2018; Liz Sly, "The Jihadists No One Wants," *Washington Post*, December 21, 2018.

23. The eviction of the Arabs was made possible in part by the 2000 elections, which swept the SDA out of the municipal government that administered Bočinja. The Social Democratic Party, which was nominally non-nationalist but mostly had Bosniak voters, argued that restoring homes in Bočinja to their Serb owners would only increase pressure on Serbs to allow Bosniaks to return to their former homes. Seven families from the Bočinja džemat ended up staying, as they purchased their homes from their Serb owners.

In the words of one International working on property issues at the time, the Bočinja evictions were a way of "kick-starting the system" of refugee returns. Charles Philpott, "Though the Dog Is Dead, the Pig Must Be Killed," 20. The year 2000 witnessed a dramatic acceleration in refugee returns, and by 2004 nearly half of all displaced persons had returned to their homes. See Daniela Heimerl, "The Return of Refugees and Internally Displaced Persons."

24. See *Bosnia-Herzegovina v. Maktouf*, K-127/04 (State Court of Bosn. & Herz. 2005).

25. Bosnia's human rights court later deemed that the manner of el-Misri's denationalization did not conform to the relevant procedures. See *Durmo*, ¶¶ 24, 26, 81–89.

26. See BH Službeni Glasnik 11/93, May 10, 1993.

27. 2005 BiH Law on the Amendments to the Law on Citizenship of BiH, art. 41(4)(a), Službeni Glasnik 82/05.

28. This was in addition to the power to revoke nationalizations obtained through fraud or by individuals committing serious crimes, which is not an uncommon feature of contemporary regimes on nationality and citizenship.

29. See Nasser Hussain, "Beyond Norm and Exception: Guantánamo"; Fleur Johns, "Guantánamo Bay and the Annihilation of the Exception."

30. "Bosnia: Citizenship Review Underway as Negative Media Attention Grows," cable by Amb. Douglas McElhaney, 06SARAJEVO1748, August 4, 2006, ¶ 11.

31. "Bosnia: Sadovic Politicizes Ministry of Security," cable by Amb. Douglas McElhaney, 07SARAJEVO1071, May 17, 2007, ¶ 6. The cable ends with a promise to "continue to engage [SDA president] Sulejman Tihic and Bakir Izetbegovic to ensure that Sadovic does not undermine progress in critical security goals in Bosnia." Id., ¶ 9.

32. "Lajčák Meets Sadović; Concerned by Developments in Ministry of Security," Office of the High Representative, July 20, 2007.

33. See "Bosnian Security Agency Heads Pledge Cooperation," cable by Amb. Douglas McElhaney, 07SARAJEVO1986, September 19, 2007.

34. See "Bosnia: Abu Hamza, the CRC, and Extremists: A Case Study in Getting to Deportation," cable by Chargé d'Affaires Judith Cefkin, 08SARAJEVO93, January 16, 2008, ¶¶ 1,8.

35. Vuković was, in the eyes of the US embassy, an "effective chairman" of the State Commission and "one of the few competent employees at the Ministry of Security." "Bosnia: Arrest of Assistant Security Minister Shocks BiH and Raises Many Troubling Questions," cable by Amb. Charles English, 09SARAJEVO101, January 26, 2009, ¶¶ 1, 3. On several occasions during our interview in December 2006, he was interrupted by friendly phone calls from embassy officials.

36. Abu Hamza al-Masri, born Mostafa Kamel Mostafa, was later extradited to the United States and convicted of various terrorism-related charges. He is currently serving a life sentence at the federal "supermax" prison in Florence, Colorado.

37. "U.S. Wrongly Identified Islamic Fighter as Convicted Terrorist: Report," Agence-France Presse, June 6, 2008.

38. See Finer; Renate Flottau, "Balkan Mujahedeens: Fundamentalist Islam Finds Fertile Ground in Bosnia," *Der Spiegel International*, September 11, 2007; Nicholas Walton, "Bosnia Fighters Face Uncertain Fate," *BBC Online*, May 10, 2007; Nicholas Wood, "Bosnia Moving to Deport Veterans of 1992–1995 Balkan War," *International Herald Tribune*, August 1, 2007.

39. "Abu Hamza Supporters Rally to Oppose Deportation," cable by Amb. Charles English, 08SARAJEVO202, February 4, 2008, ¶ 8. This description of the rally is based on interviews I conducted with the organizers, edited video footage made available by them, news accounts, and a description by a Norwegian anthropology student who was in attendance.

40. See Asim Mujkić, *We, the Citizens of Ethnopolis.*

41. In 2009, the European Court of Human Rights found the Constitution's effective exclusion of Others—in this case, a Jew and a Roma—from the presidency and the upper house of parliament to violate Bosnia's international human rights obligations, but the decision was never implemented. See *Sejdić and Finci v. Bosnia and Herzegovina*, 27996/06 and 34836/06 (Eur. Ct. H.R. 2009). Several years later, the court also ruled in favor of a Bosnian woman who was unable to stand for elections because she disclaimed any ethnic affiliation. See *Zornić v. Bosnia and Herzegovina*, 3681/06 (Eur. Ct. H.R. 2014).

42. The border of the European Union currently runs through the former Yugoslavia: Slovenia joined in 2004 and Croatia in 2013. This radically changed the status of people from other ex-Yugoslav republics who were co-citizens until a generation ago. In Slovenia, more than 1 percent of the population was stripped of residency rights overnight; more recent migrants, many from Bosnia, are now considered non-EU guest workers. See Maple Razsa and Andrej Kurnik, "Occupy Slovenia."

43. The European Court of Human Rights has generally limited power to rule in denationalization cases, so Abu Hamza's litigation was focused on ending his detention and preventing his deportation to Syria rather than on restoring his Bosnian citizenship.

44. Written Observations of Bosnia and Herzegovina on Admissibility and Merits ¶ 94, *Al Husin v. Bosnia and Herzegovina*, 3727/08 (Eur. Ct. H.R. Feb. 15, 2011).

45. See Jochen Bittner, "Hatz unter Freunden," *Die Zeit*, December 21, 2005. Years later, Seyam relocated to Syria and, according to various media reports, served as a high-ranking education official for ISIS before his death in the 2017 battle of Mosul.

46. "Tunisian Deportation: Bosnian Authorities Overcome Setbacks," cable by Chargé d'Affaires Judith Cefkin, 06SARAJEVO2042, September 5, 2006, ¶ 1. On Ferchichi's treatment in Tunisia, see "Bosnia and Herzegovina: Briefing to the UN Committee Against Torture," Amnesty International, EUR 63/005/2010, October 2010, 10; Anwar Mālik, "Awrāq ʿāʾid min bilād al-Balqān: ʿArab al-Būsna . . . hāʾulāʾi al-muṭāradūn," *al-Waṭan*, April 17, 2007.

47. See Marija Taušan, "Deportovan Alžirac Atau Mimun," *Nezavisne novine*, December 14, 2007.

48. See *Al Husin v. Bosnia and Herzegovina*, 3727/08 (Eur. Ct. H.R. 2012).

49. See Službeni Glasnik 88/15 (November 2015), 64 (amending art. 119(6) of the Law on Foreigners' Movement, Residence, and Asylum).

50. See *Al Hamdani v. Bosnia and Herzegovina*, 31098/10 (Eur. Ct. H.R. 2012).

Bibliography

ARCHIVES

Independent researchers do not currently have access to the wartime records of the various parties to the Bosnian war. The next best alternative are the materials gathered as evidence by the UN International Criminal Tribunal for ex-Yugoslavia (ICTY). ICTY investigators were able to examine and copy documents from the Bosnian army and other groups, some of which were introduced as evidentiary exhibits at trial. Accordingly, I made extensive use of ICTY holdings for the cases involving the mujahids' war crimes, namely *Prosecutor v. Rasim Delić* (IT-04-83) and *Prosecutor v. Enver Hadžihasanović and Amir Kubura* (IT-01-47). Unless stated otherwise, archival sources cited in this book are from this archive.

Materials for this book were also gathered during visits to the institutions listed below, as well as from several online collections. Acronyms are included to facilitate the tracing of archival materials cited in the endnotes.

Bosniak Institute, Sarajevo
Faculty of Islamic Studies, University of Sarajevo
Gazi Husrev-bey Library, Sarajevo
King Faisal Center for Research and Islamic Studies, Riyadh
Kulturni centar Kralj Fahd, Sarajevo
Media Centar, Sarajevo

Pontificio Istituto di Studi Arabi e d'Islamistica, Rome

Al-Qabas media archive, Kuwait

United Kingdom National Archives (UKNA), Kew, London

United Nations Archives and Records Management Section (UNARMS), New York

Wikileaks.org, online materials only

William J. Clinton Presidential Library (WJCPL), online materials only

Moreover, the following university libraries were indispensable to the research behind this book: Widener Library (Harvard), Sterling Memorial Library (Yale), Butler Library (Columbia); Regenstein Library (University of Chicago).

Archival documents, newspaper and magazine articles, and websites are cited in full in the endnotes. All other sources are listed below.

ʿAbd al-Bāqī, Miṣbāḥ Allāh. *Ḥaqīqat al-ghazw al-Amrīkī li-Afghānistān*. Cairo: Dār al-tawzīʿ wal-nashr al-Islāmiyya, 2005.

Abdul Khabeer, Su'ad. *Muslim Cool: Race, Religion, and Hip Hop in the United States*. New York: New York University Press, 2016.

Abdul Manaf Kasmuri. *Kolonel jihad: antara mitos dan realiti*. Kuala Lumpur: Nur Ilham, 2010.

Abu-Lughod, Lila. *Do Muslim Women Need Saving?* Cambridge, MA: Harvard University Press, 2013.

Abu Kalil, Šavki. *Uzroci pobjede i poraza*. Translated by Subhija Hadžimejlić-Skenderović. Zenica: Odred Elmudžahedin, under the supervision of Muftijstvo Zenica, 1995[1979].

Adanır, Fikret. "The Formation of a Muslim 'Nation' in Bosnia-Hercegovina: A Historiographic Discussion." In *The Ottomans and the Balkans: A Discussion of Historiography*, edited by Fikret Adanır and Suraiya Faroqhi, 267–304. Leiden: Brill, 2002.

Agamben, Giorgio. *Stasis: Civil War as a Political Paradigm*. Translated by Nicholas Heron. Stanford, CA: Stanford University Press, 2015.

———. *State of Exception*. Translated by Kevin Attell. Chicago: University of Chicago Press, 2005[2003].

———. *Homo Sacer: Sovereign Power and Bare Life*. Translated by Daniel Heller-Roazen. Stanford, CA: Stanford University Press, 1998[1995].

Agrama, Hussein Ali. *Questioning Secularism: Islam, Sovereignty, and the Rule of Law in Modern Egypt*. Chicago: University of Chicago Press, 2012.

Ahmad Fauzi bin Abdul Hamid. "Islamic Resurgence in the Periphery: A Study of Political Islam in Contemporary Malaysia with Special Reference to the Darul Arqam Movement, 1968–1996." PhD thesis, Political Science, University of Newcastle upon Tyne, 1998.

Ahmed, Shahab. *What Is Islam?: The Importance of Being Islamic*. Princeton, NJ: Princeton University Press, 2015.

Aidi, Hisham. *Rebel Music: Race, Empire, and the New Muslim Youth Culture*. New York: Random House, 2014.

Aigle, Denise, and Catherine Mayeur-Jaouen. "Introduction: Miracle et *karāma*. Une approche comparatiste." In *Miracle et karāma*, edited by Denise Aigle, 13–35. Turnhout: Brepols, 2000.

Akšamija, Azra. "Our Mosques Are Us: Rewriting National History of Bosnia-Herzegovina through Religious Architecture." PhD thesis, Department of Architecture, Massachusetts Institute of Technology, 2011.

Alavi, Seema. *Muslim Cosmopolitanism in the Age of Empire*. Cambridge, MA: Harvard University Press, 2015.

al-Albānī, Muḥammad Nāsir al-Dīn. *Silsilat al-hudā wal-nūr*, Vol. 80. 1992. Audio cassette recording.

Alexandrowicz, Charles Henry. *The European-African Confrontation: A Study in Treaty Making*. Leiden: Sijthoff, 1973.

———. *An Introduction to the History of the Law of Nations in the East Indies (16th, 17th, and 18th Centuries)*. Oxford: Clarendon Press, 1967.

Alibašić, Ahmet. "Traditional and Reformist Islam in Bosnia and Herzegovina." Cambridge Programme for Security in International Society, 2003.

Amīnī, Muḥammad Ṣafwat al-Saqqā. *Al-Muslimūn fī Yūghūslāfiyā*. Beirut: Dār al-Fatḥ, 1974.

Amzi-Erdoğdular, Leyla. "Afterlife of Empire: Muslim-Ottoman Relations in Habsburg Bosnia Herzegovina, 1878–1914." PhD thesis, Middle Eastern, South Asian and African Studies, Columbia University, 2013.

Amzyān, Muḥammad Muḥammad. *Al-Būsna wal-Harsak: al-Andalus al-thāniya!* Casablanca: Maṭbaʿat al-Najāḥ al-jadīda, 1993.

Anas, ʿAbd Allāh. *Wilādat al-Afghān al-ʿArab: Sīrat ʿAbd Allāh Anas bayna Masʿūd wa-ʿAbd Allāh ʿAzzām*. Beirut: Dār al-Sāqī, 2002.

Andreas, Peter. *Blue Helmets and Black Markets: The Business of Survival in the Siege of Sarajevo*. Ithaca, NY: Cornell University Press, 2008.

Anghie, Antony. *Imperialism, Sovereignty, and the Making of International Law*. Cambridge: Cambridge University Press, 2004.

Anṣārī, ʿAbd al-Quddūs. *Tārīkh madīnat Jidda*. Jeddah: Maṭābiʿ al-Iṣfahānī, 1963.

al-Arian, Abdullah. *Answering the Call: Popular Islamic Activism in Sadat's Egypt*. Oxford: Oxford University Press, 2014.

Arielli, Nir. *From Byron to bin Laden: A History of Foreign War Volunteers*. Cambridge, MA: Harvard University Press, 2018.

———. "In Search of Meaning: Foreign Volunteers in the Croatian Armed Forces, 1991–1995." *Contemporary European History* 21, no. 1 (2012): 1–17.

Armitage, David, and Jennifer Pitts. "'This Modern Grotius': An Introduction to the Life and Thought of C.H. Alexandrowicz." In *The Law of Nations in Global History*, 1–31. Oxford: Oxford University Press, 2017.

Arnaut, Fikret. *Mezhebi u Islamu*. Munich: Džema'at Sabur, s.a.

al-Arnā'ūṭ, Maḥmūd ʿAbd al-Qādir. *Sīrat al-ʿallāma al-Shaykh ʿAbd al-Qādir al-Arnā'ūṭ, 1347–1425*. Damascus: Dār al-Balkhī, 2005.

al-Arnā'ūṭ, Muḥammad Mūfākū. "Al-Albāniyyūn fī Sūriya wa-dawruhum fil-ḥayāt al-Sūriyya." Paper presented at the al-Mu'tamar al-duwwalī al-thānī li-tārīkh bilād al-Shām: 922H-1358H/1516M-1939M conference, Damascus, 1978.

Asad, Talal. "Muhammad Asad Between Religion and Politics." *Islam & Science* 10, no. 1 (Summer 2012): 77–88.

———. "Thinking About Terrorism and Just War." *Cambridge Review of International Affairs* 23, no. 1 (March 2010): 3–24.

———. *On Suicide Bombing*. New York: Columbia University Press, 2007.

———. *Formations of the Secular: Christianity, Islam, Modernity*. Stanford, CA: Stanford University Press, 2003.

———. *Genealogies of Religion: Discipline and Reasons of Power in Christianity and Islam*. Baltimore: Johns Hopkins University Press, 1993.

———. "The Idea of an Anthropology of Islam." Washington, DC: Georgetown University Center for Contemporary Arab Studies, 1986.

Auda, Gehad. "An Uncertain Response: The Islamic Movement in Egypt." In *Islamic Fundamentalisms and the Gulf Crisis*, edited by James Piscatori, 109–30. Chicago: Fundamentalism Project, American Academy of Arts and Sciences, 1991.

Aydın, Cemil. *The Idea of the Muslim World: A Global Intellectual History*. Cambridge, MA: Harvard University Press, 2017.

Azam, Abdullah. *Allahovi znakovi u Afganistanskom Džihadu*. S.l., s.a.[1983] [electronic book].
See also Azzam, Abdullah; ʿAzzām, ʿAbd Allāh

Azinović, Vlado. *Al-kai'da u Bosni i Hercegovini: mit ili stvarna opasnost?* Prague: Radio Free Europe, 2007.

Azinović, Vlado, and Muhamed Jusić. "The New Lure of the Syrian War—The Foreign Fighters' Bosnian Contingent." Sarajevo: Atlantic Initiative, 2016.

ʿAzzām, ʿAbd Allāh. *Al-difāʿ ʿan arāḍī al-Muslimīn: ahamm furūḍ al-aʿyān*. 2nd ed. Amman: Maktabat al-Risāla al-ḥadītha, 1987.

———. *Āyāt al-raḥmān fī jihād al-Afghān*. 2nd ed. Amman: Maktabat al-Risāla al-ḥadītha, 1986[1983].

———. *Āyāt al-raḥmān fī jihād al-Afghān*. 1st ed. Pakistan: Ittiḥād al-ṭalaba al-Muslimīn, 1983.
See also Azam, Abdullah; Azzam, Abdullah

Azzam, Abdullah. *The Signs of ar-Rahman in the Jihad of Afghanistan*. Translated by A. B. al-Mehri. Birmingham, UK: Maktabah Booksellers and Publishers, s.a.[1983].

———. *Dan malaikat pun turun di Afghanistan*. Translated by Wahyudin. Klaten: Kafayeh Cipta media, 2010[1983].

———. *Afgan Cihadında Rahman'ın Ayetleri*. Translated by Ahmet Pakalın. Istanbul: İslamoğlu, 1988[1983].
See also Azam, Abdullah; ʿAzzām, ʿAbd Allāh

Azzam Publications. *Under the Shades of Swords*. London: Azzam Publications, 1997. Audio cassette recording.

———. *In the Hearts of Green Birds*. London: Azzam Publications, 1996. Audio cassette recording.

Bābaṭīn, ʿAlī Bākhayyil. *Idrāk al-fawt fī dhikr qabāʾil tārīkh Ḥaḍramawt: muʿjam li-qabāʾil al-bādiyya wa-sukkān al-ḥaḍāra fī tārīkh Ḥaḍramawt*. Amman: Dār ʿAmmār, 2009.

Babuna, Aydın. "Bosnian Muslims During the Cold War: Their Identity Between Domestic and Foreign Policies." In *Religion and the Cold War: A Global Perspective*, edited by Philip Muehlenbeck, 182–205. Nashville, TN: Vanderbilt University Press, 2012.

Bādī, Muṣṭafā. *Afghānistān: iḥtilāl al-dhākira*. Vol. 1, Sana'a: s.n., 2004.

Badiou, Alain. *Saint Paul: The Foundations of Universalism*. Translated by Ray Brassier. Stanford, CA: Stanford University Press, 2003[1997].

Baer, Robert, and Dana Baer. *The Company We Keep: A Husband-and-Wife True-Life Spy Story*. New York: Crown, 2011.

Baker, Catherine. *Race and the Yugoslav Region: Postsocialist, Post-Conflict, Postcolonial?* Manchester: Manchester University Press, 2018.

———. "Opening the Black Box: Oral Histories of How Soldiers and Civilians Learned to Translate and Interpret During Peace Support Operations in Bosnia-Herzegovina." *Oral History Forum* 32 (2012): 1–27.

Bakić-Hayden, Milica. "Nesting Orientalisms: The Case of Former Yugoslavia." *Slavic Review* 54, no. 4 (1995): 917–31.

Bakrī, Ṣalāḥ ʿAbd al-Qādir. *Tārīkh Ḥaḍramawt al-siyāsī*. Vol. 2. Cairo?: Maṭbaʿat Muṣṭafā al-Bābī al-Ḥalabī wa-Awlādih, 1936.

Bâli, Aslı. "Sykes-Picot and 'Artificial' States." *AJIL Unbound* 110, no. 1 (2016): 115–19.

Balibar, Étienne. "On Universalism: In Debate with Alain Badiou." Paper presented at the Koehn Event in Critical Theory conference, Irvine, California, February 2, 2007.

Ballinger, Pamela. "Watery Spaces, Globalizing Places: Ownership and Access in Postsocialist Croatia." In *European Responses to Globalization: Resistance, Adaptation and Alternatives*, edited by Janet Laible and Henri Barkey, 153–77. Oxford: Elsevier, 2006.

Ballinger, Pamela, and Kristen Ghodsee. "Socialist Secularism: Religion, Modernity, and Muslim Women's Emancipation in Bulgaria and Yugoslavia, 1945–1991." *Aspasia: The International Yearbook of Central, Eastern, and Southeast European Women's and Gender History* 5 (March 2011): 6–27.

Banac, Ivo. *The National Question in Yugoslavia*. Ithaca, NY: Cornell University Press, 1984.

Banerjee, Dipankar. "India." In *Providing Peacekeepers: The Politics, Challenges, and Future of United Nations Peacekeeping Contributions*, edited by Alex J. Bellamy and Paul D. Williams, 225–44. Oxford: Oxford University Press, 2013.

al-Bāqillānī, Abū Bakr. *Kitāb al-bayān ʿan al-farq bayna al-muʿjizāt wal-karāmāt wal-ḥiyal wal-kihāna wal-siḥr wal-nārinjāt*, edited by Richard McCarthy. Beirut: al-Maktaba al-sharqiyya, 1958.

Barādarān, Maryam. *R*. Isfahan: Ārmā, 2017.

Barkawi, Tarak, and Mark Laffey. "Retrieving the Imperial: Empire and International Relations." *Millennium: Journal of International Studies* 31, no. 1 (2002): 109–27.

Bartulin, Nevenko. *The Racial Idea in the Independent State of Croatia: Origins and Theory*. Leiden: Brill, 2014.

Bashir, Shahzad. *Sufi Bodies: Religion and Society in Medieval Islam*. New York: Columbia University Press, 2011.

Bāwazīr, Khālid. *Mawānīʾ sāḥil Ḥaḍramawt: dirāsa ithnū āthariyya*. S.l.: Maktabat Dār al-Maʿrifa, 1996.

Bećirović, Denis. *Islamska zajednica u Bosni i Hercegovini za vrijeme avnojevske Jugoslavije (1945–1953)*. Zagreb: Bošnjačka nacionalna zajednica, 2012.

Becker-Lorca, Arnulf. *Mestizo International Law: A Global Intellectual History, 1842–1933*. Cambridge: Cambridge University Press, 2014.

Bellamy, Alex. *The Formation of Croatian National Identity: A Centuries-Old Dream?* Manchester: Manchester University Press, 2003.

Bellion-Jourdan, Jérôme, and Jonathan Benthall, eds. *The Charitable Crescent: Politics of Aid in the Muslim World*. London: I.B. Tauris, 2003.

Ben-Ari, Eyal, and Efrat Elron. "Blue Helmets and White Armor: Multi-Nationalism and Multi-Culturalism Among UN Peacekeeping Forces." *City & Society* 13, no. 2 (2001): 271–302.

Benjamin, Walter. "Theses on the Philosophy of History." Translated by Harry Zohn. In *Illuminations*, edited by Hannah Arendt, 253–64. New York: Schocken, 2007[1955].

Benthall, Jonathan, and Robert Lacey, eds. *Gulf Charities and Islamic Philanthropy in the "Age of Terror" and Beyond*. Berlin: Gerlach Press, 2014.

Benton, Adia. "African Expatriates and Race in the Anthropology of Humanitarianism." *Critical African Studies* 8, no. 3 (2016): 266–77.

Bergen, Peter, and Paul Cruickshank. "Revisiting the Early Account of Al Qaeda: An Updated Account of Its Formative Years." *Studies in Conflict & Terrorism* 35, no. 1 (2012): 1–36.

Bjelić, Dušan, and Obrad Savić, eds. *Balkan as Metaphor: Between Globalization and Fragmentation*. Cambridge, MA: MIT Press, 2002.

Blagojević, Gordana. "Savremeni stereotipi Srba o Kinezima u Beogradu: 'Kada kažeš Kina, mislim Blok 70 ili . . .'." *Zbornik Matice srpske za društvene nauke* 128 (2009): 47–61.

The Blue Helmets: A Review of United Nations Peace-Keeping. 3rd ed. New York: United Nations Department of Public Information, 1996.

Blumi, Isa. *Reinstating the Ottomans: Alternative Balkan Modernities, 1800–1912*. New York: Palgrave Macmillan, 2011.

———. "Political Islam Among the Albanians: Are the Taliban Coming to the Balkans?" In *Policy Research Series*. Prishtina: Kosovar Institute for Policy Research and Development, 2005.

Bodansky, Yossef. *Some Call It Peace: Waiting for War in the Balkans*. London: International Media Corp., 1996.

Bogetić, Dragan. "Sukob Titovog koncepta univerzalizma i Sukarnog koncepta regionalizma na Samitu nesvrstanih u Kairu 1964." *Istorija 20. veka*, no. 2 (2017): 101–18.

Bondžić, Dragomir. *Misao bez pasoša: međunarodna saradnja Beogradskog univerziteta 1945–1960*. Belgrade: Institut za savremenu istoriju, 2011.

Bonilla, Yarimar. *Non-Sovereign Futures: French Caribbean Politics in the Wake of Disenchantment*. Chicago: University of Chicago Press, 2015.

Bose, Sumantra. *Contested Lands: Israel-Palestine, Kashmir, Bosnia, Cyprus, and Sri Lanka*. Cambridge, MA: Harvard University Press, 2010.

Bougarel, Xavier. "Death and the Nationalist: Martyrdom, War Memory and Veteran Identity Among Bosnian Muslims." In *The New Balkan Mosaic: Identities, Memories and Moral Claims in a Post-War Society*, edited by Xavier Bougarel, Elissa Helms, and Ger Duijzings, 167–92. Hampshire, UK: Ashgate, 2007.

Boumediene, Lakhdar, and Mustafa Ait Idir. *Witnesses of the Unseen: Seven Years in Guantanamo*. Stanford, CA: Stanford University Press, 2017.

Bowen, John. *Can Islam Be French?: Pluralism and Pragmatism in a Secularist State*. Princeton, NJ: Princeton University Press, 2010.

Boxberger, Linda. *On the Edge of Empire: Hadhramawt, Emigration, and the Indian Ocean, 1880s–1930s*. Albany: SUNY Press, 2002.

Bray, Alan. *The Friend*. Chicago: University of Chicago Press, 2003.

Brešlić, Ivan. *Čuvari Jugoslavije: suradnici Udbe u Bosne i Hercegovine*. Vol. 3: Muslimani, Posušje: Samizdat, 2003.

Bringa, Tone. *Being Muslim the Bosnian Way: Identity and Community in a Central Bosnian Village*. Princeton, NJ: Princeton University Press, 1995.

Broadwell, Paula, and Vernon Loeb. *All In: The Education of General David Petraeus*. New York: Penguin, 2012.

Brooks, James. *Captives and Cousins: Slavery, Kinship, and Community in the Southwest Borderlands*. Chapel Hill, NC: University of North Carolina Press, 2002.

Brown, Daniel W. *Rethinking Tradition in Modern Islamic Thought*. Cambridge: Cambridge University Press, 1996.

Brown, Jonathan A. C. "Faithful Dissenters: Sunni Skepticism About the Miracles of Saints." *Journal of Sufi Studies* 1 (2012): 123–68.

Byman, Daniel. *Road Warriors: Foreign Fighters in the Armies of Jihad*. Oxford: Oxford University Press, 2019.

Byrne, Jeffrey James. *Mecca of Revolution: Algeria, Decolonization & the Third World Order*. Oxford: Oxford University Press, 2016.

Campbell, David. *National Deconstruction: Violence, Identity, and Justice in Bosnia*. Minneapolis: University of Minnesota Press, 1998.

Carter, J.R.L. *Merchant Families of Kuwait*. London: Scorpion, 1984.

Chandler, David. *Bosnia: Faking Democracy After Dayton*. 2nd ed. London: Pluto Press, 2000.

Chang, Felix. "Myth and Migration: Zhejiangese Merchants in Serbia." In *Chinese Migrants in Russia, Central Asia and Eastern Europe*, edited by Felix Chang and Sunnie Rucker-Chang, 137–52. New York: Routledge, 2012.

Chan-Malik, Sylvia. *Being Muslim: A Cultural History of Women of Color in American Islam*. New York: New York University Press, 2018.

Cheah, Pheng. *Spectral Nationality: Passages of Freedom from Kant to Postcolonial Literatures of Liberation*. New York: Columbia University Press, 2003.

Chimni, B. S. *International Law and World Order: A Critique of Contemporary Approaches*. 2nd ed. Cambridge: Cambridge University Press, 2017.

Chu, Tiffany S. and Alex Braithwaite. "The Impact of Foreign Fighters on Civil Conflict Outcomes." *Research and Politics* 4, no. 3 (2017): 1–7.

Clancy-Smith, Julia. *Mediterraneans: North Africa and Europe in an Age of Migration, c. 1800–1900*. Berkeley: University of California Press, 2012.

Clarke, Kamari. *Fictions of Justice: The International Criminal Court and the Challenge of Legal Pluralism in Sub-Saharan Africa*. Cambridge: Cambridge University Press, 2009.

Coles, Kimberley. *Democratic Designs: International Intervention and Electoral Practices in Postwar Bosnia-Herzegovina*. Ann Arbor: University of Michigan Press, 2007.

Cook, David. *Understanding Jihad*. Berkeley: University of California Press, 2005.

Cunliffe, Philip. *Legions of Peace: UN Peacekeepers from the Global South*. London: Hurst, 2013.

Dabashi, Hamid. *Authority in Islam: From the Rise of Muhammad to the Establishment of the Umayyads*. New Brunswick, NJ: Transaction, 1989.

Daly, Faïçal. "The Double Passage: Tunisian Migration to the South and North of Italy." In *The Mediterranean Passage: Migration and New Cultural Encounters in Southern Europe*, edited by Russell King, 186–205. Chicago: University of Chicago Press, 2001.

———. "Tunisian Migrants and Their Experience of Racism in Modesta." *Modern Italy* 4, no. 2 (1999): 173–89.

Dancourt, Emmanuelle. *Général Valentin: «De Sarajevo aux banlieues, mes combats pour la paix.»* Tours: Éditions CLD, 2006.

Daulatzai, Sohail. *Black Star, Crescent Moon: The Muslim International and Black Freedom Beyond America*. Minneapolis: University of Minnesota Press, 2012.

———. "Protect ya Neck: Muslims and the Carceral Imagination in the Age of Guantánamo." *Souls: A Critical Journal of Black Culture, Politics, and Society* 9, no. 2 (2007): 132–47.

Davud, Muhamed Isa. *Razgovor sa džinom muslimanom*. Translated by Mahmut Karalić. Sarajevo: Kaligraf, 2000[1992].

Debrix, François. *Re-Envisioning Peacekeeping: The United Nations and the Mobilization of Ideology*. Minneapolis: University of Minnesota Press, 1999.

Deeb, Lara. "Thinking Piety and the Everyday Together: A Response to Fadil and Fernando." *HAU: Journal of Ethnographic Theory* 5, no. 2 (2015): 93–96.

Delić, Ibrahim. *Akida ehli sunneta vel džemata*. Zenica: Emanet, 2009.

Devji, Faisal. *Terrorist in Search of Humanity: Militant Islam and Global Politics*. London: Hurst, 2008.

———. *Landscapes of the Jihad: Militancy, Morality, Modernity*. Ithaca, NY: Cornell University Press, 2005.

Dimić, Ljubodrag, and Dragan Bogetić. "La Yougoslavie et l'Algérie." In *Jugoslovensko-alžirski odnosi 1956–1979 / Relations yougoslavo-algériennes de 1956 à 1979*, edited by Miladin Milošević and Nada Pantelić, xxxiii-liv. Belgrade: Arhiv Jugoslavije, 2014.

Dirāz, ʿIṣām. *Al-ʿāʾidūn min Afghānistān: mā lahum wa mā ʿalayhim*. Nicosia: al-Dār al-Miṣriyya lil-nashr wal-tawzīʿ, 1993.

Divjak, Jovan, and Florence la Bruyère. *Sarajevo, Mon Amour*. Paris: Buchet, 2004.

Donia, Robert. *Islam Under the Double Eagle: The Muslims of Bosnia and Hercegovina, 1878–1914*. New York: Columbia University Press, 1981.

Donner, Fred. *The Early Islamic Conquests*. Princeton, NJ: Princeton University Press, 1981.

Doostdar, Alireza. *The Iranian Metaphysicals: Explorations in Science, Islam, and the Uncanny*. Princeton, NJ: Princeton University Press, 2018.

Dorronsoro, Gilles. *Revolution Unending: Afghanistan: 1979 to the Present*. Translated by John King. New York: Columbia University Press, 2005[2000].

Du Bois, W.E.B. *Black Reconstruction in America: An Essay Toward a History of the Part Which Black Folk Played in the Attempt to Reconstruct Democracy in America, 1860–1880*. Oxford: Oxford University Press, 2014[1935].

Duijzings, Ger. *Religion and the Politics of Identity in Kosovo*. New York: Columbia University Press, 2000.

Duraković, Jasmin. "Neka bude." TVBiH, 1999.

Durch, William, and James Schear. "Faultlines: UN Operations in the Former Yugoslavia." In *UN Peacekeeping, American Policy, and the Uncivil Wars of the 1990s*, edited by William Durch, 193–274. New York: St. Martin's Press, 1996.

Edwards, Brent Hayes. "The Uses of *Diaspora*." *Social Text* 19, no. 1 (Spring 2001): 45–73.

Edwards, David. *Caravan of Martyrs: Sacrifice and Suicide Bombing in Afghanistan*. Berkeley: University of California Press, 2017.

———. *Before Taliban: Genealogies of the Afghan Jihad*. Berkeley: University of California Press, 2002.

———. *Heroes of the Age: Moral Fault Lines on the Afghan Frontier*. Berkeley: University of California Press, 1996.

Efendić, Hasan. *Mudžahedini u Bosni i Hercegovini—borci ili teroristi*. Sarajevo: Udruženje za zaštitu tekovina borbe za Bosnu i Hercegovinu, 2007.

"Egypt: No Protection—Systematic Torture Continues." London: Amnesty International, 2002.

Enayat, Hamid. *Modern Islamic Political Thought*. Austin: University of Texas Press, 1982.

Erlenbusch-Anderson, Verena. *Genealogies of Terrorism: Revolution, State Violence, Empire*. New York: Columbia University Press, 2018.

Euben, Roxanne. "Killing (for) Politics: Jihad, Martyrdom, and Political action." *Political Theory* 30, no. 1 (2002): 4–35.

Evans-Pritchard, E. E. *The Sanusi of Cyrenaica*. Oxford: Clarendon Press, 1949.

Fadil, Nadia, and Mayanthi Fernando. "Rediscovering the 'Everyday' Muslim." *HAU: Journal of Ethnographic Theory* 5, no. 2 (2015): 59–88.

Faraj, Ayman Ṣabrī. *Dhikrayāt 'Arabī Afghānī: Abū Ja'far al-Miṣrī al-Qandahārī*. Cairo: Dār al-Shurūq, 2002.

Farquhar, Michael. *Circuits of Faith: Migration, Education, and the Wahhabi Mission*. Stanford, CA: Stanford University Press, 2016.

Fassin, Didier. *Humanitarian Reason: A Moral History of the Present*. Translated by Rachel Gomme. Berkeley: University of California Press, 2012.

Feldman, Ilana. *Police Encounters: Security and Surveillance in Gaza Under Egyptian Rule*. Stanford, CA: Stanford University Press, 2015.

Feldman, Ilana, and Miriam Ticktin, eds. *In the Name of Humanity: The Government of Threat and Care*. Durham, NC: Duke University Press, 2010.

Fernando, Mayanthi. *The Republic Unsettled: Muslim French and the Contradictions of Secularism*. Durham, NC: Duke University Press, 2014.

Fikes, Kesha, and Alaina Lemon. "African Presence in Former Soviet Spaces." *Annual Review of Anthropology* 31 (2002): 497–524.

Foucault, Michel. *Discipline and Punish: The Birth of the Prison*. Translated by Alan Sheridan. New York: Vintage, 1979[1975].

Freitag, Ulrike, and W. G. Clarence-Smith, eds. *Hadhrami Traders, Scholars, and Statesmen in the Indian Ocean, 1750s–1960s*. Leiden: Brill, 1997.

Fuhrmann, Malte. "Vagrants, Prostitutes and Bosnians: Making and Unmaking European Supremacy in Ottoman Southeast Europe." In *Conflicting Loyalties in the Balkans: The Great Powers, the Ottoman Empire and Nation-Building*, edited by Hannes Grandits, Nathalie Clayer, and Robert Pichler, 15–45. London: I.B. Tauris, 2011.

———. "Down and Out on the Quays of İzmir: 'European' Musicians, Innkeepers, and Prostitutes in the Ottoman Port-Cities." *Mediterranean Historical Review* 24, no. 2 (December 2009): 169–85.

Gardet, L. "Karāma." In *Encyclopaedia of Islam*, edited by H.A.R. Gibb. Leiden: Brill, 1979.

Gauvain, Richard. *Salafi Ritual Purity: In the Presence of God*. London: Routledge, 2013.

Gellner, Ernest. *Saints of the Atlas*. London: Weidenfeld and Nicolson, 1969.

Ghabra, Shafeeq. "Voluntary Associations in Kuwait: The Foundation of a New System?" *Middle East Journal* 45, no. 2 (1991): 199–215.

Ghānim, Yaḥyā. *Kuntu hunāka . . . yawmiyyāt murāsil ḥarbī fil-Būsna: al-milaff al-sirrī li-ibādat sha'b*. Cairo: Dār al-Naṣr lil-ṭibā'a al-Islāmiyya, 1993.

Ghodsee, Kristen. *The Left Side of History: World War II and the Unfulfilled Promise of Communism in Eastern Europe*. Durham, NC: Duke University Press, 2015.

———. *Muslim Lives in Eastern Europe: Gender, Ethnicity, and the Transformation of Islam in Postsocialist Bulgaria*. Princeton, NJ: Princeton University Press, 2010.

Ghosh, Amitav. "The Global Reservation: Notes Toward an Ethnography of International Peacekeeping." *Cultural Anthropology* 9, no. 3 (1994): 412–22.

Gilbert, Andrew. "The Limits of Foreign Authority: Publicity and the Political Logic of Ambivalence in Postwar Bosnia and Herzegovina." *Comparative Studies in Society and History* 59, no. 2 (April 2017): 415–45.

———. "From Humanitarianism to Humanitarianization." *American Ethnologist* 43, no. 4 (2016): 717–29.

Giustozzi, Antonio. "The Taliban's 'Military Courts'." *Small Wars & Insurgencies* 25, no. 2 (2014): 284–96.

Glück, Doris. *Mundtot: Ich war die Frau eines Gotteskriegers*. Berlin: List, 2004.

Greble, Emily. *Sarajevo, 1941–1945: Muslims, Christians, and Jews in Hitler's Europe*. Ithaca, NY: Cornell University Press, 2011.

Gregorian, Raffi. *The British Army, the Gurkhas and Cold War Strategy in the Far East, 1947–1954*. New York: Palgrave, 2002.

Gregory, Derek. "The Black Flag: Guantánamo Bay and the Space of Exception." *Geografiska Annaler: Series B, Human Geography* 88, no. 4 (December 2006): 405–27.

Gualtieri, Sarah. *Between Arab and White: Race and Ethnicity in the Early Syrian American Diaspora*. Berkeley: University of California Press, 2009.

Gunaratna, Rohan. *Inside Al Qaeda*. New York: Columbia University Press, 2002.

Gündoğdu, Ayten. "Disagreeing with Rancière: Speech, Violence, and the Ambiguous Subjects of Politics." *Polity* 49, no. 2 (April 2017): 188–219.

Hadhlūl, Ziyād Ṣāliḥ, and Muḥammad ʿAbd Allāh al-Ḥumayḍī. *Al-qiṣṣa al-kāmila lil-dawr al-Saʿūdī fil-Būsna wal-Harsak*. Riyadh: Z.S. Hadhlūl, 1998.

Hadžić, Suvad. *U kljunu zelene ptice: istinite priče o šehidima Bosne*. Žepče: Motrix, 2004.

Hafez, Mohammed. "Jihad After Iraq: Lessons from the Arab Afghans." *Studies in Conflict & Terrorism* 32, no. 2 (2009): 73–94.

Hajdarpasic, Edin. *Whose Bosnia?: Nationalism and Political Imagination in the Balkans, 1840–1914*. Ithaca, NY: Cornell University Press, 2015.

Hajir, Youssef. *Bolnica Dobrinja: monografija*. Sarajevo: EDIS, 2009.

Ḥājj, Walīd Muḥammad. *Madhbaḥat al-qalʿa wa-ghayāhib Ghuwāntanāmū: asrār shāhid ʿayān*. Khartoum: Maṭābiʿ al-Sūdān lil-ʿumla, 2009.

Hallaq, Wael. *The Impossible State: Islam, Politics, and Modernity's Moral Predicament*. New York: Columbia University Press, 2012.

Hamad, Ali. *U mreži zla: međunarodni terorizam i "Al-Kaida"*. Banja Luka: Una Press, 2007.

Hamid, Mustafa, and Leah Farrall. *The Arabs at War in Afghanistan*. London: Hurst, 2015.

Ḥamza, Amīr. *Bosniyā ke ʿarab shuhadāʾ*. Lahore: Dār al-Andalus, 2008.

———. *Qāfilah daʿwat jihād*. Lahore: Dār al-Andalus, 2004.

Ḥasan, Ṣalāḥ al-Dīn. *Al-Salafiyyūn fī Miṣr*. Giza: Dār Awrāq lil-nashr, 2012.

Ḥasanayn, al-Fātiḥ ʿAlī. *Fakhāmat al-raʾīs ʿAlī ʿIzzat Bayqawfīj ka-mā lā yaʿrifuhu al-nās*. Khartoum: Sharikat maṭābiʿ al-Sūdān lil-ʿumla, 2016.

———. *Qiṣṣat ḥarb al-Būsna wal-Harsak*. S.l.: s.n., 2016.

———. *Jisr ʿalā nahr al-Dirīnā: min dhikrayāt wa-miḥan al-Muslimīn fī Ūrūbbā al-sharqiyya*. Khartoum: Sharikat maṭābiʿ al-Sūdān lil-ʿumla, 2010.

———. *Lamaʿān al-burūq fī sīrat mawlānā Aḥmad Zarrūq: huwa al-ʿārif billāh muḥtasib al-ʿulamāʾ wal-awliyāʾ wa-ṣāḥib al-sharīʿa wal-ḥaqīqa Abū al-Faḍl Shihāb al-Dīn Abū al-ʿAbbās Aḥmad ibn Aḥmad ibn Muḥammad ibn ʿĪsā al-Fāsī al-Barnusī*. 3rd ed. Khartoum: Sharikat maṭābiʿ al-Sūdān lil-ʿumla, 2008[2002].

———. *Mawsūʿat al-usar al-Maghāribiyya wa-ansābihā fil-Sūdān*. Vol. 1. Khartoum: Sharikat maṭābiʿ al-Sūdān lil-ʿumla, 2007.

Hatina, Meir. *Martyrdom in Modern Islam: Piety, Power, and Politics*. Cambridge: Cambridge University Press, 2014.

Hayden, Robert. "Antagonistic Tolerance: Competitive Sharing of Religious Sites in South Asia and the Balkans." *Current Anthropology* 32, no. 2 (April 2002): 205–31.

Hećimović, Esad. *Garibi: Mudžahedini u BiH 1992–1999*. Zenica: Fondacija Sina, 2006.

Hegghammer, Thomas. "Introduction: What Is Jihadi Culture and Why Should We Study It?" In *Jihadi Culture: The Art and Social Practices of Militant Islamists*, edited by Thomas Hegghammer, 1–21. Cambridge: Cambridge University Press, 2017.

———. "Non-Military Practices in Jihadi Groups." In *Jihadi Culture: The Art and Social Practices of Militant Islamists*, edited by Thomas Hegghammer, 171–201. Cambridge: Cambridge University Press, 2017.

———. *Jihad in Saudi Arabia: Violence and Pan-Islamism Since 1979*. Cambridge: Cambridge University Press, 2010.

———. "Jihadi-Salafis or Revolutionaries? On Religion and Politics in the Study of Militant Islamism." In *Global Salafism: Islam's New Religious Movement*, edited by Roel Meijer, 244–66. New York: Columbia University Press, 2009.

Heimerl, Daniela. "The Return of Refugees and Internally Displaced Persons: From Coercion to Sustainability?" *International Peacekeeping* 12, no. 3 (Autumn 2005): 377–90.

Henig, David. "Crossing the Bosphorus: Connected Histories of 'Other' Muslims in the Post-Imperial Borderlands of Southeast Europe." *Comparative Studies in Society and History* 58, no. 4 (2016): 908–34.

Henig, David, and Karolina Bielenin-Lenczowska. "Recasting Anthropological Perspectives on Vernacular Islam in Southeast Europe." *Anthropological Journal of European Cultures* 22, no. 2 (2013): 1–11.

Heo, Angie. *The Political Lives of Saints: Christian-Muslim Mediation in Egypt*. Berkeley: University of California Press, 2018.

Higate, Paul, and Marsha Henry. *Insecure Spaces: Peacekeeping, Power and Performance in Haiti, Kosovo and Liberia*. London: Zed, 2009.

al-Hindī, ʿAlī bin Farīd al-Kashjanwarī. *Mukhtaṣar al-aḥkām al-fiqhiyya*. Cairo: Dār al-iʿtiṣām lil-tabʿ wal-nashr wal-tawzīʿ, 1984.
See also el-Hindi, Ali bin Ferid

el-Hindi, Ali bin Ferid. *Skraćena zbirka fikhskih propisa*. Translated by Hasan Makić. S.l.: Organizacija Preporoda Islamske Misli-Kuvajt, s.a.[1984].
See also al-Hindī, ʿAlī bin Farīd al-Kashjanwarī

al-Hindukūshī, Abū al-Shuqarāʾ. *Mudhakkirātī min Kābul ilā Baghdād*. 2007 [electronic book].

Hirschkind, Charles. *The Ethical Soundscape: Cassette Sermons and Islamic Counterpublics*. New York: Columbia University Press, 2006.

Historical Record of the 4th Battalion 16th Punjab Regiment. S.l.: s.n., 1931.

Ho, Engseng. *The Graves of Tarim: Genealogy and Mobility Across the Indian Ocean*. Berkeley: University of California Press, 2006.

———. "Empire Through Diasporic Eyes: A View from the Other Boat." *Comparative Studies in Society and History* 46, no. 2 (April 2004): 210–46.

Hoare, Marko Attila. *How Bosnia Armed*. London: Saqi, 2004.

Holbrooke, Richard. *To End a War*. New York: Random House, 1998.

Hong, Young-Sun. *Cold War Germany, the Third World, and the Global Humanitarian Regime*. Cambridge: Cambridge University Press, 2015.

Honig, Bonnie. "The Miracle of Metaphor: Rethinking the State of Exception with Rosenzweig and Schmitt." *Diacritics* 37, no. 2–3 (Fall 2007): 78–102.

Höpken, Wolfgang. "Yugoslavia's Communists and the Bosnian Muslims." Translated by Caroline Sawyer. In *Muslim Communities Reemerge: Historical Perspectives on Nationality, Politics, and Opposition in the Former Soviet Union and Yugoslavia*, edited by Andreas Kappeler, Gerhard Simon, Georg Brunner, and Edward Allworth, 214–47. Durham, NC: Duke University Press, 1994[1989].

Hurd, Ian. *After Anarchy: Legitimacy and Power in the United Nations Security Council.* Princeton, NJ: Princeton University Press, 2007.

Hussain, Nasser. "Beyond Norm and Exception: Guantánamo." *Critical Inquiry* 33, no. 4 (Summer 2007): 734–53.

Hussin, Iza. *The Politics of Islamic Law: Local Elites, Colonial Authority, and the Making of the Muslim State.* Chicago: University of Chicago Press, 2016.

Ibrahimpašić, Emira. "Women Living Islam in Post-War and Post-Socialist Bosnia-Herzegovina." PhD thesis, Anthropology, University of New Mexico, 2012.

Iqtidar, Humeira. *Secularizing Islamists? Jamaʿat-e-Islami and Jamaʿat-ud-Daʿwa in Urban Pakistan.* Chicago: University of Chicago Press, 2011.

Jackson, Jeffrey. *The Globalizers: Development Workers in Action.* Baltimore: The Johns Hopkins University Press, 2005.

Jackson, Sherman. *Islam and the Blackamerican: Looking Toward the Third Resurrection.* Oxford: Oxford University Press, 2005.

Jahić, Adnan. *Islamska zajednica u Bosni u Hercegovini za vrijeme monarhističke Jugoslavije.* Zagreb: Islamska zajednica u Hrvatskoj, 2010.

Jakovina, Tvrtko. "Yugoslavia on the International Scene: The Active Coexistence of Non-Aligned Yugoslavia." In *Yugoslavia from a Historical Perspective*, 461–514. Belgrade: Helsinki Committee for Human Rights in Serbia, 2017.

———. *Treća strana Hladnog rata.* Zagreb: Fraktura, 2011.

Jamal, Arif. *Call for Transnational Jihad: Lashkar-e-Taiba 1985–2014.* New Delhi: Kautilya, 2015.

Jansen, Stef. *Yearnings in the Meantime: "Normal Lives" and the State in a Sarajevo Apartment Complex.* New York: Berghahn, 2015.

———. "After the Red Passport: Towards an Anthropology of the Everyday Geopolitics of Entrapment in the EU's 'Immediate Outside'." *Journal of the Royal Anthropological Institute* 15, no. 4 (2009): 815–32.

———. "The Privatisation of Home and Hope: Returns, Reforms and the Foreign

Intervention in Bosnia-Herzegovina." *Dialectical Anthropology* 30, no. 3–4 (2007): 177–99.

Jarrār, Māhir. *'Abd al-Raḥmān Munīf wal-'Irāq: sīra wa-dhākira*. Casablanca: al-Markaz al-thaqāfī al-'Arabī, 2005.

Jašarević, Larisa. *Health and Wealth on the Bosnian Market: Intimate Debt*. Bloomington: Indiana University Press, 2017.

———. "Interplanetary Present: On a Spectacle of Mass Healing and Gifting in Bosnia." *Anthropological Forum* 24, no. 4 (2014): 427–39.

Jeffrey, Alex. *The Improvised State: Sovereignty, Performance, and Agency in Dayton Bosnia*. Chichester, West Sussex, UK: Wiley-Blackwell, 2013.

Johns, Fleur. "Guantánamo Bay and the Annihilation of the Exception." *European Journal of International Law* 16, no. 4 (2005): 613–35.

Jouannet, Emmanuelle. "Universalism and Imperialism: The True-False Paradox of International Law?" *European Journal of International Law* 18, no. 3 (2007): 379–407.

Kābilī, Wahīb Aḥmad. *Al-ḥirafiyyūn fī madīnat Jidda fil-qarn al-rābi' 'ashar al-hijrī*. Jeddah: s.n., 2004.

Kahn, Paul. *Putting Liberalism in Its Place*. Princeton, NJ: Princeton University Press, 2005.

Kaiser, Wolfgang, ed. *Le commerce des captifs: les intermédiaires dans l'échange et le rachat des prisonniers en Méditerranée, XVe-XVIIIe siècle*. Rome: École française de Rome, 2008.

Kamberović, Husnija. "Between Muslimdom, Bosniandom, Yugoslavdom and Bosniakdom: The Political Elite in Bosnia and Herzegovina in the Late 1960s and Early 1970s." In *The Ambiguous Nation: Case Studies from Southeastern Europe in the 20th Century*, edited by Ulf Brunnbauer and Hannes Grandits, 57–76. Munich: Oldenbourg Verlag, 2013.

Kantorowicz, Ernst. *The King's Two Bodies: A Study in Mediaeval Political Theology*. Princeton, NJ: Princeton University Press, 1957.

Karčić, Fikret. *Šerijatski sudovi u Jugoslaviji 1918–1941*. Sarajevo: El-Kalem, 2005[1985].

———. "Administration of Islamic Affairs in Bosnia and Herzegovina." *Islamic Studies* 38, no. 4 (1999): 535–61.

———. "Islamic Revival in the Balkans 1970–1992." *Islamic Studies* 36, no. 2,3 (1997): 565–81.

Karpat, Kemal. *The Politicization of Islam: Reconstructing Identity, State, Faith, and Community in the Late Ottoman State*. Oxford: Oxford University Press, 2001.

———. *Ottoman Population, 1830–1914: Demographic and Social Characteristics.* Madison, WI: University of Wisconsin Press, 1985.

Kellogg, Thomas, and Hossam El-Hamalawy. "Black Hole: The Fate of Islamists Rendered to Egypt." New York: Human Rights Watch, 2005.

Kent-Payne, Vaughan. *Bosnia Warriors: Living on the Front Line.* London: Robert Hale, 1998.

Khalidi, Omar. "The Arabs of Hadramawt, South Yemen in Hyderabad." *Islam and the Modern Age* 18, no. 4 (November 1987): 203–30.

al-Khālidī, Sāmī Nāṣir. *Al-aḥzāb al-Islāmiyya al-siyāsiyya fil-Kuwayt: al-Shīʿa, al-Ikhwān, al-Salaf.* Kuwait: Dār al-Nabaʾ lil-nashr wal-tawzīʿ, 1999.

Khalili, Laleh. *Time in the Shadows: Confinement in Counterinsurgencies.* Stanford, CA: Stanford University Press, 2013.

Khan, Hira. "Pakistan Army as Peacekeepers: A Case Study of Bosnia." MPhil thesis, Political Science, Government College University (Lahore), 2014.

Khan, Naveeda. *Muslim Becoming: Aspiration and Skepticism in Pakistan.* Durham, NC: Duke University Press, 2012.

Khuri-Makdisi, Ilham. *The Eastern Mediterranean and the Making of Global Radicalism, 1860–1914.* Berkeley: University of California Press, 2010.

Kinsella, Helen M. *The Image Before the Weapon: A Critical History of the Distinction Between Combatant and Civilian.* Ithaca, NY: Cornell University Press, 2011.

———. "Gendering Grotius: Sex and Sex Difference in the Laws of War." *Political Theory* 34, no. 2 (April 2006): 161–91.

Kirasirova, Masha. "The Eastern International: The 'Domestic East' and the 'Foreign East' in Soviet-Arab Relations, 1917–1968." PhD thesis, Departments of History and Middle Eastern & Islamic Studies, New York University, 2014.

Klamberg, Mark. "International Criminal Law in Swedish Courts: The Principle of Legality in the *Arklöv* Case." *International Criminal Law Review* 9, no. 2 (2009): 395–409.

Knaus, Gerald, and Felix Martin. "Travails of the European Raj: Lessons from Bosnia and Herzegovina." *Journal of Democracy* 14, no. 3 (July 2003): 60–74.

Kohlmann, Evan. *Al-Qaida's Jihad in Europe: The Afghan-Bosnian Network.* Oxford: Berg, 2004.

Kolind, Torsten. *Post-War Identification: Everyday Muslim Counterdiscourse in Bosnia Herzegovina.* Aarhus: Aarhus University Press, 2008.

Kovačević, Almir. *Iskre svjetlosti: istinite priče o šehidima Bosne.* Zenica: BZK Preporod, 2005.

Krishnasamy, Kabilan. "Pakistan's Peacekeeping Experiences." *International Peacekeeping* 9, no. 3 (2011): 103–20.

Krislov, Samuel. "The Amicus Curiae Brief: From Friendship to Advocacy." *Yale Law Journal* 72, no. 4 (March 1963): 694–721.

Kulić, Vladimir. "Building the Non-Aligned Babel: Babylon Hotel in Baghdad and Mobile Design in the Global Cold War." *ABE Journal: Architecture Beyond Europe* 6 (2014).

Kullaa, Rinna. *Non-Alignment and Its Origins in Cold War Europe: Yugoslavia, Finland and the Soviet Challenge*. London: I.B. Tauris, 2011.

Kumar, Radha. *Divide and Fall? Bosnia in the Annals of Partition*. New York: Verso, 1997.

Kurtović, Larisa. "What Is a Nationalist? Some Thoughts on the Question from Bosnia-Herzegovina." *Anthropology of East Europe Review* 29, no. 2 (2011): 242–53.

Laclau, Ernesto. "Universalism, Particularism and the Question of Identity." *October* 61 (Summer 1992): 83–90.

Lacroix, Stéphane. *Awakening Islam: The Politics of Religious Dissent in Contemporary Saudi Arabia*. Translated by George Holoch. Cambridge, MA: Harvard University Press, 2011[2010].

Lamberger Khatib, Maja. "Social Networks Among Arabs in Slovenia." *Razprave in gradivo* 58 (2009): 140–58.

Larise, Dunja. "The Islamic Community in Bosnia and Herzegovina and Nation Building by Muslims/Bosniaks in the Western Balkans." *Nationalities Papers: The Journal of Nationalism and Ethnicity* 43, no. 2 (2015): 195–212.

Latić, Nedžad. *Boja povijesti: Izetbegoviće godine 1983–2003*. Electronic ed. Brčko: Vatan, 2009[2003].

Lauzière, Henri. *The Making of Salafism: Islamic Reform in the Twentieth Century*. New York: Columbia University Press, 2016.

Lav, Daniel. *Radical Islam and the Revival of Medieval Theology*. Cambridge: Cambridge University Press, 2012.

Lazić, Milorad. "Neki problemi stranih studenata na jugoslovenskim univerzitetima šezdesetih godina XX veka, s posebnim osvrtom na afričke studente." *Godišnjak za društvenu istoriju*, no. 2 (2009): 61–78.

Li, Darryl. "From Exception to Empire: Sovereignty, Carceral Circulation, and the 'Global War on Terror'." In *Ethnographies of U.S. Empire*, edited by Carole McGranahan and John Collins, 456–75. Durham, NC: Duke University Press, 2018.

———. "Jihad in a World of Sovereigns: Law, Violence, and Islam in the Bosnia Crisis." *Law & Social Inquiry* 41, no. 2 (Spring 2016): 371–401.

———. "Taking the Place of Martyrs: Afghans and Arabs Under the Banner of Islam." *Arab Studies Journal* 20, no. 1 (2012): 12–39.

———. "A Universal Enemy?: 'Foreign Fighters' and Legal Regimes of Exclusion and Exemption Under the 'Global War on Terror'." *Columbia Human Rights Law Review* 42, no. 2 (2010): 355–428.

Lia, Brynjar. "Islamist Perceptions of the United Nations and Its Peacekeeping Missions: Some Preliminary Findings." *International Peacekeeping* 5, no. 2 (Summer 1998): 38–63.

Lidy, A. Martin, David Arthur, James Kunder, and Samuel Packer. "Bosnia Air Drop Study." Alexandria, VA: Institute for Defense Analyses, 1999.

Lipman, Jana. *Guantánamo: A Working-Class History Between Empire and Revolution*. Berkeley: University of California Press, 2009.

Lockwood, William. *European Moslems: Economy and Ethnicity in Western Bosnia*. New York: Academic Press, 1975.

Lockwood, Yvonne. *Text and Context: Folksong in a Bosnian Muslim Village*. Bloomington, IN: Slavica, 1983.

Luthar, Breda, and Maruša Pušnik, eds. *Remembering Utopia: The Culture of Everyday Life in Socialist Yugoslavia*. Washington, DC: New Academia Publishing, 2010.

Mac Con Uladh, Damian Henry Tone. "Guests of the Socialist Nation? Foreign Students and Workers in the GDR, 1949–1990." PhD thesis, German, University College London, 2005.

Maher, Shiraz. *Salafi-Jihadism: The History of an Idea*. London: Hurst, 2016.

Mahmood, Saba. "Secularism, Hermeneutics, and Empire: The Politics of Islamic Reformation." *Public Culture* 18, no. 2 (2006): 323–47.

———. *Politics of Piety: The Islamic Revival and the Feminist Subject*. Princeton, NJ: Princeton University Press, 2005.

Maine, Henry Sumner. *Ancient Law: Its Connection with the Early History of Society and Its Relation to Modern Ideas*. 10th ed. London: John Murray, 1908[1861].

Makdisi, Ussama. "Ottoman Orientalism." *American Historical Review* 107, no. 3 (June 2002): 768–96.

Malet, David. *Foreign Fighters: Transnational Identity in Civil Conflicts*. Oxford: Oxford University Press, 2013.

Malik, Inam-ur-Rahman. “Pakistan.” In *Providing Peacekeepers: The Politics, Challenges, and Future of United Nations Peacekeeping Contributions*, edited by Alex J. Bellamy and Paul D. Williams, 204–24. Oxford: Oxford University Press, 2013.

Malkki, Liisa. *The Need to Help: The Domestic Arts of International Humanitarianism*. Durham, NC: Duke University Press, 2015.

Mamdani, Mahmood. *Saviors and Survivors: Darfur, Politics, and the War on Terror*. New York: Pantheon, 2009.

———. *Good Muslim, Bad Muslim: America, the Cold War, and the Roots of Terror*. New York: Pantheon, 2004.

Mandal, Sumit. *Becoming Arab: Creole Histories and Modern Identity in the Malay World*. Cambridge: Cambridge University Press, 2018.

Manger, Leif. *The Hadrami Diaspora: Community-Building on the Indian Ocean Rim*. New York: Berghahn, 2010.

———. “Hadramis in Hyderabad: From Winners to Losers.” *Asian Journal of Social Science* 35, no. 4–5 (2007): 405–33.

Maqḥafī, Ibrāhīm Aḥmad. *Mawsūʿat al-alqāb al-Yamaniyya*. Vol. 1, Beirut: al-Muʾassasa al-Jāmiʿiyya lil-dirāsāt wal-nashr wal-tawzīʿ, 2010.

March, Andrew. “Genealogies of Sovereignty in Islamic Political Theology.” *Social Research* 80, no. 1 (Spring 2013): 293–320.

Marshall, Ruth. *Political Spiritualities: The Pentecostal Revolution in Nigeria*. Chicago: University of Chicago Press, 2009.

Marx, Karl. *Capital: A Critique of Political Economy*. Translated by Ben Fowkes. Vol. 1. London: Penguin, 1976[1867].

Marzouki, Nadia. *Islam: An American Religion*. Translated by C. Jon Delogu. New York: Columbia University Press, 2017[2013].

Masco, Joseph. *The Theater of Operations: National Security Affect from the Cold War to the War on Terror*. Durham, NC: Duke University Press, 2014.

———. *The Nuclear Borderlands: The Manhattan Project in Post-Cold War New Mexico*. Princeton, NJ: Princeton University Press, 2006.

al-Maṣrī, Aḥmad bin Ḥāzim bin Muḥammad Bek Tawfīq. *Tajliyat al-rāya*. S.l.: s.n., s.a.

Massad, Joseph. *Colonial Effects: The Making of National Identity in Jordan*. New York: Columbia University Press, 2001.

Matović, Jovan. *Vojni poslovi Jugoslavije i svet XX veka*. Belgrade: Tetra GM, 2003.

Mauss, Marcel. “Techniques of the Body.” *Economy and Society* 2, no. 1 (1973[1934]): 70–88.

Mazower, Mark. *No Enchanted Palace: The End of Empire and the Ideological Origins of the United Nations*. Princeton, NJ: Princeton University Press, 2009.

McKenna, Thomas M. *Muslim Rulers and Rebels: Everyday Politics and Armed Separatism in the Southern Philippines*. Berkeley: University of California Press, 1998.

al-Mdaires, Falah Abdullah. *Islamic Extremism in Kuwait: From the Muslim Brotherhood to al-Qaeda and Other Islamist Political Groups*. London: Routledge, 2010.

Mégret, Frédéric. "From 'Savages' to 'Unlawful Combatants': A Postcolonial Look at International Humanitarian Law's 'Other'." In *International Law and Its Others*, edited by Anne Orford, 265–317. Cambridge: Cambridge University Press, 2006.

Mehtić, Halil, and Hasan Makić. *Upute Muslimanskom borcu*. Zenica: Ured Mešihata Islamske Zajednice, 1993.

Merry, Sally Engle. *Human Rights and Gender Violence: Translating International Law into Local Justice*. Chicago: University of Chicago Press, 2006.

Mesarič, Andreja. "'Islamic Cafés' and 'Sharia Dating': Muslim Youth, Spaces of Sociability, and Partner Relationships in Bosnia-Herzegovina." *Nationalities Papers: The Journal of Nationalism and Ethnicity* 45, no. 4 (2017): 581–97.

———. "Wearing Hijab in Sarajevo: Dress Practices and the Islamic Revival in Post-War Bosnia-Herzegovina." *Anthropological Journal of European Cultures* 22, no. 2 (2013): 12–34.

Messick, Brinkley. *Sharīʿa Scripts: A Historical Anthropology*. New York: Columbia University Press, 2018.

Metcalf, Barbara. *Islamic Revival in British India: Deoband, 1860–1900*. Princeton, NJ: Princeton University Press, 1982.

Miéville, China. *Between Equal Rights: A Marxist Theory of International Law*. Leiden: Brill, 2004.

Miller, Alyssa. "Kin-Work in a Time of Jihad: Sustaining Bonds of Filiation and Care for Tunisian Foreign Combatants." *Cultural Anthropology* 33, no. 4 (2018): 596–620.

Miller, Brenna. "Faith and Nation: Politicians, Intellectuals, and the Official Recognition of a Muslim Nation in Tito's Yugoslavia." In *Beyond Mosque, Church, and State: Alternative Narratives of the Nation in the Balkans*, edited by Theodora Dragostinova and Yana Hashamova, 129–50. Budapest: Central European University Press, 2016.

Miller, Kathryn. "Reflections on Reciprocity: A Late Medieval Islamic Perspective on Christian-Muslim Commitment to Captive Exchange." In *Religion and Trade: Cross-Cultural Exchanges in World History, 1000–1900*, edited by Francesca Trivellato, Catia Antunes, and Leor Halevi, 131–49. Oxford: Oxford University Press, 2014.

Mišković, Nataša, Harald Fischer-Tiné, and Nada Boškovska, eds. *The Non-Aligned Movement and the Cold War: Delhi-Bandung-Belgrade*. London: Routledge, 2014.

el-Misri, Imad. *Shvatanja koja trebamo ispraviti*. Travnik: Islamski Centar Travnik, 1993.

Mittermaier, Amira. *Giving to God: Islamic Charity in Revolutionary Times*. Berkeley: University of California Press, 2019.

———. *Dreams That Matter: Egyptian Landscapes of the Imagination*. Berkeley: University of California Press, 2010.

Mlivončić, Ivica. *Al Qaida se kalila u Bosni i Hercegovini: Mjesto i uloga mudžahida u Republici Hrvatskoj i Bosni i Hercegovini od 1991. do 2005. godine*. Split: Naša Ognjišta, 2007.

Moin, Azfar. *The Millennial Sovereign: Sacred Kingship and Sainthood in Islam*. New York: Columbia University Press, 2012.

Moore, Adam. *Peacebuilding in Practice: Local Experience in Two Bosnian Towns*. Ithaca, NY: Cornell University Press, 2013.

Moore, Pete. *Doing Business in the Middle East: Politics and Economic Crisis in Jordan and Kuwait*. Cambridge: Cambridge University Press, 2004.

Mubārak, Hishām. *Al-irhābiyyūn al-qādimūn: dirāsa muqārana bayna mawqif 'al-Ikhwān al-Muslimīn' wa-jamā'āt al-jihād min qaḍiyat al-'unf (1928–1994)*. Cairo: Markaz al-Maḥrūsa lil-nashr wal-khadamāt al-ṣaḥafiyya, 1995.

al-Mubārakfūrī, Ṣafī al-Raḥmān. *Al-raḥīq al-makhtūm: baḥth fil-sīra al-nabawiyya 'alā ṣāḥibihā afḍal al-ṣalāh wal-salām*. Mansoura: Dār al-Wafā' lil-ṭibā'a wal-nashr, 1984[1976].

See also el-Mubarekfuri, Safijurrahman

el-Mubarekfuri, Safijurrahman. *Er-rahikul-mahtum: Zapečaćeni džennetski napitak*. Translated by Subhija Hadžimejlić-Skenderović. Revised ed. Travnik: Muftijstvo Travnik i Zenica, 1995[1976].

See also al-Mubārakfūrī, Ṣafī al-Raḥmān

Mujkić, Asim. *We, the Citizens of Ethnopolis*. Sarajevo: Sarajevo University Human Rights Center, 2008.

Mulić, Jusuf. *Elči Ibrahim-Pašina medresa u Travniku (1705–1939); Niža okružna medresa u Travniku (1939–1946)*. Sarajevo: Jusuf Mulić, 2014.

Munīf, 'Abd al-Raḥmān. "Taqdīm: Īvū Andrītsh wa-ḥikāyāt min al-Būsna." In *Ḥikāyāt min al-Būsna*, edited by Ivo Andrić, 5–22. Beirut: al-Mu'assasa al-'Arabiyya lil-dirāsāt wal-nashr, 1996.

Munir, Muhammad. "The Layha for the Mujahideen: An Analysis of the Code of Conduct for the Taliban Fighters Under Islamic law." *International Review of the Red Cross* 93, no. 881 (2011): 81–102.

Musharraf, Pervez. *In the Line of Fire: A Memoir.* New York: Free Press, 2006.

Mušinbegović, Hasib, Hamza Višća, Fikret Tabaković, Kemo Bećirević, and Šefkija Biogradlić. *Monografija Zlatni Ljiljani i odlikovani pripadnici Armije R BiH 1992.-1995.* Sarajevo: ZK Vojske F BiH, 2000.

Muslim Human Rights Forum. "Horn of Terror: Report of U.S.-Led Mass Extra-ordinary Renditions from Kenya to Somalia, Ethiopia and Guantanamo Bay, January-June 2007." Nairobi: Muslim Human Rights Forum, 2007.

Naber, Nadine, and Amaney Jamal, eds. *Race and Arab Americans Before and After 9/11: From Invisible Citizens to Visible Subjects.* Syracuse, NY: Syracuse University Press, 2008.

Najznačajnija dostignuća Visokog saudijskog komiteta za pomoć narodu Bosne i Hercegovine od oktobra 1993. god. do kraja 1998. god. Sarajevo: Visoki Saudijski komitet za pomoć Bosni i Hercegovini, 1999.

Nakissa, Aria. "An Ethical Solution to the Problem of Legal Indeterminacy: Sharīʿa Scholarship at Egypt's al-Azhar." *Journal of the Royal Anthropological Institute* 20 (March 2014): 93–112.

Nambiar, Satish. "Reflections on the Yugoslav Wars: A Peacekeeper's Perspective." In *Yugoslavia Unraveled: Sovereignty, Self-Determination, Intervention*, edited by Raju G. C. Thomas, 343–61. Lanham, MD: Lexington, 2003.

———. "India: An Uneasy Precedent." In *Kosovo and the Challenge of Humanitarian Intervention: Selective Indignation, Collective Action, and International Citizenship*, edited by Albrecht Schnabel and Ramesh Thakur, 260–69. Tokyo: United Nations University Press, 2000.

Naqqāsh, Muḥammad Ṭāhir. *Bosniyā ke jihādī maidānoñ meñ.* Lahore: Dār al-Iblāgh, 2002.

Navaro-Yashin, Yael. *Faces of the State: Secularism and Public Life in Turkey.* Princeton, NJ: Princeton University Press, 2002.

Nkrumah, Kwame. *Neo-Colonialism: The Last Stage of Imperialism.* New York: International Publishers, 1965.

Ochsenwald, William. "The Financing of the Hijaz Railroad." *Die Welt des Islams* 14, no. 1/4 (1973): 129–49.

Odred Elmudžahedin. *Podsjelovo/Fethul mubin.* 1995. Video cassette recording.

Omerdić, Muharem. *Imami šehidi—monografija*. Sarajevo: Udruženje ilmijje Islamske zajednice u BiH, 2005.

O'Neill, Bruce. "Of Camps, Gulags, and Extraordinary Renditions: Infrastructural Violence in Romania." *Ethnography* 13, no. 4 (2012): 466–86.

Østebø, Terje. *Localising Salafism: Religious Change Among Oromo Muslims in Bale, Ethiopia*. Boston: Leiden, 2012.

Ould Mohamedou, Mohammad-Mahmoud. *Understanding Al Qaeda: The Transformation of War*. London: Pluto Press, 2007.

Pahuja, Sundhya. *Decolonising International Law: Development, Economic Growth and the Politics of Universality*. Cambridge: Cambridge University Press, 2011.

Paik, A. Naomi. *Rightlessness: Testimony and Redress in U.S. Prison Camps Since World War II*. Chapel Hill, NC: University of North Carolina Press, 2016.

Pandey, Gyanendra. "'Encounters and Calamities': The History of a North Indian *Qasba* in the Nineteenth Century." In *Selected Subaltern Studies*, edited by Ranajit Guha and Gayatri Spivak, 89–128. Oxford: Oxford University Press, 1988.

Partridge, Damani. *Hypersexuality and Headscarves: Race, Sex, and Citizenship in the New Germany*. Bloomington, IN: Indiana University Press, 2012.

Petersen, Marie Juul. *For Humanity or for the Umma? Aid and Islam in Transnational Muslim NGOs*. London: Hurst, 2016.

Petrović, Vladimir. *Jugoslovenska stupa na Bliski Istok: stvaranje jugoslovenske bliskoistočne politike 1946–1956*. Belgrade: Institut za savremenu istoriju, 2007.

Philpott, Charles. "Though the Dog Is Dead, the Pig Must Be Killed: Finishing with Property Restitution to Bosnia-Herzegovina's IDPs and Refugees." *Journal of Refugee Studies* 18, no. 1 (2005): 1–24.

Pickering, Paula. *Peacebuilding in the Balkans: The View from the Ground Floor*. Ithaca, NY: Cornell University Press, 2007.

Pierre, Jemima. "Race in Africa Today: A Commentary." *Cultural Anthropology* 28, no. 3 (2013): 547–51.

Pitter, Laura. "Delivered into Enemy Hands: US-Led Abuse and Rendition of Opponents to Gaddafi's Libya." Human Rights Watch, 2012.

Potts, John. *A History of Charisma*. Houndmills, Basingstoke, Hampshire, UK: Palgrave Macmillan, 2009.

Prasad, Nita Verma. "Indian or Arabian? The Construction of Territorially Based Identities in the Raj, 1866–1888." *Cultural and Social History* 9, no. 2 (2012): 187–205.

Prashad, Vijay. *The Darker Nations: A People's History of the Third World*. New York: New Press, 2007.

Pugach, Sara. "African Students and the Politics of Race and Gender in the German Democratic Republic." In *Comrades of Color: East Germany in the Cold War World*, edited by Quinn Slobodian, 131–56. New York: Berghahn, 2015.

al-Qaḥṭānī, Saʿīd bin ʿAlī bin Wahf. *Ḥiṣn al-Muslim: min adhkār al-kitāb wal-sunna*. 9th ed. Riyadh: Maṭbaʿat safīr, 1992[1988].

———. *Al-dhikr wal-duʿāʾ wal-ʿilāj bil-ruqā min al-kitāb wal-sunna*. Riyadh: Maktabat al-Rushd, 1988.

Qaṭarī, Ḥamad, and Mājid al-Madanī. *Min qiṣaṣ al-shuhadāʾ al-ʿArab fil-Būsna wal-Harsak*. 2002 [electronic book].

Radonjić, Nemanja. "A Socialist Shaping of the Postcolonial Elite: Students from Africa in Socialist Yugoslavia." Paper presented at the Spectrum of Communism conference, Budapest, November 2017.

———. "'From Kragujevac to Kilimanjaro': Imagining and Re-Imagining Africa and the Self-Perception of Yugoslavia in the Travelogues from Socialist Yugoslavia." *Godišnjak za društvenu istoriju* 23, no. 2 (2016): 55–89.

Ralph, Laurence. *Renegade Dreams: Living Through Injury in Gangland Chicago*. Chicago: University of Chicago Press, 2014.

Ramet, Sabrina P. *The Three Yugoslavias: State-Building and Legitimation, 1918–2005*. Bloomington, IN: Indiana University Press, 2006.

———. "Primordial Ethnicity or Modern Nationalism: The Case of Yugoslavia's Muslims, Reconsidered." In *Muslim Communities Reemerge: Historical Perspectives on Nationality, Politics, and Opposition in the Former Soviet Union and Yugoslavia*, edited by Andreas Kappeler, Gerhard Simon, Georg Brunner, and Edward Allworth, 111–38. Durham, NC: Duke University Press, 1994[1989].

Ramić, Jusuf. *Bošnjaci na El-Azheru*. Sarajevo: Rijaset Islamske zajednice u Bosni i Hercegovini, 1997.

Rana, Junaid. *Terrifying Muslims: Race and Labor in the South Asian Diaspora*. Durham, NC: Duke University Press, 2011.

Rana, Muhammad Amir, and Mubasher Bukhari. *Arabs in Afghan Jihad*. Lahore: Pak Institute for Peace Studies, 2007.

Rancière, Jacques. *Disagreement*. Translated by Julie Rose. Minneapolis: University of Minnesota Press, 1999[1995].

———. "The Cause of the Other." *Parallax* 4, no. 2 (1998[1997]): 25–33.

al-Rasheed, Madawi. *A Most Masculine State: Gender, Politics and Religion in Saudi Arabia*. Cambridge: Cambridge University Press, 2013.

al-Rawḍān, ʿĪd Kāmil. *ʿAmaliyyāt quwwāt al-umam al-muttaḥida li-ḥifẓ al-salām: tajriba urduniyya*. Abu Dhabi: Markaz al-Imārāt lil-dirāsāt wal-buḥūth al-istrātījiyya, 2004.

Razack, Sherene. *Dark Threats and White Knights: The Somalia Affair, Peacekeeping, and the New Imperialism*. Toronto: University of Toronto Press, 2004.

Razsa, Maple. *Bastards of Utopia: Living Radical Politics After Socialism*. Bloomington: Indiana University Press, 2015.

Razsa, Maple, and Andrej Kurnik. "Occupy Slovenia: How Migrant Movements Contributed to New Forms of Direct Democracy." In *Border Politics: Social Movements, Collective Identities, and Globalization*, edited by Nancy Naples and Jennifer Bickham Mendez, 206–29. New York: NYU Press, 2015.

Redfield, Peter. *Life in Crisis: The Ethical Journey of Doctors Without Borders*. Berkeley: University of California Press, 2013.

Reill, Dominique Kirchner. *Nationalists Who Feared the Nation: Adriatic Multi-Nationalism in Habsburg Dalmatia, Trieste, and Venice*. Stanford, CA: Stanford University Press, 2012.

Riexinger, Martin. "How Favourable Is Puritan Islam to Modernity? A Study of the Ahl-i Hadīs in Late Nineteenth/Early Twentieth Century South Asia." In *Colonialism, Modernity and Religious Identities: Religious Reform Movements in South Asia*, edited by Gwilym Beckerlegge, 147–65. New Delhi: Oxford University Press, 2008.

Riles, Annelise. "Anthropology, Human Rights, and Legal Knowledge: Culture in the Iron Cage." *American Anthropologist* 108, no. 1 (March 2006): 52–65.

———. *The Network Inside Out*. Ann Arbor: University of Michigan Press, 2001.

Rizvi, S. Haider Abbas. *Veteran Campaigners: A History of the Punjab Regiment, 1759–1981*. Lahore: Wajidalis, 1984.

Robinson, Cabeiri deBergh. *Body of Victim, Body of Warrior: Refugee Families and the Making of Kashmiri Jihadists*. Berkeley: University of California Press, 2013.

Ron, James. *Frontiers and Ghettos: State Violence in Serbia and Israel*. Berkeley: University of California Press, 2003.

Rothman, E. Natalie. *Brokering Empire: Trans-Imperial Subjects Between Venice and Istanbul*. Ithaca, NY: Cornell University Press, 2012.

Rougier, Bernard. *Everyday Jihad: The Rise of Militant Islam Among Palestinians in Lebanon*. Translated by Pascale Ghazaleh. Cambridge, MA: Harvard University Press, 2007.

Rubin, Barnett. *The Fragmentation of Afghanistan*. New Haven, CT: Yale University Press, 2002.

———. "Arab Islamists in Afghanistan." In *Political Islam: Revolution, Radicalism, or Reform?*, edited by John Esposito, 179–206. Boulder, CO: Lynne Rienner, 1997.

Rubinstein, Alvin. *Yugoslavia and the Nonaligned World*. Princeton: Princeton University Press, 1970.

Rubinstein, Robert. *Peacekeeping Under Fire: Culture and Intervention*. Boulder, CO: Paradigm, 2008.

Rudy, Sayres. "Pros and Cons: Americanism Against Islamism in the 'War on Terror'." *The Muslim World* 97 (January 2007): 33–78.

al-Sadḥān, ʿAbd al-ʿAzīz. *Al-Imām al-Albānī: durūs wa-mawāqif wa-ʿibar*. Riyadh: Dār al-Tawḥīd lil-nashr, 2008.

Said, Edward. *Orientalism*. New York: Vintage, 1978.

Ṣalāḥ, Muḥammad. *Waqāʾiʿ sanawāt al-jihād: riḥlat al-Afghān al-ʿArab*. Cairo: Khulūd lil-nashr, 2001.

Salaymeh, Lena. *The Beginnings of Islamic Law: Late Antique Islamicate Legal Traditions*. Cambridge: Cambridge University Press, 2016.

Salih, Ruba. *Gender in Transnationalism: Home, Longing and Belonging Among Moroccan Migrant Women*. London: Routledge, 2003.

Salomon, Noah. *For Love of the Prophet: An Ethnography of Sudan's Islamic State*. Princeton, NJ: Princeton University Press, 2016.

Šamić, Jasna. "Les Naqshbandî (plus particulièrement ceux de Visoko) et leur relations avec d'autres ordres Soufis." In *Naqshbandis: cheminements et situation actuelle d'un ordre mystique musulman: actes de la Table ronde de Sèvres, 2–4 mai 1985*, edited by Marc Gaborieau, Alexandre Popovic, and Thierry Zarcone, 669–79. Istanbul: Isis, 1990.

Samour, Nahed. "Modernized Islamic International Law Concepts as a Third World Approach to International law." *Heidelberg Journal of International Law* 72 (2012): 543–77.

Scheppele, Kim Lane. "The International State of Emergency: Lawscapes after 9/11." Paper presented at the Yale Legal Theory Workshop conference, New Haven, CT, 2006.

Schielke, Samuli. "Living with Unresolved Difference: A Reply to Fadil and Fernando." *HAU: Journal of Ethnographic Theory* 5, no. 2 (2015): 59–88.

Schindler, John. *Unholy Terror: Bosnia, al-Qaʿida, and the Rise of Global Jihad*. St. Paul, MN: Zenith, 2007.

Schirazi, Asghar. *The Constitution of Iran: Politics and the State in the Islamic Republic.* London: I.B. Tauris, 1998.

Schmitt, Carl. *Theory of the Partisan: Intermediate Commentary on the Concept of the Political.* Translated by G. L. Ulmen. New York: Telos Press, 2007[1963].

———. *The Nomos of the Earth in the International Law of the Jus Publicum Europaeum.* Translated by G. L. Ulmen. New York: Telos Press, 2003[1950].

———. *Land and Sea.* Translated by Sonia Draghici. Washington, DC: Plutarch Press, 1997[1954].

———. *The Leviathan in the State Theory of Thomas Hobbes: Meaning and Failure of a Political Symbol.* Translated by George Schwab and Erna Hilfstein. Westport, CT: Greenwood Press, 1996[1938].

———. *The Concept of the Political.* Translated by George Schwab. Chicago: University of Chicago Press, 1996[1932].

———. *Political Theology: Four Chapters on the Concept of Sovereignty.* Translated by George Schwab. Cambridge, MA: MIT Press, 1985[1934].

Schwab, Wendell. "How to Pray in Kazakhstan: *The Fortress of the Muslim* and Its Readers." *Anthropology of East Europe Review* 32, no. 1 (Spring 2014): 22–42.

Scott, Joan Wallach. *The Politics of the Veil.* Princeton, NJ: Princeton University Press, 2007.

Sekkaf, Hasan Ali. *Vehabizam/selefizam: Ideološka pozadina i historijski korijeni.* Translated by Jasmin Merdan and Adnan Mešanović. Sarajevo: Srebreno pero, 2005.

Shah, Niaz. *Self-Defense in Islamic and International Law: Assessing al-Qaeda and the Invasion of Iraq.* New York: Palgrave Macmillan, 2008.

Shay, Shaul. *Islamic Terror and the Balkans.* New Brunswick, NJ: Transaction, 2007.

Sherman, Taylor. "Migration, Citizenship and Belonging in Hyderabad (Deccan), 1946–1956." *Modern Asian Studies* 45, no. 1 (2010): 81–107.

Ṣiddīqī, Khālid Ḥanīf. *Tarājim-i ʿulamāʾe Ahl-i Ḥadīth.* Delhi: Markazī Jamʿiyyat Ahl-i Ḥadīth Hind, 2008.

Simpson, Audra. *Mohawk Interruptus: Political Life Across the Borders of Settler States.* Durham, NC: Duke University Press, 2014.

Slobodian, Quinn. "Bandung in Divided Germany: Managing Non-Aligned Politics in East and West, 1955–63." *The Journal of Imperial and Commonwealth History* 41, no. 4 (2013): 644–62.

Smiley, Will. *From Slaves to Prisoners of War: The Ottoman Empire, Russia, and the Making of International Law.* Oxford: Oxford University Press, 2018.

Sorabji, Cornelia K. "Muslim Identity and Islamic Faith in Sarajevo." PhD thesis, Anthropology, King's College, Cambridge University, 1989.

Spaskovska, Ljubica. *The Last Yugoslav Generation: The Rethinking of Youth Politics and Cultures in Late Socialism*. Manchester: Manchester University Press, 2017.

Stenersen, Anne. *Al-Qaida in Afghanistan*. Cambridge: Cambridge University Press, 2017.

Strick van Linschoten, Alex, and Felix Kuehn. *An Enemy We Created: The Myth of the Taliban-Al Qaeda Merger in Afghanistan*. London: Hurst, 2011.

Subotić, Jelena, and Srđan Vučetić. "Performing Solidarity: Whiteness and Status-Seeking in the Non-Aligned World." *Journal of International Relations and Development* (2017).

Sullivan, Gavin. "Transnational Legal Assemblages and Global Security Law: Topologies and Temporalities of the List." *Transnational Legal Theory* 5, no. 1 (2014): 81–127.

al-Ṭabarī, Abū Jaʿfar. *The Foundation of the Community*. Vol. 7 of *The History of al-Ṭabarī, an Annotated Translation*. Translated by M. V. McDonald and W. Montgomery Watt. Albany: SUNY Press, 1987.

Tankel, Stephen. *Storming the World Stage: The Story of Lashkar-e-Taiba*. London: Hurst, 2012.

al-Tayyeb, Ghazi. "Jordanian Participation in PKO & Future Outlook." In *Challenges of Peace Support: Into the 21st Century*, edited by Wijdan Ali, 53–60. Amman: Jordan Institute of Diplomacy, 1999.

Tekin, Mehmet Ali. *Bosna Şehidlerimiz*. Istanbul: Beka Yayınları, 2014.

Terović, Taib. *Sedma*. Zenica: Naša Riječ, 2006.

Thomson, Janice. *Mercenaries, Pirates, and Sovereigns: State-Building and Extraterritorial Violence in Early Modern Europe*. Princeton, NJ: Princeton University Press, 1994.

Toal, Gerard, and Carl Dahlman. *Bosnia Remade: Ethnic Cleansing and Its Reversal*. Oxford: Oxford University Press, 2011.

Todorova, Maria. *Imagining the Balkans*. Revised ed. New York: Oxford University Press, 2009[1997].

Toholj, Miroslav. *"Holy Warriors" and the War in Bosnia and Herzegovina*. Belgrade: Igam, 2001.

Tønnesson, Stein. "A 'Global Civil War'?" *Security Dialogue* 33, no. 3 (2002): 389–91.

Toth, James. "Islamism in Southern Egypt: A Case Study of a Radical Religious Movement." *International Journal of Middle East Studies* 35, no. 4 (November 2003): 547–72.

Tsing, Anna. *Friction: An Ethnography of Global Connection*. Princeton, NJ: Princeton University Press, 2005.

Vah Jevšnik, Mojca. *Building Peace for a Living: Expatriate Development Workers in Kosovo*. Ljubljana: Slovenian Migration Institute, 2009.

Verdery, Katherine. *The Political Lives of Dead Bodies: Reburial and Postsocialist Change*. New York: Columbia University Press, 2000.

Vidino, Lorenzo. *Al Qaeda in Europe: The New Battleground of International Jihad*. Amherst, NY: Prometheus, 2006.

Viscomi, Joseph John. "Between Italy and Egypt: Migrating Histories and Political Genealogies." In *International Migration in the Euro-Mediterranean Region*, edited by Ibrahim Awad, 15–33. Cairo: American University in Cairo Press, 2019.

Vitalis, Robert. "The Midnight Ride of Kwame Nkrumah and Other Fables of Bandung (Ban-doong)." *Humanity: An International Journal of Human Rights, Humanitarianism and Development* 4, no. 2 (Summer 2013): 261–88.

Volpp, Leti. "The Citizen and the Terrorist." *UCLA Law Review* 49, no. 5 (June 2002): 1575–1600.

al-Wādiʿī, Muqbil Bin Hādī. *Maqtal al-Shaykh Jamīl al-Raḥmān*. Sana'a: Dār al-Hilāl lil-ṭibāʿa wal-nashr wal-tawzīʿ, 1991.

Wagemakers, Joas. *Salafism in Jordan: Political Islam in a Quietist Community*. Cambridge: Cambridge University Press, 2016.

Wagner, Sarah. *To Know Where He Lies: DNA Technology and the Search for Srebrenica's Missing*. Berkeley: University of California Press, 2008.

Weber, Max. "The Sociology of Charismatic Authority." In *From Max Weber: Essays in Sociology*, edited by Hans Gerth and C. Wright Mills, 245–52. New York: Oxford University Press, 1946[1922].

West Ohueri, Chelsi. "Mapping Race and Belonging in the Margins of Europe: Albanian, Romani, and Egyptian Sentiments." PhD thesis, Anthropology, University of Texas at Austin, 2016.

White, Joshua. *Piracy and Law in the Ottoman Mediterranean*. Stanford, CA: Stanford University Press, 2017.

Wiktorowicz, Quintan. "Anatomy of the Salafi Movement." *Studies in Conflict & Terrorism* 29, no. 3 (April 2006): 207–39.

Witt, John Fabian. *Lincoln's Code: The Laws of War in American History*. New York: Free Press, 2012.

Wool, Zoë H. *After War: The Weight of Life at Walter Reed*. Durham, NC: Duke University Press, 2015.

Yasmeen, Samina. *Jihad and Dawah: Evolving Narratives of Lashkar-e-Taiba and Jamat ud Dawah*. London: Hurst, 2017.

Yurchak, Alexei. *Everything Was Forever, Until It Was No More: The Last Soviet Generation*. Princeton, NJ: Princeton University Press, 2005.

Yūsuf, Muḥammad Khayr Ramaḍān. *Tatimmat al-aʿlām lil-Ziriklī: wafayāt 1397–1415 H/1977–1995 M*. Vol. 1. Beirut: Dār Ibn Ḥazm, 1998.

———. *Tatimmat al-aʿlām lil-Ziriklī: wafayāt 1397–1415 H/1977–1995 M*. Vol. 2, Beirut: Dār Ibn Ḥazm, 1998.

Zaidan, Ahmad Muaffaq. *The Afghan Arabs Media at Jihad*. Islamabad: The Pakistan Futuristics Foundation & Institute, 1999.

Zaytūn, ʿAbd al-Wahhāb. *Al-Būsna wal-Harsak: Filasṭīn ukhrā fī qalb Ūrūbbā*. Beirut: al-Manāra, 1995.

Životić, Aleksandar. *Jugoslavija i Suecka kriza: 1956–1957*. Belgrade: Institut za noviju istoriju Srbije, 2008.

Zohry, Ayman. "The Migratory Patterns of Egyptians in Italy and France." In *CARIM Research Reports*. Florence: European University Institute Robert Schulman Centre for Advanced Studies, 2009.

Zontini, Elisabetta. *Transnational Families, Migration and Gender: Moroccan and Filipino Women in Bologna and Barcelona*. New York: Berghahn, 2010.

Zulfiqar, Adnan. "Jurisdiction Over *Jihād*: Islamic Law and the Duty to Fight." *West Virginia Law Review* 120, no. 2 (2018): 427–68.

Zyla, Benjamin. *Sharing the Burden? NATO and Its Second-Tier Powers*. Toronto: University of Toronto Press, 2015.

Index

Page numbers in italics refer to figures.

Abdel-Razek, Hussein Ali, 180, 290n29
Abdul Manaf Kasmuri (Abu Muhammad the Filipino), 186–88, 292n51
Abu ʿAbd Allah al-Libi, 93, 188, 270n35
Abu ʿAbd al-ʿAziz, *30*, *37*; accusations of publicity-seeking against, 42, 237n44; in Afghanistan, 40; on casualties at battle of Ilijaš, 91–92; author's interview of, 36–37, 40, 43; author's research on, 34, 36; background of, 36, 38–40; on relationship between daʿwa and jihad, 57; birth name of, 37; and Bosnian War, 29–30, 41; career with Saudia Airlines, 39–40; diasporic sensibility of, 42–44; first marriage, 40; frequent travel by, 39–40, 42–43; fundraising for jihad, 33, 41–42, 44, 237n44, 261n66; and global jihad, 29–30, 35; humor of, 36, 42; instructions for ansar recruits, 89–90; internet activism of, 42; and Lashkar-e-Tayyiba/Markaz-i Daʿwa wal-Irshad, 33, 41, 42, 235n26, 236–37n40; media interest in, 29, 31; on medresa in Travnik, 246n32; misidentification by Western terrorism experts, 34–35, 235n25; comparison of Afghan and Bosnian jihads, 47; and Muslim Forces, 41, 64, 67; in Pakistan, 40–41, 42; recruiting for jihad, 41, 43–44; request for al-Albani's support, 57–58; on mujahids' marriages of convenience, 272n58; ties to Ahl-i Hadith, 41; time in prison, 36; turn to jihad in middle age, 40–41; and universalism, 29, 31, 35, 36, 43, 238n47;

relations with Gulf donors, 95, 96, 278nn36–37; response to war crimes allegations, 138
Abu Muʿadh al-Kuwayti, 111, 269–70nn32–3
Abu Muhammad al-Fatih (Hamad bin Khalifa Al Khalifa), 92, 258n47
Abu Muhammad the Filipino. *See* Abdul Manaf Kasmuri
Abu Omar (Hassan Mustafa Nasr), 48, 240n61
Abu Saʿd, Mustafa, 181–82
Abu Shahid al-Tunisi, 127
Abu ʿUmayr al-Jiddawi, 118–19
Abu Usayd al-Madani (ʿUmar al-Habashi), 237–38n46
Abu al-Zubayr al-Ha'ili: and Bosnian family, 185–86; mujahid group led by, 88, 89, 116, 175, 257n38, 278n37
Abu al-Zubayr al-Madani (Muhammad al-Habashi), 237n46
Active Islamic Youth, 128
Adilović, Ahmed, 63
"Afghan Arabs," 231n9, 255n24, 262n77, 286–287n6
Afghan jihad (1979–1992): 3, 8, 41, 95, 141, 255n23; ʿAzzam fatwa on, 84–85, 86, 254nn18–19, 255n21; Jeddah residents' support for, 40; comparisons to Bosnian jihad, 46–48, 54, 87, 88, 113, 271n46, 272n58; migratory ties feeding, 40, 41; miracle accounts during, 86, 251n5; Muslim critiques of, 47, 54, 57, 113, 261n67; overstated connection to Bosnian jihad, 32; veterans of in Bosnia, 29, 46, 88, 111, 118, 204, 237n46, 268n24, 269n32; and nation-state system, 85, 255n23; US support for, 40, 221n3. *See also* Services Office
Afghanistan, and GWOT, 7, 122, 140, 197, 198, 199
Agamben, Giorgio, 196, 253n12, 294–95n6
Agrama, Hussein Ali, 257n35
Ahl-i Hadith: 41, 236n39; in Afghanistan, 249n57, 269n32; in India, 71; in Pakistan, 41, 237n41
Ahmad, Babar, 45, 229n43
Ahmed, Shahab, 232n13
Ahsan, Talha, 229n43
akhlaq (virtues): as cherished quality among mujahids, 109–12; discussion of in Afghan jihad, 268n25; etymology of, 268n26; as goal of Katiba religious training, 112–14; masculinity and, 111; processing of difference through, 109–12, 115–16
al-Albani, Muhammad Nasir al-Din, 33, 57–58, 71, 233n16, 248n49
Alexandrowicz, C. H., 16
Algeria, civil war in, 95, 140–141, 145
Algeria, and GWOT, 198, 199, 295n15; "Algerian Six," 7–8, 17, 198, 201, 223n13, 259n50, 277n29
amicus curiae, 21
ansar: Abu ʿAbd al-ʿAziz instructions for, 89–90; Arabs in Bosnia as, 32, 232n11; Arab students from former Yugoslavia as interpreters and guides for,

with author at Livade mujahids' cemetery, 101–3, 125; with author in Bočinja, 125–26; as Bočinja resident, 126; Bosnian suspicion of, 137; on departure of mujahids, 192; and disbanding of Katiba, 191; on jihad as activity rather than identity, 24; imprisonment of, 195; marriage of, 120; and prisoner exchange negotiations, 137; resistance to deportation, 205, 216; sense of humor of, 101, 162; turn to jihad in Bosnia, 162–63
ʿAzzam, ʿAbd Allah: and Afghan mujahideen, 255n24; background of, 84, 265–66n13; fatwa on Afghan jihad, 84–85, 86, 254nn18–19, 255n21; and *al-Jihad* magazine, 268n25; and nation-state system, 85; political theology of, 86–87; and purported ties to al-Qaʿida, 233–234n20, 254n18; translated writings of, 86, 256n27; writings on miracles, 86, 257n34
Azzam.com website, 229n43

Badiou, Alain, 256n30
Badr, battle of, 80
Bahadhiq, Ahmad, 38
Bahadhiq, Khalid Muhammad Ahmad, 36
Bahadhiq, Mahmud Muhammad Ahmad. *See* Abu ʿAbd al-ʿAziz
Bahadhiq, Muhammad Ahmad, 38, 39
Bahadhiq family: migration to India, 36, 38; migration to Jeddah after Indian independence, 39; origin in Hadramawt (southern Yemen), 36; residence in India, 36, 235n30; branch in Java, 235n30
al-Bahri, Nasir (Abu Jandal), 233n16, 261n66
Baker, Catherine, 223n11, 280n6
Balibar, Étienne, 225n23
Balkan Pact of 1953, 281n9
Ballinger, Pamela, 242–43n12
Banja Luka: during Yugoslav period, 165; ethnic cleansing of Muslims from, 50, 165–166; after Bosnian war, 167
Belhadj, Abdelhakim, 169, 285n47
Ben Ali, Zine El Abidine, 46
Benjamin, Walter, 84
Bhatti, Raja Aziz, 289n22
Bikoši massacre (1993), 136
bin Baz, ʿAbd al-ʿAziz, 70, 123–24, 241n1, 247n46
bin Essa, Khalid al-Sultan, 261–62n71
bin Laden, Osama: ʿAzzam and, 84; criticisms of House of Saud, 95; and Hadrami diaspora, 36; training camps financed by, 40
Bočinja, 125–29; author's visit to, 125–26; mujahids' occupation of abandoned Serb homes, 125–26; postwar džemat in, 126–28, 212; NATO eviction of Arab ansar from, 128, 192, 200, 297n23; Serb-Muslim tensions in, 126; transnational family connections of mujahids in, 127–28
Bonilla, Yarimar, 252n7
Bosnia-Herzegovina: constitution of, 6, 76, 189, 206, 250n63, 299n41;

declaration of independence by, 41, 66; debates on role of Islam in, 224n19; as early GWOT battleground, 7; early lack of military, 66; elections of 2000, 297n23; elections of 2010, 75–76; and ethnic Others, exclusion from some elected offices, 206, 299n41; as exemplar of ambiguities of nationalism and universalism, 61; as EU immigration buffer zone, 194, 206–7; EU influence under Dayton Peace Agreement, 189–90; expulsion of Arabs after 9/11, 2–3, 8, 201–6; expulsion of Arabs prior to 9/11, 192, 200; High Representative power over, 189; Islamic organizations in, 128; mix of Serbs, Croats, and Muslims in, 58, 221n1; time spent by author in, 17. *See also* Arabs in Bosnia, post-9/11 denaturalization and deportation of; Dayton Peace Agreement (1995)

Bosniaks. *See* Bosnian Muslims

Bosnian Army: ansar complaints about lack of support from, 91–92; complaints about mujahids' unruliness, 92, 259n51; secularism of, 64; tensions with Katiba, 91–93, 259n54, 260n58

Bosnian Muslim/Bosniak nationalism: as an alternative to Islamic extremism, 57; discrediting of as political force, 74; in Yugoslav constitutional order, 58–59; multiple universalist idioms employed by, 61; *vs.* Muslim question in South Asia, 243n16; and pan-Islamic movements, as mutually reinforcing, 62; professional classes leading, 59; range of postwar views on, 74–77; and liberal universalism, 57; Serb and Croat views on, 61, 244n24

Bosnian Muslims: Bosniak as term for, 58; crossover voting in 2010 election, 75–76; diaspora of, 54, 60, 64, 128, 250n66; lack of designated national homeland for, 58; Muslimani as term for, 58; Ottoman legacy and, 57, 242n10; and pan-Islamic support, 61–62; perception as less Muslim than Arabs, 104, 265n10; racialization of in Yugoslav collapse, 163–64; revivalist movement of 1990s, and Katiba, 55; serving in Croat forces, 66; universalism claimed by, 54; whiteness of, 8, 67, 103, 104, 142, 265n10; women's relations with Arab ansar, 120–25

Bosnian War (1992–1995): atrocities in, 6, 9, 136, 274–75n7; as both Bosnian nationalist and universalist Muslim project, 82–83, 88, 89–91; and ethnic cleansing, 6, 156, 165, 223n8, 284–85n42; labeling as jihad, 24; Muslim media audiences and, 8–9; and nation and religion in flux, 62; pan-Islamic mobilizations in, understudied influence of, 8; and reclaiming of public spaces as Islamic, 63

Bossman, Peter, 155

Boumediene v. Bush (2008), 7–8, 227n34

Bray, Alan, 271n50

163; collapse into sectarian strife, 156–58; founding of, 153; number of states in, 153–54; and opposition to Islamism, 283n26; and use of pan-Islamism, 158; political goals of, 150; transregional circuits in, 152–55

Non-Aligned Movement, and Yugoslavia: Arab students remaining in Yugoslavia, 155; flow of Arab students to Yugoslavia, 150, 151, 155, 280n6; and marginalization of non-Slav populations, 156; and mobility to both east and west, 152–53; NATO destruction of records on, 168; nostalgia of Arab migrants for, 152–53, 156; notable successful migrants in Yugoslavia, 155; remnants of, after Yugoslav collapse, 158–59, 168–69; and welcoming of all races to Yugoslavia, 153; and Yugoslav global influence, 154; Yugoslav educational travel to Arab world, 282n15; and Yugoslav ties to Arab countries, 154–55; Yugoslav whiteness as issue in, 154, 281n10; Yugoslav workers in Non-Aligned countries, 155

Non-Aligned Movement, as universalism, 150–51; and ambiguities of nationalist projects, 156; and overlaps with pan-Islamism in Bosnia crisis, 151–52, 158–63; as state-driven internationalist project, 151, 156

Notions That Must Be Corrected (Imad el-Misri): as adaptation of al-Qahtani's *Fortress of the Muslim,* 70–71; analysts' focus on introduction of, 69; body of text, religious practices outlined in, 69–70; Bosnian critiques of, 53–54, 60–61; constitution through local practices, 55; design for portability, 71; Heritage Society and, 53, 241n1; origin in Balkan scholarship, 71; and Salafi efforts to purify Bosnian Muslims' faith, 53–54, 60–61, 69; transliteration practice in, 248n50; utility for religious practice as valued quality in, 70

Odred Elmudžahedin. *See* Katiba

Office of the High Representative, 189, 195, 204, 292n54, 292n56

Operation Karama, 94

Organization of the Islamic Conference, and Bosnian War, 62

Osman, Hassan Hussein, 283n29

Østebø, Terje, 271n46

Ottoman Empire: Bosnia and tanzimat reforms in, 244n17; Bosniak nostalgia for, 76; transregional histories of, 233n15; Salafi attitudes toward, 242n10; and Turkish geopolitical ambitions, 290n39

Pahuja, Sundhya, 226n26

PAKBAT-1, 289n25

PAKBAT-2, 175, 178

Pakistani military: and co-optation of Lashkar-e-Tayyiba, 41; as frequent participant in UN peacekeeping, 177, 288n20; in SFOR peacekeeping

Stanford Studies *in* Middle Eastern *and* Islamic Societies *and* Cultures

Joel Beinin and Laleh Khalili, editors

Waste Siege: The Life of Infrastructure in Palestine 2019
SOPHIA STAMATOPOULOU-ROBBINS

Heritage and the Cultural Struggle for Palestine 2019
CHIARA DE CESARI

Banking on the State: The Financial Foundations of Lebanon 2019
HICHAM SAFIEDDINE

Familiar Futures: Time, Selfhood, and Sovereignty in Iraq 2019
SARA PURSLEY

Hamas Contained: The Rise and Pacification of Palestinian Resistance 2018
TAREQ BACONI

Hotels and Highways: The Construction of Modernization Theory in Cold War Turkey 2018
BEGÜM ADALET

Bureaucratic Intimacies: Human Rights in Turkey 2017
ELIF M. BABÜL

Impossible Exodus: Iraqi Jews in Israel 2017
ORIT BASHKIN

Brothers Apart: Palestinian Citizens of Israel and the Arab World 2017
MAHA NASSAR

Revolution without Revolutionaries: Making Sense of the Arab Spring 2017
ASEF BAYAT

Soundtrack of the Revolution: The Politics of Music in Iran 2017
NAHID SIAMDOUST

Copts and the Security State: Violence, Coercion, and Sectarianism in Contemporary Egypt 2016
LAURE GUIRGUIS

Circuits of Faith: Migration, Education, and the Wahhabi Mission 2016
MICHAEL FARQUHAR

Morbid Symptoms: Relapse in the Arab Uprising 2016
GILBERT ACHCAR

Imaginative Geographies of Algerian Violence: Conflict Science, Conflict Management, Antipolitics 2015
JACOB MUNDY

Police Encounters: Security and Surveillance in Gaza under Egyptian Rule 2015
ILANA FELDMAN

Palestinian Commemoration in Israel: Calendars, Monuments, and Martyrs 2015
TAMIR SOREK

Digital Militarism: Israel's Occupation in the Social Media Age 2015
ADI KUNTSMAN and REBECCA L. STEIN

Official Stories: Politics and National Narratives in Egypt and Algeria 2014
LAURIE A. BRAND

The Reckonings of Pluralism: Citizenship and the Demands of History in Turkey 2014
KABIR TAMBAR

Refugees of the Revolution: Experiences of Palestinian Exile 2013
DIANA ALLAN

Citizen Strangers: Palestinians and the Birth of Israel's Liberal Settler State 2013
SHIRA ROBINSON